BREAKING IN

Breaking In: Tales from the Screenwriting Trenches is a no-nonsense, boots-on-the-ground exploration of how writers REALLY go from emerging to professional in today's highly saturated and competitive screenwriting space. With a focus on writers who have gotten representation and broken into the TV or feature film space after the critical 2008 WGA strike and financial market collapse, the reader will learn from tangible examples of how success was achieved via hard work and specific methodology. This book includes interviews from writers who wrote major studio releases (*The Boy Next Door*), staffed on television shows (*American Crime, NCIS New Orleans, Sleepy Hollow*), sold specs and television shows, placed in competitions, and were accepted to prestigious network and studio writing programs. These interviews are presented as Screenwriter Spotlights throughout the book and are supported by insight from top-selling agents and managers (including those who have sold scripts and pilots, had their writers named to prestigious lists such as The Black List and The Hit List) as well as working industry executives. Together, this expertise and practical know-how, along with the author's extensive experience in and knowledge of the industry, will inform the reader about how the screenwriting trade REALLY works, what it expects from both working and emerging writers, and how a writer can best negotiate the field in order to move their screenwriting career forward.

Lee Zahavi Jessup, author of *Getting It Write: An Insider's Guide to a Screenwriting Career*, is a highly sought after screenwriting career coach with 20+ years of industry experience. Lee's clients include writers working in film and television, participants in the prestigious television writing programs, contest winners and many more. An invited speaker at the WGA, NBC, UCLA and countless screenwriting conferences, Lee is a contributor for *Script Magazine* and has been interviewed by many screenwriting-centric television shows, web series and podcasts.

BREAKING IN

Tales from the Screenwriting Trenches

Lee Zahavi Jessup

Routledge
Taylor & Francis Group

NEW YORK AND LONDON

First published 2017
by Routledge
711 Third Avenue, New York, NY 10017

and by Routledge
2 Park Square, Milton Park, Abingdon, Oxon OX14 4RN

Routledge is an imprint of the Taylor & Francis Group, an informa business

Library of Congress Cataloging in Publication Data
Names: Jessup, Lee Zahavi author.
Title: Breaking in : tales from the screenwriting trenches /
Lee Zahavi Jessup.
Description: New York : Routledge, 2017. | Includes index.
Identifiers: LCCN 2016041946| ISBN 9781138679115 (hardback) |
ISBN 9781138679122 (pbk.) | ISBN 9781315558561 (e-book)
Subjects: LCSH: Motion picture authorship. | Television authorship. |
Screenwriters—Interviews.
Classification: LCC PN1996 .J47 2017 | DDC 808.2/3—dc23
LC record available at https://lccn.loc.gov/2016041946

ISBN: 978-1-138-67911-5 (hbk)
ISBN: 978-1-138-67912-2 (pbk)
ISBN: 978-1-315-55856-1 (ebk)

Typeset in Bembo and Stone Sans
by Florence Production Ltd, Stoodleigh, Devon, UK

Dedicated to my Safta

CONTENTS

SPECIAL THANKS

Special thanks to everyone who participated in this book and made it what it is:

The writers: Erin Cardillo, Kirk Moore, Marissa Jo Cerar, Terrell Lawrence, Eric Koenig, Greta Heinemann, Chandus Jackson, Melissa London Hilfers, Moises Zamora, Joe Webb, Barbara Curry, Diarra Kilpatrick, Tawnya Bhattacharya and Ali Laventhol, Isaac Gonzalez, Danny Tolli and Michael Perry.

The Executives: Adam Perry, Ally Latman, Chris Coggins, Chris Cook, David Boxerbaum, Evan Corday, Janine Jones-Clark, Jarrod Murray, Jason Scoggins, Jeff Portnoy, Jennifer Au, Jennifer Titus, Jewerl Ross, John Zaozirny, Jon Karas, Josh Adler, Kailey Marsh, Lee Stobby, Mike Woodlief, Ryan Cunningham, Ryan Saul, Scott Carr, Sean Barclay and Zadoc Angell.

Great thanks to the people who inspired this book and helped it become a reality:

My editor, Emily McCloskey who gave me the freedom to write the book I wanted to write.

Aaron Schuelke who provided me with insight, perspective and encouragements.

The brilliant and generous Eileen Jones, Greta Heinemann and Patrick Mahon, without whose insights, ever-present support, brilliance, candor and practical assistance this book literally could have never been completed.

My Wednesday-nighters. Or as one of you coined, my army of writers. Couldn't have done this without you. You know who you are.

The whole team at Akasha Café, including Rhianne, Mary, Dustin, Drew, the rest of the Barista gang, as well as the great Akasha Richmond herself, who have continued to welcome me to my usual corner table through the writing of two books now and countless client meetings over the years. You guys are my home away from home.

And of course, my family:

To my father, who instilled in me the love of visual storytelling and introduced me to this industry, and to my mother who gave me the courage and passion to pave my own path within it.

To my children, Lennon and Lula, who humble me, teach me, guide me, inspire me, humor me and light up every corner of my life.

And to my husband, my best friend and the love of my life, Tony, who gives everything meaning and helps me grow, dream, believe and rise. There is no one else with whom I would want to go on this ride.

INTRODUCTION

The idea for this book was seeded on April 2, 2015. That was the day that I interviewed Markus Goerg, partner in and manager at Heroes and Villains, for Final Draft's online blog. I had been talking to my friends and colleagues in the industry and gathering information for years about all it took for emerging writers to become professional. For some reason, on that day it all coalesced for me: in an industry of opinions, I realized I was quickly becoming the hoarder of pure gold. What if there was something other than an interview that could come out of the information and relationships I had been cultivating all these years? The next morning, I told my husband about my idea for this book, and knowing that I am not one to keep dormant once a challenge presents itself, he completely understood. I also told him that I was in trouble—and it turns out I was right. Outside of raising children, this is by far the biggest project that I ever undertook.

With every screenplay, there is always the question: Why now? *Why Now?* In terms of the story. *Why Now?* In terms of the industry. As I set out to write a book chock full of practical, no-nonsense, industry-driven insights, I realized I had to answer that very same question for myself: Why this book at this time?

There are endless celebrated stories out there about how many of our most famed professional screenwriters broke in in the 1980s and 1990s. You can read about them on websites, listen to their unique, enviable tales of meteoric success again and again in speeches and podcasts, read about their paths to screenwriting triumph in a myriad magazine profiles and online biographies. The story of writers breaking into the industry—effortlessly and seemingly by miracle—was once again shared when I interviewed Scott Alexander and Larry Karaszewski (*The People Vs. Larry Flynt*, *The People Vs. O.J. Simpson*, *Man In The Moon*, *Big Eyes*) at Story Expo in Los Angeles a few years back. But as soon as Larry and Scott shared how they wrote a script in college and promptly had industry doors open for them, they went on to tell our standing-room only audience that how they broke in in the 1980s has absolutely no bearing on the path to breaking in and becoming a professional screenwriter in the industry as it operates today.

And they were right. As I talk to my friends in the professional space, I often hear about how, after the 2008 WGA strike and financial market collapse, along with the onset of television's golden age and retraction of the spec market, everything changed. Became harder. People talk about how the rules from the 1990s and early 2000s simply no longer apply. Often, I am told by producers, agents, managers and executives that it's never been harder to sell a spec script; that getting a deal for a pilot from an unknown writer is near impossible; that breaking a new writer into the industry is just so blood-sweat-and-tears tough. And yet, from my day-to-day involvement with emerging and professional screenwriters, I know that new writers are breaking in all the time.

That is why this book at this time: to inform scribes everywhere, both emerging and professional, how writers are breaking in to the screenwriting space RIGHT NOW. If everything has changed, if the spec boom of the 1990s is long gone, and the ways writers broke in in the 1980s and 1990s no longer apply, how are hardworking, talented, ambitious screen and television writers becoming working professionals in the new millennium?

Don't look for this book to illuminate the one sure path to screenwriting success. That path doesn't exist. Sure, it makes for a good story, but as most screenwriters know, most great stories don't stick very closely to the truth. So if that's what you're looking for—the easy path, the magic formula—let's establish right now that this book is NOT for you. It will NOT outline how to build a screenwriting career in twelve steps or twelve months. It will not tell you how easy it is, how everyone can do it. Because this is demanding work, requiring dedication, consistency and talent. And if this book will illuminate one thing, it is that each writer gets made following his or her own unique path.

So instead of looking for this book to spell out a foolproof generic plan, think of it as a three-layer cake full of straightforward insight and guidance. You read that right. A three-layer cake. And here is how it breaks down:

The first layer, and the foundation on which the cake is standing, is its SCREENWRITER SPOTLIGHTS: interviews with sixteen working television, film and new media writers and content creators who have broken into the industry after the famed 2008 strike, and who, with hard work, perseverance and determination, managed to get their careers off the ground. In the Screenwriter Spotlights, you will learn about each writer's unique journey to becoming a screenwriting professional, what they experienced and learned, and how they came to work in the film and television industry today.

The writers chosen for this book are all hard working. They are all talented and distinctive, with a strong voice and a specific point of view. The one thing they are not? Overnight successes turned screenwriting superstars. Don't get me wrong: they have created the sort of success and opportunity that many people marvel at and long for. But I selected them for this book because of the consistent work they did over many years to get to where they are today.

The truth of the matter is that I am not interested in what it takes to become a phenomenon. The practicalities of some seemingly meteoric rise are near impossible to pin down. Those stories are so inimitable, so specific, and more often than not so circumstantial, that there is little to nothing we can learn from them. Instead, I am interested in what it takes to foster, create and sustain a screenwriting career. The writers spotlighted in this book are ones who have gone from emerging to professional not by some miracle or magic act, but by sheer will, talent, dedication and tough grind.

They are:

Erin Cardillo, the creator and EP of The CW's *Significant Mother* (along with TV writing partner Richard Keith). Her feature *Isn't It Romantic?* sold to New Line in 2015. Erin is also the EP of *The I Do Crew*, which is being developed by The CW. She is represented by UTA and The Cartel.

Kirk Moore, NBC Writers on the Verge alumni, is a writer on *American Crime* and also wrote on Netflix's *13 Reasons Why*. He is represented by The Kaplan Stahler Agency.

Marissa Jo Cerar had her script *Conversion* appear on both The Hit List and The Black List in 2012. Marissa appeared on 2013's Young & Hungry List, spent three years on Freeform's *The Fosters* and is a co-producer on FOX's television series *Shots Fired*. In between television gigs, Marissa spends her time on writing assignments. She is represented by ICM and Heroes & Villains.

Terrell Lawrence wrote on *Your Family and Mine* and *Undateable*. He is represented by ICM.

Eric Koenig sold his Tracking Board Launch Pad competition placing spec script *Matriarch* to Paramount for mid-six-figures. He is represented by Paradigm and Madhouse Entertainment.

Greta Heinemann was accepted to the CBS Writers Mentoring Program and Humanitas New Voices program. She is a writer on *NCIS: New Orleans*, and is represented by UTA and Madhouse Entertainment.

Chandus Jackson is an alumnus of Universal Pictures' Emerging Writers Fellowship. His screenplay *The Muti Killings* made The Hit List in 2015, and currently has Djimon Hounsou attached. Chandus is represented by WME and Circle of Confusion.

Melissa London Hilfers sold her spec script *Undone* to Parks/McDonald. She is developing *The Recessionistas*, a book adaption for television, for USA. Melissa is represented by Paradigm and Alan Gasmer & Friends.

Moises Zamora is a lauded Mexican novelist and award winning filmmaker. He is currently staffed on *American Crime* and is repped by Silent R Management and CAA.

Joe Webb has developed television pilots for Fox, Sony and Fremantle Media, and currently works on the staff of Fox's *Sleepy Hollow*. He is represented by WME and Primary Wave Entertainment.

Barbara Curry wrote Universal Pictures' *The Boy Next Door* (which was named to The Blood List), starring Jennifer Lopez, as well as Hallmark's *Anything But Love*, starring Erika Christensen. Most recently, Barbara sold her pilot *Reversible Error* to NBC. Barbara is represented by Paradigm and Heroes and Villains .

Diarra Kilpatrick is the creator of the web series *American Koko* and was a staff writer on NBC's *The Mysteries of Laura*. She is currently developing original content for F/X and Amazon Streaming, and is represented by CAA and Gotham.

Tawnya Bhattacharya & Ali Laventhol are a writing team and alums of NBC's Writers on The Verge. They have written on shows such as *The Night Shift*, *The Client List*, *Perception* and *Barely Legal*. Currently, Tawnya & Ali are writers/producers on Freeform's *Famous in Love*. They are repped by ICM.

Isaac Gonzalez has written on such shows as *Legends of Chamberlain Heights* on which he became an Executive Story Editor in 2016, *Community*, *Welcome to the Family* and Seth MacFarlane's *Bordertown*. He recently sold a pilot to NBC called *The Great Brown Hope*. He is repped by CAA.

Danny Tolli participated in NHMC's TV Writing fellowship. Danny got into the room as an assistant on CBS's *Stalker*, and has since gone on to write on Shondaland's *The Catch*. He is represented by Verve.

Michael Perri is alum of both NBC's Writers on the Verge and NHMC. He has written on *State Of Affairs* and *Blindspot*, and is represented by The Kaplan Stahler Agency and Echo Lake.

The second layer of this cake is its *Executive Insights*: here, you will read observations from literary agents and managers, development and network executives, as well as subject matter experts. While not always in agreement, each of these executives provides an individual point of view, crafted by years of experiences working day-to-day with writers and success in today's distinctive industry microcosm. With the agents, managers and executives who so generously agreed to sit down with me for this book, I explored questions about breaking new writers, selling specs and pilots, representation relationships, the validity of contests and television writing programs, and much more. Their knowledge, opinions and impressions will be scattered throughout the book.

The executives interviewed for this book are:

Adam Perry, Literary Agent, APA

Ally Latman, VP (Head of Television), Blondie Girl Productions

Chris Coggins, VP of Development, EuropaCorp

Chris Cook, Literary Manager, Skyway Entertainment

David Boxerbaum, Literary Agent, Paradigm

Evan Corday, Literary Manager, The Cartel

Janine Jones-Clark, Director, Creative Talent Development & Inclusion, Disney/ABC Television Group

Jarrod Murray, Literary Manager, Epicenter

Jason Scoggins, Creator of The Scoggins Report, General Manager of Slated, Spec Scout

Jeff Portnoy, Literary Manager, Bellevue Productions

Jennifer Au, Literary Manager, Untitled Entertainment

Jennifer Titus, Senior VP On-Air Creative, CW

Jewerl Ross, Literary Manager, Silent R Management

John Zaozirny, Literary Manager & Producer, Bellevue Productions

Jon Karas, Literary Manager, Infinity Management

Josh Adler, Literary Manager, Circle of Confusion

Kailey Marsh, Literary Manager, Kailey Marsh Management and creator of The Blood List

Lee Stobby, Literary Manager, Lee Stobby Entertainment

Mike Woodlief, Literary Manager, MSW Media Management

Ryan Cunningham, Literary Manager, Madhouse Entertainment

Ryan Saul, Literary Agent, APA

Scott Carr, Literary Manager, Management SGC

Sean Barclay, Literary Agent, Gersh

Zadoc Angell, Literary Manager, Echo Lake Entertainment

Finally, the third layer of this cake of a book is (drum roll please . . .) Little ol' me.

A little about me, in case you are not familiar: by day, I am a career coach for professional and emerging screenwriters, and by night I am a hoarder of information, a lover of statistics and a rabid fan of strategy and well-made plans. Having started out as a writer myself, I was lucky enough to find some early modicum of success when a feature script of mine got picked up and plunged me into development hell, where I quickly discovered that I had no interest in working as a screenwriter long term. Instead, I jumped over to development headfirst. I went on to run ScriptShark.com where I created a series of business of screenwriting seminars—a venture co-run with Final Draft and sponsored by *The New York Times*—that ultimately went national. In 2008 I started taking on private coaching clients . . . and never looked back.

Think of me as a guidance councilor, support system, cheerleader and advisor for writers working in—and working to break into—the professional screenwriting space.

In this book, I am harvesting and synthesizing the same invaluable, screenwriter-specific industry information that I've brought into my coaching practice and building on it, in a manner that will help you learn more about the practical ways in which writers have broken into the industry following the famed 2008 WGA strike. While many chapters conclude with advice to help you construct appropriate next steps to elevate your own path, I've sown insight and guidance from yours truly throughout. My hope is that when you finally put this book down, you are not only inspired for your journey, but also armed with real-world, usable information that will inform future decisions and empower you to make the most of your screenwriting endeavors.

Enjoy!

SCREENWRITER SPOTLIGHT #1: Erin Cardillo

Erin Cardillo was raised in Greenwich, CT and has a Bachelor of Science in Performance Studies from Northwestern. After college, Erin moved to New York and worked extensively on stage as an actress, but a decision to pursue a career in film and television brought her to Los Angeles. She was the writer/producer for a feature film she developed at Warner Loughlin Studios called *Speak Now* (Audience Award: Austin Film Festival, 2013) and her original feature script, *Isn't It Romantic?* developed with Little Engine Productions and Broken Road Productions, was purchased by New Line in 2015. Also in 2015, Erin was hired to write a live action feature for Disney, which she is developing with Mandeville Entertainment.

On the TV front, Erin partnered up with Richard Keith in 2012. Cardillo & Keith won the 2013 New York Television Festival and subsequently received a development deal at FOX. Shortly thereafter, they partnered with Alloy Entertainment to develop *Significant Mother* for CW Seed, which was later picked up to series and premiered on The CW in 2015. Also in 2015, Cardillo & Keith sold an original pilot to The CW called, *The I Do Crew*, which is currently in development. In 2016, the pair joined the writing staff of Fuller House season two for Netflix as Co-Executive Producers.

Lee   You started out as an actor. Can you tell me a little bit about your life as an actor?

Erin: I went to Northwestern University and was studying acting there, mainly because my mother told me that I couldn't do it until I graduated college. Northwestern had an incredible theater program that drew me in very quickly. I feel like everybody should have that college experience. So I went there and ended up sort of falling in love with performance studies, which was performance art and adaptation of books to theater and adaptation of poetry and dance and all this stuff. So after school, I went to New York and tried to do experimental performance art in the Lower East Side, which was amazing and paid nothing. So (two years later) I started auditioning for TV and film. My first job was *Law & Order* in New York. And then right before 9/11—I'm dating myself—I had decided to come out to LA to just check it out because I'd never been here before. I had some friends from college who were out here, so I thought I'd come and check it out and see how it was going, what it would be like out here. And then 9/11 happened and . . . I ended up losing my job there, I was in this play that ended up closing because it was down in Soho, and I was just feeling a pull to move. So I just got rid of my apartment and packed up and moved to LA. And I had never been here before. So that was an adventure. Because of Northwestern, I had a nice network of people out here. So that made things a little bit easier. I started auditioning for film and television and working a bit and found myself a couple years later on a soap opera where I was having the most fun of my life because they literally let me do and say anything I wanted. I was sort of the comedic relief on a very campy soap opera called *Passions*.

Lee: So you could try on every human emotion.

Erin: I did. She was just such a fun character, and I got to wear fabulous clothes, and I improv'd half of what her dialogue was. But because I was contracted on that show, I had a lot of downtime, as well. I was a sidekick character, so I was on enough to be making a good living, but I had a lot of free time. I had an idea for a pilot and started talking to a friend who was further along in his writing career than me. We decided to pair up and write that show together, and it got some attention. It's one of those almost-got-made stories.

So (then) I decided to write a feature by myself. I had a story that I wanted to tell, so I decided I would try it out and see how it went. I had another writer friend who was mentoring me on that project and we ended up sharing story-by credit—a really great writer named Austin Winsberg, who's a TV/film writer/producer. I gave it to the agency that repped my previous writing partner. I gave it to the TV side because I didn't know anybody on the feature side—and they liked it and passed it to the feature side. And all of the sudden, I had fifty meetings all over town. And so it really was just one of those, I wrote a script that people liked, and then I got invited to play.

My goal in those meetings was I tried to turn as many of those meetings into—to close the deal in as many of those meetings, whether it was, let's do another project together or have you hire me to do something else. It was sort of my goal to not just have coffee or go to their office for five minutes, but to kind of say, how can we work together—if I felt like there was a vibe there.

So I started developing a couple things with a few different producers at that time. One of the women I met with was Gina Matthews (*13 Going On 30*, *What Women Want*), who I adored and became a mentor and a champion of mine, and that's the feature that I developed with her starting back in 2010. We developed it slowly because I was working on a couple other things, as well, but it's now at New Line—they optioned it and then asked for a rewrite and sort of a revamp. Now Rebel Wilson is attached, and we'll see what happens.

Lee: How long have you been working on it?

Erin: It's about six years, since Gina and I started talking about the idea for the project. I was writing another feature at the time, as well, so I was sort of writing two. But my main source of income then was acting, so all of this was on spec. And I was auditioning and going through pilot seasons and working on Disney's *Sweet Life On Deck* for three years. So I was busy as an actress, and so the writing took longer than it would if that was my main focus.

Lee: What became of the original script that got you a bunch of meetings?

Erin: Nothing. It got me a bunch of meetings.

Lee: Which is great.

Erin: Salma Hayek was attached for a minute. Jenn Todd was attached to produce it for a minute. There was all this activity and it was a romantic comedy that was like *Love Actually* in terms of multiple storylines and it started going out right around the time that Garry Marshall started his *New Year's Eve*. I think because he had so many stars and so many people attached, there was talk of, Well, we're not really doing that, *he's* sort of doing that. So then it just kind of died on the vine. So I just started working on other things and using the momentum of it as opposed to being attached to that script having to get made. I was told early on from my friend who I did that first pilot with (Michael Weiner, a successful Broadway writer and just amazing), and one thing that he said that stuck with me was he was always doing twelve projects at once. And he just was like, You have to output as much as possible, throw as much against the wall as possible, because you never know what's gonna hit. So I sort of went into that mentality and was just going with, Okay, I did that one, we'll see what happens. What are the next five things I'm doing?

Lee: The agent that you met through your previous writing partner—did they become your permanent agent? Are you still with them?

Erin: No. They were my permanent agents for a little while, but at that moment I had written three features—I'd written the first one that got me meetings, the one with Gina, and then a third one with the management company that I was with at that point attached to produce it. A friend of mine who was a writer who had also only written features at the time had an idea for a pilot, and he asked me if I wanted to write it with him. And I loved the idea, I thought it was really fun and funny, and I had never written a half hour before, but we both had come from writing romantic comedies. So we wrote this half-hour spec together, and it was another situation where a lot of people liked it, and it was hard because we were partners on this project, but we didn't know if we were going to keep working together, so we had five sets of reps and lawyers and different people, and it was kind of complicated because people kept saying, Well, are you a team now? Or are you not? But from that one spec we had a bunch of meetings and turned two of them into viable development things. We were developing something with Mandeville Television. That executive ended up leaving, so our project there sort of died. But we really liked it. Our managers weren't really getting it—one manager liked it, one didn't. It was just hard to get anything going with it. So Rich— Richard Keith is my current TV partner's name—was like, Let's admit this to the New York Television Festival. Because we both thought it was good, but nobody was paying attention to it. Our reps were sort of lukewarm on it. So we applied to the New York Television Festival—this was 2013—and this was the second spec that we had written. So we actually ended up winning the New York Television Festival Fox Comedy Pilot Competition. And with that came a development deal at Fox, and we had meetings with CAA and with WME—all in New York—and it was sort of this moment where it seemed like there was momentum and something was happening.

We ended up signing with CAA mainly because I remember them saying to us: Well, what else do you guys have? And we listed like twenty ideas. And they were like, Oh wow, you guys have a lot of work! So I think one of the things that helped solidify signing with them was the idea that we didn't just have this one spec. We'd been sort of doing it for a minute and maybe this was the momentum we needed.

At that time, Alloy Entertainment had an idea that they'd brought us in to development. But it was for a web project, and the project had sort of died. When we won the competition and signed with CAA, Alloy was like, Oh, maybe we can use the buzz or the momentum to revisit that project! And they knew that CW Seed was an activate participant in the New York

Television Festival, so they called the CW Seed people and said, These guys just won the Fox competition, but we have a pitch with them, can we come in? So we won the festival in late October. We pitched CW Seed in early November, and they bought the show like two weeks later. It was another one of those moments where they said, "Okay, you guys have sixty minutes of content, and you can break it up however you want. You can do ten-minute episodes or five-minute episodes or whatever." And we had this thought of like, Well, we're going to take this opportunity and make the most of it, so we're going to make three twenty-minute episodes that are ready to air. And we got very lucky, made those episodes for very little money, and they ended up not airing on Seed because CW really liked them, and they ended up getting us picked up to the network, which never really happens. Our intention was to take the smaller opportunity and turn it into a bigger opportunity.

Lee: And that show was . . .

Erin: *Significant Mother.*

Lee: Which started out as *Motherfucker.*

Erin: Which was our web title. The moment we went to network, we got way more PG, which was actually a bit of an issue for this show, because Seed had pushed it to be as raunchy as possible. And when we got picked up to network, we had to soften things, but we also didn't have the time or the budget to completely rework the episodes that we had shot for digital. So we had to keep a lot of what we had and just soften it.

Lee: What was it like working on the first show that you wrote for network?

Erin: It was surreal and sort of amazing. Being on set, for me, felt like it was a synthesis of all of the training I'd ever had. Like being on set as an executive producer and doing the writing aspect and working with the actors and overseeing production—it took all of my creative skills and managerial skills and for the first time, I had this sense of, Oh, this makes sense—it's like all of those divine moments where you feel like my life makes sense. And then it doesn't again five minutes later.

Lee: Not every writer out there gets to EP their first show.

Erin: You want to know how that happened?

Lee: Please!

Erin: We have very good lawyers, that's how it happened. We'd been making the deal for the digital series, and in the contract for the digital series were the clauses of what happens if it gets picked up to network. And our lawyers pushed to get us EP if it got picked up to network. And we believed that nobody actually thought it was going to get picked up to network because that had never really happened. So they just, in an effort to close the deal, were like, Okay fine. That's what we think happened. I don't know for sure. But we know that it is not the standard practice of the studio to do that. Part of the reason was because we did deliver three fully-produced episodes, so

I think they said—well, they did executive produce three episodes that you're willing to put on air, so . . . It's not like a crapshoot. You know what they can do, so just let them keep doing it.

Lee: Did you bring other writers into the room?

Erin: We didn't have a room because it was really low budget. The show did set a precedent for being the lowest budget show on television. We were able to hire a few freelance writers who wrote two episodes of the nine that were picked up, and Rich and I wrote the other seven.

Lee: That's a lot of work. And now you're waiting to hear on season two. What else are you up to?

Erin: Rich and I sold another show to The CW—a pilot. We pitched it this fall—an idea for an hour-long dramedy, and they bought the pitch, and so we just turned in the pilot. Now we'll wait to see if they're going to want to make that pilot. We developed the pitch with Gina Matthews and her husband Grant Garbo, who were the ones that I had the New Line movie with. It was an idea that Rich and I had, and we'd been looking for something to do with Gina. And so we went in and talked to her about developing the pitch, and we were very lucky to have her guidance because Rich and I had never pitched an hour-long before. And the format for pitching that is much different than comedy. Comedy you pitch the characters, you pitch the world, you pitch the dynamics that are sort of never going to change because half-hour tends to not be as serialized. It's a lot more straightforward. With the hour, we were pitching sort of long story arcs and mystery and we pitched a five-season concept. We also pitched ideas for marketing and how we would do web tie-ins with extra content. Having come from *Significant Mother*, we knew that was something The CW was interested in. Knowing the industry or how it's veering towards consuming television online, we built that into the pitch component.

The pitch was 20 minutes long. We went in and met with three people at the network. We ended up going directly to the studio, which is not usually the case. Usually you go to a studio first and then the studio takes you to different networks or maybe to the one that they have a deal with and then to others. Because we had worked with CW before and it was actually very late in the buying season—because we were doing *Significant Mother* in the summer, which was an off-season show, Rich and I didn't have a lot of time to develop for this pilot season. Because it was last minute and because they liked it, they just took it off the table so we didn't end up pitching it anywhere else. And then we met with Warner Brothers and CBS to decide which one would be our studio. We ended up going with Warner Brothers. It was a very hard decision, which I'd never had to make—but we went with Warner Brothers because *Significant Mother* was with them, too. We felt that it would be good to cultivate that relationship because we hadn't worked with anyone on the drama side over there, so we decided to build that relationship, and they've been really great partners in that development process.

Lee: It sounds like it.

Erin: And then, in the fall, I also got an assignment from Mandeville Films. They have a project that has been floating around that they were completely revamping—like a page one rewrite situation. I didn't even read the original script, they just gave me one sheet on what they wanted the concept of the movie to be. And I developed a pitch for them in the fall with Mandeville, and then went in and pitched Disney—because this would be a Disney movie—and ended up getting that assignment job. I've gone out for a lot of writing assignments before—not a ton, but the ones I've resonated with— and it's like the longest audition of your life. It's months of work to develop the pitch, and then you go in, and hope that you get picked out of however many writers they're seeing—and you don't ever know how many writers they're seeing—so I felt very lucky to get that project.

Lee: So that's your first big assignment? Congratulations.

Erin: It happened at exactly the same time that Rich and I sold the pilot, and that feature I was doing on my own, so I ended up in the fall having to write the movie and co-write the pilot at the exact same time. I was like, How did I get two of the biggest opportunities at the exact same time?

Lee: Well, seeing as you did them side by side, shall we compare a bit the process of writing a pilot a network is waiting on versus writing a feature for a studio? Is it the same process?

Erin : Very different, actually. They bought the pitch—it was a pretty well thought-out pitch, but it wasn't outlined. They didn't know what every scene was going to look like. So I just ended up with eight weeks to write it. It was just, go off, write this thing, turn it in. And now I'll be getting notes, but that first draft was just on your own.

In TV, you're doing three layers of notes at every stage. So we sold the pitch, and then we wrote—well, we have a production company, which is why it's three layers. If you sell to a studio, it's just two layers. But then you write a page of the story, and then you turn that in. So we would turn that into our producers, get notes, rewrite, all agree, then turn that into the studio, get notes, rewrite, then turn it into the network, then get notes, rewrite, then get approved to move on to outline. And that process goes through the outline stage—the same level of everybody weighing in at every stage— and then first draft is the same thing. So TV is a way more hands-on, by-committee process in my experience than features. But the good part about TV is if it actually goes, you're way more involved than you are in features.

Lee: I'm sure that your lawyers did what they did the first time and got you in a good position for this new pilot.

Erin: Yes, we're in good shape for the new pilot. We would be executive producers if it went . . . There was something else I was going to tell you . . . Oh! When

Rich and I executive produced *Significant Mother*, we had our producing partner because we had never run a show before. And we're technically the showrunners of that show, so if we get a second season, we'll have a little more responsibility, but because we didn't come up through the normal channels, it's been sort of difficult for us—we're learning as we do it. It used to be that you went through all the different levels of staff writer and all of that, but the industry is really changing and there are 400 TV shows currently on air and not all of those people are journeymen writers, so Rich and I now are taking the WGA showrunner training program. It's amazing. We just started, and if we get a season two or this show, it's literally saving our lives. They're amazing. Carole (Kirschner) is amazing. The program they've created is incredible. We had our first class last Saturday—it's a six-week, eight-hours a day kind of thing. But we got there and they were like, Okay, so the morning lecture is John Wells, and then in the afternoon, you'll have a panel with Carlton Cuse and Marti Noxon and Craig Daniels . . . Oh my God. You got to hear how all of these different people run their rooms and run their shows, how they manage, how they do time management and all of these things. It's already invaluable, and we've only had one class. So I'm excited about that.

1

UNDERSTANDING THE INDUSTRY

Profession Evolved: Screenwriting Through the Ages

Now nearly 100 years old, the profession of screenwriting has shifted and changed through the ages. Reflecting fluctuations in society, in the industry from which it was born, in response to maturing audiences as well as socio-economic ups and downs, the role of screenwriter continues to evolve dynamically as the industry continues to grow, shift and mature in its own way.

For the record: I am a big believer in context. In understanding where you come from, in order to aptly recognize what brought you to where you are now as well as accurately plan for where you might be going. Therefore, it's important that we break down the story arc of this near-century-old profession. While I am not going to school you on the entire history of film (if you haven't already, I do hope you make an effort to uncover it utilizing your screenwriter-mandatory tendency towards the autodidactic) I do want to take a beat to explore where we are this particular moment in time:

With the arrival of the "talkies" (*The Jazz Singer* was released in 1927) came the golden age of film, just two and a half decades after *A Trip To The Moon*—black and white and without any dialogue—introduced audiences to a whole new way of consuming stories. And with the golden age of film, the time in which MGM, Fox and Warner Bros thrived, came the flourish of the screenwriting profession.

At that time, screenwriters were salaried employees, getting paid per week, month or even year while contracted to churn out script after script for the magic moving pictures. In on-the-lot writer's buildings and bungalows, they punched keys and produced pages, finishing one script only to start the next. At that time the only writers working "on spec" (writing speculatively, not on assignment or for a paycheck) were writers trying to crack the system, to produce a sample good enough to land them a coveted screenwriting position.

The very first significant spec sale on record came in the form of *The Power and The Glory* from Preston Sturges, which sold in the early 1930s for $17,500, a sum many considered too small to shake up what was a convenient situation for contracted studio writers. The threat presented was simple: if studios agreed to pay writers per completed script, the comfortable studio contracts many screenwriters enjoyed would be at risk of elimination. So when the movie was released and tanked at the box office, many a studio screenwriter breathed a sigh of relief. The decision for the studios was easy: keep writers on contract, which allowed executives to influence the direction, subject matter and casting options presented in any individual work, rather than pay for individual scripts written without studio directive.

In the late 1940s and into the 1950s things began to change. Studios no longer held a monopoly on production and distribution. Movies were no longer automatically successful, and as the possibility of failure loomed, the number of movies produced per studio per year dropped significantly from one decade to the next. Screenwriters moved out of bungalows and writers' buildings. Development Hell—in which screenplays fighting for a shrinking number of green lights often got buried in endless rounds of notes—was born. The Golden Age of film became a thing of the past.

As the 1960s came, screenwriter William Goldman made the ambitious decision to write his next screenplay, *Butch Cassidy and the Sundance Kid*, outside of the studio system. The script sold, and fast. Every studio in town seemed to want a piece of it. The movie went on to become the highest grossing film of 1969. Despite Goldman's glowing success, screenwriters were slow to adjust, and collectively seemed to reject the idea of writing without receiving upfront pay. Instead, pitching became the name of the game: writers pitched projects to studios, received a green light and a paycheck, and went to work. With the exception of a few spec sales each year, screenwriters continued to work with contracts in hand well into the 1980s.

Television became, for lack of better words, the screenwriter's desk job—if you got that coveted job, you kept it. There were only so many shows and so many jobs for writers to populate. Television writers became part of the larger corporate machine, many dabbling in screenplays speculatively (assuming they had big screen aspirations) during downtime or on hiatus.

And then came 1988 and with it the WGA strike. Studio contracts were suspended. Writers stood on the picket line, and when they did not, they went home to write. When the strike was over five months later, in came the flood: an influx of available, quality content written off contract by some of the biggest names in the business, available for any buyer willing to pay a competitive price.

Into the 1990s, Hollywood became the wild screenwriting west, in the best ways, as the spec market exploded. Aggressive ticking-clock strategies were deployed in order to sell a spec to the highest bidder in the shortest amount of time. It was not unheard of to have a hot spec delivered on Tuesday by messenger who would then watch over the executive as he read from first page to last, not allowed to make copies before the script was once again whisked away. Bidding wars became the norm, occurring through the night and often at a frenzied pace.

In *Vanity Fair*'s March 2013 article *When the Spec Script was King* Margaret Heidenry wrote: "Not only were spec sales the industry's own version of a Hollywood ending, they also broke in a passel of Oscar winners: Alan Ball, who sold American Beauty to DreamWorks for $250,000 in 1998; Callie Khouri, who sold Thelma & Louise to Ridley Scott's production company for $500,000 in 1990; Ben Affleck and Matt Damon, who were movie extras before they sold Good Will Hunting to Castle Rock Entertainment for $675,000 in 1994."

Price tags rose higher and higher and the market hit its 1990s peak when Shane Black's *The Long Kiss Goodnight* sold for 4 million dollars.

As the 1990s came to a close, the proposition of another WGA strike loomed over television broadcasters. If television writers chose to strike in order to affect what was perceived to be unfair distribution of residuals from non-traditional distribution sources, networks would have to roll out a fall television schedule without any new series or new episodes for its returning hit shows. In order to curtail the potential effects of this looming problem, networks concocted a WGA-writer-free solution to keep the show on the road: reality television was born. And while the WGA strike of 2000 was ultimately averted, reality television seemed to—at least for a moment—take over the world.

As the new millennium made its grand entrance, all major studios but one (Disney) became at least partly owned by major corporations. Wild spending on spec screenplays slowly waned. The previously dependable home video market was no longer a safe bet. In fact, in just a few short years the home video market all but went away. With the advent of emails, Tracking Boards and text messaging, bidding wars and ticking clock strategies could no longer be deployed to the same effect. Confusion, once so key for generating the sort of excitement that lead to spec sales, was eliminated; agents were no longer able to create hype and buzz as they once had, and by the time the 2008 WGA strike kicked off, the spec market was on its very last legs.

Once the picket lines were dismantled and the dust settled, the 2008 WGA strike became known as one in which writers won a pyrrhic victory. Won the battle, lost the war. Yes, some paths for residuals were strengthened and clarified, but the strike also commenced the spec market's death rattle. In addition to bringing the industry to a halt for a good few months, the strike also allowed studios, now well under corporate management, to do some accounting. This quickly uncovered some undeniable facts: most screenplays purchased on the spec market never made it to screen. The ones that did rarely produced the sort of revenue that would justify the cost for which they were purchased. Therefore, new purchasing directives were initiated, ones much more aligned with the new corporate strategy to develop and capitalize on existing IP.

EuropaCorp's Chris Coggins explained:

> When we actually did strike, it was bad. It was really, really bad. Couldn't get anything made. But also studios went back into their libraries and things that had been in development for a long time were put into production because that's what they had. Turned out some good movies and some not so good movies. But really, after the writers' strike, there was a definite shift with the studios in that we have to make movies that can definitely sell. One story that I heard coming out of the writers strike was that it turned out to be very good for television because when all the writers were on picket lines together, they were sharing ideas they had, and a bunch of great writers from different shows got together to work on one show. Like *Modern Family* was a couple of different great writers, and that's how that show came to be. There was a couple of other collaborations that really came out of that strike, and it seemed to be much better for television than it was for features.

As the spec market was retracting and Open Writing Assignments were becoming few-and-far-between, newly developed DVRs started making their way into the homes across America. Content creators such as Vince Gilligan, Kurt Sutter and Matthew Weiner, previously orphaned by the deep-pocketed mainstream networks, found homes with smaller cable companies who offered less money but great promise of allowing them to create their unique content with little executive interference. As cable networks and digital streamers explored various paths to grow their subscription base, the concept of original non-network episodic content—both long and short—became a "thing." And the ongoing advances of digital equipment continuously made visual storytelling, a previously expensive endeavor, an available opportunity, not only on the tube or big screen, but now also on the web.

And that is where our story—if you will—begins.

The Industry Today

I've heard it said a million times: "It's never been harder to get a movie made." "It's never been harder to break a new writer." "It's never been tougher to sell a script." I've heard it from friends, from colleagues, from acquaintances at large dinner parties and in one-on-one afternoon coffee. I've heard these statements for decades now, and still movies are being made, and writers are breaking in, and a few of them are even managing to sell spec scripts.

Even so, it's important to recognize where the industry stands—as it relates to the screenwriter—at the time this book is written:

Most notably, we are in the time of what FX Networks CEO John Landgraf termed PEAK TV—a period of over-abundance in original scripted episodic programming, predicted to be followed—some time around 2019—by a period of natural contraction. Peak TV could be blamed—if you need to blame anyone for the profusion of scripted programming out there—on both changing viewer behavior (in 2010, there was no such universal concept as highly-accessible and widely available "binge viewing"), as well as the play made by digital streaming services to get into the original content game (in just two short years, Netflix went from 0 hours to 450 hours of original programing). In 2015, 409 original scripted programs hit the air. In 1999, and not counting HBO, we had all of 29 original primetime programs. In 2016, the number is expected to hover around 450, and includes programming on broadcast networks, cable networks and digital outlets. For 2017, the estimate is roughly 500 scripted programs, with numbers only expected to rise from there, until the inevitable bubble burst, after which they are expected to settle somewhere around the 400 original scripted programs per year.

But does this mean that networks are picking up shows left, right and center? At the time this book is written, broadcast networks are expected to generate roughly 150 original scripted programs per year. The outlets that are making the play for both market share (i.e. viewership) and prestige (award recognition) and have therefore seen significant growth, are cable networks (both basic, such as AMC and FX, and pay, i.e. HBO, Showtime and Starz) and digital outlets (such as Netflix, Amazon and Hulu), each developing unique content appropriate for its varied audience. By the end of 2016, pay cable, basic cable and digital outlets are expected to double the number of original scripted shows that broadcast networks deliver within a calendar year.

The feature spec market, as we know, has retracted. Not only has it retracted following the 2008 strike—with slight fluctuations, it has continued to retract in the years that followed, in a manner that left many writers who broke through selling specs confounded. Jason Scoggins, of The Scoggins Report, Spec Scout and Slated, had this to say:

> I've been having reps and people talk to me about how basically the spec market has disappeared and what I find interesting is that that was a prediction that was coming out of the writers strike period in 2007 and '08, when the writers strike happened, and then later in 2008, the actors were threatening to strike, so that really had a dampening effect on spec market activity. And then the recession hit. Those components led to this completely different environment for spec sales, where it was no longer a seller's market, it was definitely a buyer's market, and the studios basically shifted what kinds of movies they were making, all of which is to say that the spec market as we used to think about it—as almost this auction space, where agents and managers would take material into the marketplace and try to get as much momentum around it as possible in order to create an auction—that environment basically just went away. With some notable

exceptions. Every year, there's a handful of 7-figure sales that have multiple studios or multiple buyers bidding for them. That used to be the norm. After the writers strike it really became very much the exception.

In 2016, the most impressive seven-figure sale came in the form of *Bright*, a spec script written by Max Landis (who already had a significant number of impressive spec sales to his name), which sold to Netflix for over 3 million dollars, with Will Smith and Joel Edgerton attached. It was a spec sale that everyone talked about for two reasons: 1) that sort of sticker price is rarely observed in a spec sale these days, even with high profile attachments, and 2) the multi-million dollar purchase came from a digital outlet rather than a studio, a shift that Landis, a celebrated disruptor, deliberately orchestrated. But in the bigger picture, if the 1988 strike cracked open the seller's market, the 2008 strike closed the doors on it, and made the market very much a buyer market, where the buyer—for the most part—could be highly selective and incredibly demanding.

For a while now, we all have been hearing (and, let's face it, seeing the proof) that studios are interested in superhero movies and franchises, and little else. Gone are the days when a studio would make *When Harry Met Sally*, *Forrest Gump*, *Se7en* or *American Beauty* on any sort of a regular basis. Even the hyper successful *Straight Outta Compton*—which had, incidentally, a built-in audience—was put into turnaround by New Line (whose marketing and distribution is handled by Warner Brothers) when its budget ballooned to 29M. Ironically, when the film was picked up and released by Universal, its opening weekend take was over 60M, proving that a relatively small, special-effects-free movie can still find an audience.

The point here is simple: if one looks to the product available in their local Cineplex, it is easy to assume that over the past twenty years studios have shifted their buying directives. Therefore, I wanted to know: are studios still in the spec business? Once again, Jason Scoggins brought his useful data to the table:

The number of studios is consistent and the number of projects they collectively purchase year over year is within 20 percent. It doesn't really go crazy. If a given studio decides that they have plenty of original material and they're just going to develop internally, they might buy significantly fewer specs—that happens with Sony, actually, you can see the pattern where in a given year they might buy 6 or 8 or more specs, and then the following year, buy 1 or 2. Disney on the other hand, has only bought 1 or 2 specs each year for the last 6 or 7 years. And there's everything in between. I think Warner Brothers bought a huge number of specs for a couple of years running, and it was the number one studio buyer, and then kind of stopped doing that altogether. So the things that affect what the studios are doing change, but as a group, they tend to buy the same amount. To some extent the question is, are there other non-studio buyers that are going to swoop in? Or, are the previous buyers still around who are going to step back up? It's impossible to say. However, from the time that I started doing The Scoggins Report back in 2009 until now, the consistent thing I keep hearing from everybody involved in the feature side of the business is: We're looking for great material. It's impossible to find great material. Great material, the definition of that changes from person to person based on what they're doing. A producer might be looking for just strictly a really great script. A studio executive might be looking for a great package, where the script plus the actor plus the director make them go, Holy crap, we have to get involved. But the consistent thing that you hear is how hard it is to find great material and how desperate people are to find it.

These changes have been observed far and wide, not just by data geeks such as the likes of Scoggins and I. If the spec market moved fast in the 1990s, in the new millennium and the years that came after the writer's strike it was the industry—not the market itself—that has continued to shift and change actively and dynamically. Gersh agent Sean Barclay, who has been an agent for more than a decade, provided his perspective on the changing nature of the industry, and the speed with which it moves:

> There are changes happening, maybe not every day, but every few months you look back on the many days and you say: "Oh my God, that happened." On the movie side, the independent film has kind of moved onto television, right? *Breaking Bad* could have been a Sundance movie fifteen years ago. But meanwhile it's actually become a real independent film world where the studios are now in the acquisitions business and so there's actually more independent movies being made than ever before and there's more money sources than ever before. So writers have that playground, where there are barely any rules. But meanwhile on the TV side, you have 400+ shows on TV hiring writers. There are 48 entities that can write a check to a TV writer. So I would just say there's volume on both sides, one with guaranteed distribution (pretty close to guaranteed distribution, anyway) and one with the opposite of that.

Today, the market is continuing to shift and change, not only in what Studios and Networks produce or the new players that sprout to contend for market share, but also in how content is now finding its audience. Where in the 1990s and early 2000s it was the direct-to-video market that enjoyed a boom and offered an alternative to broad studio projects, today outlets such as VOD (Video on Demand), Amazon, Netflix, Hulu and even Xbox put endless content, from movies to traditional series to web series, at the fingertips of the audience.

In the current climate, the various digital content providers out there attract high profile storytellers with the promise of more creative freedom and greater control of their product. Unlike the broadcast network process for creating new shows, here writers, directors and showrunners seeking to tell their story in episodic format are offered full season orders, rather than just the opportunity to make a pilot and then hope for more. This is, however, not a new approach: just a decade ago, basic cable networks—then significantly less popular than broadcast networks as well as their pay cable counterparts such as Showtime and HBO—attracted name showrunners such as Kurt Sutter, Matthew Weiner and Vince Gilligan with offers to tell their stories with significantly less network oversight, which in turn grew the reach of cable networks, and made outlets such as AMC, USA and FX a must-have in homes across America, while the programs themselves became both award contenders and licensing candy all around the world.

With digital players fighting to lay claim to their rightful place in the growing market, content creators have come to recognize the freedom given to them by these non-traditional outlets. Woody Allen, who for decades rejected television, brought his first episodic venture to Amazon. Independent darlings The Duplass Brothers—who already have a deal for episodic content with HBO—signed a multi-picture deal with Netflix. The distributors of quality content have diversified, and literary talent has swiftly found its way to opportunity.

EuropaCorp's Chris Coggins shared her point of view:

> I think Netflix is the biggest game changer. They sort of paved the way, too, for Amazon, and Amazon is doing really well now, but also Amazon is doing much better in TV than they are in features. I'm sure Facebook has got their division ready to go. The YouTubes and the Awesomeness TVs, those are all interesting. I think *Beasts of No Nation* was a good experiment for Netflix, and I think it paid off a little bit with the SAG Awards (where supporting actor Idris Elba was bestowed with an award). Some people still thought of Netflix as just television. They didn't know that *Beasts* was a theatrical release. They know now, so the next couple of years, Netflix movies that get theatrical distribution could get some major awards attention. That's a huge game changer. And of course VOD is a really big business. I think *The Interview* did pretty well—it did have a lot of extra marketing and advertising around it, but I think it proves you can release a high quality studio movie on VOD and people will see it. VOD is a really good business, especially for the indie film market. With the VOD market and Amazon and Netflix being in everybody's home, the indie market could go bigger than it was.

Becoming a Screenwriter in Today's Industry

Throughout the years, what it meant to be a screenwriter, and what was expected from anyone attempting to own that moniker, has changed and shifted along with the shifts and changes in the industry.

In the years leading up to the 1988 strike, the screenwriting brass ring was the studio contract, but what came after that? The spec boon of the 1990s brought with it what became known as the "one-and-done" screenwriting model: an industry climate where material was flying off the shelf and screenplays were purchased more for concept then execution. In this unique environment, unknown screenwriters could emerge, going from complete unknowns to bona fide screenwriters with a studio sale on their hand in a matter of months, weeks, or even days. The down side? Many such screenwriters became one-hit-wonders (hence the term "one and done"), having achieved a single success that was never again repeated, only to then once again fade into the obscurity from which they came.

In the 1990s, there was little opportunity for inexperienced, unknown screenwriters to emerge in television. While agents and managers have long understood that consistent money is in content created week after week for the small screen and positioned their clients accordingly, many a screenwriter considered television to be—for the most part, though there certainly were exceptions—the place that writers went to die, until shows like *The West Wing*, *The Sopranos* and *The Wire* changed all of that. Until the early 2000s it was nearly unheard of for an un-established writer who has not worked their way up the television ranks to write an original pilot and see it go somewhere, let alone attempt to staff on a series without previous success or substantial relationships to their name. Today, with the arrival of peak TV driven by cable and digital outlets seeking the sort of scripted content that would help them expand and solidify their viewership, writers are finding varied avenues to break into that space. In the time I've worked with writers, I've gone from working with 20 percent TV writers and 80 percent feature writers, to 60 percent TV writers, and 40 percent writers writing strictly in the feature space.

Indeed, things have changed. The one-and-done model is gone, television is a huge growth sector, and many writers seeking to build and sustain steady screenwriting employment have taken on the new moniker of content creators, exploring every format from feature, to traditional episodic, to the ever-growing platform that is the web. With access to digital equipment, and the ability to make a web-series with little more than a few enhanced iPhones and a Final Cut Pro, many writers have explored their voices—and built their cinematic communities—with the creation of innovative, unique web content, made on a budget and put together with like-minded friends as well as family resources, all of which allowed them to explore new facets of visual storytelling and generate the sort of content that could help them stand out in a space saturated with product. Using digital distribution channels, content creators have been able to gain attention through less-traditional work (*Too Many Cooks*, anyone?) expressing their unique visions and parlaying their success to more traditional projects, while establishing a strong following and brand identity through ingenuity and hard work.

Whether telling stories in screenplay, long-form episodic or web format, the industry has turned its eyes to the career screenwriter—one who is not seeking to sell the one script quickly or tell their one story, but rather make the sort of go of screenwriting that would hopefully keep them busy, employed and collecting paychecks for years down the road.

Because of this, in today's career-centric industry space many agents and managers seek out writers with multiple pieces of industry-ready material to their name, proving that the writer is able to repeat what they've done well again and again. Executives are known to ask the ever-popular question: "what else do you have?" at every meeting and every turn, always in search of the next great writer, the next big idea, and the creative partner they may want to get into business with long term. Relationships are forged with writers who commit to writing script after script until they find success, only to then return to their computers for the next script and the one that will come after that, continuing to produce the sort of work that will keep them front-of-mind with the industry, and electrify their growing fan base. Today, the search is on for the writer who will not only excite with the script at hand, but also present the promise of what they may write in order to fuel the sort of screenwriting career that could last for years on end.

SCREENWRITER SPOTLIGHT #2: Kirk Moore

Kirk Moore is an NBC Writers on the Verge (2014–2015) Fellow. He was staffed on ABC's critically acclaimed *American Crime*, and is currently writing on Netflix's teen drama series *13 Reasons Why*, based on the YA novel by the same name.

Lee: When did you start writing? Did you always know that TV was where you wanted to be, or did that reveal itself later? And if so, how?

Kirk: I started writing in high school not long after a personal tragedy. When I was 14, I lost all vision in my right eye after a freak accident. I wasn't able to do much physical activity for months, so I began writing angry poetry and short stories. Those poems and stories later became a one-man show and my first original theatre production at the Alliance Theatre in Atlanta, Ga. I can't say I always wanted to be a TV writer, but I knew wanted to WRITE.

Lee: Gotta ask . . . Why television?

Kirk: For me, television writing gives me a freedom that I couldn't have in film. It's more inclusive, and I'm able to tell different types of stories. Plus, I'm a big fan of collaboration. TV is all about being collaborative, sharing ideas and receiving different points of views.

Lee: Once you decided you wanted to write professionally, what steps did you take to become the best writer you could be?

Kirk: First, I consulted friends who were making strides in television. I need advice and mentorship. Then I read tons of produced pilot scripts. I also took a Script

Anatomy class with Tawnya Bhattacharya. Her course was so helpful on a professional and creative level.

Lee: If you could retrace your steps . . . what did you do to prepare yourself for a career in the industry?

Kirk: It may sound clichéd, but . . . I learned to love myself and trust my instincts. This isn't an industry where self-doubt helps anyone soar. Also, I learned the business. Well as much as I could learn. I read the trades like *Variety* and *Hollywood Reporter*. I frequented sites like Deadline and Hit Fix. I wanted to know what projects were being bought. I wanted to know the producers and writers. You can't be a TV writer and know nothing about the business.

Lee: You first surfaced through the television writing programs; what was that experience like for you, and how important do you think those programs are for breaking into television?

Kirk: I think fellowships are very important. They provide a door of opportunity that some writers may not have otherwise. I submitted to the fellowships three years in a row. My first two tries, I was a finalist at ABC/Disney and NBC *Writers on the Verge*. One my third try, I was one of the eight chosen for *Writers on the Verge*. *Writers on the Verge* was a very rewarding challenge for me. I was working a full-time job, so I had to juggle quite a bit. I learned to write faster and to really trust my instincts.

Lee: Did you go directly from *Writers on the Verge* to staffing? And if so, what was that experience like?

Kirk: When *Writers on the Verge* ended in late January I was already going on general meetings with production companies and studio executives. I had already secured my agent and manager during the fellowship. It was quite an experience, because there is so much uncertainty and rejection in the staffing process. Showrunners are looking for something specific. They want someone special who speaks to their show's needs. If I'm being honest, it was tough. But ultimately, I landed a staff writer position on *American Crime*.

Lee: When and how did representation come into your journey and how did you decide to go with your rep?

Kirk: The moment I was announced as finalist for *Writers on the Verge*, people started reaching out to me. I found it strange and hilarious. After years of trying to get agents and managers to read my work, they were coming to me. I sat with a few agents and several managers. I told them what I wanted for my career, and then I listened to what they could do for my career. What stuck out for me most was how they critiqued my writing sample(s). I paid close attention to how they gave me notes. I wanted to hear how their perspective and point of view aligned with mine. We didn't necessarily have to agree, but I wanted to make sure I respected what they had to say.

Lee: Tell me a bit about the experience as a first-time TV-staff writer on *American Crime*. How was it for you?

Kirk: I pinch myself everyday, because my experience as a first-time TV-staff writer was truly amazing. I didn't have much experience in scripted, so I was a bit nervous. But the other writers on staff were so welcoming and helpful. We have a very seasoned and diverse writing team. John Ridley, our showrunner, was very specific about his expectations, so that made the process much easier for me. I know how to follow instructions. In the room, I pitched as much as I could and found ways to bring my personal experiences to the story. As time went along, he assigned episodes, and I was lucky enough to write my own episode. That is a big deal as first-time writer.

Lee: How does your life change after your first staff writing position—are jobs just handed for you, or do you have to work for them? And—assuming you do have to work for them—what does "working for them" look like?

Kirk: Well I go on a lot of meetings. A lot of meetings. I have to know the execs and producers who are creating content and looking for new writers with fresh voices. Nothing is handed to me. I still have to write new material. I still have to pitch myself. I will say, working on a show like *American Crime* does add tons of sheen to my resume.

Lee: How do you keep yourself busy (creatively and professionally speaking) between TV seasons and staffing gigs?

Kirk: Right now, I'm writing a new pilot. I have set times where I dedicate myself to nothing but writing. I treat the process as if it's a regular 9 to 5. I'm a busy body, so I have to be doing something. If I'm not writing, I'm reading. I read several articles a day, who knows what I'll stumble across. I'm also very active on social media, specifically Twitter.

Lee: Is it important for TV writers to live in Los Angeles? And if so, why?

Kirk: I think it's important for TV writers to live in Los Angeles. Yes, I can write anywhere, but a TV writer needs to be where everything is happening. That's here in LA. A writer needs to network, build relationships and possibly start a writers group with peers. Also, most fellowships want you to reside in LA. It shows you're serious about the profession and your career.

Lee: In your estimation, how long did it take you to break into the industry from the time you set your sights on a career writing for television, and what did you do during that time?

Kirk: It took me a little over three years from the time I wrote my first TV spec (*Southland*) to the time I was chosen to be in *Writers on the Verge*. Then three months later, I was staffed on my first series. I, initially, set my sights on getting into one of the fellowship programs. My biggest hurdle was learning how to pitch myself. I've never been the type to open up to strangers, but that's what you have to do as a TV writer. I had to learn it's OK to be vulnerable, because my personal story makes me valuable.

Lee: If there was one thing you wish you knew when you got started that you know now, what would it be?

Kirk: TV writing is very personal. Don't be afraid to be transparent.

2
YOUR CRAFT

The Importance of Craft

When I proposed this book to my publisher, one question came back: this is not a book about screenwriting technique. Lee is not a screenwriting instructor. Why, then, is this book going to include a whole chapter about screenwriting craft?

The answer is simple: because you can't talk about building a screenwriting career without putting some much-needed emphasis on the importance of the writer's screenwriting prowess. Becoming a working screenwriter requires producing exceptional screenplays or outstanding original television pilots, or both. Big ideas may get the glory, but screenwriting success is all about execution. In order for you to succeed in this industry, you're going to have to write a script, or a number of scripts, that are not only good, but rather are GREAT. So while I am not going to belabor craft itself, wax poetic about the intricacies of character arcs or aim to summarize the keys to great screenwriting in this chapter (because first, that's not the focus of this book and, second, many other great books have already been written and will be written about just that, so if that's the insight you're looking for go ahead and pick up any number of those) it is of critical importance that we all recognize how integral craft is to this process.

As Manager Chris Cook put it:

> At the end of the day, you need a great screenplay and you need a modicum of luck. But you are mitigating the luck by getting better and better and better and working harder and harder.

In his book *Outliers: The Story of Success*, author and journalist for *The New Yorker* Malcolm Gladwell said: "Researchers have settled on what they believe is the magic number for true expertise: ten thousand hours." Your screenwriting craft is no different. It demands hours, days, weeks, months and years of outlining, writing and rewriting in order for you to attain the sort of mastery that can one day bring you great success.

The consensus in the industry is that in order for a script to gain traction, it has to be GREAT. Not just good. Therefore, I turned to Jason Scoggins, once an agent and now the GM of Slated, who spent ample time studying the market, for insight about writing a great screenplay:

> It takes years of practice to get to the point where you're writing anything good, let alone great. I mean, draft after draft of brand-new material. You've got to start from scratch 6 or 7 or 8 times. When I used to represent screenwriters I used to say that it's not worth your time or my time to work together unless you have at least six scripts in your drawer because it takes that amount of time just to get good at screenwriting in the first place. And then all of the elements have to come together so perfectly for a screenplay to be great, it's just really hard getting all of those elements to line up. And not everybody's going to respond the same way to any piece of material. Even if everybody agrees that it's good writing, not everybody is gonna get super excited about it. There's subjectivity to assessing material and deciding whether you want to spend multiple years of your life pushing it forward. At the core, the answer to the question is it's just really difficult to write great material and if it was easy everybody would do it.

Mastering screenwriting craft is not just about writing. It's about learning structure, decoding character arcs and internal/external journeys in whatever is your preferred format, and figuring out how to raise stakes, create effective escalation, keep your protagonist active, and so much more. You can learn auto-didactically by breaking down scripts on your own (though not everyone is equipped for that), reading books, taking classes online or in person, enrolling in an MFA program or by any other method. Many of the executives I spoke to touted academic programs; not necessarily because of the quality of education you receive (though that certainly was not disputed) but due to one simple truth: programs make you write pages. They force you into discipline. They leave you no choice but to absorb method.

The point is: whether through academia or on your own, you have to do it. You have to learn structure, develop the capacity for storytelling and have the tools to identify what is and isn't working in a script, whether it's someone else's or yours. You have to read other screenplays—preferably unproduced, such as those that are named to The Black List, The Hit List and The Blood List every year, and form educated opinions about them that help you understand the craft. It's also about reading pilots, as many as you can get your hands on, and learning what the television microcosm is shaping up to look like, so that you can develop a better understanding of the landscape that you are trying to break into.

Or even more bluntly: the industry is on the lookout for screenwriting professionals, or in the very least writers with the talent, dedication and discipline to become that. Agents, managers and executives are seeking to work with scribes who don't only rely on their talent, but also understand the critical importance of ability to back it up and catapult them to the next level. While talent is critical, learning your techniques, understanding structure inside out (even if you then make the educated decision to go against it or throw it out) and having the training and discipline for the format is what will make you shine as you become a screenwriting professional. This is why, then, we have to have a whole chapter about craft.

One of the managers I spoke to asked me to keep his name off this very simple quote he gave me: "The problem is," he said, "that everyone thinks that they're above average, but very few actually are." Learning, dissecting and diligently challenging your growth in the development of your craft is how you begin to set yourself apart.

As noted above, there is no one way, or only way, to learn screenwriting craft. Manager Lee Stobby is a fan of Academia. He told me:

> I have more writers who have English degrees than Screenwriting degrees. Or they will have English degrees but then they'll get a MFA screenwriting degree. I think those MFA screenwriting degrees, especially the ones from UCLA or LMU are really good. Not because they are necessarily going to teach you what to write and what not to write but they are going to force you to crank out scripts. You're going to be in a program for three years? You need to write one script every three months. So, if you're doing it right, you come out of and you have eight scripts. I can deal with somebody who's written eight scripts. So, if you don't think you have the discipline to do it without someone forcing you to do it, then you should go to school and have someone literally force you to do it. Because then, when I'm forcing you to do it or somebody else is forcing you to do it, you understand how that works. It's one thing to say you are a writer but it's another thing to actually sit down and write for twelve hours every day. Versus if you've been casually writing a script over two years or whatever—then you're not a real writer. That's not going to prepare you.

Like Stobby, Manager Scott Carr is a believer in craft, dedication and discipline. Once again, Scott emphasized the importance of superior execution:

> If someone's got a really strong understanding of craft and a great voice, we can work through the other things a lot more smoothly. If the writing isn't there, then sadly good ideas don't really matter as much. I work in a literary capacity, so in order to convince people to spend two hours of

their busy lives to read something, it's gotta be a great read. While reading a screenplay to evaluate the level at which a writer is at, that's when it comes down to the execution and how well they tell a story. The quality of the structure, the way in which they hit the beats that move the momentum of the story forward while still subverting my expectations on where I think the story is going. And that's something that usually requires a writer to be very good at rewriting. Because, usually, first passes are more like a vomit draft, the most banal way to tell the story. So I prefer that the writer go in and challenge and question the way they are telling the story and ask themselves if they really are doing it in the most original and effective way.

Years ago, I was in New York teaching a business of screenwriting seminar. As I did at every such day-long session, I asked my students to introduce themselves, and tell their classmates why they decided to get into screenwriting. A couple of the writers in the room told me how they always loved movies. How they wanted to contribute to the conversation on the silver screen. Another was an NYU film student. A fourth was blunt and brave enough to tell me that she was taking classes but still figuring it out. And one of them—whom I will never forget—told me that he started out writing novels. But then he got his hands on a screenplay, and thought that it was so much easier, so much less work (because most of it is just dialogue, right? It's not like you even have to really fill up those pages) and so he decided to forget the novel and go the easy route. To which all I can say is: Good luck with that.

If you take anything away from this section, let it be this: it takes a lot more than writing ninety pages (or thirty-two pages or fifty-eight pages if you're a TV writer) in Final Draft in order to master the craft of screenwriting. As you go through this journey from emerging to professional your mastery will be challenged at every turn. It only gets harder, more exciting and more demanding, when industry folks start to pay attention. Therefore, the period when you are learning your craft, when you're figuring out structure and character and voice, when you are finding your brand and getting confident with your chops is the time to immerse yourself in all things screenwriting and work up—one hour at a time—to those all-important ten thousand hours.

Screenwriting Advice from Industry Professionals

For further, non-technical screenwriting guidance, I turned to my industry colleagues, in the hopes of gleaning some inspiration and direction for the readers of this book. After all, there is no building a screenwriting career without that outstanding, unique, exciting script, regardless of how much determination and ambition you bring to the table. At the end of the day, every single screenwriting career that is launched these days starts with a great screenplay.

With that in mind, my friends in representation, discovery and development shared with me their best advice, aimed at inspiring emerging screenwriters towards their very best work.

Passion is something you will hear about in this book again and again. As I often remind my writers, there is little of more value that you can offer in the context of screenwriting (foundational screenwriting knowledge not withstanding) than your passion on the page. Paradigm's David Boxerbaum spoke to that:

> First and foremost, always write from a place of passion. I always say great writers write. So if you're a writer, you should always be writing no matter what. It should be your job 24/7 to be sitting down and writing and focusing on furthering your career, furthering your craft. Because it is a craft and it's a talent. Most people say they're a writer because they wrote one script and that's that, and now I'm a writer. Well, if that's your job, that's what you want to call your craft, you should be continuing to hone that craft every day.

It is important to remember that agents, managers and executives read hundreds of scripts every year, whether for projects that they are developing, clients who they are representing, or new writers who they are considering for representation or development. If they don't HAVE to read the entire work for notes or feedback, the executive usually makes a quick assessment: Is the material well written? Does it offer something unique, interesting? Has it managed to grab me by page 5, 10 or 25? If the answer to any of these questions is No, the material will likely be set aside sooner rather than later, and the executive will turn their attention to the next script on their iPad or in their pile. Because of this, it is critical that the writer is able to deliver the sort of stellar work that, for all the right reasons, stands out. EuropaCorp's Chris Coggins explained:

> I want something that will punch me in the face, if that makes sense. Something that will grab me right from page one, either a character that has really interesting dialogue, a set-piece or an action scene that I haven't seen before, something that surprises me. Nothing really surprises me lately. Something with some personality—strong personality to it—it doesn't always have to be good, but a personality that comes off the page is what I look for the most. And then after that, something that's very high concept. Something that's easy to sell. A project with a really good hook because you can make a great movie all day every day, but if nobody goes to see it because nobody knows what it is because you can't sell it with the hook, it's really unfortunate.

During her many years in the industry working with TV lit clients, The Cartel's Evan Corday, too, has done her share of reading, appraising original pilot script after original pilot script. She has seen every type of procedural, and like many agents and managers out there, is looking to get excited by either an entirely new take on old standards, or, better yet, a pilot that takes her on a whole new journey that she has not yet seen.

> There is literally no cop show that you can pitch me that I haven't heard and so if someone actually comes up with something I haven't heard before, that is exciting. But to me, it's more that cable/digital voice that's really gonna go the extra mile. We heard a pitch recently from a non-client that was like the Indiana Jones young sexy version of Darwin and I was like, OK, that's interesting, I want to read that. I've just never heard that before. My client, who actually was my former assistant who I love, wrote an insane dark drama about a junkie tooth fairy who's grinding up the teeth and snorting them. So she starts stealing teeth from kids and it ends up in this really dark place where she hooks up with a dentist who has a sex addiction so she gives him what he wants and he extracts teeth for her. So it's insane. It'll never get made. But it's the best thing to open doors because you are like, "You have never read anything like this" to the buyer.

When it comes to television, it's the broadcast networks—for the most part—who have been in the procedural business, often turning to proven procedural content creators to reinvent the genre, or else repeat it well. Cable networks and digital outlets are much more aggressively seeking out serialized narratives both in one-hour and half-hour formats, with potential season procedural elements as seen in shows such as *True Detective*, *Stranger Things* and *Top Of The Lake*.

Both in features and television, just as important as understanding the mechanics of your script, is to know whom your audience is. Some years ago, one of my writers wrote an adult comedy with a few horror elements and a juvenile tone to it. Well received though the material was, executives couldn't wrap their brain around the screenplay's potential audience: Teenagers or adults? Sophisticated or silly? The screenplay, ultimately, never found a home. Knowing your audience doesn't only speak to understanding who it is that will be turning on the television or walking into the movie theater to watch your work. It's also about understanding what you can and can't get away with, based on adoption and audience behaviors.

That simple lesson is one that Ryan Saul of APA spoke to:

> I teach a screenwriting class, and one of the things I always tell my students is, when you're coming up with your ideas, before you start writing, know who your audience is. If you're writing a family movie, you need to reach 4-quadrants of families. You need to reach everybody. Or if you're writing a movie for younger boys then know that your budget is going to be capped at a certain level because there's a finite amount of people who are going

to see that movie. Or if you're doing an Academy-type movie, that's prestige and you're going for adults, which is why they have to be cheaper to make. If I'm making SPOTLIGHT, I know I can't have a scene that's gonna have a car chase in it. That's a contained adult movie and only certain people are going to see that movie. So you have to write to that audience.

Manager Jeff Portnoy of Bellevue Productions broke down the industry's different expectations from pilot and feature film scripts:

> On the TV side, it's extremely competitive so it's really all about the hook, the concept, the world, the characters, something's gotta stand out, it's gotta be something we haven't seen before. It's better to think about worlds that have never been explored before, character types that have not been explored before or stories that really make your eyes go wide. Those things kind of apply in the feature space for the most part but here it's more about the plot. It's better to write something that you are passionate about and that has a really unique concept that's intriguing. From my experience, that studio, network, or production company executive would rather enjoy their read and really be blown away by a script, even if it's something they would never make, and then bring that writer in for a general meeting, get to know them and then give them an assignment or hire them to be a staff writer on a show.

Like many managers out there, Jeff understands many emerging writers' desire to write the perfect studio script. However, as the studios have been in the franchise/IP game, he cautioned:

> The studios are not looking for new IP. They can remake any film, reboot any film, do a prequel or a sequel of any hit film; they own hundreds and hundreds of bestselling books, articles, and true stories. It's better to write something that really blows them away, even if it's very small and completely off the radar. And then get them excited. That's exactly what happened with *The Wretched Emily Derringer* (by Bellevue client Chris Thomas Devlin). It's a script the studios would never make but they loved it so much and it's gotten the writer dozens of studio meetings and he's being considered for studio projects. If the writer had written a script that was a 100-million dollar sci-fi action-adventure, the studios already have that. So they would rather just read something they really enjoy and then put that writer on to the next big thing that they control, the IP that they control.

Just as important as passion, execution and uniqueness to a screenplay's success is the writer's voice, that hard-to-delineate factor, which we will seek to break down and explore later in this chapter. Literary manager Jewerl Ross spoke to the importance of a writer's voice:

> One of my favorite quotes is—I don't know if this is an Oprah quote or who this quote comes from—"Who you are speaks so loudly, I can't hear a word that you're saying." I think that relates to writing, as well. How talented you are, your point of view on the world, your prejudices, your inner demons . . .all of that stuff will end up on the page when you are writing a screenplay. I think it's impossible to not share who you really are if you spend 4 months or longer writing something and getting it onto the page. The truly talented people share a lot of themselves every time they write. It's impossible not to.

Finally, Jason Scoggins who knows all too well about the micro when it comes to writing, opted to offer his two cents looking at the macro:

> Everybody is looking for great material, whether it's packaged up or not. And so to a certain extent, worrying about the numbers, worrying about what the studios are buying, worrying about all of the stuff that I tend to focus on, it's all noise. And until you have a bunch of great material that you've written, all you should be focusing on, really, is writing great material. Your job is to amass a bunch of material that people are hungry to buy from you. And I think that between companies like Slated and The Black List website and Tracking Board and SpecScout and the other discovery mechanisms in the space that have popped up over the last 2 or 3 or 4 years and become a real presence, I think it's easier to get discovered now than it has been. There are companies whose reason for being is to find good material. And specifically to help executives and producers find good material. So don't worry so much about getting signed and selling and following the marketplace. Again, most of that is noise. And when you have a bunch of great material, there's ways to get it out in front of people. And if it is as great as you think, then everything else will fall into place. Just focus on the writing. That's what matters.

But . . . Is it Ready?

You finished a screenplay—congratulations! It's an exciting and rewarding moment, and you should celebrate it. But once the celebration is over, how do you know if the screenplay is, indeed, ready for the industry? If you've workshopped your material with a seasoned screenwriting instructor, or gotten ongoing feedback from other professional writers or writers' groups populated with writers who are a step or two ahead of you, it is likely that the screenplay is further along than it would have been had you written it in a bubble.

Remember, the key to accelerating the writing process and challenging yourself to the best screenplay or original pilot you could write is early-and-often exposure of the material, at all stages, from idea, to outline, to draft.

A number of years ago, I sat down with a writer who was convinced that his screenplay, written and re-written, was indeed ready for showtime. The screenplay, after all, was developed with his writers' group, and so the writer was perplexed as to why, after reading it, I was not persuaded that his script was the screenwriting equivalent of THE ONE. His writers' group loved it. He consulted with them every step of the way. It was only upon further investigation that I found out where the problem lay: the writer did the right thing assembling a writers' group, there's no question about it, but it was the other members of the group who gave me pause: one was a retired community theater actor; another made his money as a plumber. None of them have ever worked in a professional environment. None have read extensive screenwriting books or even taken class. None of them have read scripts or watched movies or shows on a regular basis. This, then, turned out to be a classic case of the blind leading the blind.

Like this particular writer, not every writer out there has a built-in screen-writing community. Many write in solitude, without experienced eyes to which they can turn for feedback. In those scenarios, non-industry friends and family often become touchstones for logic and quality control, but it is important to remember that they are, for all their story instincts and good intentions, not seasoned industry professionals. Therefore, before you unleash your material on the professional space, it's important to find out whether it does, in fact, pass industry muster.

> Jason Scoggins of Slated told me: the problem becomes when you're the writer and you've been working on a given thing for so long you just can't see what's working and what's not anymore. So feedback from people like you Lee, from professional development executives, whether they're at companies or doing it on a freelance basis for screenwriters, that kind of feedback is hugely helpful. The coverage product that SpecScout developed and is now at Slated is hugely helpful. The whole point of it is to indicate what's working and what's not. It's difficult to see the forest through the trees if you're the person who's written the material but if you're looking at somebody else's material, I think it's a pretty well understood question of what's good or not. We see it a lot at SpecScout, projects that are good with some clear paths to make it much better. But the process of solving the existing problems creates new problems—that's sort of the nature of development hell, where you, in the process of trying to fix one or two or more issues with a script, you create another couple, and you just get in this cycle where you keep sort of fixing and breaking and fixing and breaking. I wish I had a good solution to that, although I do think that guidance from professional development executives can be very, very

helpful. We do see at SpecScout score improvements more consistently when a third party is helping to develop a piece of material rather than the screenwriter basically working in a vacuum, even working off of good notes. It's just finding the solution that doesn't break other elements is something that is challenging and having a guide to help you get there can be super helpful.

A caveat: while the majority of my client base is made of writers either professional or just about ready and positioned to break, I read screenplays from new screenwriters who just completed their first-, second- or third-ever screenplay on a regular basis. And I can tell you unequivocally that material from writers who have not done the legwork of exposing their screenplay to individuals in the know is almost never industry ready, despite the writer's hard work, passion for the subject matter or conviction in the material.

One path to developing your craft with ongoing, constructive feedback and insight is the MFA programs at higher learning institutions across the country. While each program operates in its own unique way, many offer mentoring from experienced Hollywood screenwriters, while providing a demanding incubator environment to help the writer develop craft on a rigorous, demanding schedule. Even though the strengths and focus of these programs vary, many of them are sure to make you do one thing: write pages, while receiving ongoing, knowledgeable feedback. Any writer participating in such a program can be expected to come out with a stronger handle on the craft, as long as they do the work.

Regardless of your path to screenwriting education, be it independent, in an MFA program, through self-created course work or via non-university affiliated screenwriting classes, the process of gathering outside opinions and verifying that the script stands a solid chance of meeting and/or surpassing industry standards is the all-important process known as VETTING. While it is true that this is a business of opinions and that everyone will not likely agree on any particular script, your job is to seek out reputable industry sources whose opinions and taste levels have been well established, and assess their reaction to your work.

Over time, the argument of whether one should spend money on coverage and script consultants has raged on. My take on it? If you are well connected in the industry, with working friends and colleagues who have a firm, proven handle on story, willing to give you in-depth feedback, there is no need for you to spend money on consultants or coverage. HOWEVER, most emerging writers are NOT positioned to seek out in-depth coverage from other writers, development executives, agents, managers and producers working in the industry today, and many of my pro writers continue to pay for notes in addition to seeking those out from their industry contacts. At the end of the day, there is plenty to be gained from a set of notes from someone who knows story but doesn't know you, and therefore can't anticipate your intention. Therefore, screenplay coverage and insights provided by reputable screenwriting consultants can be a much-needed, unabashed reality check, as well as provide valuable guidance for next steps.

However—and this is a big HOWEVER—not all screenwriting consultants, screenplay coverage services, screenplay readers or even screenwriting programs are created equal. As someone who ran a leading coverage service for over six years, I can tell you unequivocally that no two script readers, for example, are the same. Experience, taste level and sensibilities all play a part in how their opinions are constructed. As a screenwriter or television writer seeking to challenge his writing and demand the most growth of his work, your job is to find the readers, consultants and teachers who are likely to be most demanding of your work. They will be the ones who will challenge you and ultimately—if they do their job right and if you are receptive to notes—be able to push you to your next writing level.

The consultants, readers and instructors you should seek out are:

- Ones who have a solid and current industry track record. Whether they are working writers themselves or have been reading, consulting and teaching for years and years, the road that brought them to your consideration is clear.
- Ones whose taste level you agree with. This likely means that you respond to similar work. Whether or not you will agree on your script remains to be seen.
- Ones who have read thousands of scripts, or taught hundreds of students with some great results.
- Ones who have endorsements from writers working in the industry. While naysayers are everywhere, the readers, consultants and instructors you should work with are ones who should be able to produce notable endorsements from other writers you respect or whose shoes you'd be happy to walk in.

The consultants, readers and instructors to avoid are:

- Ones who have been doing this only for a short while, with a somewhat confusing track record behind them. The coverage/consultant space has been saturated for some time, with many inexperienced aspiring consultants emerging and demanding the sort of payment that their experience level simply doesn't justify. So before you settle on a reader or consultant, do your research.
- Ones whose experience is adjacent, but not industry specific. This can include novel and playwriting instructors and consultants, for example. If you look closely you will clearly see that their experience, while seemingly impressive, does not apply.
- Ones who are fighting to remain anonymous. If you don't know the reader or consultant's track record, experience and taste level, you can't pay too much heed to the notes that they give you.

Over my years working with screenwriters and television writers, I have made it a practice to crowd source my recommendations. This means that many of the readers, screenwriting and television writing consultants and screenwriting and television writing programs that I now recommend to my writers regularly include ones I came to know because a writer of mine took their class, gave it a glowing recommendation, and caused me to investigate it further.

Here are the vetting resources I regularly recommend to my writers:

Screenplay and Pilot Readers:

- **Andrew Hilton**, Screenplay Mechanic
  Andrew is a talented, repped writer in his own right, and a reader who has read upwards of six thousand screenplays and television pilots professionally, for almost every major movie studio.
- **Rob Ripley**, The Third Act
  Rob has been reading screenplays within the studio system for many years. He ran the story department for Cruise/Wagner, read for every major studio, and currently reads for ABC television. Like Andrew Hilton, he is a talented writer himself.

Screenwriting and Television Writing Consultants

- **Pilar Alessandra**, On The Page
  Pilar started as a story analyst at Amblin Entertainment, and from there went on to run the story department at DreamWorks. She has taught at such institutions as UCLA Extension and Writers Boot Camp, and today works exclusively out of her On The Page studio, where she conducts private consults and teaches classes (so expect to see her name again on this list!)
- **Jen Grisanti**, Jen Grisanti Consultancy
  Once a VP at Spelling Television, Jen now shares her wealth of knowledge with screenwriters via private and ongoing script consults. In addition to teaching NBC's *Writers on the Verge* fellowship, Jen is known for her discerning taste level and dedication to her writers.
- **Ruth Atkinson**
  A former development executive and one who is instrumental to both the Sundance Screenwriting Lab and Film Independent's Project Involve, Ruth is known for doing extensive work with her clients from top to bottom, taking them from concept all the way to draft.
- **Hayley McKenzie**, Script Angel
  Hayley is the over-the-pond equivalent to Los Angeles-based Ruth Atkinson. Previously a Development Executive for UK's ITV and the BBC, Hayley is known for her nurturing touch with her writers, with whom she develops work step by step.

Screenwriting and Television Writing Programs & Instructors

- **Pilar Alessandra**'s On The Page
  On The Page offers six-week writing courses throughout the year both in person and online, as well as weekend intensives, all of which are taught by the indelible Pilar Alessandra.
- **Script Anatomy**
  Script Anatomy, which focuses exclusively on writing instruction for television writers, produced a number of successful, working writers in the television field. Working television writer Tawnya Bhattacharya—who is also featured in one of our Screenwriter Spotlights—developed the Script Anatomy program. All classes are taught by working and up-and-coming television writers, and take place here in Los Angeles and online.
- **Jen Grisanti**'s Storywise Teleseminar
  The ten-week teleseminar, which launches in March every year, takes writers through spec and pilot writing for television. Writers may participate at various levels, some of which include ongoing feedback from the illuminating Jen.
- **Corey Mandell**
  A screenwriting veteran, Corey has written projects for Hollywood's A-list. Today, he shares his knowledge through his intensive, multi-level online courses, which have produced dozens of industry success stories.

Decoding the Voice

In today's industry the term THE VOICE has been used endless times. "The writer has an amazing voice." "The script wasn't there, but I signed the writer because of the voice." "Does the writer have another sample in that voice?" An enigmatic term, for sure. But this book being what it is, it is also one I wanted to decode. For which—you guessed it—I turned to my industry colleagues. Here's what they had to say:

Skyway Entertainment's Chris Cook told me:

> Well, it's like the Supreme Court definition of pornography—I can't tell you what it is, but I know it when I see it. Unfortunately there's a little bit of that (in defining the voice). The voice can be as simple as a new way of saying something that's been said before. It can be a certain confidence that you can read in the pages. If I read your screenplay, and I instantly know your characters as well as you do, that's an issue. You should know your characters inside and out, every which way. Voice comes out of a confidence of going off the beaten path. It's like knowing the rules and knowing that you have them sort of nailed, that you can then be ultimately just more interesting.

Paradigm's David Boxerbaum added:

> A voice is a unique point of view to a storytelling process. Someone that takes a character and layers it in a way that is different from what I've read in the past. Someone that takes a story and adds an element to it that we haven't seen before. I know it sounds so cliché, but it is something that you know it when you read it. It stands out to you. When I read David Guggenheim's draft of *Safehouse*—just to use that as an example—there was a voice to his action, there was a voice to his character work that spoke to something I had not read in many action movies—two-handers especially—in the past. So to me, that's what a real definition of a voice is. Someone that takes a character, takes dialogue, takes structure, takes all of that and elevates it to a different level.

Untitled Entertainment's Jennifer Au had this to contribute:

> For me, it's akin to a point of view. You know? It's distinctive. It's me saying, "I know who this person is, I know where they've come from based on what's on the page." It's the opposite of generic. It's the farthest thing from generic. It's literally the difference between paint by numbers and Warhol. But it's something that, if I read a script and it's so completely by the beats and anyone could have written this, then that's not a voice. That's not an identity. Writing is very personal, and it's a reflection of someone's self and their mind and their process. The more someone knows themselves and what makes them tick, the more of a voice I generally see.

Madhouse Entertainment's Ryan Cunningham said:

> The voice is a couple of aspects. One is literally the way the writer writes words on the page. Frequently that doesn't actually translate into what the movie or the TV show looks like, but at the very least, it makes the reading experience more enjoyable because they describe certain things or point out certain details or have certain turns of phrases in their dialogue that make it feel more authentic or surprising in some way—usually those go hand in hand. The other part of it—which doesn't exactly apply to what the words look like—is literally what they're choosing to write about and who they're choosing to write about and the way they choose to do it. And that can be anything from somebody who takes a really standard love story, but tells it out of order, like *500 Days of Summer*, and that's a really unique experience to enjoy, no matter how you absorb it. To me that's part of the voice. Or it could be just, you tell a story from a character's point of view that people wouldn't normally think of that story being told from, and that can be pretty unique—I consider that part of the voice, as well.

Manager Scott Carr of Management SGC added:

> I think the most exciting new writers are the ones that write material in a way that kind of subverts the expectations of what material is in the market. Like a *Lars and the Real Girl*, or *500 Days of Summer*, writing something that just feels uniquely special is something that writers should be considering rather than just trying to go with the grain of what they think Hollywood is about or what kind of films just get made. They should really embrace the identity of their voice and just be super creative. Like—as an example—the way that Diablo Cody wrote *Juno* involved a lot of phrases and lexicons and writing elements that really just sparked something, almost like her own little universe that she occupied, and as a result it was very indicative of the personality of that writer and thus she became a prototype for a number of films that people wanted to replicate in that space. And that's a good place to be, for a writer to be the prototype of what people are looking for when it comes to hiring someone. And that comes with a very stand out piece of material. So that in turn allows people to embrace the unique stories that they have to tell versus the ones that they think are going to appeal to a mass audience. There is value in breaking in with a script that might not necessarily be the movie that's gonna keep Universal's lights on but it might be the thing that gets them working at Universal.

SCREENWRITER SPOTLIGHT #3: Marissa Jo Cerar

Marissa Jo Cerar is a film and television writer who grew up in a family of eight adopted kids in rural Illinois. After writing a handful of award-winning scripts, her project *Conversion* was selected for the Hit List and the Black List in 2012, and Marissa Jo was included on the Young and Hungry List the following year. *Conversion* sold to indie financiers KperiodMedia in 2016.

From 2013—2016, Marissa Jo wrote for the critically acclaimed television series *The Fosters*. She's currently a writer and co-producer on the new Fox series, *Shots Fired*, set to premiere in Spring 2017.

Lee: You once told me that you knew from a very early age that this was what you wanted to do. How did you know?

Marissa: I grew up as an adoptee in rural Illinois. Movies and television were my connection to the world, and the only way I saw people who looked like me. I had a lot going on inside my brain that I couldn't—or wasn't brave enough—to share, so I got lost in books, movies and television. It's cliche, but in my case it's the truth: I started writing to escape.

Lee: You came to Los Angeles with your film school's screenwriting program and never left. How important was your college experience for your transition to Los Angeles?

Marissa: My college experience was very important, because the "Semester in LA" screenwriting program allowed me to settle in, meet people and get acquainted with the city and the industry without as much pressure as moving here jobless, friendless, and clueless. I learned how to write coverage and break down scripts. I met my first screenwriting mentor, I had a small community of screenwriters, all new to the game, screenwriters I could confide in and share my frustrations and small victories with—it was essential to my journey.

Lee: Right out of school, you got a screenwriting mentor. How did that relationship work, and how instrumental was it to your current success?

Marissa: I wrote Thank You notes to the professional writers who spoke with us at my Semester in LA. And while many of them promised to connect with us and offer guidance if we reached out to them, only one actually kept his promise. He had a few projects being independently financed, and he needed a freelance/occasional writer's assistant, so I was able to learn while getting paid. That's pretty rare in this industry; most would've called it an internship to avoid paying me to learn. And that is why relationships are priceless. When you meet good people, keep them in your life. Learn from them, and give back. Never forget who helped you on your way up.

Lee: You were selected as a fellow for Film Independent's Project Involve. Could you tell me a bit about that experience, including having one of your short scripts produced?

Marissa: I submitted an indie feature script to the program, a very personal script I wrote titled *Human Resources*, after it placed in a few screenwriting contests. That submission—along with an essay and interview—secured my spot in Project Involve. It was a wonderful program where I not only learned a lot about festival submissions and indie financing, I made some of my dearest friends—friends still in my life years later. Having my short script *Steps* produced was quite the learning experience—but I didn't realize that at the time. Years later, I've written seven episodes of television, I now understand how impossible it is to get your *exact vision* from script to screen. When you hand in your material, even if you're attached as a producer, even if you're on set during production, you're giving it to the director, the crew, the financier, the editor and the actors. I had a wonderful director for *Steps*, and I was pleased with the end product, fortunately, but my time in the program gave me my first lesson in letting go.

Lee: Prior to your big break, were you working in the industry, or did you make a living in an unrelated field? How important was it for you to stay involved with the industry despite not yet having earned the label "working screenwriter"?

Marissa: I guess I've just never taken my eye off the prize, and my "day jobs" have all been in the industry. I interned in development, worked as a writer's assistant, an executive assistant to a producer, and I did freelance script consulting and coverage. Working in the industry made it possible for me to read current TV and film scripts. I met people, some I've collaborated with, I joined a writer's group, learned from (what to do and what NOT to do), and etcetera. There are some drawbacks to being totally focused on one thing your entire life. I feel I missed out on *living*—and that means I missed out on moments in life I could've used in my writing. Most of the writers I've met had other careers or took other paths before they ventured into writing seriously, this means they're experts in other fields that can be a bonus in terms of pitch meetings and writer's rooms.

Lee: In addition to becoming a Project Involve Fellow, you also placed in a number of screenwriting competitions. How integral were those placements to moving you forward?

Marissa: If it's a fellowship like Nicholl, Disney, or a writer's lab like Sundace, being in such company proves your work is well-received, polished and professional. It can help secure representation, in some cases. Placing in contests got my script into more hands, and in a few cases helped my dwindling bank account with prize money, but it's mostly encouragement to keep fighting and writing—if you've won or placed in one of the big contests, you're on your way. I suggest paying the extra $ for coverage or script notes from the contests that offer it. It's another way of getting feedback from an objective reader.

Lee: You met your manager through a referral. Could you tell me a bit about who the referral came from, and how your life as a writer changed once you had your manager on board?

Marissa: The referral came from a fellow TV writer who was working as a PA who saw me writing on Final Draft. At the time I was an executive assistant at a TV production company. He asked to read my work, liked it and submitted it to his managers. They had just opened at the time and were actively seeking to build a client roster, so I was very lucky. It's one of those "right place, right time" moments.

Lee: Did your managers at Heroes & Villains introduce you to your ICM Agents? And speaking of agents . . . Can you speak a bit to what your managers do for you, as well as what your agency does for you?

Marissa: My managers submitted my material to a few agencies and ICM was the first to show real interest. Once I met them I knew they "got me." They understood my voice, and worked very hard to get me my first TV gig within months of signing with them and finishing my first pilot. Before I landed my first paid gigs my managers did a lot of development with me, but now that I've been on a show for three years and had a couple feature assignments they submit my material for potential projects and help me make career decisions. Agents generally handle deals and fight to get you the best script fees and contracts.

Lee: Before you had your first "big break" you had both features and a TV pilot to show. How important do you think it was for you to have both?

Marissa: It's only important if you want to work in both worlds. I started as a feature writer and was advised to get into TV because of the changing climate in television. TV is more character driven than movies, and I write character-driven material. I'm fortunate in that I have done feature assignments on my TV hiatus. I will always write both. They are such different mediums and experiences and fulfill different creative desires.

Lee: In late 2012, your screenplay *Conversion* was named to The Black List. Was that a game changer for you? What sort of effect did it have on your career?

Marissa: Being on The Black List brought more attention to my script, and personally served as validation of my hard work. About a year after being on the list I sold the script to an indie financier and recently attached an amazing producer.

Lee: Shortly thereafter you got staffed on *The Fosters*. I was lucky enough to have dinner with you the night you got the call. How did that job come about?

Marissa: My TV agents at ICM worked very hard to get me read because they knew I had a personal connection to the concept. As soon as my agents heard about a new show that had a lot of similarities and connections to my own family they jumped on it, got me read and set up meetings. I then met network executives, producers and creators who responded to my material, and I did my best to convince them I could do the job even though I'd never been staffed before. It all happened very fast, and I couldn't have been staffed on a better show. Three years later, I'm about to start season four as a co-producer.

Lee: Now three seasons in, you've done seven of your own episodes. What's it like, moving up the ranks and being a part of bringing your words to life?

Marissa: Most low level writers stay in the room, but I've learned so much from running set during each of my episodes. It's invaluable experience that will make a world of difference when I have my own show one day.

Lee: In addition to your work on *The Fosters*, you've continued your work on the feature front, selling an indie spec, as well as doing some rewrite assignments. How do you juggle the two?

Marissa: I am a workaholic. I don't sleep much, but I chose this life and am lucky enough to be employed, so I'm taking advantage of every opportunity that comes my way. During hiatus I have to keep busy and I was lucky enough to rewrite an indie movie during my last hiatus. I came from a working class family, so I understand the value of a dollar and know that I need to save in case of emergency. I work to make sure I'm doing as much as I can to remain relevant in the movie world when I'm on a break from the show.

Lee: And speaking of juggling . . . On top of everything else, you are also a working mom with a newborn baby. How do you manage?

Marissa: Returning to work so soon after my daughter's birth, she was only nine weeks old, was the hardest thing I've ever done, but I have an amazing husband who stays home with her. When I need to write, he's there. And my baby is pretty amazing, if I do say so myself. She sits with me in my office and lets me write from time-to-time. It is not easy, but nothing worth fighting for ever is. If you want a career, you'll make it work. You won't sleep much, but you can sleep when you're unemployed. In the past five months, I gave birth, did a rewrite of a movie and wrote an episode of television. I'm exhausted, but it's an investment in my future—and worth every second.

Lee: When you're not "in the room," do you still try to write a lot? Do you go on a lot of industry meetings? What are those like?

Marissa: I take a lot of feature meetings when I'm on hiatus. I get a lot of material sent to me—from producers who want to hear my take on material they've purchased and/or are developing. I have formed some pretty great relationships in the movie world the past few years, and when you deliver on a writing assignment producers want to work with you again.

Lee: You are a Los Angeles transplant. Do you think it's important for writers to live in Los Angeles? And, if so, why?

Marissa: If you're a TV writer, YES. You have to be in the writer's room, and most of them are in LA (or NYC). If you're writing features I'd say: YES, live where the work is. You have to take meetings and give pitches—especially when you're first starting out. You can leave town when you have a few hits under your belt, but you have to be available, even in this world of FaceTime and Skype.

Lee: If there was one thing you know now that you wish you knew when you first came to Los Angeles, what would it be?

Marissa: If you can, have a year's worth of income in the bank so you can explore the city, see movies and soak up the culture. I love this city and wish I had explored more when I was fresh off the plane.

Lee: In your estimation, how important were the relationships you built in this industry for the construction of your screenwriting career?

Marissa: Relationships are everything, from my first screenwriting mentor to my managers and my writer's group—navigating this business can be tough, especially if you don't have a great support system who understands rejection and the amount of work a screenwriter must do to finish a script. It can take a year (or longer) to finish a script, and it can "die" in a flash. That can be devastating.

Lee: Do you have any advice for readers of this book who are aiming to construct a screenwriting career of their own?

Marissa: Work hard. Be nice. You should really take the time to learn about the people you're meeting. Making a good impression counts. Read pilots.

Watch TV and movies. Read the scripts on The Black List and Nicholl Fellowship if you can. Read the pilots getting picked up. Study your medium. Surround yourself with a team of reps that know your voice and share your vision. Join (or create) a writer's group. I can't stress enough how important personality and professionalism are. Be polite in emails. Be nice to readers, receptionists and assistants. Meetings are auditions for future writing gigs. Be nice. Be nice. Be nice! Execs are more likely to fight for you and your material if you're a pleasant person.

3

SO . . . HOW DO YOU BREAK IN?

Breaking In—Insights from the Industry

You've heard it said a million times: breaking into the entertainment industry, going from emerging screenwriter to professional, has never been an easy feat. It takes time, effort and luck, not to mention blood, sweat, tears and years. And yet, from vast personal experience working with writers for many years I can tell you with absolutely certainty that it is indeed happening. All the time. Hard-working, talented writers, including those spotlighted in this book, have found a path to making their screenwriting aspirations a reality.

But in a feature market that is retracting and a television market that is only becoming more competitive, how are they doing it? In order to illuminate what it takes to break in and what one can expect to encounter within the changing industry in their quest for breaking in, I turned to my industry colleagues:

Literary agent David Boxerbaum of Paradigm spoke about the effects that changing studio directives—which we explored in previous chapters—and the emergence of new buyers are having on the shifting feature film market:

> Less movies are getting made. I think it's more about the brand now. You look at what's happening in the box office and you see original material that comes out that's just not working, and so therefore it scares off studios from making original material and going more towards things that are built-in brands, built-in IPs, ones, twos, threes and fours, sequels, prequels, all that—that's changed the landscape of the feature business tremendously because it changes what writers are working on, what they're doing, and how you sell it in the marketplace. So it's been difficult in that sense. It's opened up a whole new world for us to sell to, which is great, but at the same time it cut out a lot of opportunities in the marketplace. Less specs are getting done, less specs are getting sold, and less jobs are out there for

the writer. So now it's much more concise in how you dictate a client's career. There's a lot more engineering and maneuvering than in the past.

In essence, the biggest difference between today's challenging spec market and that of the over-abundant 1990s is that there is now little allowance for throwing everything—every script, good or bad—at the wall and seeing what sticks. The retracting spec market that is today's reality rarely allows reps to get writers into the professional space without first identifying market need and constructing thoughtful strategy, both for the writer and for their material. The same can be said for television: while that market is thriving, it is also much more competitive, as more writers are fighting for each available opportunity that promises stability and employment for years to come. With that in mind, agents and managers are being more thoughtful than ever, working hard to position their clients for success.

Manager Jewerl Ross provided his perspective about breaking new writers in the market:

> People talk a lot about how hard it is to break into the business. People talk a lot about that it's harder today than it was a year ago or five years ago or ten years ago. People talk a lot about the growth of TV over film. All of those things are worthy conversations. Yes, it's harder today than it was yesterday. Yes, there's an expansion in television. But none of these big picture ideas matter. The most important ideas are, Am I talented? Do I have a passion for film? Do I have a passion for TV? Can I produce material at a certain level? Can I produce enough of it? Am I a social person? Those internal, smaller, micro ideas dictate your choices, not macro ideas. I often tell people that the writers who follow trends are often hacks. I'm not looking to represent a trend-following-hack. I think making it in the business, no matter if it was ten years ago or today, in TV or film, is fucking hard for anybody. It's really about where your talent is and what you can produce. I really think that whenever anything good happens in ones' career, it's magic. It needs luck and happenstance and timing and so many things that we have no control over. The one thing you do have control over is your talent.

What Jewerl is speaking of is the writer's mission to listen to his own drummer; to shut out the noise of the industry that so often influences the direction of the writer's work in order to challenge one's self towards his or her best work, best ideas, most disciplined work ethic. While industry trends, and the lamenting of the people working with it, can easily affect the writer's trajectory, the real challenge is to become the very best writer you can be in the face of it.

In today's industry, breaking a writer in is not as simple as getting them a high profile spec sale after high profile spec sale. In fact, only a select few writers have been able to make a living in today's industry selling specs. While—on the features front—spec sales get the glory, the reality is that over 90 percent of screenwriters who make money in the feature space do so via writing assignments and delivering on pitches, rather than selling their wares.

Jason Scoggins, of The Scoggins Report and Slated, elaborated:

> As a screenwriter, you get paid in two basic ways. Either people buy your material that you've already written or they pay you to write material. Products and services. So the spec market is the first of those. You write a piece of material with the hope of somebody buying it from you. If you don't sell it, the secondary hope is that your rep will take your material out to the town in order to introduce you to everybody. Writing a spec for somebody who's already broken in can be a way of rekindling relationships, it can be a way of changing people's perspectives of you as a writer—what you're good at, what you tend to do, what lists you should be on internally at the studios. The way professional screenwriters get paid is writing drafts. And that can be something that would be an original project that the writer has come up with and just pitches, or it can also be internal material that a given production company or studio is developing and they need somebody to do a new draft or part of a draft, a polish, et cetera, and that is what most working screenwriters do.

There are a number of truths you will hear touted again and again through this book. One of them is: despite the golden age of television, which spurred many more writers to try to break into that space, it is much harder breaking a writer in television than it is breaking a writer in film. Manager Scott Carr spoke to this:

> Breaking a writer in features is much easier than breaking a writer in TV because a writer in features really just needs to have a great spec script and there's a system in place with which we can expose that spec script. An original TV pilot is only like 1 percent of what that show needs to be in order to be successful. Television is a very competitive industry that is already virtually staffed right across the board because a lot of these staff writers just bounce from show to show because shows get cancelled all the time. When a show gets cancelled that's 10 available writers, almost all of which are gonna have a better chance of getting the next shows that are getting picked up than the guy that's trying to break in. Because having experience on a show means a tremendous amount to the way the hiring process happens. So getting that first job in television is the watershed moment that is just very challenging to accomplish.

Perhaps one of the reasons that screenwriters who are seeking to break into the industry set their sights on television now more than ever before—outside

of the abundance of jobs available in the space (over 4,100 WGA men
income from television in 2014, while only roughly 1,800 WGA
so from film)—is the reality that while film was always considered a ᴅᵤᵣ
medium, in television writer is king. Only a few people remember that celebrated
director Rian Johnson (*Looper, Star Wars: Episode VIII*) directed *Breaking Bad*'s
final season episode, *Ozymandias*, which was considered by many to be its
preeminent episode. Instead, everyone remembers that the show was created by,
and that its very last episode was written by, the great Vince Gilligan.

To this, Manager Mike Woodlief commented:

> The great thing about the television business is that it's a writer driven
> medium. And in the writer driven medium you're going to have most of
> the control. And it's on you to develop and create a world and an outline
> that is worth that world and the characters. I think we're in the heyday of
> television and the bubble is going to burst at some point. That said, writers
> can write themselves out of a hole, but say you're a director, producer, or
> line producer you're at the whim of everyone else. I tell my staff writers:
> You're getting your own first job. It's coming through relationships. It's
> coming through you willing to continue to write and write and write.
> Because you've gone out to all the mixers, you've done all the heavy lifting,
> you continue to follow up. You've gone through being a PA to working
> your way up and hoping that you bet on the right horse and then it's luck
> and timing. UGH! It's all such a crapshoot. I wish there was some formula.

While the competition for every screenwriting job remains fierce and breaking
a screenwriter in television even in the days of PEAK TV is in no way easy, the
recent growth in the television sector has given many a manager reason to be
optimistic. Echo Lake's Zadoc Angell explained:

> Things have gotten a lot better because there's twice as many television
> shows as there was I think even 3 or 4 years ago. So when you have that
> many shows in production, you have that many more writing staffs and
> writers assistant jobs and PA jobs and actor jobs that are available to people.
> So it's actually a great time. We're probably in a bubble that will burst a
> bit in a while. I hope not, but now's actually a good time because there
> are more jobs, and the business has been in an expansion mode, not a
> contraction mode. When I was coming up, it was contracting. So that just
> means more opportunities.

Yes, there is talk about the television bubble bursting. But those who mention
it are, in all likelihood, just not that worried. After all, nobody is talking about
going back to 2013 numbers, when we topped out at 343 original scripted
programs on air. Even if (or when) we do see the number of original scripted

programs on television retract—which is right now expected to happen some time around or after 2019—the anticipation is that the retraction would be in the 15 percent to 20 percent range from the anticipated high of 500 original programs, likely ending up somewhere around 400 original scripted programs per year. To put the aggressive growth in perspective: back in 2009, we had 211 original scripted programs on the air. That number nearly doubled in just six years.

From 2009 until today, basic cable and digital outlets (also known as online services) have taken on the bulk of the growth. Broadcast, too, has exhibited growth, but according to John Landgraf and the good people at FX, the growth from 2011 to 2015 has been roughly 29 percent, while the growth rate for pay cable (such as HBO and Showtime) has been all of 12 percent. Meanwhile online services (such as Amazon and Netflix) and basic cable (such as AMC and FX) have each grown over 60 percent.

On the feature front, the story has been a stark contrast to the explosion happening in television. Don't get me wrong: I am in no way saying that features are dead. In fact, they remain a solid and often more accessible way for breaking writers into the professional space. But the reality is that for every open writing assignment, for every dollar available to purchase specs, there seem to be more and more eager, talented feature writers trying to break in. So who gets through? Which is the writer who manages to break through the noise, and stand above the rest? The cartels Evan Corday gave me her take:

> There are 50,000 completely talented fine writers, it's that 1 percent of that group that's gonna rise to the top because they have it all. Because they have the voice, because they have the talent, because they have the drive and because they keep being in a room where people want to be with them. And when you read them and you meet, you know, that magic, that thing happens and you're like, oh yeah, I gotta work with that person.

Another truism is that today's screenwriters, whether they are trying to break into the feature or television market, are underserved by the available information out there regarding what it really takes, TODAY, to break into the industry. While stories of celebrated screenwriters who broke in in the 1980s and 1990s have been explored in interviews, profiles and articles, there is little out there regarding the current realities facing screenwriters aiming to break into the industry at this moment in time, which manager and Blood List founder Kailey Marsh commented on when we conducted our interview for this book:

> I'm glad that someone who's actually working in the industry is writing this book. Because I feel like the books that writers are reading are so archaic. The days of the feature spec sale or the quote "overnight success" . . . it's just not here anymore. I'm as optimistic as anyone. I work for myself and

I'm strictly commission based so I have obviously seen the ups and downs. But I've also seen the reality that it is really hard but it is possible, which is why I stay in the industry.

Kailey is right: if there is one undisputed proof that writers are, despite all the noise you hear about how hard it is to break into the industry, indeed breaking in, it is managers, who largely work on commission only (and about whom you will learn more in Chapter 4). The managers most dependent on their writer's success are the likes of Kailey Marsh, Lee Stobby, Scott Carr, Chris Cook and Mike Woodlief: single manager operations, who don't have any of the benefits of a larger company to rely on, even though those too are usually limited to expense accounts and office space. The bottom line is: if writers didn't succeed, didn't break in, these managers, working on their own or as part of a larger company, wouldn't be able to make a living.

However, just because writers are breaking in—and their managers, by extension, are collecting their 10 percent—doesn't mean that breaking in is by any means easy. Untitled Entertainment's Jennifer Au spoke to the effort, diligence, determination and consistency it takes to build a career in today's industry.

> It's going to be so much harder than I think people anticipate. It takes 120 percent. And I mean that across the board, whether you're trying to be a feature writer, television writer, work in the digital space, an author. It really takes diligence and it takes work. I remember when I first started—and I think it's still fairly accurate—that to become a working writer from the point someone gets to me, on average is five to seven years. A lot of people underestimate how much they're going to have to pitch and actually be in rooms and in-person. If you want to just be writing and not have to have that interaction, the book space is more for you. But if you're going to work in this business, a lot of your job is going to be pitching, and that's not just on assignment. That's your own originals. If you're going to sell a show, someone is going to read your pilot and ask you to meet, and you're going to have to talk about the series. And you're going to have to learn how to be presentable in a room, have great energy, have those people want to work with you. Because not only are you meeting with them to talk about that project, you're meeting with them as an impression of yourself and you're representing yourself as a brand and a business.

Gersh's Sean Barclay talked to me about how, in today's environment, a new, emerging writer can best stand out from the rest and break through the barriers:

> The easiest way to get into professional baseball is to be a left-handed pitcher, because that's the shortage. I think a new voice absolutely has a leg up at

this moment in time. And there are a few factors to that. One is the kind of history of Hollywood and that being a perennial experience, the new voice, the hot writer, the new director that pops, the overnight success stories—we always promote that. But the other thing about new writers and new voices is that they have no quotes (i.e. established price point) and they are inexpensive. So if I was a Studio executive on the movie side I could bring a new writer in, pay them WGA scale to create the bones of a big Studio movie based off of a sample that was pretty damn good, kind of a "wow" sample. And then a hundred thousand dollars into the development I could bring in a character guy, or, you know, my action guy—or whatever that is—and pay them 250 (thousand) a week.

Sean Barclay was not the only rep I encountered who felt that today's new writers are arriving at the cusp of an exciting opportunity. To give you a little background, I first met Infinity's Jon Karas at a Final Draft lunch some years ago. Everyone was going around the table and introducing him or herself. I don't remember exactly how it came to be—if Jon was asked a question or decided to volunteer the information on his own—but at some point even before the main courses arrived Jon went on a tangent about what an exciting time it is for screenwriters in the industry at this particular moment. It impressed me then, and that much more so when he graciously agreed to sit down with me for this book and share his consistent and well-substantiated positive outlook.

It's a time of major opportunity and the only limitations to that opportunity are lack of originality, lack of intensity and focus and lack of persistence. What do I mean by that? There are so many outlets now, especially with the rampant growth in cable television and streaming content that there is an incredible need for fresh new voices, original storytelling in cool arenas that people haven't seen before, or cool ways to do familiar arenas. So I think that it is a time of amazing opportunity. If somebody says: "I can't get a job," or "I can't get my material out there," to me that's a lack of persistence and, or, a lack of quality in what they are presenting. My belief is that the cream rises to the top. It's just a question of time and access. Well, access is easier than ever before because there's a whole bunch of people that one can access. In the old days, you had to have an agent, and the way that you got an agent was often through friends, family or entertainment lawyers. Now there's a whole wave of people, who call themselves 'Managers', some more connected than others, all of whom have a desire to help people rise up. So I think there's a lot easier access to the buyers than there ever has been before so that confluence of factors creates a time of amazing opportunity.

Jon Karas and Sean Barclay were not the only industry professionals to whom I talked who hold that perspective. In fact, most of the agents, managers and executives who took the time to talk to me spoke to this being a time of great opportunity at some point of our interview, as did agent Ryan Saul of APA.

> In a lot of ways it's a great time to be a writer because there's a place for every story. Whether it's something along the lines of a 6-hour biopic mini-series set in the 1100s—there's a place for that, or something like *Mr. Robot*—that project floated around, everyone passed on it, and then USA picked it up because they wanted to go darker. It started off as a feature and then it became what it is now. You still gotta write a spec. That's still the way to get in. You have to show that you can write. But it's an exciting time to be a writer. It's not a great time to be a writer who is in the middle. Like everything in this country, the middle class is shrinking. So you either are a million-dollar Aaron Sorkin type or you're the young writer who can give a first draft for cheap.

Specifically when talking about feature film, the very concept of "breaking in"—going from emerging writer, one who is juggling writing and a day job, to a well paid professional who no longer needs a day job to support his screenwriting habit—may not be as linear as one might think. In today's industry, breaking in doesn't necessarily mean an instant payday, or a direct path to significant revenue, at least not immediately. Unlike the days of the spec market boon of the 1990s, today's measurable success for a feature film writer is not all about quick financial gratification. But just because the money—or at least the up front money—is not what it used to be, doesn't mean that writers are not getting significant opportunities. Bellevue Production's John Zaozirny explained:

> It's easier to break a writer these days than it used to be. I'll put it like this: it's harder to make money immediately from a writer, like you could previously when the spec market was very hot, back then you could sell a great script and suddenly these people were hot. But I think the creation of The Black List has allowed different voices to get in there and people to be aware of the screenwriters who are writing interesting screenplays. Also, there is less of a fixed idea of who these people are, that these are the closers, these are the people that studios will only work with. For better or worse, they'll now take a chance on an up-and-coming writer. The writer is much cheaper, they'll give you guild minimum to do something as opposed to a writer who might be $500,000 for a draft. So I think it's easier to break writers and get them well known, it's harder to get them paid. Those things seem counterintuitive. You have a lot more opportunities to make money but the money will not be as huge at first, necessarily.

For television writers, the barrier to financial gain is quite different. Once you are staffed, the weekly paychecks start rolling in. If selling a pilot, the writer will get paid a lump sum for the script, in addition to potentially collecting producing fees (more of this in Chapter 10). In television, getting paid is not the problem; the challenge itself lies in simply breaking in.

Back in the feature world, there is one thing that everyone agrees is indeed dwindling: the studio movie, and with it the studio writing assignment. As mentioned earlier, studios are no longer making the movies they used to, and for the movies they are making—for the most part superhero and big blockbuster fare—they are traditionally turning to a very defined, highly proven A-List that has become very hard to crack. Sure, new writers do get in on occasion, but for the most part these studio executives are turning to their proven writers again and again, betting on a tried and true path. So I asked manager Lee Stobby: for a new writer to be considered for a studio writing assignment, what is it going to take?

> You know how you get *The Hunger Games*? By not writing anything like *The Hunger Games*. Honestly. You write something like, for example, my *Bubbles* writer (2015 topper of The Black List Isaac Adamson) writes a biopic of Michael Jackson's chimpanzee. And then he writes a football movie. And then he writes a contained thriller. These are book adaptations and true-life stories for studios. Nothing like *Bubbles* at all. But the people who read, read *Bubbles*. They see the voice. They see his ability to push something beyond the boundaries. The way that he can deal with humor and tone and character. People in Hollywood are very risk averse; they're trying to keep their jobs. It doesn't benefit them to hire somebody who has never gotten hired to write a job before. It really doesn't. The only reason they are going to hire you is because you're cheap. And that's it. They think that they are gonna get a better product out of you for less money. So you have to prove yourself to them. You have to do something that's gonna set you apart. They're not going to take a flyer on you unless you show them that you are doing something different. You have to be very distinctive in what you are doing because if you are not distinctive you are not going to stand out. A studio executive or an agent or a manager is going to say they don't know what to do with that person because they are just doing what everyone else is doing. Writing takes a long time. Right? So don't write something because you think that, "Oh I have something that is totally like *Taken.*" Don't even bother. They've already made *Taken*. As soon as you start trying to chase that kind of dragon, the dragon's already way ahead of you and you are never going to catch up to it. You have to pave your own kind of path. You know, the most successful writers just do their thing and they do it really well and eventually it will work out. It might be your first script, it might be your seventh script, but it has to be about you being truthful. And it only takes one person. But you have to inspire that one person. People are motivated by passion.

Bellevue Production's John Zaozirny also spoke about the viability of writing directly at the studios when an emerging writer seeks to break into the feature space:

> The idea that what you are writing is something that a studio is going to want to buy is an even more far-fetched notion than it was 10 years ago. I get people sending me query letters saying, "Oh, I've written this fantasy series that's in the vein of *Lord Of The Rings.*" Well nobody wants your fantasy series because they already have *Lord of the Rings*. They also have *Harry Potter*. You look at all the people who are making these huge movies now, you look at the guy who wrote and directed *Safety Not Guaranteed* (Screenwriter Derek Connolly). People are paying attention to these people who are making these smaller movies and they're drafting them to make huger movies. Your better shot of working with a studio is writing a really great smaller movie and people noticing it. Or writing a script for a really great small movie that maybe doesn't even get made. But look at what your best shot is to actually get a movie made. The guy who wrote *Prisoners* (Aaron Guzikowski), before *Prisoners* had even got made, he'd written a Mark Wahlberg movie called *Contraband*. And *Prisoners*, this dark drama about a father searching for his missing daughter, is what got him that job before that movie was even made. So I would be like: How do I write something really interesting? As opposed to trying to write a 100 million dollar epic that A) Tends to be based on a pre-existing IP and then B) Competes with huge incredibly talented writers like David Keopp and John Logan. Don't assume that the rules don't apply to you because they absolutely do. And everyone in Hollywood is aware of them and plays by them. It doesn't mean that exceptions can't occur but more often than not, it's kind of like the old line, everybody thinks they're above average. And I'm not telling people to scale down their dreams, I'm telling them to recalibrate them, There are a lot of different ways to get your career going.

Even though screenwriters are breaking in and the industry—outside of the studio system—continues to be rife with opportunity, there are certainly more scribes out there slaving over scripts than there are writers able to make a real go of it. While tens of thousands of scripts get registered with the WGA every year, fewer than 6,000 WGA members are collecting screenwriting income year over year. While additional screenwriters—specifically on the feature side—who are non-WGA members manage to sell feature scripts to and do writing assignments for non-WGA-signatory companies (usually for significantly less money), the simple truth is that there is no sure fire path to building a screenwriting career. Circle of Confusion's Josh Adler elaborated on this:

> To be honest, if there were a tried and true way to do it, then it wouldn't be as difficult as it is, and everybody would go do the steps that are required

to become successful writer. So it's different for everybody. But there's two aspects, one of which is the writing on the page and the other being the personality of the writer, which is obviously different for film and television. First thing is the writing. 100 percent. So if you have a great script, it will get read, it will get noticed, it will find its way into the right hands. It always does. Before I was in representation, I worked in development, and all we would do would be talk to each other. What have you read? Anybody read anything good? So if somebody reads something and it's great they will mention it to other people, and it will find its way to people and permeate the industry. That being said, it has to be great. Good doesn't cut it anymore. And then when you're deciding what to write, if you're looking to break as a writer, write whatever you're the most passionate about. Don't write to the marketplace. Don't even worry about getting your movie made. You should be worried about getting read and getting people to know you as a writer. So whatever the idea is, regardless of how commercial or uncommercial you think it is or people are telling you that it is, if you are super passionate about it, write that. Because you can look at The Black List—the majority of those movies don't get made. If you've got a writer who says, "I've got this idea, I know it's not what I should be writing right now, but I've gotta get this off my chest. I really believe that I could knock this out of the park." Great! Go write it. Nine times out of ten, it's awesome. Because it was a passion.

At the end of the day, success in this industry is all about your writing, the quality of the pages that you generate. For those who thrive that's where it starts, and for many who don't, that's where it ends. But it's not JUST about that. Breaking in is also about the hard work that you put into it. It's about consistency, and flexibility. It's about determination. For some, it's even about sacrifice, be it the sacrifice of long nights of sleep or relaxed weekends. Once again, Josh Adler of Circle of Confusion explained:

> There is an element of luck in this business. Sure. But the rest of it is a lot of really fucking hard work. It's a lot of keeping your chin up in the face of rejection and saying, "You know what? It didn't work on that one. Fuck it. Let's try it on this one." And forging ahead and having that day job where you work 9 to 6 but instead of waking up at 8 to make it to your job by 9, you wake up at 5 so you can write for three hours before you go in to work. Most of the people that make it in this business have a passion and a drive to be in this business and are willing to do whatever it takes to make it and stay in this business. I've had clients that had three jobs, who worked all day and on the weekends, they were driving an Uber just to be able to pay rent and so they could write for an hour a day at night when they got home and they were exhausted at midnight—and did

that for ten years before they broke. It's different for everybody, but most people don't make it without a lot of hard work.

Reverse Engineering Your Break

A few months before I started working on this book, I sat down with a writing team who was at the time seeking guidance on how to break into the professional screenwriting space utilizing their recently completed historical family feature script. While the screenplay was well executed and tightly written, it presented some obvious challenges right off the bat: period, which means expensive, not to mention not prime product for the 18–24-year-old sect. And . . . It was a family movie. Potentially an animated family movie, no less. Yikes.

As the writers and I got deeper into conversation, I quickly realized that the marketability of the material at hand was not the biggest hurdle to the writer's trajectory. Instead, the challenge was this: while they had a perfectly presentable (albeit not exceptional) family screenplay on their hands, the writing team had no long-term interest in writing in the PG family space. Or the film space, in fact. Instead, the writers were really interested in writing television, in the adult, one-hour drama space.

It's not unheard of for screenwriters to write in one format in order to break into another, specifically when talking about television. Screenwriters with a standout feature-length writing sample have been read by showrunners. A strong one-act play or essay has been known to get writers into rooms friendly to that sort of material, so long as an in-format sample was also available. But breaking into this industry is too demanding, too full of challenges, for writers to take a hard left when the intention is to veer right. Therefore, it is important that you write with a specific destination in mind. In other words, the wise business decision is to write exciting original content that is in the very least in the general vicinity of the space in which you want to work. Don't get me wrong: I am not suggesting that in order to become a studio writer you should create the next *Star Trek*. Write characters, write technology, but write it on a smaller scale, and most importantly make it exciting, original work. The important thing is to write yourself into a spot that you can leap out of in the direction you want to go when the opportunity does indeed present itself.

Before we go any further, let's break it down: What is a writing sample? A writing sample is any screenplay or original television pilot that puts the writer's voice, skillset and originality on display. While most every writer is eager to see his screenplay or original pilot positioned for a sale, 99 percent of the time they come to serve the writer as a sample, a piece of work to be read by development executives, producers, showrunners and network executives as an introduction to the writer himself, rather than a piece sent into the market for sale. In the simplest terms a strong writing sample is a conversation starter. The writer's calling card. It is the thing that gets you invited into those all-important rooms, where careers begin and important connections are made.

Therefore, it is important to consider what your ultimate writing destination is when you are deciding what to work on next. While a new writer should certainly take the time to explore various genres and formats to uncover where they are at their best, it's important to remember that every project you take up, every story and format into which you invest yourself represents a business decision made for the career that lies ahead. Therefore, if you want to end up in one-hour television drama, be sure to write the sort of character-and-world-building material that lends itself to that space; learn the structure that must be adhered to and the rules of that universe. If you are seeking to write in the 1/2-hour comedy space, take sketch comedy classes, maybe even do a little bit of stand-up. And if you want to write feel-good, uplifting movies, try not to break on the merit of a dark thriller where all your characters end up gruesomely murdered. You will likely be able to pivot later, but that initial leap may be harder to construct than you anticipate.

Ask yourself this: if I want to end up writing X (fill in the blank: feature comedies, dramas, thrillers, halfhour comedies or one-hour dramas), what sort of body of work and experience should I amass in order to effectively get there?

Or as John Zaozirny of Bellevue Productions put it:

> Are you aware of what you want to be, of who you want to be? Do you want to be a commercial writer? Do you want to become a writer/director? Because that makes a big difference. If I'm meeting with someone who wants to write sci-fi but they also wants to write broad comedy, that's a little troublesome. It's better to be really really good at one thing than to be mediocre at a number of things. And also, to be fair, the skillsets that are required to be really good at writing sci-fi and to be really good at writing broad comedy don't necessarily transfer over to each other.

Luck Favors the Prepared

During the interviews I conducted for this book, manager Chris Cook shared this anecdote:

> I heard Ted Elliott and Terry Rossio (writers of such Box Office hits as *Shrek* and the *Pirates of the Caribbean* series, to name a few) speak once. When they first realized they wanted to be writers, they decided they were going to write five things before they were going to show anybody on the planet two things. Look, when you finish your first screenplay, there's such a feeling of, Oh my gosh, I did it! You should be proud when you finish your first script. But what they were talking about was that when someone writes their first script, even though there's a feeling of accomplishment, when you write your third script and go back and read

your first script, you're probably going to cringe because you've become such a better writer.

While not every writer has written five scripts before picking the two they should share, one of the common threads among many of the screenwriters spotlighted in this book is that they wrote, and often wrote A LOT, before they arrived at their big break. With that in mind, let's break down the various ways in which a writer can and should prepare for the professional space:

Brand

Your brand, in practice, is a simple thing: the genre space and potentially format in which you are at your writing best. Providing a strong and well-defined brand delivers a sense of clarity about the writer sitting across from the executive, the agent or the manager. Failing to brand yourself effectively (i.e. writing across every genre and format) implies that you yourself lack clarity about what it is that you do best. If you are not sharp about the areas of writing in which you most excel, how can you expect the industry to know when and where to best put you up at bat? Make no mistake about it: writing thrillers is entirely different from writing comedies. Sure, story is story is story, but comedic timing and effective tension building require largely different skillsets. And very few writers can truly execute both to same effect.

As Echo Lake's Zadoc Angell told me:

> One of the frustrations I have about new writers is that they're often writing all different kinds of genres—features, TV, comedy, sci-fi, horror, they're all over the place. And as a representative, it's very hard to represent someone who's not established who does everything. I don't care how good you are, no actor can play all parts well. And writers need to write enough to start to figure out where your writing is best, right? So maybe you write a bunch of scripts in different kinds of genres, and then you realize, okay, I'm really, really good at writing high-concept genre or science fiction. So then write several great scripts in that wheelhouse. They don't need to be identical to each other, they should be cousins to each other. There are so many different kinds of TV shows and movies, so especially in the beginning you have to pick the lane you want to be in. You can always reinvent yourself later through writing. But you've gotta be great at something at the beginning so that you can brand yourself to the community and then get advocates in the community—friends, fellow writers, agents, managers, lawyers, people to advocate on your behalf, because they know what they're advocating. We know we're advocating for X writer who's really great at doing Y and Z. Go. If I can't kind of categorize a young writer, then I don't even know where to begin.

Added Paradigm's David Boxerbaum:

> If you're known to be someone that's great with comedy, great with character, great with dialogue, that's a real benefit to the marketplace these days. Having your brand—having a built-in area that your expertise is in is really important when studios are trying to nail down what they're looking for. When someone calls and is like, I just need a great family voice, someone who can take like two, three weeks to work on this script. Who's great with family and heart? Okay, well, you know the brand of writers you represent and your client stable, so who has that brand behind them? Who's done that and has a track record with that kind of success?

John Zaozirny of Bellevue Productions agreed:

> If you're really good at writing sci-fi and you want to move into thriller writing, ok, that's kind of a cousin. Or if you write comedy and you want to move into action-comedy, Okay. The line between writing a comedy and then writing *Oceans Eleven*, or *The Italian Job*, it's not incredibly that far off. But if you have clarity of what kind of writer you want to be that's good because it's not my job to turn you into that person. I'm looking for writers who have clear ideas of who they are. And so if you are trying to be all things to all people, I know that that might seem like you are being very open and you are trying to be broad but in essence it makes you a jack of all trades, master of none.

And Ryan Cunningham of Madhouse Entertainment added:

> I might sign somebody off of a really great horror script they wrote. And if I talk to them, and they're like, I wrote this one-off horror, but I really don't like horror, I don't want to write it anymore—well, then that's very different. Because what you don't want to do is send out a piece of material in a particular space, get every producer and development exec excited to meet this person, and then all of a sudden, that's what you're being expected to generate in this bubble at least at the beginning, and if you don't want to be in it, that's going to create more issues in the long run than anything else.

Let's break it down: Why the brand? It's simple, really. The industry wants to understand what sort of writer you are, in the most specific (though not myopic) ways. Agents and managers want to strategize how to best sell you to the industry, whether it's shopping your products (screenplays) or your services (writing services, which come into play with Open Writing Assignments) to a potential fan base. That potential fan base will be constructed of producers, executives, production companies, studios and networks that work in the same or a similar space. Consequently, when those same producers seek to do rewrites on a thriller, they will put together a list of thriller writers whose work they responded to in the past. Every time, those will be writers well vested in that particular brand of storytelling, which then makes them viable for collaborative work in the space. Showrunners too are going to seek out new writers whose writing samples fall within the brand of the show whose positions they are now trying to staff.

Though genre selection may be the most obvious path through which to brand oneself, other thematic and message-driven choices made by the writer may also come into play when constructing the brand. In television, the sort of world, characters and themes explored with any consistency may help define and enforce the writers' brand as well.

As your career progresses, you will find more out-of-brand opportunities for your craft. You are, after all, a storyteller, and the stronger you get in one area of the craft, the more occasions you will find to stretch your screenwriting legs. Flexibility is one of the many perks that come with success. However, at the outset of your career, it is important that you identify where you are at your screenwriting best. Not only will it help you define and develop your voice and your screenwriting brand, it will provide a clear understanding of your value proposition for agents and managers considering you for representation, and instill confidence in those considering you for collaboration, staffing and assignment work.

Body of Work

If your job is to construct a road to your screenwriting career, then every screenplay or original pilot written is a brick laid in that road.

As discussed in an earlier chapter, gone are the days of the one-and-done screenwriting model; this is very much a career-oriented time for those taking on the moniker of SCREENWRITER, whether in the feature or television space, or both. And a career screenwriter is one who can generate high caliber work at a regular clip again and again. Therefore, an agent or a manager is likely to ask to see all of your available work prior to deciding whether to take you on for representation. Because of this, it is advised that before an aggressive approach into the screenwriting space is deployed (anything beyond contest and submitting into the television writing programs, really) you construct a cohesive and compelling body of work so that you are always able to effectively answer the industry's ever-popular question: "What else do you have?"

Consider yourself ready for the space once you have at least two to three scripts in the same or like genre (i.e. comedy, thriller, horror, etc.) that you feel confident enough to share. That means two to three feature scripts, one-hour dramas or half-hour comedies that aptly put your skillset and voice on display.

Is the writer allowed to vacillate between formats and genres? Yes, but with a caveat. If you are writing in the thriller space, you can do so in both the feature and television space, so long as you have mastered the structure in both and identified which story is best served by which format. However, vacillating wildly between genres and formats—for example, having a body of work comprised for a raunchy comedy feature, a horror feature and a one-hour family drama—often does much to confuse the message about the writer at hand.

Once again, I turned to my industry colleagues to get their thoughts about the writer's body of work:

Manager Kailey Marsh told me:

> I usually like there to be—not a plethora of material—but at least something else so that if I'm sending out the script and it doesn't sell then there's something else to bounce back on. Or something that we could do some work on and then go back out with. You're going to send the script out and you hope that it's going to sell. But most of the time it doesn't. Even if it does "sell" it's usually an option or if it's a pilot it's an If/Come deal (for more on If/Come deals, check out Chapter 10) so you're not getting paid. Because I'm commission-based I don't really want to take on people that have only one script because then that means they're one hundred percent developmental. Whereas some people I've taken on have already staffed on shows, or have prior reps, or have six samples they can send out.

John Zaozirny of Bellevue Productions provided his take:

> It's perfectly fine to be like, "Hey I'm a TV guy but I also do write features on the side but TV's where I want to focus." Or a features guy, "I'm open to TV down the road but features is really where I want to stick." But if you're kind of in the middle that's a confidence issue. And that unnerves us. We're like, well if this guy doesn't know what kind of writer he wants to be, whether it's TV or features, then that's problematic. Because if you can't make that decision, I don't want to make that decision for you.

John also talked about the importance of developing your craft from script to script:

> There are people that write their first couple of screenplays and they emerge born. But that's rare. I wouldn't say that if you've written 20 screenplays that suddenly you're a better writer. But as a general rule, you want someone who has written a fair amount and it's not his or her first screenplay. They're able to look at it and be objective about it. They're not blinded by, "This is the greatest thing that's ever been written" or "My mom says I'm a great writer."

While emerging television writers used to be expected to have spec episodes for existing shows in their arsenal (usually both network and cable in their respective space), recent changes in the industry have effected the requirement on the TV writers' body of work.

Said Blondie Girl Production's Ally Latman:

> Ten years ago it was like, Oh, let me read that person's *Lost* spec. Or let me read that person's *Everybody Loves Raymond* spec. And now we need originals. No one is writing specs for existing shows anymore. I mean, specs exist. But no one is writing them. There's no longer like, what's the hot spec of the season? It's, Do you have an original pilot, play, screenplay? Whatever it is. It's just changed enormously. It's more and more ways that you have to find to stand out.

Manager Evan Corday agreed:

> It used to just be about a spec script. You know you had to write your Barney Miller spec to be able to have anybody read you and suddenly, maybe 15 years ago, it finally became about the voice of the individual writer and not so much about being able to copy the voice of the showrunner. 99 percent of the people we deal with now want to read original material. Again, there are some old school showrunners who still want to read specs. But most people are more interested in what the writer is thinking and diving into. Because most younger writers write from personal experience. So you're getting a little bit of glimpse into that person and maybe their upbringing and maybe their passions.

Expertise

If brand speaks to what it is that you are writing, expertise speaks to the knowledge you possess about the space you are writing in. Movies, television shows, documentaries, books and even articles, plays and podcasts that pertain to the space are game. Think about it as the passion and inspiration that complement, influence and inspire your work.

Remember, executives want to work with writers who are smarter than them. In the very least, the hope is to find a bond and common ground in movies and TV shows in a particular genre that both writer and executive are fans of. And little is better than a writer introducing an executive to an obscure movie, television show, book or even podcast in the space of which they then become a fan. That is a great way to establish your mastery of your field in an elegant way.

Beyond knowing material with similarities to your own work (be they audience, genre or story), you also have to know who in the industry is making the movies, television shows and new media content in your space. Make it a point to study up on current showrunners, screenwriters and directors making waves. Know the production companies, studios, cable and digital outlets as well as networks with whom your work would be a natural fit. One day—if you are so lucky—you will get sent out to a slew of industry meetings on very short notice, in which you will have to put on display your knowledge of the players and the space again and again. And the one thing that becomes plainly evident when such opportunities arise is this: those are the sort of opportunities for which one can't simply cram. You have to knowledge-gather for months, and sometimes even years, in order to show up prepared.

Your Personal Narrative

As you read on, you will discover that both the writers and executives interviewed for this book speak extensively about the importance of meeting, impressing and building relationships with people in this industry. If getting a job in today's industry, and specifically in television where a writer's personality heavily influences hiring decisions, does not start and end with what's on the page, you have to impress as much in person as you did in your work.

Echo Lake's Zadoc Angell shared his thoughts:

> You know, I can send a writer into a general meeting and if they kind of give a boring general meeting with the executive, it's not really memorable for the executive, it's going to be hard for me to get that executive to recommend that writer to one of her shows down the road because the writer didn't make a strong impression. And they meet tons of writers, right? So you kind of have to stick out. You have to be memorable. You have to be outgoing and high-energy and charming and it's often hard for writers to do that because most writers are naturally introverted and kind of live in their minds, and so it's hard to be that outgoing, that social, and sell yourself with regularity. But you have to. If you really want a long-term career in the business, you have to learn to do that. You can't just hide behind the writing. Most of the time, people are going to read you and judge you for your material and then decide whether or not they want to meet you. And then once they meet you, hopefully they've already read your material, so they like the material. So the in-person meeting is about whether or not you can walk and talk and are personable and can hold up a conversation and be someone that I really want to invest in and that I can get excited about.

Often, writers new to the game ask me: What happens in these meetings? What am I supposed to talk about? Do I just ask questions? What do I tell them about myself? We will dig more into the dance of the general meeting in Chapter 11, but for now, this is where your personal narrative comes in.

Your personal narrative or personal story is the story you will share with listening executives, showrunners, producers and even representatives upon initial meeting, to tell them a bit about who you are in a unique and memorable way. Remember, these people sometimes meet upwards of twenty new writers a week. The personal story is what can set you apart from the rest and make you uniquely memorable long after your meeting is wrapped up. If your writing resonated (which likely put you in that room in the first place) and you were able to share a specific story, experience or point of view, executives will remember you when a project for which you may be a fit rolls by weeks or even months after you initially met.

So what makes for a unique and memorable personal story?

- **Give your story a clear beginning, middle and end.** Remember, your own story is your most important story, so telling it in a succinct, focused and enthralling way is key. The name of the game here is ENGAGEMENT. You want to get their attention, and keep it as long as you can with effective, specific, personal story telling. After all, if you can't tell your own story effectively, it is likely that executives won't trust you with material you know less intimately. Therefore, and whether you choose to share a personal journey of sorts (either physical or metaphorical) or a life event, be sure you go from a set up of your story all the way through to an effective conclusion. When telling your personal story, meandering is your enemy: The last thing you want to see is an executive's eyes glaze over as you search for a next story turn, not sure what is this ride on which you are taking them. That is when you have, effectively, lost them.
- **Your life's chronology is not your story.** The story of how you grew up in Minnesota, went to school in Florida and then moved to Los Angeles in search of your screenwriting dreams is neither memorable, nor is it going to get anyone's attention. Remember, most writers walking into a room will have studied somewhere or another. Most made the move to Los Angeles. Therefore, those sorts of life milestones are not specifically memorable. While they all hold importance and relevance for you, they are not the sort of unique life events or experiences that are going to be memorable in the long run to the person sitting across from you.
- **Memorable does not mean spectacular.** Not everyone gets to tell the story of how they ran away with the circus at the age of nine. But that doesn't mean that those without that sort of unique on-the-road experience have no way of being memorable or setting themselves apart. Instead, find an unusual defining moment, a life experience that informed who you are as a person and as a writer, that infused your writing with theme, that created a focus for the sort of material you're interested in writing. Steer clear of the sort of stories you are likely to hear from many other writers out there, specifically the ones about growing up lonely, feeling misunderstood and an outsider, with television your only friend, reflecting a world in which you

knew you would belong. Find dynamics and experiences to focus on that can only be told by you, and that are decidedly your own.

- **Don't be afraid to let a bit of your insides show.** Writers interviewed for this book used such words as "transparent" and "vulnerable." After all, it's your personal experiences and themes that resonate with you that you are going draw on for your screenwriting, so don't be afraid to share a bit of those with the executives listening to you. You want them to leave the room feeling as if they got to know you—that comes from specificity and transparency. That said, be careful not to over-share. This is not a therapy session. Therefore, you should not venture into personal stories that could make the listener highly uncomfortable, unless you are ready to handle them with humor and grace, and surprise the listener with the ease and comfort with which you can speak to them.

- **Imply wound.** A big part of creating an effective personal story is revealing something of yourself to which the executive listening is able to connect. While your wound should not be put widely on display, if you are able to find a way to share a bit about a wound that has helped form who you are as a person and a writer today without turning the meeting into a difficult and thereby highly uncomfortable session, your story would greatly benefit from it. Do what you can to imply, without spelling anything out. One of my clients had done well telling the story of his reunion with his birth mother. While the story itself was a happy and clarifying one, it also alluded to the inevitable wound created by having been abandoned by his birth mother as an infant.

Remember, finding a way to summarize who you are in just a few minutes can often feel significantly more daunting than writing an effective screenplay, or even a logline. Some people refer to this as "finding your nuggets" while others simply talk about making the most of your personal story. No matter what you call it, your job here is not to summarize. It is to come up with a few anecdotes that can specifically speak to the essence of who you are as both a person and a writer that will be specific enough to be memorable for the person listening to you, be they an executive, a showrunner or a rep, sitting across.

SCREENWRITER SPOTLIGHT #4: Terrell Lawrence

Terrell Lawrence grew up in the backwoods of Georgetown, SC. After blatantly being told that he was unfit for an Engineering career, he graduated from the University of South Carolina–Columbia with a Bachelor's degree in Media Arts. Shortly after graduating, he relocated to LA in pursuit of a writing career with a car crammed with clothes and a heart jammed with fear. Luckily within a few short months, he obtained a job at ICM Partners in the Contract Admin Department, primarily focusing on Film and Television allowing him to pay at least half of his bills. During his tenure with the agency, he continued to hone his writing chops by overdosing on writing classes, podcasts and numerous networking events. Eventually all of these actions aided in landing his very first staffing job on TBS' *Your Family Or Mine* and later on NBC's *Undateable* where he currently serves as a Staff Writer and hopes to never wake up from this dream.

Lee: When did you start writing, and did you always know you wanted to write for television?

Terrell: I grew up in South Carolina in a very rural area, and I always loved reading and writing. But over there and in other places outside of Hollywood, you really don't know that you can do it professionally. So it was something I was always interested in as a kid. And then what happened was I got to take a screenwriting class in college at USC in Columbia, South Carolina, and I fell in love with it. After I graduated, I moved out here, tried to make it happen. At first I didn't know whether I wanted to do features or TV—until I went to a panel one time and someone was talking about the differences between them—features are more visual, TV is more dialogue driven—and I realized that I like dialogue more. And that's when I realized I wanted to do TV writing and started going after that specifically.

Lee: When did you move out to LA?

Terrell: I moved to LA in August of 2006.

Lee: Was it a shock to the system moving out here? Or easy to adjust to?

Terrell: It was a little bit of both because it's so different—the climate, the people. It's more diverse, which I love. But I guess it was a little bit of a shock because of the uncertainty of it all. I moved over here without knowing anybody, without having a job lined up. I was really fortunate to get in contact with a producer before I moved over here—what I did was I got the *Variety* production lists. I don't know if they still have those or not, but I literally wrote down all of those numbers, it was over 100 numbers, I put them all in an Excel sheet, and I marked every time that I called people. I called everyone on that list, and three people were really nice enough to call me back, and one of them was super, super sweet. She told me a story about how she was a producer on *Golden Girls* and *Benson*, and she was telling me about how at one point she was living in her car for a while, and she really, really motivated me to come out. She said, "Hey, when you come over here, let's get coffee," and that's exactly what I did, and we're actually still really cool to this day. She really helped guide me, and in that regard, she really helped me make it a smoother transition.

Lee: Did you always know that it was going to be comedy for you?

Terrell: I always gravitated more towards comedy, automatically. I come from a very silly, fun family, and I always loved weird, crazy movies like *Naked Gun* and *Top Secrets*. They're very slapsticky, and I always loved that stuff.

Lee: A little while after you got out here, you got a job working for ICM, right?

Terrell: Correct, yes.

Lee: But it wasn't in the talent or lit department, it was in accounting?

Terrell: Yes, it was in accounting. When I got the job at ICM, at the time, I just needed a job. I was like, I'm over here, the rent is still due, and I didn't have any income at the time. Luckily, my friend (the producer of *Golden Girls*) told me about this website called entertainmentcareers.net, so I saw a posting on there, met with them, and got the job. I still wanted to be a writer, but I was just happy to be able to pay the bills. But then, while I was working there, I would still go to classes, I would still go to panels, I was writing on the weekends and on my lunch break. Just to really study and get better. I kept writing (original) specs and entering writing programs. I worked there for eight years before I started getting any traction.

How I transitioned into becoming a client was that I got really cool with one of the other clients, who was a bigger guy, and we have a mutual friend. And I was working with him the entire time—all eight years—I was working with him personally, but I never wanted to cross that professional line, like, "Hey, I'm a writer, too, can you please help guide me or something?" But luckily we have a mutual friend, and she was like, "Oh my gosh, I'll totally send him an email and let him know that you're a writer and maybe you guys can get some coffee." And I said, "Okay, that would be great", because I didn't want to do that. I didn't want to be pushy about it. So she did that, and I met up with him for coffee. And he was like, "Hey, so do you have anything you would like to send me?" And I said, "Oh yeah." I had just written a *Big Bang Theory* (spec) a year before and had gotten into the Austin Film Festival and became a second rounder. So I said, "Okay I have this script, it got a little bit of traction, I'll send that to you." And he said, "Great, okay, I'm not going to read it, but I'm going to send it to my agent, and we'll go from there." I said, "Okay, great!" He did that, he sent it to his agent, who's a bigger agent (Ted Chervin at ICM), and Ted sent it to a newly-minted agent at the time, Laura Gordon, so she read it, called me, and said, "You know, I really like this, do you have a pilot?" And I said, "Actually I do!" You know, I was actually just finishing up a pilot I was working on, so I made a few tweaks and sent it to her. And she liked that, too. So she started sending me out for jobs. And everything happened so quick. I met with him for coffee in January 2014. I sent her my scripts in February, and she started sending me out in February, and I got my first staffing meeting a couple weeks after she started sending me out. And that one didn't go, but then I had a general meeting with Bill Lawrence, and it went incredibly well. He was so nice, so cool. He didn't have anything to staff at the time, so he referred me to another friend of his who was on *Your Family and Mine* on TBS. I met there and got staffed. I got my first job—all of that started in January, the meeting with the coffee, and I got staffed July of that year, 2014. That was my first staffing job.

Lee: What's it like being a staffer for the first time?

Terrell: So great. Especially for me. I'm a quiet person. And of course, you can't really be quiet, especially not in the comedy world. You have to be fast. As long as you know your lane—you know when to pitch and what to pitch, because everybody can contribute in their own way. But the first time is so nerve-wracking, because you just don't know exactly what to do. I just decided I'm gonna be quiet and observe for a while and learn people's rhythm. But I was so terrified. Every time I had a pitch—any kind of pitch—my heart would race so bad. You could probably see my chest jumping up and down. And my voice would crack. I was like—wha-at if we did thi-is? It was so nerve-wracking.

Lee: You went from a cable show to a network show. How are the two different? Or are they very much the same?

Terrell: Weirdly enough, it seemed like it didn't change very much in terms of content—the raunchiness of it all and the subject matter that we deal with. But the biggest thing is that the show that I'm on now is completely live. Everything is done in real time. What you see is what you get. And we have to do more pre-editing before they actually air, which is a little different. So we spend a lot more time leading up to taping instead of, while we're taping, making changes.

Lee: So once you get your first job as a staff writer, how does your life as a writer change? Is getting the next job that much easier?

Terrell: Yeah. I'm actually still learning and getting familiar with that, too. I keep hearing that getting your second job is almost harder than getting your first sometimes.

Lee: You got that out of the way—you got the second job.

Terrell: Whew! Thankfully. Wipe the sweat off my forehead. But yeah, there's a lot of uncertainty because you just don't know if your show's gonna be back, and then will they bring me back, and then of course you have to worry about your option. Will my option get extended? It's a series of worries. You worry if you're going to get staffed. You worry if you're gonna stay on the job. You worry if your showrunner's gonna be a scumbag—there's a lot of that. And, from what I hear from veteran writers, that never goes away. Until you get to a certain point and you're creating stuff and you're pretty much set because you're developing constantly, non-stop.

   I think the more you do it and the more you work with people, too—there are people who will look out for you. I have found there are so many people who look out for me. Bill Lawrence looked out for me in a crazy way because he got me my first job and then he brought me onto this one. And I don't know what's next, but I could not be more grateful. And I have to keep writing. Every hiatus I'm gonna make sure I'm still creating new material so just in case something happens with this show, I have something new to pass around with my agent. Always keep that mentality, there's a lot of hustle mentality in the writing world. You can never stop. You can never stop or get too lax or too comfortable.

Lee: You worked for a long time before you started to surface as a writer. Did that feel at any point like, Oh my God, I'm never going to get there?

Terrell: Yeah, there were so many times when I was like, Okay, I came over here when I was 23—right before my 24th birthday—and I told myself, you know what, if I'm not a writer by the time I'm 30, I'm gonna go to Africa and take care of orphans and I'm gonna say forget it! Of course, then 30 came, and I was like, yeah, no, that's not happening. But while I was sitting in the accounting department at ICM, there were ebbs and flows. There were moments where I felt like I had some momentum . . . and then it goes away. Oh, here's another opportunity! Oh . . . okay never mind. So it was a whole rollercoaster of emotion going on with this thing. And there were plenty of times when I thought, Okay, it's just not going to happen.

And then once it did start to happen, it was at that same moment I was like, okay, my head is down, I'm working, I'm doing the work. If something happens great, if not, my head is still down and I'm just going to do it. And when that momentum started happening, I still kind of had that mentality like, Okay, well, great. I told my friends, Oh yeah, I'm sending my stuff to an agent . . . Okay, oh, you know she liked it, we'll see. . . . Oh okay, she's sending me out. So everything was kind of tampered down. They were like, No, dude, stuff is happening! And I was like, No, I gotta keep focused, I gotta keep working! But I'll never forget when I met Bill Lawrence—the day I met Bill Lawrence, I thought Oh my God, this could be the meeting that changes your life.

But before then, I was just putting in the work. There was literally a year where I wrote nothing because I just didn't have anything—I didn't know what to write. I wasn't getting into any of the programs—I applied to all of the writing programs every year, never got into any. Not that I deserved to— I was still learning. I think my first year, I wrote a multi-cam, but it was in single-cam format, but I didn't even know the difference. There was a lot I had to learn. But yeah, there was a lot of uncertainty. The big thing is just to keep writing—and it sounds so clichéd—but you have to. I think that's why it's clichéd because it's true and so real. You have to keep writing. You have to. Regardless of what's going on.

Lee: Is there anything that you know now that you wish you knew in those moments where you felt like it wasn't going anywhere?

Terrell: Hmm. That is such a good question. One of the biggest things is I guess just to never give up. I will say that I feel like I could have been a little more aggressive being at an agency. I could've possibly gotten there quicker if I was a little more aggressive about it. But at the same time, when I say that, well, it happened when it was supposed to happen because (before that) I wasn't ready. Luckily, at the time when I was asked to send material in, it was ready—it was where it needed to be. And I'm not sure it would've been where it should've been had it happened earlier. I needed to learn more and grow more. So I don't know. But I still feel like I could've been slightly more aggressive.

Lee: Do you have an agent and a manager?

Terrell: I do not. I only have my agent Laura Gordon who I love so much. That's my bestie there.

Lee: Why did you make the decision to only work with an agent at this time?

Terrell: I keep having this conversation with more seasoned writers, and most of them—I would say 90 percent—say not to get a manager. Unless you're a feature writer or you have some material that you're trying to adapt or once you get to that creative level, then maybe bring someone on. I guess at the staffing, baby writer level, a lot of them don't advise it. But I know some people who have managers and they love them, and the managers do a lot of work for them. So it's weird. Me and my agent had a conversation last year, when *Your Friend and Mine* ended, if nothing happens, then maybe we'll bring a manager onto the team to see if we can use some other relationships that the agency doesn't have and the manager might have so they can get in there. But then I got staffed, so I was like, Okay, well, maybe we'll just nix the manager conversation for now. But I'm still asking a lot of those questions, too.

Lee: How do you work with your agent? What does she expect from you? What do you expect from her?

Terrell: My agent, especially when it comes time for a new pilot, is so awesome. She gives really good notes, which I know is kind of rare—a lot of agents don't really read stuff. But she does. And she's always honest with me. That's one of the biggest things that I love with my agent. She's very honest. Then again, I guess all agents say they are, but she really is honest. Any time I have any questions at all, I email her and she's really quick to respond. And I appreciate that. Because I know, there have been some friends of mine who have representation and at points, they were trying to reach out to them and couldn't get them for whatever reason, and it's nerve-wracking for them. And fortunately I don't have to deal with that. But any time there's an issue, she always lets me know, and I like that openness with our relationship. I think that's one of the best ways that we work together. And asking her opinion on things. Because this is all still new to me and I got so much more to learn. So I love being able to have that relationship with her and going to her for that. And if she doesn't know something, she's like, You know what, let me ask someone. Because she's a young agent, too. But it's really cool, we're growing up in the business together basically.

Lee: So what's next for you?

Terrell: Well we're about to wrap on this season of *Undateable Live*, and right now, we don't really know if we'll get another season, so that's going to be in limbo probably until about May or so. And in the meantime, I'm going to work on another pilot just to keep that hustle mentality—you gotta keep working—and I'll probably take a couple generals just to see what's going on out there, and wait 'til we see what the official word is with this show, and then after that, I'll probably try to go out for some new stuff. But I love this show. This show is so fun. So if I can go back to it, I will be so happy. But if not, that's the nature of the beast. I wanted in the game, so here it is.

4

GETTING REPRESENTATION

Agent, Manager or Both?

For many writers looking to break into the industry, landing representation can be perceived as the first critical step to "arriving." And with good reason: When doing his or her job well, a reputable, well-connected agent or manager can become the writer's most powerful advocate in the industry.

As Blondie Girl Productions' Ally Latman put it:

> As difficult as this can be, get a manager. Get an agent. Get somebody who will be fighting for you. Because it's ridiculously tough to be noticed and seen.

Reps offer a direct path into the industry, opening doors for their writers that were likely previously closed. As many industry companies, including studios, networks and many production companies, don't accept unsolicited material, strong reps can quickly and effectively eliminate those barriers. It's the rep who will make the calls, the rep who will facilitate introductions, the rep who will attempt to play matchmaker between writer and job, the rep who will expose a feature or original TV spec until it is widely read or, in the best case scenario, finally set up or sold. Whether pushing a script up The Black List or helping their writer land their first or next TV writing gig, when writers' careers move forward on the studio or network level, an agent or manager is almost always involved.

It used to be that agents were the name of the game. Back in the 1990s, for many a young writer it was a big-time agency or bust. But as the new millennium came and with it brought the spec market crash, which minimized a new writer's sales potential, many agents found themselves challenged by the retracting space, and were therefore forced to substantially grow their lists in order to continue to make their same numbers. While literary managers began to break out from agencies back in the 1990s, and many made a name for themselves early in the game, they did not become the staple gateway for new literary discovery—especially in television, which has until recently been almost exclusively an agent's playing field—until well into the 2000s. This was born of a simple reality: with aggressive sales goals and quotas, agents could no longer afford the years it often took to develop a new writer for the marketplace. Instead, their energy became almost entirely devoted to booking revenue and finding work for proven "earners." Therefore, it fell to managers to identify and cultivate strong talent with promising industry potential, while the role of the agent became to service their existing, working clients, manufacture new opportunities, and negotiate, negotiate, negotiate.

Many screenwriters and television writers, however, remain confused about the differences between agents and managers. Here, Zadoc Angell of Echo Lake Entertainment aimed to clarify some of the key differences for me:

> On the surface, agents and managers perform very similar functions, and there is a lot of overlap in what we do and what our tasks are that makes it very confusing to people. But one of the things that I've found as an agent was there's just very high volume. High volume and very bottom-line oriented. So as an agent, your job is to book clients into jobs and to make money, and to go on to the next client who needs a job and book them and make money, and move on. So there's not a lot of time or space for the creative. I always gave notes as an agent. I was always very hands on and creative with my clients. But I was working in a culture that really didn't value that. If you're on the phone giving notes for an hour with a client, to an agency point of view, that's a loss because you're not spending an hour making phone calls and selling people and making submissions and finding potential income. When I went into management, creative was a big part of it—something I took a lot of pleasure in. When you have a smaller client list, and you're not servicing an entire agency department's client list, you have a lot more time and investment in the people you are caring for. And so, by virtue of that, I feel much closer to my clients as a manager. I talk to them more often. I know what's going on in their lives. It's a people business, and I feel closer to the people I'm representing than I could as an agent.

Even though responsibilities vary, what makes a good rep is fairly straightforward. Jason Scoggins, once a rep himself and now at the helm of Slated and Spec Scout explained:

> This is in no order, but the most important elements are: passion for a given project or for the writer him or herself; deep and longstanding relationships

such that the rep can help the writer get a job; whether that's to sell a piece of material or get in a room to pitch on a project; and for lack of a better term, a great work ethic. By which I mean, I don't have a lot of patience for that common complaint about agents in particular not returning phone calls or emails to clients. That definitely happens, but there's a reason for it. They tend to be very busy. They've got stuff to sell. But that doesn't excuse a given rep from not doing their work, which is to say getting material out there, setting meetings, basically being an advocate of the writer and the piece of material that they're trying to sell. You're looking for somebody who works their ass off. The good ones all do. So that's really it: Passion, relationships, and then the willingness to work their tail off to get stuff done.

Ally Latman of Blondie Girl Productions, which is housed on the Warner Bros. lot, put the difference between the agent and manager approach into perspective:

> Managers tend to be more focused, so they don't just send you everybody they're trying to get work. Agents tend to be like, Oh, we have these five people. Managers are like, Look, I just want you to hear this one idea that is so great and so perfect. They tend to cater a little bit more to the needs of what I've just said we're looking for.

In a perfect world where all parts work in harmony, there are certain things you can expect from both your agent and manager: facilitating introductions, advocating for you in the space, setting meetings and exposing your work to their industry contacts. Both are expected to—in their own unique capacity—help push your screenwriting agenda forward.

However, there are also differences, with one rep complementing and supporting the other's work. Gersh agent Sean Barclay elaborated:

> Managers are more important than ever. There's very few, if any, boutique agencies in the competition. Obviously there's the big three now, versus the big five. As a result of the siloed agency ecosystem, we need managers now more than ever as partners who work under a different route. And those managers have taken on traits of the agents and I do think that great agents have some traits of the managerial spirit.

Although nothing is black and white, it is important to understand not only the similarities, which often tend to overlap, but rather some of the key differences between agents and managers both practical and functional, which will help inform your decision about what might be right for you at each stage and each station of your screenwriting career.

Literary Agents

An agent serves as the writer's most vocal business advocate, making the kind of introductions and facilitating the sort of deals that will keep the writer working in the professional space for the long term.

Agents, as part of larger agencies, are licensed and operate under very strict parameters. Because of this, licensed agencies and the agents working within them cannot be attached as producers to material, nor are they able to collect out-of-pocket fees from their clients. At least not on the up-and-up. Agencies do, however, collect packaging fees from networks and studios when packaging material for the screen.

Agencies are legally allowed to procure work for their clients. That means that an agent is permitted to submit a stack of potential writers for a job, an especially important capability when it comes to television staffing, where agents take on the lion's share of the work.

Bellevue Productions' Jeff Portnoy spoke to the effectiveness of agents when pursuing television opportunities for their writers:

> Agents and then agencies are very helpful in terms of staffing, they track all of the shows that are getting ordered to series, they reach out to all of the showrunners, producers, network executives that are working on those shows and then they submit staffing samples for all of those shows. And they have a very formidable organized machine that does that. So for staffing you really ultimately want an agent. Managers also do staffing but it just depends on the size of the company. The bigger the management company, the more like an agency it functions, the more staffing they do.

Jeff went on to say:

> If I find out a show is getting ordered to series and I think a client would be perfect for it, if the client has an agent I'll reach out to the agent and then together the agent and I will reach out to the showrunner, or the executive producers of the show. If they don't have an agent I'll reach out to the show directly, tell them about the client, tell them how great the sample is, how perfect for the show it is and then submit it. Hopefully they love you in the meeting, they love your pilot or your original samples, and then you get the job and we're off to the races.

As part of their job, agents are assigned studios and networks to "cover." This means that rather than just servicing their clients, these agents are tasked with staying abreast of developments within a particular studio or network, as well as working their relationships with network and studio executives.

Chris Coggins of EuropaCorp shared with me how she works with her contacts in the agencies:

I talk to our covering agents at agencies at least every week, give them the updates on our projects, if Luc (Besson) or whoever has a new idea that I need to find a writer for, I'll tell them, "Hey I need a writer who can write female point of view, scifi action thriller," and they'll send me samples of people who can write in that genre for that idea. Conversely, they'll call me and say, "I have this new writer, I'd love for you to read this script." Hopefully I read it and like it and we work on another project together. So agents and managers are very instrumental in anything they might want me to read and anything that I need to find.

Agencies provide their agents with a base salary, on top of which commission is paid, typically a percentage of the commission an agent's clients have brought in, though some agencies do have a profit-sharing model in place, allowing for agents to more willingly see their clients vacillate between formats (in the agenting world, a writer is likely to have a film agent AND a television agent if working in both. If the agency does not have a profit sharing model in place, the TV agent gets commission on the writer's work in the TV space, while the film agent collects commission on work done and projects sold in the feature space). Because of this, agents tend to be more beholden to the goals and quotas set by their companies than managers.

Additionally, agents tend to "load their rosters," handling forty, fifty or even seventy writers at a time in order to meet the aggressive revenue goals set for them. The more clients an agent has that they can book revenue through, the more easily they can meet and exceed their sales goals. That means that—with the busier agents—a lower priority writer is less likely to get their agent's attention on a regular basis, while writers signing with a junior agent, or an agent still building up his list (which can occur when an agent moves from one agency to the next) are likely to receive more career-building helpfulness. Of course, there are exceptions. A handful of agents at the very top of their powerful agencies have been known to take on "projects," i.e. emerging writers whom they would like to shepherd. This, though, does not happen often, as these very powerful agents tend to take on one or two emerging clients at a time, if any.

There are still agents—albeit few and far between—who are known for developing their writers. But more often than not, those who wanted to focus on the terms of the deal, on covering the studios and networks, on negotiations and client servicing became agents, and those who wanted to be more closely connected with cultivating new talent, handling the day-to-day and thoughtfully developing the writer's chops and brand, became managers.

While many writers are eager to sign with a big-name agency, the reality is that when your career is at its infancy, it's about the agent rather than an agency. The full power of an agency—which includes packaging capabilities and high-value introductions—does not come into play until the writer has begun building a name for himself in the industry. Ryan Saul, literary agent at APA, concurred:

When you're a new writer I believe it's about the agent and not the agency. We all know the same people. If you have an agent that really believes in your material and can be the Sherpa for you and has the time to focus on your career, then that's the guy you wanna be with.

While every writer wants an agent, the reality is that not every new writer is ready for such representation. Manager Kailey Marsh shared with me her point of view on when a writer should engage the services of an agent:

I think you should be at a certain level before you need an agent. I usually tend to go out with brand new scripts to agents if the client doesn't already have one. Mostly because I'd like to tag team the town, it basically cuts my job in half going out with a spec. But an agent has five times more clients then us and is being pulled in a bunch of different directions and they can't be expected to care about your problems or give extensive notes on your script or prepare you for meetings. That's more of a manager's job, which is why managers can produce and agents can't. Agents are more checks and balances and we're more about building you up into who you need to become as a writer.

Which brings us to . . .

Literary Managers

Today, managers are considered to be at the forefront of talent discovery, serving as scouts for the agencies, the studios, the networks and production companies. It is their job to find the diamonds in the rough, then develop and prepare them for the working industry.

Jon Karas of Infinity Entertainment broke down the job of a manager:

Management has 'The Three S's of Management'. We sign, we sell and we service. So signing isn't just about, 'hey come on in and sign your contract'. It's about figuring out who to work with and why they are special, and deciding that they are worthy of your time and attention. Selling is a lot broader than just: "Hey, I'm gonna take your stuff and show it to all these buyers." It's a lot more than that and before you can get to selling, this sort of fits into the Service category as well, we have to shape what we will sell, we have to make sure we put the best foot forward and the most unique original special version of whatever it is any particular writer does. And then the goal is having a really thorough approach to selling. For us, most of our clients also have agents. And agents do things a certain way and we do things a bit of a different way. But together we cover the universe even more thoroughly.

Unlike their agent counterparts, managers are not licensed, and therefore can attach themselves to a client for representation, or to the client's project for the production of that particular piece of material, or to both. Additionally, managers or management companies can take a project on for production, but opt not to take the writer on for representation. Producing a client's project allows the manager or management company to collect a larger "producer's fee," which thereby demands that they waive collecting 10 percent directly from the writer (managers are only to be paid once, either as a rep OR as a producing entity).

Ryan Cunningham of Madhouse Entertainment, which produced client projects including *Prisoners* and *Creek*, spoke of the manager-producer hybrid:

> When we produce, it's almost exclusively material that was our idea to begin with (i.e. it originated with one of the managers/producers at the company), which we then took to writers. The same goes with books or articles or IP that we've sourced and brought to the writer. We'll develop a pitch, develop a pilot, develop a feature speculatively, then take it out and try to sell it, which usually involves packaging with elements and so on and so forth. The benefits of it are the fact that because we're involved, we add another voice to the process that is almost always aligned with the clients—because we broke it open creatively together to begin with, we have the same point of view on the material. So creatively it's good. Monetarily it's good for the writer because if the movie goes or the TV show goes, we don't commission the project so the writer saves 10 percent on it that way. And even if, on the feature side, you sell a spec to a studio, the writer does some rewrites, the studio decides they still want to bring on another writer, maybe just because they have a huge name and they like to do that before they go to directors. Because we're still involved in the process as a producer, we're able to keep the client more informed of what's going on and hopefully keep their vision of the project intact going forward. Whereas, if we are just managing the writer, our hands are essentially wiped clean of it at that point.

While agents are legally allowed to procure work for their clients, managers are not. They can only pursue these opportunities on a one-off basis, facilitating introductions and submitting a writer of interest to a producer or a showrunner, rather than a packet of potential writers for a job. For this reason, agents tend to be more instrumental for television staffing, which can become a numbers game.

Contrary to agents, managers tend to be mostly—if not all—commission based. While a few of the bigger shops offer their managers a base salary plus commission, most operate on commission alone, some profit sharing and—if part of a larger operation—a generous spending account, depending on the size of the company. Because of this, managers have a longer runway for developing new talent; while agents need to see returns and quick, managers may opt to develop talent and material over time in order to deliver just the right career-making impact. In the management scenario, and because of the lack of company-wide sales goals, each manager sets his own limits for how long he will work with a writer before the client books a job or sells either a pilot or a spec.

Even though some managers develop with their clients—sifting through loglines to select the writer's very best next project, providing constructive feedback on outlines and beat sheets before diving into pages—others prefer to send their writers off to develop their work without oversight. Neither approach is right or wrong; one may take longer and cause some frustration in the earlier stages of development, but ensure that the manager is invested in the final product, while the other dictates that the writer write for an initial audience of one: either the manager loves the work or . . . not so much, and it's back to the drawing board. The writer may, of course, opt to take the material to his agent should his manager reject it, but that on its own already presents a big hurdle for taking the material out to market.

Unlike agents, managers tend to work with a smaller roster of clients, in order to be able to give each one the time and attention they deserve. Because of this, managers are likely to have fifteen, twenty or thirty clients at most, allowing them the bandwidth to read scripts, give notes, prep for meetings, escort clients to high-priority meetings if needed and check in on a regular basis. Managers who do not develop or do not develop significantly (i.e. read scripts but don't work draft-to-draft or give in-depth notes) are likely to have more clients on their roster, as their development time is limited. Managers at larger management firms may appear to have even more writers on their list, but in fact are sharing some clients with another manager, which helps carry the load of day-to-day servicing.

Managers are also helpful when it comes to managing relationships; if a relationship with a producer becomes strained or if an executive has to be pushed to an answer, being it on an open writing assignment or staffing opportunity, managers are great when it comes to working in your best interest. Additionally, managers can help prod an agent along (and vice versa) when their writer is not getting the attention that he or his work warrants.

Choosing Your Rep

When you sign with representation, it is of the utmost importance that you uncover via simple, direct questions what your agent or manager is intending to do for you, and what they will not. For example, some managers breaking new writers seek to introduce them to network executives as up-and-coming-writers to watch, in the hopes that the writer would be considered should a staffing opportunity that is right for them surface. Other managers find those sorts of introductory meetings ineffective, and prefer that their writers work independently in pursuit of their first staffing gig. Some agents and managers believe in setting up tons of generals; others do not. Some managers are all about selling your original pilot, and have no interest in staffing you. Neither path is the "right" one, but it's your job to determine whether your manager—or for that matter your agent—will deliver (or attempt to deliver) what you are looking for. While you don't get to dictate how they do their job, it is critical that you know their approach and agree that it is right for you.

Zadoc Angell of Echo Lake said:

> If you're signing with a manager, I would encourage any writer to be really clear about what he or she is offering and what they do because management is a rapidly growing field that is changing a lot. Agents will give you a couple notes, a couple thoughts, a couple changes, but traditionally they're not going to do hours of notes calls and be in the weeds the way we work in management. Some lit managers really do just focus on the creative. They work on scripts and generating material for their clients, and then it's the agent's job to go sell that material and negotiate and make deals from it. I'm someone who used to be an agent—I was an agent for 3 years and worked at an agency for 7 years total—and there are a lot of former agents who are managers in the business, and it's hard to totally shift your training. We all know how to sell. We know how to cultivate relationships with showrunners, we know all the executives in town, and we want to get our clients jobs. And, by and large, that's what writers want—they want to work. They want to be paid to write, and sometimes it's hard to find that work. So the sort of manager that I am is a hybrid of a traditional manager and I would say like a boutique agent, where I am not only working with my client creatively, but I'm also selling him or her in the marketplace, and that's something that me and my team at Echo Lake really pride ourselves on. But it's not the style of every management company. I would actually say very few management companies really offer what we offer. But that's why, if you're going to sign with a manager, you should talk to them about what they do or what they don't do. What you can expect from them. Because each management company kind of defines itself and brands itself differently.

The most important thing about any agent or manager you are considering working with is that they are excited about you and your writing, and eager to do what it takes to get you read, and get relationships forged on your behalf. That means introductions, general meetings, network meetings, sitting down and talking with anyone who responded to your work. At the end of the day, you can sign with a marquee agent or manager in a name company, but if they don't really get what you do or lack the bandwidth to do what it takes to help a new writer break, there is only so much that they will be able to do to move your screenwriting career forward.

When I met with Blondie Girl Productions' Ally Latman, she told me:

> So many times I've heard a writer sit here and say that they're repped by—
> I'm just going to pull out the first agency I thought of—CAA. They're
> repped by CAA, and they're like, I don't feel like they're working for me.
> And it's because they're a baby writer at an agency that probably has some-
> one like J.J. Abrams, and they're not going to get the attention they need
> when their agent also represents some huge name. Which is understandable.
> But that's when a manager can come in and be like, I have a great baby
> writer.

Zadoc Angell of Echo Lake elaborated:

> Management has a responsibility to find the diamonds in the rough—to
> cultivate new talent—because agencies aren't doing it. Agencies used to
> when there were a lot more literary agencies and there were more literary
> boutiques out there, but in the last ten or twelve years, virtually all of the
> agencies have become big, high-volume corporate kind of places that value
> making money. So they're not going to sign a baby writer hoping that two
> years of investment will turn into a staff writer job. That's just not their
> business model, and that opened up a real vacuum in the business. Well,
> who is doing that work? Who is finding the next generation of
> showrunners? And that's where, often, managers really win because we find
> that new talent, we cultivate it, we put in the hard years and build a person's
> career and get them launched.

Commission

Across the board, both agents and managers collect 10 percent from their clients.
That means that, until they book you on a job, get you staffed or make a sale
on your behalf, they are, like the writer, working on spec. While there have
been rumors of managers raising their rates to 15 percent across the board, I find
that this is a claim made largely by "fringe" managers, i.e. managers who are
unconnected and without great level of respect or influence, who try to convince
their unsuspecting new writer clients that 15 percent is indeed the new standard.
The only occasion in which 15 percent becomes acceptable is IF the writer refuses
to take on an agent when their manager recommends, and the manager is therefore
charged with overseeing negotiations on their client's behalf.

While 10 percent or even 20 percent of a big fat zero may seem entirely
palatable now, believe me when I tell you that paying an agent and a manager,
after paying your taxes and your WGA fees, will put more than a small dent in
your wallet, so be prepared. Every emerging writer just making their way, whether
landing their first writing assignment or TV staff writer job, feels it. Therefore,

you want to make sure that your agent and your manager each have defined roles as they relate to your business operation. Remember, having an advocate, or a couple of strong advocates in the industry is invaluable, and very much worth the spend. Particularly for a new writer coming up, this expense is instrumental for introducing you to the industry and keeping you in front of potential buyers and employers.

Constructing Your Team

As a writer's career begins to take off, many writers seek to construct the team that represents them, rather than remain with a single industry advocate. Within this construct, and when the writer's career requires it, the writer should seek to have business handled by agents in the film or television space, or in both. Development, relationship management and meeting prep should all be handled by the manager, while any and all legal responsibilities would then fall on the writer's lawyer.

Agent Ryan Saul of APA provided further insight about the construction of the writer's team:

> You want to match the strengths of your manager with the weaknesses of your agent or vice versa. So if you have a manager who's at one of maybe the bigger management companies, you don't really need to be at a CAA, WME or UTA. Or an APA. If you have a manager that's maybe kind of a one-person shop, then maybe you could use the power of some of those bigger agencies. It's all about the personality fit and how it fits together with your team. And if I'm a writer, I'm putting together my board of directors for my business, and the CEO is the agent. The president of my company is the manager. Business Affairs is my lawyer. You want all of those cogs in the wheel to work together and be in synch and those are the careers that I see rise the fastest. When your team is in synch and gets it.

Jeff Portnoy of Bellevue Productions spoke of the writer's best approach to representation:

> I think it's a smarter strategy to find a manager first and then workshop the material, have the manager read everything, decide what's the best piece of material to lead with when we are introducing the writer to the town and decide which agency would be right for the writer, helping them navigate the space. Typically the biggest difference between managers and agents is that managers are more about being in the business of development, discovering writers, and then developing material with them. With agents it's more about selling and putting them up for jobs. So I just think that

naturally it is a better fit to do manager first, polish the material, get the best work, choose what the best thing to go out with is, get an agent onboard and then go out and try and sell that piece of material.

While every writer wants a team, a manager as well as an agent or multiple agents working to get his career off the ground and keep it moving, the reality of the matter is that multiple team members is not always a good thing. In fact, having multiple reps on your team may create hurdles that you may not anticipate. Manager Jewerl Ross shared with me his perspective about just that:

> You assume that when you get an agent, your agent is going to love your stuff and send it to people, but that's not always the case. The agent is another test for any piece of material. Not only do I (the manager) have to love it, but then the agent has to love it for it to see the light of day. Not every young client needs another test before their material reaches the market-place. Not every young client can handle the politics and the parameters that come with having another layer, you know? With me, on the face of it, my rules are very simple. I must have an emotional connection to this material and think it's good, and then I'll send it to everyone I've ever met. With the agent, their rules are sometimes about: is it commercial? How many of these ideas have I seen before? Will people think it's better than the last thing? You have the added complication of: Did they really read it well? Do they really have good taste? Are they smart? So in some ways I'm a good insurance policy, because if an agent passes, I can still send a script out to whomever I think is worthy. But that requires me navigating some politics. Because I have chosen to be in business with this agent, I also want to maintain a good relationship with them, so I have to make sure they're eventually on board with my plan for sending it out. I have to either frame it in a way that is unthreatening to them or frame it in a way that they can get excited about the fact that someone who is not them is gonna send a script that they do not like out to people. That requires forethought and maneuvering and motivation on my part. So, when someone asks me, Oh does this client want an agent? I have to think about all these things. Do I think the client can handle another barrier? Do I have the strength to navigate tricky political waters for this particular client? Do I have the strength, or the time, or the desire to handle those machinations for this particular client? It's not just about having more hands to help you. Because under that scenario, yes, I want all my clients to have agents. But the reality is, more people, more problems.

Ultimately, each writer's unique circumstance requires a unique team to be assembled for him or her. Gersh's Sean Barclay explained:

Every client needs a strategy and every client is different. Certain clients want to talk to one person. Some clients want to know the culture and interface with multiple agents. A lot of it is tied to what that client is doing. If it's a writer who gets so hot that the movie business starts calling and they have a show on the air and they launch a production company and they're producing books and they want to option books and they have that one act play they want to launch in New York, then you start grabbing from multiple departments. So it is really driven by the game plan. And then, this is the most important part, how that game plan changes and how you adapt to that.

What Agents and Managers Look For

In representation, discovery is often the name of the game. Everyone in representation is on the lookout for a stand-out writer who is dynamic in the room and—of course—on the page. But agents and managers usually begin to respond to writers at different stages of their career. Although there is no doubt that the hotter you are the more attractive you will be to both—and the less effort it will take to get their attention—there is also the reality that agents and managers work in accordance with specific standards dictated by their field. Manager Chris Cooke of Skyway Entertainment told me:

> What you're looking for is the writer's ability to write," You have less clients as a manager than an agent. You have less keeping up with what the industry is doing on a daily basis. Again, none of these things are black and white, but what you're looking for as a manager is more the raw talent than the sculpture.

Madhouse Entertainment's Ryan Cunningham added:

> People with something unique to say are few and far between, and people that, in their writing, manifest that in a unique and interesting way are few and far between, so it's reading a lot of material. A lot of times it's bad. A lot of times it's good . . . but not amazing. And I try to hold out for the stuff that's amazing, which to me, speaks to the uniqueness of the voice.

Ryan went on to speak about how he works with writers through the development process:

> I got into management because I love the process, soup to nuts, of working with writers. So I'm in there in the idea stage and I want to go through dozens of ideas with them before we find the right one. And then through the outline and scripting stages, I want to dig really deep with the writer, and I want them to not be afraid of getting challenged, I want them to

have a point of view when they get notes back from me and from others, but at the same time, they've got to be collaborative. Because usually if myself or if multiple people are giving them the same note, it means there's merit to it, and some people dig in their heels and refuse to acknowledge it, and some people honestly are so wishy-washy that almost any note you give them, they'll take literally and put it in there, which sometimes isn't what we're looking for, either. So I'm looking for somebody that's strong but open to constructive feedback, which, for any movie or TV show, is going to involve dozens if not hundreds of people sometimes. As far as what I expect, it's positive attitude, flexible, hard-working, prolific, always trying to improve themselves, always getting out there and trying to experience new things, so they actually have something interesting to write about, and they're not just recycling the same tropes or stories or characters in everything they do. And they've got to have a lot of fortitude, because there's ups and downs even for the best ones. Even if you sell a million-dollar spec right out of the gate and have the best team around you and all the things go your way, you're gonna have ups and downs. And some people collapse under that. And others rebound and do really well. It's all part of the process.

John Zaozirny of Bellevue Productions told me:

There are two things every representative looks for in a client. The first one is talent, which is the most obvious one, and somewhat ephemeral. The second thing is drive. The first one is straightforward: "Are you a talented writer?" Is there something on the page, something that often gets called a 'voice'? And the second thing is drive. Which is basically someone who is a hustler, someone who is hard working. I think the simplest way to put it is: "Do you want to make a living as a writer?" The question is less: have you written a lot? And more: are you committed to becoming the best version of a writer? Which is a working writer essentially. And that is also are you someone who's open to collaboration and working with myself, an agent, producers, directors, down the line. Because this business is a deeply collaborative one. It can also be, "Are you open to working on your own material and getting it into the best shape possible? Are you open to recognizing that it may take months, more likely years, to get to a point where you can financially support yourself solely through your writing?" You know, it's the hustle; it's grinding it out there, and recognizing that nothing is given to you. The talent, that's really important. But I would rarely, if ever, sign anyone until I met them in person because someone could be incredibly outrageously talented but then you may meet them and realize they have no desire, they don't take this seriously or they have no desire to hear other people's opinions, or anything like that. If I had to choose between the two things, I'd rather take someone who is more driven and less talented over someone who's more talented and less driven.

Of what he expects of his clients, John said:

Whether we're developing something brand new, or we're revising something that's pre-existing, I expect them to be open to collaboration. Open to the idea that we are going to keep working on something until it's the best. And they're not going to just be like, "OK, I've put two months of work into it, I want to get this script out right now because I want to prove something to my parents, or my girlfriend, or my boyfriend, or my family, or to myself." I expect them to recognize that this is a business, it's not Art or Emotion, there are artistic aspects to it but at the end of the day when people are paying you hundreds of thousands of dollars for something they're not doing it because they love your art, they're doing it because there's a product that they think they can make money off of.

When it comes to what TV lit agents are looking for, John's Bellevue counterpart Jeff Portnoy advised:

The bigger that agency, the less likely they are to take you on without any prior staffing experience. The smaller the agency, the more likely they are to take a risk on you and believe in you and sign you and go out with your material, even though you have no prior or present staffing experience. For the bigger agencies, the exceptions might be if you qualify for diversity, if you have credits on the feature side, or there's some type of heat surrounding something you've written. It's not easy. The agencies tend to be more interested in you when you've just been promoted to staff or are currently working as a writer's assistant on a show and are close to getting promoted. It's more of a sure bet that you're going to be staffed so that's what they're interested in. But like I said, every agency is different, every agent is different, they are looking for diversity, and the smaller shops are likely to take chances and believe in you if they like the material and go out with it. Also, if you have a manager you're going to be perceived differently than if you don't. If you're diversity you'll be perceived differently than if you're not. If you have any track record in features, or in TV selling a pilot, you'll be perceived differently.

And Gersh's Sean Barclay concluded:

It needs to be on the page, writers need to be able to execute at a level, they need to be what people call "being good in the room", they need to be able to articulate what they have written and what they are about to write. And of course every agent says they want someone to be a nice person—that's not really true—but they want someone to have some kind of business person's hat.

Attracting Representation

As I conducted interviews for this book, many agents and managers shared with me that, with a market flooded with scripts on a regular basis, it is now nearly unheard of for name reps to bring an entirely unknown, unvetted writer into their stable of clients without a modicum of success to their name. Success, however, doesn't have to mean having a staff-writing gig or a spec sale under your belt. Instead, managers (and sometimes agents) seeking superior new voices look for success in screenwriting contests, film festivals, TV writing programs or even listing services such as The Black List website (all of which you will find information about in consequent chapters) to confirm that the writer can indeed garner the sort of interest that could make a difference in the marketplace.

Most reputable agents and managers find their clients through one proven path: Referrals. Said Echo Lake's Zadoc Angell:

> It's a referral business. How does a baby writer get on my radar? It's someone in the business that I talk to with regularity saying, "This is someone that I think is exciting, and I've read their material myself and I think it's great, and I think you'd be a match, and you know, you should look at this." That's one way. And there's also, of course, the network and studio writer programs and diversity programs, because they read a lot of the new talent out there and cultivate a class of writers every year and are invested in staffing them, and so of course you sign people out of those programs, because they've already been selected in some fashion.

Added long-time manager Jon Karas:

> Referrals are important for a number of reasons. One, somebody already cares about that writer. Usually it's someone that we like, respect and are friendly with. So referrals are most important because if it's an agent or a lawyer—which they often are—it's people that we already respect, admire and want to keep working with. And then, if it comes from a producer or a studio executive that's also good because typically they're like "We like this person and we want to help them succeed and we know that you'll help them succeed and we know that you'll help to support, encourage, stimulate, refine their material and their career choices."

Manager Scott Carr concurred:

If something comes through a referral of someone I trust it does mean that I will probably read the material either faster and also with a higher expectation because I think there's gonna be quality there because it was pre-vetted by someone I trust and think has good taste. So if the writers do have access to executives and producers and people they feel can better facilitate conversations with executives then I encourage them to go those routes and exploit those relationships.

While you will on occasion hear of a writer who got signed off a single writing sample—either an original spec pilot or a spec screenplay—most agents and managers will ask to read at least a couple of scripts from the writer's body of work before the decision to sign—or not—is made. Being able to fulfill this request, and show more than one completed and vetted writing sample, signifies that the writer is able to produce more than one screenplay (i.e. this is not a situation of one-and-done) and is serious about his craft, thereby raising his chances to become a career screenwriter rather than being a writer with one story to tell.

Attracting Representation—Do's And Don'ts

As you seek to stimulate interest from representations, there are some things you should always do, while others you should avoid at all cost. Here is a quick list of do's and don'ts:

- DON'T reach out to representation, or have someone refer you, until you have material that is vetted and ready to show, and a body of work behind it.
- DO vet material before you send it to representation for consideration. Remember, unless the rep loved the concept and gives you specific notes (which hardly ever happens with non-clients) you don't get a re-do.
- If an agent or manager agrees to read your script DON'T pester them. Even though they requested the material or gave you permission to send it, they do not owe you a read. Follow up a few times (I usually recommend three to four soft email follow ups over a ten-week period), but if they don't get back to you, then you ultimately have your answer.
- DON'T assume that if you haven't heard back from a rep then they hated your materials. Industry folks generally let you know when they did the work, even if they didn't respond to the material. The more likely assumption is that the script was deprioritized as time went by, and probably never read.
- DO present yourself professionally. Reps are looking for clients whose calls or emails they are happy to receive, rather than ones who annoy them before the relationship has been cemented.
- Unless you've already secured their services, DON'T call an agent or manager. They have a long phone sheet to attend to every day, and your

name on it will only provide a distraction and take valuable time from their day. The best follow up is done via email.

- If an agent or manager provides feedback on your script, DO accept it graciously, even if you don't agree with it.
- DO start fostering the sort of industry relationships with other writers or industry executives that can become valuable referrals now, even if your material is not yet ready for showtime. Remember, people want to help others who they like, rather than those who reach out only when they need something.
- If querying an agent or manager (which you will learn more about in Chapter 12) DO lead with the headline: what competitions you've won, what programs you were granted entry to or which film school you just graduated from.
- If querying an agent or manager DON'T bother mentioning any successes that may be meaningful to you but not to the industry (such as winning an unknown screenwriting competition or only making the quarter or semi-finals in a highly regarded competition).
- DO send thank you cards after initial meetings and holiday cards every year. Little gestures can go a long way in the industry.
- DO keep potential reps in the loop on recent successes. Placed well in a highly regarded contest? Finished a new script that's getting a lot of positive feedback? Drop a quick line to a rep that might have shown interest in the past. Even though they will likely not respond, they are keeping an eye out for writers who are prolific, determined and consistent.
- DON'T take rejection as an end to the relationship. Even if an agent or manager says that your material is "not for me" or that they "couldn't connect with it," they may welcome you to send them your next script, which you should take them up on!

The Writer/Rep Relationship

With any luck, your relationship with your agent or manager will be a long lasting and productive one. In order to ensure this, be certain to have a clear understanding of what your reps will, and will not, do for you. As mentioned in an earlier section, understanding the parameters of your relationship is going to be key to managing those relationships to satisfaction long term.

Said David Boxerbaum of Paradigm:

> An agent guides someone's career in the writing business, meaning that they will be helping the writer to choose the types of stories they should be telling, and then telling the writer what the marketplace is looking for, marketplace being the studio world, independent world . . . Making sure the writer is writing from not only a place of passion but a place that

can hopefully further their careers, so a script that can help generate opportunities to rewrite scripts. Basically, everything that comes to help guiding them in the right direction, keeping them on track—that's what an agent does every day. You hope, at least.

No matter what stage of your career you are in, you must always remember this one simple fact: despite the highly social nature of this industry, your rep is not your friend. Your rep is your business partner, your liaison to the industry, and you must always handle that relationship professionally. As such, that relationship has to be managed to make sure that you remain top-of-mind when it really matters.

I asked Gersh's Sean Barclay how to set the proper expectations for the writer/rep relationship.

> Expectations can be the engine for the relationship or they can be the pitfall. Right? It's the hard work, putting pen to paper, it's the networking and reporting back, it's the partnership aspect of it—for example, if a writer has a meeting, goes into that room and then comes and says: "I didn't know what it was about." That's not on anyone except the client who should never walk in the room without knowing the agenda. So it's a whole list of things that lead to professionalism and communication.

As far as what his writers expect of him, Sean had this to contribute:

> There's more talent out there than there are agents who can properly represent them. That's why a lot of writers have had to develop a new skill set: representative awareness, if you will, where you really know what your partner is going through. As a writer, I know that my agents are in more staff meetings than ever. So I'm going to make sure I email them before I call them, with bullet points. That was never done ten years ago. I mean the culture now is . . . (and this is obviously a joke) it used to be ten years ago the client called the agent and said "Why haven't you gotten me a job?" and now, in 2016, the agent calls the client and says "Well why haven't you made me any money?" And that is a bizarre reversal, which is probably tied to the Super Agent and agents being in the spotlight now more than ever. But you know, my system is honesty and over communication and transparency and just trying to get it all done.

Ryan Saul of APA shared his insight about how to remain a priority for your agent or manager:

> They need to write. They can't rest on a spec that got them there five years ago. They need to keep writing. They need to keep re-inventing.

They need to keep creating. The biggest issue that I have is when a writer calls me and says, "Hey, why did Joe Blow get this assignment and not me?" Well you haven't given me new material in three years. I need something new. I need stuff to sell. The writing assignment game, that's probably changed the most. There's just not a lot of assignments out there. So if you want to play that game, you have to keep writing. And you have to keep selling. Or write something that blows people away and then they come to you. Then that's an incoming phone call business.

It is your job to stay top-of-mind for your rep. That is accomplished not by calling and nagging, but by delivering new, exciting, high quality content on a regular basis, building new business relationships and pursuing opportunities outside of the rep/writer relationship. While you certainly want to see your rep setting up industry meetings for you, you always want to contribute by networking and making valuable contacts whenever the opportunity presents itself.

If your reps are not getting you out there as you had expected, be it for generals or even pitch meetings, it is up to you to connect and explore whether there is something your rep needs from you that you are not delivering. Is there a certain type of script you should be writing? Does the execution need to be elevated? Is there a small project, like a web series, they would like to see you get on its feet? Never hesitate to have the big strategy talk, with openness to hearing what more you could be doing for your rep to be able to do their job for you. However, if your rep gives you specific instruction about what they need from you, you are going to have to follow through.

The longer you are with a rep without producing tangible, revenue related results, the more likely they are to begin to lose interest. It's a simple equation of money over time: The longer a rep works for you without getting paid, the less money they will have made from you per year in the end. While managers tend to stay on the ride longer without immediate expectations of financial returns, agents who are investing their time in you will likely ease their efforts on your behalf if working for you doesn't produce results and instead keeps them from making their numbers at the end of the day.

As Sean Barclay of Gersh suggested, always be strategic with your communication, not just what you're communicating, but also when and how often. Don't let your manager or agent get in the habit of deleting or ignoring your emails because they know another one—on an entirely different topic—is just around the corner. Instead, prioritize what it is that you are looking to communicate to your rep. Is there a new TV show that just got picked up that you would love to meet on? Are you looking for an update on a spec that went out a few months back? Are you seeking feedback on an outline? Identify your top priority, and pursue it until you have your answer.

Remember, failure to communicate from the rep side doesn't always have to mean a loss of interest or your lack of importance. Instead, it could mean that your rep has not yet gotten the answer they've been pursuing on your behalf, or is working on something and will get back to you once they are able to deliver. In their mind, if the choice is between pursuing an opportunity or calling you/ answering an email from you, unless the matter requires immediate attention, they are going to focus on the opportunity at hand.

When developing new material, which will happen with the involvement of management much more so than an agent, be sure to listen to your managers' instructions. If you are tasked with delivering ten new ideas, don't deliver just the one you are crazy about. If you're in outline, and your manager is asking that you deliver—in outline—just the first act, be sure to deliver just that and not jump ahead. You may think that delivering a full outline rather than just Act 1 is ambitious; a manager may think that this deems you non-collaborative, and cause them to wonder whether you want to listen to them, or just do your own thing. And if your rep gives you notes on a screenplay or television pilot, be sure to either address them or else discuss them if you decided against incorporating them. The worse thing you can do is entirely ignore them.

Of course, there are those times when emails and phone calls stop being returned. Your rep didn't fire you, but you seem to no longer be a priority in any way. If this behavior is consistent over weeks and months, and even after new work is turned in remains unchanged, then it might be time to consider whether you and your rep are, indeed, a fit. There has been more than one occasion when a rep took on a client hoping for specific results, and when those didn't materialize turned his attention to the next. In other scenarios, the writers' and reps' expectations of the relationship may have changed, or else writer and rep may not have been able to agree on the quality or direction of the work. If that turns out to be the case and the relationship does not change course, it may be time to make a change.

Representatives on Representation

Once again, don't take my word for it. Here is further advice, guidance and insights from agents and managers:

Said Paradigm's David Boxerbaum:

> The thing to getting an agent (or manager) is don't give up. I mean, so many writers get told no once, twice, three, four times, and they give up. You're going to get told No a million times, and that's not an exaggeration. You will. The people who make it and want to stick in it overlook No to find that Yes. I get told no every single day and rightfully so, it's that one yes that I come to work for everyday that I get that makes it worth it. It's the same thing for a writer. They have to be focused on that Yes from whoever and the validation that that will bring to them, rather then only focusing on the negative of a No, which you're going to hear time and time again.

Added Gersh's Sean Barclay:

> I work with a lot of young writers. A lot of baby writers, as you say. I call them new voices. It's still a hot commodity in our business. A fresh new voice. It's probably not the best business model for an agent to represent, you know, the playwright out of New York, or someone not established, but it is also the most rewarding when you break somebody that you know has something special. And part of your job is to launch them and protect them. Very time consuming but a direct correlation to the feeling of reward.

Infinity's Jon Karas had this to add:

> If you're functional, aggressive, enthusiastic, intelligent, collaborative, it gives you a chance to be a writer as a starting point to build a real business in the entertainment business and that's a big piece of what we do. We build businesses around our clients.

Circle of Confusion's Josh Adler contributed:

> Just getting a rep doesn't guarantee anything. Not to allay it off on a writer, but as a rep, there's only so much that we can do. We're not miracle workers—same thing with agents. We can connect dots, but unless you're funneling us the material and unless you're giving us great material, there's only so much we can do. So a lot of it is on the writer to write material and to keep writing material. There are writers who'll write something and get so hung up on that one thing that they're excited about that they keep coming back: What's going on with this project? What's going on with this project? What's going on with this project? And two years later, they haven't written anything else. I'm not saying that you shouldn't be passionate about the things that you write, but keep creating. Because if you get a rep, they take your script out, and nothing happens with it, have the next thing. Be writing the third thing. And just keep that supply chain of material coming so that the rep has something to work with.

Untitled Entertainment's Jennifer Au provided this insight into her work:

> Part of my career up to this point has been building my own relationships, and I'm known for my taste, so when I send a writer out, whether it's their piece of material or I'm sending them into the room to pitch or for a general, that person is speaking for me, too. So that's why I spend so much time practice pitching with people or talking with them about ideas or reading their work—I want it to be as strong as possible. What I'm

looking for is someone who is willing to put in that work and has great quality in them and also is a good person. Life's too short, you know? I never want to cringe when I have someone on a phone sheet. I want to be able to pick up a phone and have a conversation, and I think it's really about wanting to put in the time and build the relationship with this person—the investment, because it is an investment. Because I don't get paid hourly. I get paid when my client gets paid, and for a young emerging writer, sometimes I work my ass off for years, and I don't get paid. So it's about, Am I ready to take this journey? Am I going to say, "I think, later down the road, this person is going to be a star"?

Jeff Portnoy of Bellevue Productions told me:

Managers tend to serve as, to use a sports analogy, scouts for the agencies. It's our job to be out there, judging screenwriting competitions and TV writing competitions, meeting writers and developing material. And then when we feel the writer is ready we reach out to the agencies and the agencies hopefully will sign them, and then together as a team we go out to the town with the material and get the writer meetings.

APA's Ryan Saul added:

My job is part psychologist, part Sherpa, part lawyer, even though I'm not one, and a big part being a sales person. There's a lot of psychology involved. Even with working writers. I have a writer who's working on three different projects, none of them are studio projects –and he's feeling like "I have to write a big studio project." And I'm like "you're making a nice-mid six-figure sum for doing these three projects, let's work on these . . ." He also has two movies that have recently been made. So you kind of have to look at the big picture. Where do we want to be in 2 or 3 years? The Sherpa part of it is making the plan. You wouldn't climb a mountain without a Sherpa or a guide, because they know where the pitfalls are. My job is to know what those pitfalls are and know the right place to hang your rope when you're mountain climbing, and allow you to take that step. Where do we wanna be in 3 years? Where do we wanna be in 5 years? The lawyer part is the negotiation. That's where I get to yell. But I also understand the argument from both sides especially since the deals are different now than they have been before. There are deals that I'm doing now that probably 10 years ago I would've said, "pass." But you have to figure out a creative way of getting to a number if that movie gets made even if you have to take less up front. And that's the dance I think a lot of agents are doing now and I think why a lot of feature departments are shrinking. At all of the agencies. The big and the small. And then there's development too. I develop a lot with my clients whether they want my notes or not. I let it be known to them when we sign that I come from a film background, I come from a theater background, I've read more plays and scripts than I can count. I'm sure it's in the thousands at this point. And probably more. Structure is easy to teach. But if you have a voice, that's what I'm looking for. So those are the facets of being an agent, although nowadays I think agents are becoming more producerial than ever before. Because selling a spec is like a freaking mitzvah. I have to put things together.

And manager Jewerl Ross added his two cents:

As it relates to starting off a career for a writer, what I do for them in the beginning is simple: I fall in love with the material and I send it to a lot of fucking people. There isn't any magic or voodoo in that. I know a lot of people, even if I don't know someone, I'll call them. I'm lucky that a lot of the people that I don't know who I can cold call have heard of me or my clients. And so, you know, it's simple work, it's exciting work, everybody wants to read something that's new and fresh and interesting. It's easy. Making a list of 20 or 30 or 40 or 80 people to send something to—I can do that in a day and send it to people. Where does it get hard? Having a reputation whereby the people you are calling will actually read it. Where does it get hard? Following up with people to make sure they've read it. There's nothing sexy about calling someone once a week, three or four or five weeks in a row to say have they read a script. There's no panache or gold stars or blue ribbons or articles in trade magazines about calling someone once a week to make sure they've read a script. That is sort of the nuts and bolts of pushing a writer's career forward who has never done anything. I love that element of the job because it is so simple. I love it because I know that many of my competitors will forego that very simple thing because it's so unsexy. But it really takes time and the will to do it. I will often ask agent friends of mine did they follow up on X submission? And they're like, "Oh, if I haven't heard from them, they've passed." And I'm like, "Really?" I've had executive after executive tell me that they're overwhelmed with material. That they don't have time to read everything that they've been sent. Outside of my reputation, the reason they read my stuff is because they know they're going to get a call from me on Monday morning. The truisms that we learned in kindergarten are true today. The squeaky wheel gets the oil. I am a professional squeaky wheel. But doing the nuts and bolts work of following up on submissions and seeing what people really thought, that's where the magic happens. So there's magic in the reading and there's magic in the doing.

Positioning Yourself for Representation

Every time I sit down with a writer who is relatively new to the industry, I hear the same question: What do I need to do to get an agent or a manager? You will read more about the various paths to breaking in as the book progresses, but it's your own positioning, delivering the goods that could potentially make you attractive to a rep, that we can begin to explore right here.

It is true that not all agents and managers are on the lookout for new clients. Some are servicing large rosters made of big players already, and don't have the bandwidth to bring a new, unproven quantity into their stable. But others, from managers to junior agents, are always on the hunt. After all, they are in the business of discovering new talent, identifying the next class of showrunners, finding exciting original voices and material that can gain traction and provide a fresh new voice in the space.

You can begin to learn about some of the agents and managers working in representation today by listening to the following podcasts:

- **Scripts and Scribes**, which provides a library of in-depth interviews with a number of exciting managers and agents.
- **Selling Your Screenplay**, another great resource for learning more about what reps are looking for in the space.

If there is one thing you can take for granted in your search for representation, it is this: both agents and managers working in the industry have a pile of scripts needing to be read virtually staring at them every day. These are scripts given to them by their clients, scripts of writers referred to them, scripts that they can't even remember how they got on their desks. It is up to you to provide the answer—which goes beyond a logline—that will make your script and your own pedigree as a writer stand apart from the rest. But how do you do that? You don't have the luxury of jumping up and down yelling "Look at me! Look at me! Look at me!" and even if you did, it would likely be less appealing, more scary. So what's a new screenwriter to do? Consider these industry-acceptable alternatives:

Referrals continue to be the number one way to get an agent's or a manager's attention. If you can get someone trusted from within the space—be they a lawyer, an executive or even another writer who is a few steps ahead—to pick up the phone or send over an email suggesting that you are a writer who should be read, that would go a long way. Remember: The industry is a bit like the mafia. We need someone to vouch for you before you are made.

Listing services such as The Black List and Spec Scout, which is a hybrid listing, evaluation, and marketplace website, are useful when a script garners high scores and scouting qualifications. As you will learn later on in this book, these are services that the industry has come to rely on as experienced vetting services.

In the coming chapters, we will be exploring contests, television writing programs and feature fellowships and writing labs. While winning or placing in them (as a finalist, semifinalist or quarterfinalist, which most name competitions do rank) does not guarantee you immediate entry or an immediate path to representation, surfacing in those does serve as a confirmation that you may just be a writer worth looking at.

SCREENWRITER SPOTLIGHT #5: Eric Koenig

Eric Koenig was born in southern California in 1973. After graduating from high school in Portland, Oregon, he enlisted in the U.S. Air Force where he served for ten years before deciding to pursue his education. After obtaining a B.A. in Biology from San Diego State University and a D.M.D. from The Arizona School of Dentistry, Eric once again joined the U.S. Air Force, this time as an officer and general dentist. So what does all that have to do with screenwriting? Other than amassing a trove of life experience, absolutely nothing! Eric caught the "screenwriting bug" while practicing dentistry and hasn't looked back since. His thriller spec script *Matriarch* sold to Paramount for mid-six figures, as well as made the 2014 Black List. Eric is represented by Madhouse Entertainment and Paradigm.

Lee: There's a perception that you just sort of "appeared" one day in the industry, sold a script and became a screenwriting star. How close is that to the actual reality of things?

Eric: I actually "appeared" many, many years ago in 1973 actually. My mom tells me she remembers it well—imagine that. I guess from an industry standpoint, I did just kind of appear, but as we all know there are no overnight successes, or at least very few and I certainly wasn't one of them. Perhaps because I wasn't involved in the industry in any form or fashion before selling *Matriarch* it makes my appearance seem like a bigger deal than it is, but I'd say many if not most aspiring screenwriters are not actively working in the industry when they get their big break. As for screenwriting star . . . I'm still pursuing that aspect! While selling a single script to a major studio is a dream come true, a star has sold multiple projects, has numerous produced credits (all of which were huge blockbusters and loved by critics), and has at least two Oscars on their mantle. Now that's a star.

Lee: It took you three years from the time you started writing to the time you were discovered via Tracking Board's Launch Pad contest. That is lightning fast by industry standards. Can you share a bit about how you developed your craft and industry know-how during that time?

Eric: If you only knew how much writing I did in those three years!! But seriously, I do recognize that is fairly quick in comparison to many others and I'm grateful for it. More importantly than how quick you break-in though is: are you capable of sustaining it? Are you a one-hit-wonder or can you make a career outta this? That is the real challenge. Everyone wants to break-in as soon as possible, understandable, but you've gotta be ready for what that means and what's expected of you once you do. In that regard, I think it's a good thing that most writers don't get their break six months after finishing their first script. If it had taken me seven years, I'd probably be a better writer because of it. Alright, back to your question. I'm a biology major and practicing dentist, so no film school background. When I decided I wanted to write screenplays a few years back, I think I read every book and blog on the topic to educate myself. I also read screenplays, but credit much of my success and learning the craft to simply just writing—lots of it. That's what we do, right? That's what we call ourselves, writers. So if you truly don't enjoy sitting down and cranking out pages, because that will always be the expectation, then you may have a long road ahead of you.

Lee: When you write . . . What is your process, and how do you ultimately make sure that your final draft is as good as can be? Do you get notes? Have a trusted circle of readers or . . . ?

Eric: Every writer has their own little unique quirks when it comes to how and when and where they write and I love that about this profession! Personally, I need silence and almost always write when I'm alone and sitting at my desk at home. When I was starting out, yes, I'd use several different pay services to read my stuff and provide feedback. Some were better than others. Some were more expensive than others. But it was all valuable and unequivocally improved my work and strengthened my skills as both a writer and storyteller. I know not every novice writer has the income to do that, so I feel very blessed to have a career where I could afford to get notes.

Lee: What was your experience of placing Top 25 in Tracking Board's Launch Pad contest?

Eric: The Tracking Board contest changed my life and I will forever be indebted to them. I tell them that all the time too! Placing in the Top 25 was still enough for *Matriarch* to get the attention of a producer who then took it to my reps. Not having a single Hollywood contact when I was trying to get my stuff read, entering contests seemed like the best and perhaps only way for me to break-in. Contests can be great exposure for aspiring writers and I'd encourage people to enter. There are a wide variety of contests, but what I like about The Tracking Board is that they offer representation to the winners, not a financial reward. Not gonna lie, both would be awesome, but what I think everyone really needs who's entering contests is representation and The Tracking Board has a great track record of getting that for their winners. Heck, you don't even need to win the thing.

Lee: You quickly got signed after that, after a producer read your script and passed it on to your current reps. How does your life as a screenwriter change once reps are involved?

Eric: I've got two great managers at Benderspink* and two great agents at Paradigm. Things are definitely different once you have reps, but that doesn't mean they are easier. I think that's a common misconception. Yes, I have people who will read whatever I write now, which is amazing. It's what every aspiring writer dreams of when they start out—just having someone in the business to send their material to! But that doesn't mean everything I write gets sold or even passed around town. Once repped, the bar actually gets set even higher for what you're expected to turn-in. Landing a manager and/or agent does not mean you're set for life—not even close, and I can personally attest to that. What's nice is that everyone on the team is striving for the same goal: selling specs or landing assignment work. They look out for your career and arrange meetings. Because *Matriarch* was a thriller, they've encouraged me to stay in that genre, which is fine because that's what I'm naturally drawn to. In fact for me, the darker the better.

Lee: Was Launch Pad the first exposure that *Matriarch* had in the industry, or did you try sending it to people prior to the contest placement? And, if so, what was the response?

Eric: Truth be told, I entered *Matriarch* in another contest as well as The Tracking Board and in that one it didn't even advance! Just goes to show that every reader is different and what one is drawn to may not connect with another. So don't ever take "no" for an answer. Believe in your script. Trust your gift as a writer. Doesn't mean it can't be improved because everything can, but know that a single "no" is not the end. There are countless Hollywood stories of a writer or director or producer getting passes on their idea or project, sometimes dozens upon dozens of times, yet they stick with it and eventually someone loves it and the next thing you know they've got a hit movie on their hands. Had I entered *Matriarch* in just the one contest, I might not be writing this paragraph today.

Lee: *Matriarch* ultimately went on to sell to Paramount—for most writers, selling a feature spec is a dream come true. So . . . Could you tell me a bit about what the experience of actually selling a spec to a major studio is like, and what sort of doors it may (or may not) open for you?

Eric: I'm extremely grateful to the producers who took it to Paramount and for the execs there at the studio who believed in and bought my script. Everyone has a different story, but for me, everything happened really quick. We're talking lightning fast. Immediately after signing with my reps, they gave me a few notes, which I implemented over a weekend and that Monday they

---

* Since this interview, Eric switched management from Good Fear Films (previously Benderspink) to Madhouse Entertainment.

took it out wide and Paramount bought it only a few days later. It was less than two weeks from the time I was sitting at home, eagerly waiting for The Tracking Board to announce the Top 25 to the time I learned Paramount made an offer to buy my spec. Amazing experience. Very exciting. It definitely opened doors, but selling a spec to a studio is truly just the beginning. We've all heard it before and it's the absolute truth: once you break-in, the real work is just beginning.

Lee: Being named to The Black List is so coveted by so many writers. As you said, it was also a goal of yours. Could you tell me a bit more about what happens once your name and screenplay are put on that list? Do more doors open for you?

Eric: I imagine every writer has a different story about what making The Black List did for them or the script or their careers. For me, I didn't garner any work directly from it, but it's definitely a badge of honor. I'm proud of that one. The scripts that make the list every year are supposed to be those that folks around the industry enjoyed reading, the ones they remembered or were entertained by, and that means the world to me. One of the cool things was how they announced the list that year. For *Matriarch*, there was a short video by Reese Witherspoon, Bruna Papandrea and Laura Dern and they just very briefly mentioned my name and the name of my screenplay, but I have three younger sisters and they went absolutely nuts when they learned Reese Witherspoon had actually said my name. To them, so I sold a screenplay, blah blah blah . . . To them, so I made The Black List, blah blah blah. . . . But Reese Witherspoon saying my name?! I was finally the cool brother. Thanks Reese—I owe you one!

Lee: We often hear about writers going on "Generals." I am assuming that since *Matriarch* blew up, you've been making the industry rounds. Can you share a bit about what that experience has been like for you?

Eric: Following the sale, my reps arranged a bunch of general meetings around town and I finally got to experience what I had been reading about for years. Mostly producers and production companies that had read *Matriarch* and wanted to know what else I was working on. They'd tell me what kind of material they were interested in. All of it was very relaxed. These weren't pitch meetings. I wasn't trying to sell them any ideas. Just forming a relationship in the hopes of working together in the future.

Lee: Since you've sold your script, you've kept your day job as a dentist on an Air Force base. How do you manage to juggle the two very demanding responsibilities?

Eric: Yeah. This one's tough. I'm a single guy, so no wife or kids, which is probably the only way I'm able to do this. I'm currently active duty Air Force stationed at a base a couple hours north of Los Angeles. My military commitment always comes first, so I practice dentistry during the week. Evenings and weekends, however, are my dedicated screenwriting time and that's when I get to sit down at my laptop and bang out pages. It's definitely a challenge juggling the two careers. Both are very demanding, but luckily writing is something I can do anytime. I love being a dentist, but I also love storytelling. The two are so very opposite that it's kind of nice in the sense that I'm constantly taking a break from one or the other. I'm fortunate to have a career—and by that I mean dentistry—that provides a comfortable income, but the time commitment to do both that and writing is grueling. I don't believe you can have a successful career as a Hollywood screenwriter while also maintaining a completely separate one in a different field. I have a big decision to make in the summer of 2016 when my contract with the Air Force ends. Military dentist or screenwriter? Teeth or character arcs? Root canals or re-writes. Hmmmmmmm.*

Lee: You were just named to Launch Pad's annual Young & Hungry list. What do you think placing on a list like this says about you?

Eric: The "young" aspect is highly questionable and could probably be considered outright fraud. Guess I'm young in my screenwriting career, so that much is accurate. But I'm definitely "hungry." I'm eager to write and hungry to build new worlds and create new characters. I want nothing more than to have something I've written actually get produced. It's always an honor to be on a list with so many other extremely talented individuals.

Lee: Now that you've gone from "aspiring" or "emerging" to "professional," how has your life changed?

Eric: I'd say the expectations I have of myself and my writing have increased. My writing has to be at a higher level now, that of a professional. I have different goals. Whereas the goal before was to gain representation and sell a spec, now it's get something produced. Life is still pretty much the same. Really all it boils down to is that a professional is getting paid for what they write and an aspiring writer isn't. That does not mean there's necessarily this huge difference in quality. Professional writers can still write a crappy script and a novice can still write something that wins an Oscar.

Lee: Do you go up for open writing assignments, or are you focusing on your next piece of original material?

Eric: I personally have not gone up for any open writing assignments. Much of that probably has to do with the fact that I have a day job, so I'd be unable to do so unless a studio wanted to have a weekend meeting with me—not surprisingly, that hasn't happened yet. I do really enjoy creating original material. That's what excites me. I mean, that's one of the most enjoyable aspects of being a writer. Waking up in the middle of the night with this great idea for a new script. Coming up with an amazing and imaginative set piece. A violent and inventive new kill. A hilarious meet cute. The nastiest

---

* In the summer of 2016, Eric made the move to Los Angeles in order to pursue screenwriting full time.

villain you've ever seen on film. An ending that leaves you in tears. The *WTF?!* twist no one saw coming. Right?! All that stuff. Heck, I'm getting excited right now just thinking about it! So that's what I enjoy. There's an endless number of stories I want to tell, I just need the time to get them all down on paper. Doesn't mean they'll all sell, or that any of them will sell, but I genuinely enjoy the process and that alone keeps me sane.

Lee: While you are not in Los Angeles, you are in close proximity to it. Is being in or near Los Angeles an advantage for an aspiring writer in your opinion? And, if so, why?

Eric: I can be in Hollywood in one to three hours depending on traffic and let me tell you, even that isn't close enough if you really, truly want to make this a career in my opinion. I was recently listening to the On The Page podcast (#340) where you (Lee) were being interviewed, and you hit the nail on the head. You can break-in to screenwriting from literally anywhere in the world, but to make a career out of it, to take the meetings, to go up for the assignments, to write for television, to form the friendships and contacts, you gotta live in Los Angeles. Period.

Lee: Based on your screenwriting journey, what advice would you give other writers aiming to break into the industry?

Eric: Enjoy the process of banging out pages. Tell your mom you love her. Be passionate about the characters you create and the voices you give them. Smile more. Trust your gift as a writer. Pursue whatever it is in life that makes you happy, be it writing or otherwise. Never take a "no" as the final answer. And lastly, *always* brush and floss at least twice a day—this will only help you once you do finally sell your spec and are taking meetings.

5

WINNING A SCREENWRITING COMPETITION

Screenwriting Competitions as Vetting Avenues

Screenwriting competitions have been around for what seems like FOREVER. The first major screenwriting competition, The Nicholl Fellowship, which is operated by the Academy of Motion Picture Art and Sciences, opened to all US citizens in 1989, and, now accepting screenplays from writers all over the world, is still considered the most prestigious of all screenwriting competitions. In the new millennium, many screenwriting competitions previously friendly to screenwriters in the feature film space only have expended their competition models to include awards for television writing as well.

Over the years, the industry has come to turn to trusted competitions in order to identify emerging writers of worth. Like Eric Koenig, featured in Screenwriting Spotlight #5, competition winners and placers have gone on to sign with representation, get staffed on television shows, get their TV pilots picked up and even sell feature specs. In this chapter, we will explore the relevance of such competitions to the industry, as well as which competitions—in my humble opinion—are worth the price of entry.

When The Nicholl Fellowship launched in 1986, it received all off ninety-nine entries, which included full-length screenplays, teleplays and spec TV episodes. It has since changed its model and now accepts only feature film screenplays. Today, the biggest screenwriting competitions receive anywhere from 7,000 to 8,000 submissions every year. This is emblematic of the growing number of fledgling screenwriters hoping to be discovered as they aim to penetrate the field. To put it in perspective, if any agent, manager, executive or producer attempted to read all of those scripts in one year, they would have to read roughly 20 scripts a day, every day, for 365 days.

While in the 1990s—when a lot fewer writers were trying to break in—agents, managers, producers and executives relied on query letters to decide what they should read, today it's often trusted screenwriting competitions that identify which of 7,000 scripts should be worth the precious (and often lacking) time of an executives. While some competitions—such as The Nicholl Fellowship—pique the industry's interest as soon as they release their list of quarter-finalists, others begin to garner pedigree and gain interest for its winners' circle with the announcement of semi-finalists, Top 25, Top 10, Top 5 and Top 3. To put it in the simplest terms: competitions are there to help sift through the endless amount of material flooding the industry, and surface quality scripts for reps and executives.

Make no mistake about it: good scripts can and do fall through the cracks. Competitions are in no way infallible. They simply provide a shortcut for industry professionals to identify material capable of rising through the ranks. Much as in Eric Koenig's case, where *Matriarch* failed to crack the quarterfinals in one competition but placed Top 25 in another and went on to become the subject of a high profile spec sale, these things are known to happen as judging competitions does rely on the individual reader's taste level, sensibilities and experience. But part of the reason that screenwriting competitions hold such an appeal is because agents, managers, producers and executives know that the scripts have had many sets of eyes on them before they got to the winners' circle. For example, getting to the Top 3 in Final Draft's Big Break Competition requires that the script pass muster with at least four layers of readers. That implies—almost instantly—that there must be something there in order for the screenplay to graduate from stage to stage.

The Screenwriting Competitions that Matter

Not all screenwriting competitions, either for features, TV scripts or both, are created equal. In fact, if you research the screenwriting competition landscape you will quickly discover that most are not worth the financial investment they require or the suspense they generate, if only because there are SOOOOOOO many of them out there. I'm not going to call every lesser screenwriting competition out on these pages because, well, there are just too many and even if there weren't, I am not that kind of girl, but I will say that if you are looking for a screenwriting competition to produce results for you, to do more than provide a boost of confidence and a copy of Final Draft, you are going to have to jump into the deep end. Standing out via a high-profile competition placement or win is a big-fish-big-pond sort of game.

So what does set a screenwriting competition apart from the rest? In two words: Track Record. And not just a track record of getting writers repped; a track record of breaking new writers into the professional screenwriting space in a very real, result-driven way. Here, in no particular order, are just a few examples of screenwriting competitions that—year over year—did just that:

- **Final Draft's Big Break Screenwriting Competition** made a splash when its 3rd place winner, Larry Brenner, sold his competition—placing screenplay *Bethlehem* to Universal Pictures.

  - This competition accepts both feature and television script.
  - Submissions are usually accepted through early summer.
  - Final round read by panel of industry insiders, mostly on representation side.
  - Competition organizes scripts by genre, both in the film and television space.
  - The competition produces eleven winners in all, including one in each category and two grand-prize winners in the film and television space.

- **Tracking B's TV Script Competition** surfaced Mickey Fisher's *Extant*, which aired on CBS with Steven Spielberg as Executive Producer.

  - While *Extant* won the TV Script Competition, Tracking B also offers a highly reputable feature script competition.
  - The TV competition closes in the spring, while the feature competition accepts submissions through summer.
  - Final round read by panel of industry insiders, mostly on representation side
  - Tracking B is a popular subscription-based industry Tracking Board.

- **Script Pipeline's feature competition** broke Evan Daugherty, who was plucked out of the competition by manager Jake Wagner, and then went on to write the screenplays for *Divergent* and *Snow White and The Huntsman*.

  - Script Pipeline offers both feature and television writing competitions.
  - Both competitions open for submissions in late summer/fall.
  - Script Pipeline also offers Script Notes and Coverage.
  - Additional competitions include the Big Idea competitions (film & television) and the First Look project.
  - Final round read by panel of industry insiders, mostly on representation side.

- **Tracking Board's Launch Pad Feature Competition** helped surface Eric Koenig's *Matriarch*, which sold to Paramount.

  - Like the providers mentioned prior, Tracking Board offers both a feature and a television writing competition.
  - Feature competition accepts submissions through the fall.
  - Pilot competition accepts submission through spring.
  - Launch Pad also offers a manuscript competition.
  - Competition ranks Top 75, Top 50 (quarter finalists), Top 25 (semi finalists), Top 10 (finalists) and three Grand Prize winners.

– Final round read by panel of industry insiders, mostly on representation side.

- **Austin Film Festival**'s 2010 finalist Christopher Cantwell had his television pilot *Halt and Catch Fire* ordered to series by AMC.

  – Accepts feature film and television submissions.
  – Announces 2nd round, semi-finalists, finalists.
  – Submission deadline traditionally in May.
  – Writers placing in competitions gain entrance to exclusive panels and classes during annual festival.
  – Offers free reader notes to submitters.
  – Specific awards (drama screenplay, comedy screenplay, horror screenplay, one-hour pilot, etc.) granted by such relevant companies as AMC, Sony Pictures Animation, WGAEast, etc.
  – Semi-finalists read by agents, managers, producers and development executives.
  – Finalists read by category-appropriate industry judges.

Other high-profile competitions worth considering include:

- **The PAGE International Screenwriting Awards,** which has a slew of success stories to its name and accepts both feature and television submissions.

  – Like Final Draft competition, screenplays categorized by genre.
  – Accepting submissions usually through spring.
  – Announces quarter-finalists, semi-finalists, category winners and Grand Prize winners.
  – Offers judge's feedback for additional fee.
  – Semi-final round judged by literary agents, managers and development executives.
  – Final round read by panel of producers and production executives.

- **The Nicholl Fellowship** is open to feature screenplays only, and to this day is considered the one to rule them all.

  – Submissions usually accepted through the beginning of May.
  – Up to five fellowships are awarded every year.
  – Also announces quarter finalists, semi-finalists and finalists.
  – Conducts both ceremonies and seminar for selected fellows.
  – Brief reader comments are available for purchase.
  – Semi-final rounds judged by members of Academy; final round judged by Nicholl Committee.

But Are They Worth It? Industry Perspective

Don't take it from me. For more insights on screenwriting competitions, I turned to some of my industry colleagues wanting to know: Are screenwriting competitions important? And if so, why? Manager Jewerl Ross told me:

> You win the Nicholl, a lot of people have read your script in order for you to win, so maybe your script is worthy. People need something to talk about when they call me or when they send me a letter in the mail. Everyone thinks that their writing is good, so talking about how good your writing is is a waste of everyone's time. Telling me your great idea also is a waste of time—a good idea doesn't mean good writing, a good idea doesn't mean good execution, a good idea doesn't mean you know what the fuck you're doing. You need something to prove to me that you are worthy. You win a contest, maybe you're worthy. You win five contests, maybe you're worthy. You need something to talk about that's more than just your opinion or your idea. The better the contest, the sexier it looks. I'm a snob. I didn't go to Yale because it was in Connecticut. I went because it was the best school I got into. I'm going to pay attention to the person who wins the Nicholl more than I am the person who wins some random screenwriting contest. So if you don't know anyone in the business and you are in Ohio and you can't get a script to anyone based on a referral, you have to do something. Anyone can send a script to a contest and pay the $20 or the $40 or the $60 and see if their script can do something.

Paradigm's David Boxerbaum said this of his company's perspective on screenwriting competitions:

> Our younger agents here peruse them or read them and kind of are our first line of defense. We've found some obvious successes from that and there's definitely some value in that for sure.

Circle of Confusion's Josh Adler, who judges for at least one highly regarded industry competition, had this to advise:

> If you have $100 in your pocket and that's all you've got to play with, and there's 2 competitions to choose from, one that has a $50,000 prize and one that has no prize but guarantees your script will get read by this list of people that work in the business, and both of them are $100 to enter, enter the one with the list of people because that's worth way more. Yeah, $50,000 is nice, but that's just some guy sitting in his apartment reading a bunch of scripts saying, "Yours is the best, and here's the prize." There's legitimate ones out there that get read by agents, managers, producers, and we all get

together and have a big dinner and everybody talks about what they've read. That's what you want. Go where you get the most amount of exposure for your money, not the most amount of money for your money. It's a quick Google search and you can find out the good ones to enter. And the ones that say, "Hey! You'll be read by some people who work in the industry!" Maybe, maybe not. But if they say, "Hey, here's the list of the judges on our panels," and it's this person from this agency, this person from this management company, this person from this studio, and they actually say these are the people who are going to be reading your scripts, it's probably a worthwhile investment of your $100, because if the script is great, one of those people will recognize it and will do something with it. Whether it gets made or not, who knows, but it will at least advance you in the right direction towards having your career in this business. It will get you that foot in the door.

John Zaozirny of Bellevue Productions had this to add:

I've found writers through screenwriting competitions by being a judge. One of the writers I signed ended up not even winning; he ended up just being a finalist. So I think competitions are useful. Certainly as a concept I can't argue against them. I think it's good to be a finalist because that might get you read by a bunch of people in the industry but I don't think winning them is automatically a ticket to anything. The best thing you'll ever get out of it is industry people reading your screenplays. And that's kind of the goal of the script that you're trying to get out there, to get a manager or get an agent, to get you in the room or on the phone with a potential representative. But if you win, riches and fame are not going to come your way automatically.

Infinity's Jon Karas contributed:

Competitions are important. They are really important. Competitions are one way of seeing what stood out to some segment of the informed, or somewhat informed, population. For example, The Final Draft Big Break Competition (which Jon judges), by the time we as judges saw the scripts that were in that one, x-thousands of entries had been filtered by who knows how many people to get to a number of finalists that we ultimately read. There weren't any bad scripts that we read as finalists. But to be honest, the last number of years it was very clear which scripts were the best on both the film and TV sides. Some a little closer than others. Now, even a win in a lower tier competition is helpful for confidence building and to show that somebody somewhere liked what you were doing. On the flipside,

I have a script that it took me 8 years to sell, the client would not give up on it, he re-wrote it 4 times. I think to date it's won 9 competitions and we're gonna get it made someday, it hasn't been made yet.

Jeff Portnoy of Bellevue Productions added:

Competitions are important just because managers, agents and representatives in general just don't have the time to read the thousands, possibly tens of thousands of screenplays and teleplays that are out there so we depend on them to vet, to screen. Think of the Nicholl, there are 7,500–8,000 applicants every year, they bring it down to 10 finalists and 5 winners. So it just makes sense, based on the fact that our time is valuable, that we would rather wait for the Nicholl to vet and screen those. We would rather read the top 10, 15 or 20, or the semi-finalists. It's a better use of our time to let all these reputable established vetting sources like the competitions, the fellowships, do the screening for us. And the Austin Film Festival, PAGE Awards, Final Draft Big Break, Screencraft, The Black List website, we use all of these and the list kind of goes on from there. We depend on those. And reading the finalists in all those is enough for a whole year of reading. You know?

Madhouse's Ryan Cunningham provided this:

Competitions serve to give a little bit of legitimacy and exposure. It certainly is a culling process from unwatched writers. And something like the Nicholl especially—because everybody reads the finalists—it just gives the writer exposure very quickly to people who normally wouldn't care that much. But there are a lot of competitions that aren't really legit that are just there to take your entry fee. So find the competitions that are actually connected. I would say the Nicholl especially, the Tracking B competitions are pretty good because they've got a good, wide panel of judges (I'm on both panels, so I'm biased.) If you go to some sort of a film school or adjunct program like UCLA Extension, USC, NYU, they have competitions that are good, too. There are so many others, and I don't want to name names of the ones that aren't legit, but just do your research before you give them your money.

Manager Lee Stobby concluded:

I've signed a few people through Nicholl, The PAGE Awards, any of these things that filter good screenplays down. The thing to be aware of though is that you can't just submit to one competition and then think I didn't place so my script must be bad. No. Not all these competitions are created equal. The winners of competitions tend to be worse than the ones that come in tenth place. In my experience, if something has gone through fifteen layers of voters, who are bringing all different taste levels, in some ways the winner is actually gonna get kind of watered down. When you are submitting to these competitions a lot of people come tenth and then wonder why they didn't get any representation. You have to use that momentum. I love it when someone sends me a query letter that says, "Lee, I'm a Nicholl quarter-finalist with this script and I just found that out today." There's an urgency—there's something happening right now. "You should jump on this train right now because other people are going to be seeing this too. I sent this email to other people, this information's going to get out there, but I'm giving you a sneak peek." So there's a time frame. Right? If you send me a query letter that says your script won some competition three years ago, I don't know what to do with that. Because that tells me literally a bunch of people have had a shot at this and can't do anything with it. The competitions are always an avenue to get reps to pay attention to your scripts. And that's it. So whatever you can do to get a rep to pay attention to your scripts that's what you should do.

Making the Most of Your Win

When you win or place well in a high profile screenwriting competition, there are certain things you can expect: while every competition has its unique list of top prizes that may include financial rewards, gadgets and even trips to Los Angeles, each competition will seek to get your work as much exposure as it can. After all, it's in the competition organizer's best interest to have your win or placement translate to success in the screenwriting space, be it signing with representation, staffing on a TV show or selling your feature or television spec. So the one thing you can expect following a high-visibility competition placement or competition win is industry attention for both you and your work.

Over the years, I've seen competitions make significant efforts for their winners. But it's not just about what the competition will do for you. Instead, it's about the boost this win can give your own activities, your own career. Remember: no one has more to gain from your screenwriting success than you do. Therefore, as manager Lee Stobby suggested in the previous section, it is critical that you take that win or placement out for a spin.

Winning or placing in a highly regarded screenwriting competition is a conversation starter. It's that all-important answer to: "Of everything in my pile, why should I read your script?" And it's up to you to utilize this conversation starter to either rejuvenate stalled opportunities, or to create new fans within the industry. Let me break it down:

If you were previously in talks with agents or managers, but those talks didn't ultimately lead to anything, this is your way to announce: "Look at me! Still here! Still writing! Still working at it! Getting better from script to script!" Utilize your competition win or placement as an opportunity to breathe new life into once promising relationships that have since fizzled. Seize the occasion to blast anyone and everyone in the industry you've previously come in contact with, humbly and gratefully sharing the good news of your win. This will not only remind them that they knew you then, but also that maybe they were onto something because, well, others now seem to agree.

Your competition win or placement can also come in handy when seeking to build new inroads with agents and managers with whom you did not previously have an "in." Your competition placement gives you an excuse to reach out— you just placed, and you are seeking to make the most of this break. There is a feeling of momentum in the air, and you are doing your diligence to capitalize on it. Of course, your job is not only to tell the agent or manager why they should read you. You should also be sure to illustrate why you are seeking to be read by them. Do they represent someone you admire? Better yet, did they say something on a podcast or a panel that resonated? Make sure to build a real case for why you two should connect, instead of resting entirely on the placement or competition win.

While amassing a number of competition placements and wins under your belt can do nothing but help, it is also important to remember that competition wins—or at least the momentum that can be gained from them—do come with an expiration date. While you will always be able to claim that you won, were a finalist, or came in Top 3 or Top 25 in this or that well-regarded competition, the impetus of the win itself will diminish the further you get from the announcement date. The farther you get from your big competition splash without additional movement in your career, the more people will start to question: Was that script just not that good in the end? The voice not strong enough? The execution not commercially compelling? Or did the writer get the win and go MIA, thinking that all he had to do now was sit back and wait?

Because of this, you want to be sure to make the most of your win or placement as soon as it comes your way. While nothing is guaranteed, it certainly presents an opportunity to take things to the next level.

SCREENWRITER SPOTLIGHT #6: Greta Heinemann

Greta Heinemann grew up at the Bavarian-Austrian border (where they shot *The Sound of Music*) and, for the lack of parents telling her otherwise, raised herself watching an abundance of German-dubbed US TV shows by day, and action movies by night. At the age of fourteen, it was the lethal concoction of *Baywatch*, *Melrose Place* and *The Terminator* that inspired Greta to pursue a career as a Hollywood writer. Greta has since learned how to speak English and immigrated to the US in 2009. In 2013, Greta won the UCLA writing competition with two different scripts at the same time and also wrote and directed a pilot episode to a new original series. In 2014 she was chosen as one of the CBS Mentoring Program fellows and in 2015 she was announced as one of four emerging writers to receive a grant by the Humanitas Prize Foundation's New Voices Program. At the time of the interview Greta was staffed on her first job, writing for CBS' NCIS: New Orleans.

Lee: Why did you decide to move here from Germany?

Greta: I came out here to work. I always knew that I wanted to be in America to work in the entertainment industry. I didn't know exactly if I wanted to be a director or a producer or a writer, but I knew from when I was fourteen that I wanted to come here for that.

Lee: How did you decide that it's going to be writing and not directing or producing?

Greta: When I was back in Europe, I was directing and producing and everybody was like, you should be a producer because you're very organized. But I don't want to be just that person. I want to be the creative person. When I came to America, I got a job that, as amazing as it was to get me into the country and be here and be able to live here, it didn't creatively fulfill me. I took all my life savings that I had at that point and made a feature. I wrote a feature and I shot it and I realized that I'm not the best director. Not necessarily by talent but just by experience. And I realized that writing costs less. So I started writing more and more and I realized that I potentially do have a talent for telling stories.

Lee: And how old were you around the time you directed your feature?

Greta: I was 24. And it was a really, really bad feature. So then I started writing just to save some money, and I wrote a feature that got into the final selections at the Berlin Lab, which is kind of like the Sundance Lab, and it won a couple of things at festivals, and I was like . . . that's interesting! And then—oh yeah! I won a place at Outfest—and they suggested I go to this NBC Workshop where I met Karen Horne, who's the person who runs the (fellowship) program there, and she was talking all about TV, about how TV basically allows you to produce, sort of direct on the page, and write. And I thought: That's it. I should be writing for TV, because that way I get to produce and direct and do all of it.

Lee: So what do you do when you decide that you should be writing for TV? What happens then?

Greta: So I was at that workshop at NBC and Karen Horne said: It's your job to hone your craft, do whatever you have to do, take UCLA Extension classes, take whatever writing classes you want to find, read scripts, do all that jazz. I remember I was driving and telling my girlfriend I'm gonna sign up for UCLA Extension classes no matter how much they cost. And I did sign up that night.

That was my first introduction to TV writing. I took a class that was called Outlining the One-Hour Spec and instead of outlining one spec, I outlined two because I was a little overeager, and then I signed up for Writing the Draft and wrote both drafts. The great thing was, in basically two UCLA semesters I learned TV structure, how to write an episodic spec and all of that.

Lee: Did you apply to the TV Writing Programs that year?

Greta: The following year. I took the fall semester, the winter semester, the spring semester, and that's when I applied for the fellowships. I wrote a *Walking Dead*, I wrote a *Sons of Anarchy*, I wrote an original pilot, and then I wrote a *Southland*.

Lee: And . . .?

Greta: Oh. I didn't get in. Nothing happened. I still think it was a good *Southland*. I still steal ideas and then pitch them from that into my current show.

Lee: But you also entered the UCLA contest.

Greta: This was about the same time. I entered my *Sons of Anarchy* that I had and my original pilot—*Valleyhood*. I think I heard in September that I was getting on the next level, and there was like some weird selection. And then they assigned a mentor—the mentor stuff was in the fall, and I used that momentum to apply for the next season's fellowships.

Lee: You're forgetting to mention that you actually won this very prestigious contest.

Greta: I won first place on the spec and second place on the pilot.

Lee: And what came from that?

Greta: A shitload of requests to read—like legitimately a shitload. I think I got like sixty, seventy, eighty requests in a week from like CAA, Paradigm, Brooklyn Weaver, all the guys. And I sent it out, and I made a couple of mistakes then. Like I had a manager then, and I could've played it smarter. But regardless, nothing really came from it other than interest from a manager—from my next manager.

Lee: How could you have played it smarter?

Greta: I had a manager who I was very loyal to. And so when other managers reached out, I mentioned that.

Lee: How did you get this first manager?

Greta: The feature that I did had an actor in it, and the actor and I remain friends until this day, and he asked me later to get involved in a project he was doing with another actor, and they needed a writer, so I wrote the pilot, and we produced the pilot and I directed it. Somewhere in that whole weird blur one of the actresses on the pilot was so impressed with the material that she was like, "you know, my friend is a manager, she really should read you." So she gave my stuff to this person to read, and she met with me, and signed me right on the spot. She was a one-woman show. And she definitely worked her butt off to get me out there. But at the same time, people from Management 360 and Circle of Confusion were reaching out. And I was stupid enough to tell them that I had a manager, which in retrospect, you should never do. But I'm a very loyal person. So I don't have any regrets. And then the funny thing was that someone from Energy Entertainment reached out to me and wanted to read, and it was an assistant, and I was like, okay. I had read a lot about Brooklyn just on the internet. And then three days later, Brooklyn himself reached out. He had read it, and two days later, we were on the phone and he was giving me notes.

Lee: So then you went on to write another spec for the following year's fellowship season . . .

Greta: Yes. I wrote *Sons of Anarchy*.

Lee: That year you were in the very unique spot of getting into two Television Writing Programs in one cycle. Let's talk about the Humanitas Prize first. Why did you apply?

Greta: Here's the funny thing about the Humanitas Prize. I have no idea how I found out about it. It's one of the best-kept secrets in this industry. The Humanitas slogan is making the world a better place, one story at a time. And all of my stories are guns and drugs and hookers and thugs . . . So I was like, should I even bother to apply? I'm usually the person who will submit a week before the deadline because I always have my shit ready. But on that occasion, I did not have my letter of intent ready yet. It was like 11 pm— and I was like, What the fuck am I supposed to write in this? Why am I even applying to something that's clearly catering to shows like *Parenthood*? Those are their people. And I literally consciously remember thinking to myself, if you do leave this opportunity untouched, you're an idiot. It's another hour. And they can turn you down for writing about guns and thugs and hookers, but you still try. So I finished the letter of intent, and it was probably the most personal thing I've ever written. I turned it in, and to my very surprise, I got a call to come in for an interview, and then it was a very rigorous process of interviews. The first interview they told me, "You'll meet Carole Kirschner who runs the program, and you'll pitch your two ideas that you have prepared." And I'm like . . . "Wait a minute! What two ideas have I prepared? Because I don't have any." And I realized that I never actually read the thing, and the premise of the fellowship is that you prepare two pitches, and they will tell you which one you should go with. So I prepared my two pitches, and I read Carole's book within hours to prepare myself for the interview. And I took preparing for the interview very, very seriously. The pitches I took also very serious, but I would say that I probably took the personal stuff more serious because anybody is more likely to hear your pitch if they like you. So I went, and it was probably the first time that I remember being really, really, nervous going on a meeting. I'm not the person who ever gets nervous, because I speak in public a lot, but I was really nervous because it was kind of a make or break opportunity. In the end, the meeting was great. I looked like an idiot because I had a fancy outfit on. And then two days later, I got a call that I needed to come back, so I went back, and it all was a blur . . .

Lee: What you told me about that call was that they called and said, "We really like you, we didn't like either one of your ideas, so come back."

Greta: Yeah. I got a message from Carole saying, "Call me back, I'm available on Sunday." So I call her, and she says: "We really like you. We think you're very talented. Your ideas aren't quite what we're looking for." Then she says: "What I would like for you is to just get back to me on like Tuesday morning with new ideas, maybe six." And she is telling me this on Sunday! I gave them my six ideas and they picked two. I refined those two ideas, and sort of grew show ideas within two days. There were a lot of notes, and then they told me that I'm in the final selection, and they wanted to match me up with a mentor. I met my mentor and interviewed with her a couple of months later. And that was that.

Lee: While all this was going on, there were also the more traditional writing programs that you were pursuing, right?

Greta: Yes. I knew that I shouldn't get lazy because of what was going on with Humanitas. So I wrote a *Sons of Anarchy* within all this craziness, and I think I probably wrote it in four weeks. The good news was I had written a *Sons of Anarchy* before, and it's very much in my wheelhouse. I turned that into CBS and ABC and Warner Brothers and NBC.

Lee: When did you find out that you were in the running for CBS?

Greta: I got a call inviting me to an interview with the CBS Selection Committee. All of this is very short notice. You get a call, and then like two days later you go in. So I worked Facebook and my friends and got on the phone with two people who had gone through the CBS program before. I went to the interview and a week later maybe—very quickly—I heard that I got in.

Lee: How did you manage participating in two television writing programs back to back? Most people usually have to choose one.

Greta: If you have the network fellowships, they make you choose. But with regards to the Humanitas fellowship, it's a different animal. You basically develop a pilot—you don't go on a weekly thing—it's grown up studies. Independent studies. So that worked out that way.

Lee: What was the Humanitas experience like? What was it like working with a mentor?

Greta: Really, really great. The interview process was probably one of the most important experiences in my career so far. Just in terms of preparing me for meetings and for pitches and for dealing with my own nervousness. The process of working with my mentor, Pam Veasey, who is incredibly talented and a really amazing person, has been not as busy as I would've hoped for because I got staffed. And the moment I got staffed, my development got put on hold, and I was working 500 hours a week to do my best job as a staff writer.

Lee: Tell me more about working with Pam.

Greta: She was amazing. I spent one day with her on the set of CSI Cyber. First thing in the morning, she had me in her office. Her set designer came in, and it was really cool to see a showrunner decide about wall color and set design. And then we went to stage and watched Lil Bow Wow shoot some scenes. After that, we went to hide in the editing bay, and that was actually one of the most amazing experiences because I used to edit a lot back in the day, and it was really cool to see that network television has the same problems. They don't have the coverage they want. They figure it out in creative edits. And she is a wizard doing that. In the one hour I was sitting there, I learned so much. And then I thought the day was done, but then we walked through the writers' room, and this impromptu rewrite session happened, and I could sit in on that. This was the first time I sat in on a writers' room, because I never was an assistant or anything. It was really amazing to watch people work.

Lee: What was the structure of the CBS fellowship? What were the expectations? Tell me everything.

Greta: In October you hear, I think. Then you pitch pilots, because they pair you up with mentors, as well. They pick an idea with you, then you refine the idea, go to story, go to outline, and then write the pilot. By the time January comes, your pilot is technically ready. That's when the actual program starts. Once a week you meet up at the CBS lot, and they teach you a bunch of incredibly invaluable lessons all about industry savvy. They teach you about taking meetings with showrunners, executives, managers and agents. How to present yourself in a showrunner meeting. How to sell yourself. How to direct the conversation. Find the balance between small talk and personal connection. And that's what the weekly workshop is like.

Lee: While you're in CBS, what were your hopes? What were you seeking to get out of it?

Greta: They asked us that on the first night. And I said, my hope is to be in a position where I would be prepared to staff. I wanted to get the experience that I needed that would prepare me for the actual job.

Lee: So as the fellowship winds down, what happens?

Greta: Panic! So here's the thing. CBS does not promise or guarantee you will get staffed. And I actually think it's smart. Because if you're ready to get staffed, you will get staffed. And so a couple of people got staffed, and I tried really hard. I forgot to mention that I had gotten a new manger before the CBS fellowship.

Lee: Why the switch?

Greta: It was a decision of pure strategy. I wanted to plan my career as a TV writer based on working my way up, because to me, it felt more reliable to go get staffed and learn other shows, than to hope to sell my own right away. And Energy Entertainment, as prolific as the management company is, focuses mostly on selling stuff. That was the reason. So I ended up with Madhouse Entertainment. And that happened right before I started the CBS program, which was great, because I was a bit ahead of the curve. So I felt like that made a big difference, actually. It allowed my new managers to call people up and be like, "Look, this woman is about to be in the CBS Program, she's about to be announced as the winner of the Humanitas New Voices Prize," and it gives it a bit of an edge. And so throughout the program I could take meetings. I did a lot of that.

But back to your original question—when the program was coming to an end it was panic. Because at this time, I had quit my job. I saved a lot of money so I could take a year off and really try to push for this writing thing. And everything aligned perfectly because I saved up my money and just as I was about to run out, I won the Humanitas Prize, which comes with a check. So it allowed me to have literally the time—full-time—to focus on going on meetings. And that's a full time job. But by the end of the CBS program, money was running out, and the question was, Am I gonna go sign up to work at Starbucks? Or am I gonna get a writing job? Other people started getting jobs, and I was really disheartened. My management company was really strategic about who they had me meet with. I met with Jeffrey Lieber, who at the time was the showrunner of *NCIS: New Orleans*, and they had a slot open for a staff writer position. Jeffrey is the nicest guy on the face of the planet, and I used all the skills that CBS taught me—it was a great meeting. Jeffrey was really excited and said: "I really want to do this, I just need to figure out if I can get the money for you." It ultimately came down to CBS also approving of me and really liking me. And in this particular case, it was amazing because I had been in the program and everybody was all excited about me, and had my back. And that's how I got my job.

Lee: Can you talk a bit about what you call Common Sense Meeting Skills that you learned at CBS?

Greta: First of all, have a personal story ready. Talk about who you are, put it in a nutshell, make it interesting and memorable. My story is that I came from Germany, and I learned English by watching *Baywatch* and renting DVDs of *The Shield* because I wanted to work in the entertainment industry. I came over here to do that. Don't be a boring storyteller. If you're a storyteller and you're a writer, you should be telling interesting stories. Don't be too full of yourself—don't plug too much. Have questions ready. Find commonalities. Research the people you're meeting with. I think that's legitimately one of the most important things. I research everybody ridiculously before I meet them. I know what they're working on, I know what they have in the pipeline, I know what they've done in the past. I try to listen to podcasts to get a sense of the personality and the humor. In the case of my interview with *NCIS: New Orleans*, I knew Jeffrey had written a pilot that I had read a while before that was super under wraps that I loved, and so I brought that up. And then another interesting thing for interviews is to know current news. The day I went on the interview for NCIS was the day after an episode had aired that got a lot of chatter on Facebook and Twitter. So before I went on the interview, I actually read up on it, and I was able to talk about something super current that not only showed that I cared, but also showed that I was smart enough to look it up. If you go into a general, have an agenda. Figure out what you want out of the meeting. Don't ask for a job. Don't ask for a read. Don't ask for anything. These people are really, really busy, and they have too much to do to read your shit. But have an agenda of what you want them to know about you.

Lee: There was a minute there where it looked like you were going to come out of CBS and potentially not have a job. What was that like?

Greta: It was fucked up. Look, here's the thing. I worked my ass off. And I never expect to get something in return. That's the one thing that I live by. But at that time, I saw people getting staffed left and right, and it was so fucking disheartening, and I started wondering if it was me. Often, especially when you're in that spot where you're just about to jump the hurdle, it's not about you. It's about the opportunity that is there. It's about the fact that there needs to be a slot open on a show that is in your genre that can pay for somebody, and then it might even be, oh, they can only pay half, so you need to be part of a diversity program so the money can come from somewhere else—it all needs to come together. Is that truthful or am I making this up? You remember it. You were there.

Lee: If you weren't going to staff, what were you planning on doing next?

Greta: By the end of the program, when I was not sure if I was going to get staffed, I actually started lobbying to get into other programs. Because programs like Warner Brothers or ABC are much more pushy in terms of getting you staffed. And so once you're in one fellowship, you've gotten a certain seal of approval, so I tried to get in touch with the people who were running other programs. I started meeting people, and I wrote a *Bates Motel* spec. So I did write a spec. And I was also working on a pilot, and at the same time, I had written all my letters of intent. Just when I was supposed to be turning them in— like seven days before the deadline—I got my first staff writing job.

Lee: So what's it like getting your first staffing gig?

Greta: Oh Jesus, it's amazing. It's very surreal that someone would pay you for doing what you would do anyways. If I had a job at UPS, I would write anyways at night. It's super amazing to learn this much and meet other writers. And it's super challenging. It's super demanding. I'm in the room, ten, twelve, fifteen hours every day. Going from your passion to an actual job has been very interesting. It's stressful. Super stressful, especially in the first days. It's nerve wracking. I've never second-guessed myself as I have then in my life. I was sitting there wondering if, like, I should put my arms over my chest or put them on the table because I wasn't sure how I'd come across in the room, and I wanted people to like me. It was like the first day in high school. That's how it felt, and it's a very surreal thing to have that job and then also, at the same time, not to lose yourself as a writer.

Lee: You've been on the job now for six months. Do you know where to put your arms now?

Greta: Yes. I know where to put my arms. I know that people don't get my humor, but they still like me. I think. I've gotten a little more comfortable. In the six months that I worked on this show, I have actually experienced different leadership styles, different people would run the room. And that was very interesting because it literally matters—it's the difference of night and day in terms of who's running this room. And it's night and day how much you can contribute and how confident you feel about your ideas. That was an incredibly valuable lesson in terms of personalities.

Lee: What's it like going to set and producing your episodes?

Greta: Amazing. Here's the fun thing: going to set and producing my own episode of real television was the moment where I was like, okay, so I made the right decision. Because I wasn't sure if I wanted to direct or produce or write, and I go there, and I shoot my own episode, and I was just so excited to see that I can contribute. One thing that was really amazing is that when I was seven years old, I watched a movie called *Bagdad Café*, which was shot in 1982, before I was born, and it's about the friendship of a Bavarian woman who is stuck in an unhappy marriage and takes a trip to America with her husband, and when she and husband fight, and she gets out of the car, and he leaves her there. And she's in Arizona somewhere. A truck stop. And it's filled with these weird, quirky characters. And one African-American woman. So this weird Bavarian woman is striking up a friendship with this African-American woman in a deadbeat truck stop somewhere in the desert. I watched that with my mom, and I remember my mom at that time wasn't very happy, and I remembered that I felt very misplaced in my life. And I was like, oh well I should do that, I could be this woman, I could be the one who's speaking terribly broken English with a Bavarian accent and wearing lederhosen and making friends at a truck stop. And then, many, many years later, I actually did. And many, many years later, I found out that the actress who played the African-American character is CCH Pounder, who I think is one of the most terrific actresses in TV right now and in general. And she is on *NCIS New Orleans*. She sent my showrunner an email about my script when we shot my first episode, and she said, this was a really nice script. And he forwarded it to us. And that was some of the most meaningful positive feedback I've ever gotten in the entertainment industry.

Lee: How do you work with your representation now? You are still with Madhouse, and now have UTA on your team.

Greta: I try to be mindful of the fact that both my agent and my managers represent a lot of people, and I try to always be mindful of the fact that it is a professional, working relationship. So even if I feel whiny, I try to take that somewhere else, and I try to use them for what they're amazing at, which is strategically planning my career with me. I really think of it like a corporation, business plan kind of thing.

Lee: If you could go back seven and a half years to when you first got here and tell yourself something that you know now that you wish you knew then, what would it be?

Greta: I wouldn't say nothing. I honestly wouldn't, and this is not a joke. Here's the thing: The anxiety about our future is what gives us the biggest drive, so the anxiety about what am I going to do with my life? Am I working hard enough? Am I going to get a job? That's the actual self-doubt that keeps you going and that keeps you trying harder and harder and harder. And if I told myself that it's going to somewhat work out, then I wouldn't try that hard.

Lee: Looking from the sidelines, all of this happened pretty quickly, right? How long did it take for you to really—from the time you buckled down and signed up for UCLA to the time you got your staffing gig?

Greta: I started the classes 2012. So that's three years, four years. That's kind of ridiculous.

Lee: That's really fast.

Greta: It's really fast, and it's really ridiculous, but I'm also really aware that I got really lucky. For some reason, lightning struck twice with the two fellowships for me, and that's nothing that anybody could have counted on. And the fact that I got the new management company at the same time as their client was running a show that, a spot opened for a staff writer, that at the same time was on the network whose program I was with . . . I just got really lucky with that. And I'm aware of that. It takes much longer, very often.

———————————————————————

6

ACCEPTANCE INTO A TV WRITING PROGRAM

Overview: Television Writing Programs

In its October 23, 2015 issue, journalist Rebecca Sun stated in *The Hollywood Reporter*'s heavily-circulated article "TV Diversity Programs: Launching Pad Or Scarlett Letter?": "In their ideal form, the mentorship and training programs that the Big Four television networks use to identify and develop new writing talent also serve to jump-start the careers of diverse writers." Whether they are diversity driven or open to every race, gender, gender identity, sexual preference and age group, the television writing programs, also widely referred to as the TV Fellowships by TV writers everywhere, offer one thing for all who are accepted into them: opportunity.

If one removes diversity as a qualifying criterion, The Big Four transform into The Big Six: Warner Brothers Television Writers Workshop, Disney ABC TV Writing Program, NBC's Writers on the Verge, FOX's Diversity Writers Intensive (accepting writers by nomination only), CBS's Writers Mentoring Program and Nickelodeon's Writing Program. Additional writing programs include: CAPE (Coalition of Asian Pacifics in Entertainment), NHMC (National Hispanic Media Coalition), as well as non-diverse programs like Humanitas New Voices program, Sundance Episodic Lab and HBOAccess.

Some inclusion programs, such as the Disney/ABC TV Writing Program, offer pay as engagement in the program and require full-time participation, in this case for a 12-month period. The other notable program to offer a grant to its participants is Humanitas, which pairs its chosen writers with working showrunners who mentor the writers as they develop an original pilot. Other programs run anywhere from a few weeks to a few months and do not offer pay, but instead engage their participants in craft-driven coursework usually conducted in the evenings (to accommodate those juggling jobs while going through the program).

Through courses, workshops and mixers, these invaluable programs expose their participants to agents, managers and TV executives, explore life "in the room," discuss business challenges and seek to prepare the writer for the professional space.

I asked Janine Jones-Clark, of Disney/ABC's Television Group, what a writer can expect to get out of participating in the program:

> When people come through the program, we let them know yes—you have been selected. You are in this program. We are your advocates and your champions all the way through. But from the get-go, we let them know the hard work is just about to begin. Don't take a breath and feel like, "Whew! I'm in, life is easy." What they can expect is very much an intensive period of workshops, executive meetings, us prepping them so they know how to meet with executives, so they know how to convey their own personal story in 60 seconds—their elevator pitch, so to speak— to win over our executives. We put them with mentors where we expect them to develop a wonderful one-on-one relationship with a creative exec at either ABC/Disney or Freeform. And then something we introduced three years ago is they each have a mentor who is a producer on an ABC/Disney TV series. Not only are they mentored by someone who is a producer-or-above level, but they are developing a new original piece of material while they're in the program, so the goal is, by the time they get to the end of their 12-month period, they're going to have this new piece of work, which is going to be a tool we'll use for staffing. So it's a ride. There's no guarantee for staffing, by any means. But we're going to do everything we can to make it happen.

For years, the Television Writing Programs were known widely as Television Writing Fellowship, a term still often used by the writers submitting to them. However, recently, most if not all of these initiatives changed their moniker from FELLOWSHIP to PROGRAM. Janine Jones-Clark explained:

> The fellowship is gone, we now just call it the Writing Program. And if you want to know why I changed that, I changed it because perception is so important in this town. And the perception of a fellow going in a writer's room, I found that the writers were not being given the same responsibilities as a staff writer. They were almost looked at as this juvenile with their training wheels on. So once we shifted that perception, I can't even tell you the success we've had—it's crazy.

While each of these programs operates differently, in its own unique way they seek to identify writers—diverse or otherwise, in accordance with the program's specific mission and parameters—ready to take the leap from emerging scribe still honing their craft to working staff writer. Whereas one program may put emphasis on the writer's velocity, ensuring that they are gaining the skillset and discipline to develop material—from story area to outlines to scripts—at network pace, others will stress ideation (the development of concept and concept pitches), the importance of business savvy, meeting preparation, industry access or any combination of these.

Diversity and inclusion departments were created within studios and broadcast networks as a reaction to findings by different coalition groups, which uncovered a low-to-no number of diversity in Hollywood, not only on the executive level, but also in the creative space, with writers, actors and directors across the board. These departments were constructed to help their companies diversify their staffs, making the immersion of creatives from different walks of life not just good business, but basic common sense.

Today, diversity and inclusion departments in studios and broadcast networks are charged not only with running the writing programs, but also with overseeing inclusion throughout the company within which they operate. Janine told me:

> We are charged with so many different things. The Writing Program being one of them, which has been in existence for close to 30 years here. The program has the goal of really identifying individuals who are just on that cusp of breaking in to the industry, but for whatever reason, they don't have the right relationships or the contacts or maybe it's something in their skillset and how they're presenting themselves. We're almost an internal agency for all of Disney/ABC Television, where people will use us as their resource to tap into for identifying diverse talent at all levels. We're branching off into the digital space because ABC is launching a new platform. We're also an integral part with TV animation, TVA, and we help staff a few writers on that. In fact, one of the alumni from our writing program is the head writer on *Elena of Avelar*. Agents are constantly trying to put writers on our radar so that we might champion them. We have "breakage"—an allotment of money that can be helpful for productions to bring in diverse writers.

That's right. Diversity and inclusion departments across broadcast networks and studios do provide funding—independent of a specific show's budget—for staffing diverse writers on existing and new shows, hence the hope that many program participants possess the skills to ride their acceptance into the program all the way to a staffing opportunity. While inclusion departments vary the length of contract for which they will pick up the diversity writer's cost, this opportunity for a free, diverse resource in the room is something that many showrunners like to take advantage of.

This is not to say that program participants do not staff out of non-diversity program, only that the path to staffing could be made easier by the network or studio—who would pick up the burden of the writer's paycheck—should the writer qualify for diversity dollars. While there has been some pushback against diversity programs specifically from non-diverse writers, the reality is that these programs are very much needed: In June of 2016, a *Variety* investigation uncovered that 90 percent of showrunners on new Broadcast Network fall shows for the 2016–2017 season are white, with 80 percent being male. So while some writers have expressed frustration that these programs—and their consequent funding—are not open and available to all, the truth of the matter is that when it comes to diversifying writers, Hollywood still has a long way to go, and the diversity programs are very much a way to help get there.

There is a catch though, one that every diverse writer should be aware of: "Like college scholarships for minorities, these programs are all about removing as many barriers to entry as possible, including financial ones." Stated Rebecca Sun's very same *Hollywood Reporter* article cited at the opening of this chapter. "But with every good intention can come inadvertent side effects, from writers of color who are perceived as less qualified to the subsidization of first-season salaries that can lead to a 'freebie' mentality among showrunners toward those scribes." Sun went on: "A diversity hire is a minority scribe who occupies a staff-writer position that is fully network-subsidized. Showrunners are thus incentivized to take on an unfamiliar face since his or her salary isn't coming out of the show's budget." In other words, because diversity subsidized hires are perceived as free labor, their retention rates—once studio or network funding has run out and the show becomes responsible for their cost—often can and do become a problem.

Regardless of staffing results or diversity implications, getting into a TV writing program represents a clear bulls eye, a tangible, attainable result, which one can prepare for and hopefully effectively drive toward. The bad news? It's been said that it's easier to get into Harvard than it is to get into these sought-after programs.

Every year, the number of applicants for each writing program grows. A program is likely to receive anywhere from 500 submissions for the smaller programs, to 2,000 submissions or more for the programs operated by the broadcast networks. In every cycle, only a handful of writers are selected, filling anywhere from four to eight spots. That means that even with the smaller programs where one's chances improve since the competition is effectively smaller, the best-case scenario is for 1 percent of applicants to make the cut. It's easy to acknowledge that these are not great odds. But even those odds don't offset the viability of these opportunities. Unlike screenwriting contests, which have no guaranteed results even for its winners, television writing programs offer the writers fortunate enough to get into them an immediate, palpable leap forward, whether or not instant television staffing at the conclusion of the program is the result. Not only will participants gain immediate access to working television executives, they will also intrigue agents and managers on the lookout for talent poised to break through.

Television Writing Programs—Requirements

Each television writing program requires its applicants to submit some combination of scripted materials as well as essays and personal statements. While programs operated by broadcast networks started out requesting a spec episode for an existing show as its primary submission requirements, nowadays every single program operator, broadcast or otherwise, seeks to see original content representing the writer's voice, while additional submission materials may include spec scripts for existing shows.

Every year, the TV writing program cycle begins with the early onset programs (such as Sundance Episodic Lab, Humanitas and HBO Access), whose requirements focus on original content. While some may require the submission of a complete original pilot, others may request to see the first five or ten pages, as well as extensive series documentation outlining the world, primary characters, prominent themes or mythology, as well as the long term multi-season vision and arc for the show.

As broadcast networks open for submission, they may request an original pilot, a spec episode, or—more often then not—both. Just a few years ago, one of the major broadcast network programs changed its submission requirements from TV specs only to both pilot and spec just a few weeks before the submission deadline, so it is wise to assume that you will be required to deliver both and prepare yourself accordingly.

In addition to original pilots and spec episodes, all programs require some version of a personal statement, essay or letter of intent. Although those may vary in length (one program might ask for a statement that runs 250 words, while another might allow a more generous 500 words to express your point of view), all essays, statements and letters of intent should be carefully and thoughtfully crafted and come to share the applicant's unique perspective, as well as a personal story and/or anecdote that now informs the themes or areas of interest the writer sows into their work. By all accounts, these essays are CRITICAL for the writer's success in the application process, and have been said to have the ability to put the writer over the top, or else entirely eliminate them from consideration. A writer with a stellar essay may generate further consideration even if his scripted material was not as strong; a writer who bombs his essay may never get called in for an interview, even if his scripted material was powerful. So even though some applicants may leave these essays to the very last minute, they may in fact be the most important piece in the application.

Guidance on these essays and personal statements has been highly conflicting (some say to steer clear of accomplishments, and others suggest touting them; some recommend finding your wound and exposing it front and center, while others recommend to tell a lighter, more linear beginning-middle-end story). However, there is no doubt that these personal statements are integral to the success of writers in the application process. Therefore potential mentoring program applicants are advised to give themselves time to develop an effective essay or personal statement in accordance with each program's unique submission guidelines, allowing time for multiple drafts as well as peer or instructor review and insights. For writers seeking to gain entrance into these programs, it is important to do their diligence and research extensively what program operators are looking for. It can make all the difference when consideration time comes.

I asked Janine Jones-Clark: What does she look for in a potential program participant?

> I look for someone that has a story, that has an amount of depth and uniqueness, that makes me feel like, "Oh my gosh, this person is gonna make a contribution in that writer's room that no one else can give!" Because writing is such an emotional line of work. The whole job of the writer is to evoke emotion, whether it's humor or anger or laughter or sadness, whatever it might be. I feel like when I sit down and I meet with writers, even when we interview prospective writers for our program, it's really about how are they as far as telling their own story? That's essential. But, before I even agree to sit down with someone and want to know what their story is, they obviously have to have it on the page.

Janine went on to tell me:

> We look for people who have some sort of unique life experience that they can infuse into the creative process that will give a multi-cultural or diverse perspective, really. That person doesn't necessarily have to be an African American, Latino Hispanic. It can be a Caucasian person who just so happened to, let's say, grow up in The Bronx and had a totally different kind of life. Or someplace abroad. It's about the perspective that they can offer. But it is very important that they can somehow tap into content that offers a diverse or multi-cultural perspective. Let me give you an example: We had a doctor who was in the program last year. He was a medical doctor with his own practice. But he wanted to be a writer. He also happened to have been in a wheelchair—he had an accident in his teenage years, but that's another unique life experience that he brought to the room. They loved him, too, over on *Blood & Oil*. Those are the people that our showrunners and our executives really respond to.

Even though every Television Writing Program has its unique process of cataloging applications (some have gone on record saying that they will read the first fifteen pages of a script, and if the material is strong enough, it will then be designated for further reads), I wanted to know: How does it work at Disney/ ABC? Janine explained:

Our team, and myself included, will read every single piece of information we've asked for in the application. Then it will get processed, and we hire a team of readers—this is where, I think, we differ from some of the others because we have the budget to hire readers—and the readers that I tend to bring in are people who were previously creative executives. For whatever reason, they've taken time off of the business or they're working freelance. So we hire them to be our readers. They break down all of the scripts with the notes and score them for us. So they're our first line of defense. And so, literally, everything everyone submits gets read. That's where it gets kind of interesting, because that's where you kind of start gauging and scoring the material. And that's the first read. Everyone gets two reads and then potentially a third and fourth read.

Even though some writers may scoff at the idea of their scripts getting reviewed by a particular program's qualified readers—usually creative executives with time on their hands, as is the case with the Disney/ABC program, or otherwise working writers and past program participants—the reality is that this is very much the industry standard. No single program organizer can get through all of the material submitted, specifically not in early rounds.

Every year, as my emerging television writers prepare to submit to the programs, I see many of them hustle to secure industry recommendations: Who is recommending them for NBC? ABC? CBS? WB? Usually, it will be agents, managers, producers, executives and other working writers recruited to write these carefully cultivated letters and emails. Every recommendation has to be tailored. Every recommendation source has to be a known quantity to the program. But do those recommendation letters really matter? Once again, I turned to Janine, who told me:

They are suggested but not mandatory. And the reason we say that is because there are so many varying cases. The letters can be important in the sense that, if you get down to, "Wow, I've got two candidates that have the exact same writing skillset, and their backgrounds are both amazing, but I can only take one . . . Oh! Do they have letters of recommendation? Oh, who's recommending them?" And then you start reading and looking at them. So they can factor in. It's one of those things where if it gets to a point, where you're like, "Oh my God, I love both these people, what do I do, what do I do?" And then you look at the letters and you're like, "Oh wow, Shonda wrote a letter for this person . . ." Then you're like, "Huh, well, if she believes in that person . . ." There you go.

As the programs begin to narrow the competition for participation spots, each process varies. Some will ask for additional work; others will set a phone interview, to be followed up by an in-person interview for those applicants who graduate to finalists. Janine broke down how the process works at Disney/ABC:

For us, it's a three-day interview process, it's usually from 8–8:30 in the morning and we sometimes don't leave until 7 at night. We have one full day that we call our "speed dating" interviews. The writers bounce from office to office, they have five minutes to tell their story and talk and leave a lasting impression. You go through all of those interviews all day, and then you have an evening gathering where you have creative execs from across the TV group, and so the writers are mingling and the creative execs are also gauging who these people are, so that all factors in. And then we have two solid days of panel interviews, which is where the poor writer comes into the conference room with a combination of showrunners, executives and our team, and it's Q&A and they pitch an idea to us, and then boom! We have big discussions about each and every candidate, after each of those half hour/forty-five minute interviews. So it's a very long, arduous kind of process. But in the end, you benefit so much because you have a really clear sense of who the people are and who you feel you can pull into the program that given year.

Since these interviews are SO critical, and writers work so hard to nail them, I asked Janine what mistakes they should avoid coming into the room:

I think writers should avoid approaching it from a corporate perspective. I see a lot of people who come in for the interview portion and it's almost like they're tackling it as if it's a corporate interview. And it's not. A writer is very different from an executive. And when I say a corporate perspective, it means not opening up, not sharing that personal life story—that life experience—that essence of who you are and keeping that wall up. A wall up doesn't let anyone open up to be able to gauge what you can contribute emotionally. So that's probably one of the biggest mistakes.

Television Writing Programs—The Industry Perspective

For further insight, I turned to my industry colleagues. Ultimately, I wanted to know if the writing programs are viewed by industry insiders in the same fashion that they are seen by the writers trying to get into them.

Circle of Confusion's Josh Adler told me: "Writers fellowships, diversity programs, anything that you can do to get a foot in the door and start developing relationships is advantageous and beneficial."

Manager Chris Cook had his own unique take:

There's one such program, whether we want to name it or not, where pretty much everybody who's in it gets staffed every year, right? Not only getting into one of the fellowships, but getting into that exact fellowship with all of these people that are trying to get into it, with judges that you don't know exactly what they're looking for, it can be a fool's errand to put all your eggs into that basket.

But Chris also added:

Getting into one of these programs elevates your career, it's a feather in the cap, but it's not something that by virtue of you being in it, is going to put you over the edge as far as now you're winning every job on the planet or now you have to do less to win a job. That's just not the case.

Evan Corday of The Cartel advised:

The studio programs have opened the doors for a lot of people. Some of them are diversity, some of them are not. Warner Brothers is just open to anybody. The Disney program is not about ethnic diversity but life diversity. They like people from different backgrounds, who studied rocket science or medicine or something else and need a change. That's interesting for them. And the others, CBS, NBC and FOX are diversity based. And I think that's changed the landscape in the last 6 or 7 years in terms of that foot in the door because a studio pays for a staff position for 20 weeks, 13 episodes basically. So that's a really big deal. If you're a show-runner and you're looking to put your staff together and you've got, whatever it is, 70 grand (per week) to put your entire writing staff together you can add a free body and give somebody a shot without screwing with your budget. You can still have your upper level producers and then have somebody less experienced, greener, that you can give a shot to without adding to your budget. So that is a really big deal.

Bellevue Productions' Jeff Portnoy told me:

The TV writing programs are another avenue to getting staffed. The writer's fellowships are hard to get into because it's very competitive, there's a lot of applicants and only a few candidates are chosen. But if you're in those, sometimes they have you interview for staffing at the end of the program, which is a huge deal. And if they like you in the interview and they like the pilot that you wrote during the program you can get staffed that way. So, entering the writing fellowships at any of the major networks is a huge.

And Jeff's Bellevue colleague John Zaozirny added:

They're great because you're working with people who are working in the TV business. A lot of times people come out of those fellowships and get staffed on TV shows. That will definitely help you get an agent or a manager, if you don't already have one. They are very very hard to get into but if you get into them then it's definitely a ticket to getting representation, I'll tell you that much. It may not be a ticket to getting a staff-writing job immediately but it's definitely a ticket to getting representation.

Epicenter's Jarrod Murray had a slightly different perspective:

> It's sort of a double-edged sword in a way. We have someone in the Fox Writer's Intensive now—he's in the top 10. But I feel like there's a stigma—that he's a "diversity hire" or a free writer that doesn't count against the show's budget. But when that writer moves up, they will account against the show's budget so you have to work just as hard or they're not going to bring you back. Once you get in the room its all about what's on the page. But I feel like that creates an unfair stigma because the diversity writers who go on to staff are free. A lot of writers find that—when you're a diversity writer—there's still a glass ceiling when you get to a certain point.

What You Can Do Right Now to Position Yourself for a TV Writing Program

Your first action item should be obvious: write, and write, and write some more. Learn your structure, explore your themes, create exciting worlds and dimensional characters. Master your voice.

As a writer seeking to break into television through television writing programs, your next action item is to learn, learn, learn. And by learn, I mean watch A LOT of television, so that you can understand not only where the type of material you're writing "lives" (are you network, cable or digital? CBS, AMC, TNT, HULU or MTV?) but also to identify a show for which to write a spec episode that would present in harmony with your original pilot. In a perfect world, a TV spec script not only presents the very best of the show for which you are writing, but also stands to clarify what sort of writer you are. This should be evident in central themes, tone, genre and also format. Therefore, a writer submitting an original thirty-minute comedy pilot should not spec an episode of a one-hour sweeping fantasy epic. They simply don't pair well, and are more likely to confuse the message of who you are as a writer than make your case.

If a pilot's job is to put your originality, craft and voice on display, the job of the spec episode is to exhibit your ability to make the best of the structure, rules, world and characters created by somebody else, find a cool, unique, angle on the story and characters, and express your talent, skillset and creativity within those parameters. Choose the show that you are speccing thoughtfully: select a show that has been viewed widely enough to be familiar to the readers evaluating material for the program, but also one that is highly regarded, and held in high enough esteem to be impactful. You don't want to spec a show that's been on for too many seasons and has potentially grown stale. Instead, seek out quality shows that are in their second or third season if at all possible, so that the show would not have been overly specced, and the material itself still feels exciting and fresh. Perhaps most importantly, spec a show that you are entirely passionate about. Passion on the page goes a long way, and is often the best way to showcase your skillset.

Once you've selected a show to spec, the onus is on you to learn it inside and out. This means studying the season progression and understanding where your proposed episode would fit in, what loose threads it would connect, and how it would assimilate with the season narrative. If you are speccing a highly serialized show, don't count on the readers to know every narrative twist and turn that came before and after the episode that you are slotting in, and instead find a way to create an episode that adheres to the show's serialized standards while also, in some ways, standing on its own.

Then comes "breaking" a few episodes, in order to identify the consistent structure and parameters deployed by the show itself. Next, find a few episode scripts, and study the writing style deployed by the writing staff. Is it novelized or straight forward? Does it deploy act breaks or bypass them? Does the writing style take any noticeable liberties? All of those elements must be considered when developing your spec episode.

Remember: writing TV specs, while a required skillset, is an effort put towards limited opportunities. Nowadays, very few agents, managers and executives are reading them. Therefore, within months of submitting to the TV writing programs your spec script will no longer be of use to you (you have to submit a new spec for every submission season), so while dedicating it the attention required to churn out a superior episode, be sure that this effort is not one that takes many months out of your schedule. After all, when working on a network show, you may be expected to break an episode over a single week, maybe get a whole week for an outline, then write your full episode in another. If you find that it is taking you months and months to construct and execute your spec episode, this could be an indication that you are not quite ready for primetime. Assuming that you are able to generate your spec in a reasonable amount of time (I generally like to see my writers complete their specs in six to eight weeks, from concept to final draft), explore using your episode as a case study that can be translated to structuring and writing your own original content. And once your spec episode is finished, pivot right back to original content.

If you are able, conduct research and gain insights from interviews and podcasts with writers who were accepted to programs in the past. No one knows the TV writing program experience better than the scribes who have gone through them, and whatever hoops are needed to jump through in order to be able to get in, those writers have successfully navigated them. And if you are in Los Angeles, be sure to seek out live panels and mixers in which program operators will be present. It is your responsibility to get as much insider insight as you can in order to most effectively meet and impress when applications are submitted and judged.

Most importantly, make your submission effort a focused, educated and strategic one. Consider all of your choices, from the show you are speccing to the information included in your personal statement and what it says about you. Do all those things right, and you give yourself a real, fighting chance.

SCREENWRITER SPOTLIGHT #7: Chandus Jackson

Chandus Jackson is an award-winning screenwriter, having recently participated in the inaugural Universal Emerging Writers Fellowship, Disney Feature Writing Fellowship and PGA Diversity workshop. His crime thriller screenplay *Muti* was voted to the 2015 Tracking Board Hitlist and recognized as one of the top specs of the year. Chandus presently has feature and TV projects in development and is repped by WME and Circle of Confusion.

Lee: You had a number of other careers before you got into screenwriting.

Chandus: I primarily had two careers before jumping into writing. I did ROTC in college, and it was one of those things that I did because I love the military, I love travel, I love doing things as far as traversing the world and going to different places. And believe it or not, it really fed into my writing. It really opened me up to just having those different perspectives and so forth.

The other thing was working in finance. I worked in investment banking initially—in corporate finance—and that gave me a strong sense of structure and management of my time, which allowed me to basically sit down and carve out time to write, because I had this perfect nine to five finance job. So I wrote in the morning beforehand, got a lot of stuff done, went to work, and then in the evening time, critiqued and edited what I wrote.

Lee: When did you decide to get into screenwriting?

Chandus: I think it was when I met my wife. Malena will always say, "I was the reason why you're on this crazy journey." At the time, she was going to journalism school at Columbia in New York, and I started being her camera guy and all this other stuff on the streets, and she would write things out in script format, and I was like, "Oh that's pretty cool!" And so I started becoming more of a student of what she was doing in her profession. That led me to reading other scripts, and joining writing groups, and really just getting an education.

Lee: What brought you out to Los Angeles?

Chandus: I came out here back in 2007–2008 to be a writer for the Disney Writing Fellowship. It was a feature program, and they have since shuttered the program. They have a shell of it right now on The Black List where they will have one writer selected, but it's not what it was. I was an in-house writer, writing in the Disney old animation building. But the process of me getting to that was . . . I was working in finance, and I wrote this script and sent it off to the writing program and totally forgot about it. And six or seven months later, I get a call from two execs at the studio and they said, "Hey, we read your script. We think it's awesome." So I pull over on the side of the interstate while I'm driving home, and we have an interview for 30 minutes, and about two weeks later they called me back and said, "We want to fly you out to LA." And so they did and I met with about seven or eight writers in a room— I took a meeting. I didn't know I was taking a meeting, but I took a meeting. It was interesting because I was one of the very few writers who had no film experience. I had an MBA in finance and accounting, and everyone else was either at UCLA or USC or NYU. But I ended up getting the gig, and that brought me out here. I told myself I would only come out here if I had an invitation, and so I had an invitation.

Lee: Once you got into that fellowship, what was that experience like?

Chandus: The Disney fellowship was a great experience. I was just totally green about the expectations and the industry. I literally thought, "I'm in Hollywood. I'm in." And it was kind of like that in a way because I had a Disney pass, I'd drive onto the lot everyday, I had an office. I went to screenings in a private room. It was a surreal experience. And so I think for me, I got a chance to see what the creative execs were looking for in a Disney movie. How they were looking at entertainment, not just for the studio, but for the theme parks and so forth. It brought everything full circle, which as a writer, is not necessarily something that you want to think about when you're writing, but if you're going to be a studio writer, you have to take all of that into consideration.

Lee: Now, sometime into your fellowship, the fellowship was discontinued.

Chandus: Well, we had the writer's strike. And it was totally unfortunate because during that time we were told, "No, no you guys aren't in the guild yet, don't worry about it, this is an educational enclave of writers, and you're not Guild-affiliated." But lo and behold, the Guild co-sponsored the program and once the strike became something that definitely was going to happen, they made it loud and clear, like, "Look, we don't want you working for a company that we consider to be now a struck company, and if you do, that will hamper your ability in future endeavors of getting into the guild." Hollywood is a union town, and we had to respect that. So no joke, I went from writing at the old animation building to picketing outside the lot and seeing my execs go in. It was a crazy experience.

Lee: What about your family back home?

Chandus: We had two kids. We had a house back in Jersey, and Malena really didn't understand all this Disney stuff. And so I was doing the bicoastal thing.

By the time I convinced her to finally move out, and we sold the stuff and whatever, the strike happened a week later. So that wasn't the best timing.

Lee: So what do you do when your wife and your two kids have just moved here from Jersey, and you left your life back in New York to come to this fellowship that was supposed to be a certain path, and suddenly your next best option is going and picketing?

Chandus: At that point, you really have to ask yourself why are you here. Why are you doing this? But I knew that this was my passion. This was what I wanted to do. And in many ways it was freeing. I know that I really want this. I know that I have to be even more dedicated to make it happen. And so seeing that —because I have friends who have subsequently left the business and gone back to Iowa or wherever—seeing that just made me even more resolute.

Lee: Now—fast forward—in May 2014, you started the Universal Emerging Writers Fellowship. Considering your previous experience with Disney, what made you decide to apply? What was the application process like, and how did you get in?

Chandus: What made me decide to apply was that I had recently entered my script in The Nicholl Fellowship—this was, at the time, a new script, *The Muti Killings*. I had just come off of a low of being disqualified as a finalist for the Nicholl. And Greg Beal—the director of the Nicholl Fellowship—when I saw him at The Nicholl presentation, his exact words were, "Oh I enjoyed your script. You would have been a finalist. Sorry I had to disqualify you." He basically said that they considered my income, although partial income that I had received while a Disney fellow, to be a writer's income. So that in and of itself disqualified me, which is something I hadn't thought of. But that was the case, and so I entered it in a new fellowship program that I'd heard some things about—the Universal Emerging Writers Fellowship, which caters to writers with diverse experiences and unique voices and gets them into the studio system. So lo and behold, I won that.

Lee: What was the day to day of the Universal fellowship like for you?

Chandus: Day to day, they structured the program very well in that we had writers who were different genres—someone who was action/thriller (myself), someone who was comedy, someone who was a little bit more horror-focused—so we had different segmented areas for writers. We had a period within the program where they would have an entire greenlight committee come and talk to us, so we're talking about the marketing person, the finance person, the distribution person. And basically I would say the VPs—the senior most people of each of those committees—would come and talk to us about their process and how they are involved in getting the movie out.

The other part was involved in speaking with experts, who would come in and talk to us about the craft, from Craig Mazin to writer-directors who have worked for the studio, and it was awesome to see how these writers took notes. How they navigated the process of script to screen, because a lot of them had been produced several times, and so it was good to get that perspective.

Another part of it was writing. We had a writers' bungalow and were able to have a set amount of time to work on new ideas and so forth. One of the things they did our first year, which they've now changed up, is that every week we had a certain type of deliverable, meaning we had a deliverable for original ideas for one week, another week we had a deliverable for IP and public domain, another week we had deliverables for rewrites, and it was great. At the end of all these weeks of going through and sourcing things, we would come with our top three projects and then pitch them to the creative committee, and they would say, "Go off and write that." So that's how the project that I worked on, inspired by the poem *The Aeneid*, became a fellowship script that I wrote during that time period. I went in and pitched it, they said, "Hey, we want you to work on that." It was awesome.

Lee: Having gone through the program, what were its great benefits?

Chandus: Access. The toughest thing about working in the business is getting to know the buyers, who are going to purchase your material, who are going to shepherd it through production and so forth. And so the big benefit for me was knowing the creative execs inside the studio. Having a relationship with Chris Morgan, who was a mentor that I worked with during that period. Seeing the writers come in and pitch him, because he's a writer/producer, so I'd see writers come in to pitch him ideas and it really demystified a lot of that process because I was just able to see how things worked. A lot of time we are kept in the dark as to what happens on the studio side, but it's not so complicated once you get in.

Lee: You mentioned Chris Morgan, and you also mentioned other relationships with name players in the industry. Do those relationships last beyond the fellowships? Or do you kind of leave them behind when you leave the fellowship?

Chandus: I think it's up to the writer really to lead that, because these are busy guys, they have tons of stuff going on, and what you have to do is figure out a way to not be so intrusive, but to still let them know that you're out there. When I met David Goyer for the first time, I left our conversation and was like, "David, hey, as you know I was in the military—I was in the army— but I have buddies and friends that were in other facets of the Army, I have a good friend at the Pentagon, friends that were stationed in Afghanistan and Iraq. I know you've done some military-themed stuff, if you ever need any research or expertise let me know." That very next morning I get an email from David, and it's like, "Hey, I'm working on something with Navy SEALs. Do you know anyone who's a Navy SEAL?" I'm like, "I surely do."

Lee: Did the fellowship open doors to representation for you, or did that come in earlier?

Chandus: The manager thing kind of came in a little bit earlier, but the agency—
it opened doors. There was a production company on the lot that read me—
because one of the cool things about being a fellow is that you get the
opportunity to take generals with all the on-the-lot producers—and so I had
a producer read me and he said, "Hey, are you repped?" And I told him,
"Not on the agency side, no," and so he forwarded my work over to Verve
and made an introduction that way, and they were excited to meet me based
on that intro. When I had my meeting with my agency, my senior agent told
me: "Hey, one of the cool things that I like about your background is that
you were a Universal guy. They know you, they know your work. And I called
over, and I spoke with them, and they had nothing but great things to say
about your work and your work ethic and your writing and so forth, and
that's great, because I know when they have something that's open and I
know when they're looking at OWAs (open writing assignments). And since
they already know you, it just makes that relationship even better."

Lee: How did your life change from being part of this fellowship?

Chandus: This is the first time I've had my entire team in place, which is awesome.
I have agency on board, I have a top management company on board,
and I have an attorney, so I can say that's something that I did not have
before.

Lee: You've been keeping pretty busy since your fellowship wrapped up. What's
the day to day of a writer who comes out of a fellowship and has an interest
in him? What do you do?

Chandus: A big part of my day is spent writing. But it's different facets of writing.
I'm either working on something that is in the development stage, or it could
be reading a book or reading something that is a rewrite opportunity to get
my own take. Or I could be taking meetings. I've done a lot of those things
interchangeably. One of the things I've learned is that when a new writer
hits the market, everybody wants to get an understanding of who this writer
is. I think that those general meetings are equally important because it is a
relationship business. Execs want to work with someone that they know is
going to be exciting to work with and bring about that great experience.

Lee: On a busy week, how many meetings would you be out on?

Chandus: On a busy week, I'd have upwards of maybe five meetings. Over the
summer, I took over maybe fifty or sixty meetings. That's fifty to sixty first
time meetings. With one company that I'm working on a project with,
I must've had maybe sixteen meetings, lunch meetings and so forth. Post-
strike a lot of the production companies—in particular smaller production
companies—don't develop after they decide to buy. They do a lot of that
pre-development beforehand, then make the decision to actually acquire, so
you do a lot of that (i.e. upfront work without pay), which unfortunately is
the way that the industry has shifted.

Lee: You were recently named to the prestigious Hit List. What's that experience like?

Chandus: The Hit List is a roll-up of all the top spec scripts for the year, which differentiates it from The Black List, which looks at everything that's unproduced, so it could be assignment work, as well as specs. The Hit List is just specs. For me, it was great because it validated that the industry took notice, that I had some new material in the marketplace, that I was a new voice and that the industry dug what I was pushing out from a spec standpoint.

Lee: Looking back, how instrumental has your move to Los Angeles been to your career so far?

Chandus: I highly encourage someone who's looking to get into this industry to make that jump and just move out here. I initially started writing when I was back in New Jersey but when I really started making inroads to my craft, it was when I was out in Los Angeles. You have to be here. This is where movies are made. I mean, yeah of course movies are shot all over the world, but this is where the braintrust is.

Lee: Do you have any advice for writers who are reading this interview?

Chandus: Focus on the writing. When I first started out, I was reading everything. I was reading *Creative Screenwriting*, I was reading *Script* magazine. Back in the day when they were physical magazines, I would get subscriptions and they would come to the house, and I just couldn't wait to go through and read it cover to cover. And then I would get in touch with the people in those magazines—and eventually they would know me. I think if you're looking to make this something that you want to call a career, you have to start out as a student in this, because it's how you really understand what the foundation is. You can't really advance through the ranks the way you should advance because there are going to be gaps, whether it's in structure or characters, whether it's in pitching or whatever. So for me, I was a student of it for many, many years, and then one day it just all came together. And you don't know when that process will happen, but when it does come together, it's going to be a great thing. It's going to be a beautiful thing.

7

RECEIVING A FEATURE WRITING FELLOWSHIP OR LAB PLACEMENT

Breaking Down the Feature Fellowships and Lab

Emerging television writers are not the only ones allowed the opportunity to qualify for unique, carefully crafted mentoring programs, conducted within the safety of a sort of creative incubator. Though feature writing fellowships and labs vary wildly in format, structure, requirements, duration, location and opportunity and do not offer the possibility of an end-result such as television staffing, like their television writing counterparts they too provide scribes lucky enough to be granted placement a distinctive and productive environment in which to develop their craft, bolster their resume, build industry relationships and strengthen their business savvy.

Screenwriting fellowships and labs have become another important way for the industry to vet screenwriters on the verge: those who qualify, specifically to the more high profile programs, easily add a prestige factor to their arsenal, as each of these programs have not only a lofty reputation, but also an aggressive and specific weeding-out process to ensure that here too the cream will once again rise to the top. Placement in any one of these highly regarded screenwriting fellowships and labs provides the writer with a level of gravitas, a cachet that can only help set the scribe apart from the pack. And if it has not been clear so far, when it comes to breaking in, that is a big part of your test.

While each fellowship and lab has its own specific criteria for qualifying and ranking applicants, one thing seems to be almost inarguable: these programs are seeking to support and promote writers who have shown the skillset, dedication and consistency that could tangibly translate to a long and prosperous screenwriting career. Because of this, many seek to identify applicants with more than just one completed screenplay; some seek additional successes such as high profile contest placement, industry contacts or even shot material (such as a short of web series) to indicate that the writer is not a hobbyist with one story to tell, but rather a writer seeking to make a career of it for the long term. In the simplest terms, the writers sought out are those who are *right* there, and just need a boost to push them to the next level.

But don't let that scare you away! By all accounts, these programs are not seeking to get behind writers who are already, effectively, there. In all reality, most such fellowships and labs are seeking to identify, support and elevate emerging writers who have not yet piqued; as the program's missions are often— and broadly put—to help writers as they reach for the next level in their careers, scribes no longer in need of such assistance are rarely fully considered.

Although submission requirements may be lofty and the application process demanding, acceptance into one such screenwriting fellowship or lab can help the writer attain much needed respect that could make him stand out. Therefore, for any feature screenwriter who has begun to uncover their voice and make a real go of cracking his screenwriting career, these fellowships and labs come highly recommended.

The Best of the Best: Labs and Fellowships

There is no question that placement in screenwriting fellowships or lab can be— if not a game changer—a significant step forward in the screenwriter's career. It can have great positive effect both on the screenwriter's pedigree, and, therefore, screenwriting trajectory. But prior to submitting applications for every feature fellowship and lab available to feature screenwriters out there, you must consider: Which is the screenwriting fellowship or lab that is right for you?

Perhaps the oldest and most prestigious of all screenwriting mentoring programs is the **Sundance Institute Screenwriting Lab**, which holds two sessions every year, one in June by invitation only, and one in January which is open to applications. Additionally, it offers an annual screenwriting intensive held in Los Angeles in March, as well as diversity initiatives. Founded in the early 1980s to provide a concentrated experience to selected participants, the screenwriting lab invites its partaker to a week of focused meetings, discussions, learning and exploration in Park City, Utah, which is home to the Sundance Institute.

Many previous participants in Sundance's screenwriting lab seem to have been not only writers, but rather on the writer-director track. The lab appears encouraging of its attendees to develop a script following the screenwriting lab, and then submit to the directing lab as well. As with many of the other fellowships and labs out there, Sundance is known to seek out screenwriters who have already begun establishing themselves; while those don't necessarily have to be produced screenwriters, it is to the submitter's advantage if they have industry recommendations, an impressive short or a high profile contest win or placement to include with their application.

Screenwriter Jimmy Mosqueda, a finalist in the Austin Film Festival screenplay competition and Tracking B screenplay competition, as well as a Nicholl semi-finalist, who is currently repped by Jeff Portnoy and Bellevue Productions, told me about his experience with the Sundance Institute Screenwriters Intensive—2016:

> Attending the Sundance Screenwriters Intensive has been the highlight of my young career so far. It's truly an honor to be recognized by an organization like the Sundance Institute for my work. The intensive takes place over 2 days at the Sundance's offices in Los Angeles, and it's run like a mini-version of the famed Screenwriters Lab. The first day was a workshop with Joan Tewkesbury (writer of *Nashville*). In the workshop I learned many things, but perhaps the most important thing I learned is that creative development is not about brainstorming characters or story points. All of us have unique, personal experiences and emotions that can form the building blocks of a story. Joan was a master at taking us through these steps. She helped bring in even more emotional verisimilitude and weight to my screenplay, *Valedictorian*. The second day of the workshop consisted of two 90-minute meetings with my creative advisors, who had read my screenplay beforehand. I was assigned Scott Neustadter (*500 Days Of Summer*) and Kyle Patrick Alvarez (*The Stanford Prison Experiment*). I could not have picked two better advisors, to be honest. They both gave great, actionable feedback on my script. We spent a lot of time talking about the main character, her motivation, her relationships, and how she "earns" the big moments/twists in the script. Since the intensive, I've remained in contact with both Scott and Kyle, as well as the Institute staff. Once you are part of the Sundance family, you're in for life!

Like the Sundance Screenwriting Lab, **Film Independent** has created a number of screenwriting labs to support and develop its emerging screenwriter seeking the support and guidance required to take his career to the next level. While neither Sundance nor Film Independent is known for taking screenwriters with material that is overly experimental, by all accounts both are seeking out scribes with strong voices and unique points of view. The **Film Independent Screenwriting Lab**, specifically, seeks out writers with a completed screenplay that possesses an independent slant, which would then be developed and consulted on with industry advisors during the lab. The program takes place over a four-week period in Los Angeles, out of the Film Independent offices.

Project Involve, Film Independent's "other" screenwriter friendly program, is a fellowship to which emerging screenwriters, producers, directors and other creative types are invited to apply in order to participate in master-classes, take industry meetings and ultimately come together to create a strong short film project combining all of the participants' unique talents.

The newest bona fide player in the screenwriting fellowship space is the **Universal Pictures' Emerging Writers Fellowship**, which Chandus Jackson, subject of Screenwriter Spotlight #7 participated in. This program, which requires year-round participation and takes place on the Universal Studios lot offers a participation fee for each fellow as they commit themselves to the 12-month program full time and take part in workshops and studio seminars, are mentored by established studio-based filmmakers, network with agents and managers and develop new work within the program. This program, too, seeks to discover screenwriters who are ready to take their writing and career to the next level but lack the access and/or visibility required to accomplish that. In years past, the fellowship selected participants based on genre specifications (thriller, comedy, etc.), so that they may be paired with a mentor possessing a track record in the same space.

While the above labs and fellowships are likely to gain you the most prominence and prestige, others too have built a stellar reputation for discovering and supporting emerging scribes in the screenwriting space. Here are just a few more:

Hamptons International Film Festival Screenwriting Lab. The Program pairs its participants with high profile Hollywood creatives who advise the writer in a one-on-one setting over three days.

Outfest Screenwriting Lab. In operation since 1997, the fellowship selects five writers to participate in a three-day mentor-led workshop in Los Angeles.

Hedgebrook Screenwriting Lab. Operating out of Whidbey Island in Washington State, selected scribes are invited for a weeklong residency in the fall, in which they develop their work with film industry professionals.

New York Women in Film & Television Writers Lab. Fully financed by Meryl Streep, this unique, newly formed mentorship program seeks to support the development of female screenwriters over the age of 40.

The industry, too, regards these labs and fellowships with a great deal of respect.

EuropaCorp's Chris Coggins put it quite simply, with specific emphasis on Sundance: "Sundance Labs are always a great thing. If you can get into that lab, please do, it's amazing. The writers who come out of there are fantastic."

And Bellevue Productions' Jeff Portnoy had this to add:

> When someone reaches out to me and says, hey, I found this writer, their feature script got into the Sundance Lab, or got into any of these Labs, they been vetted, it has the same effect on me psychologically as if they won or placed in any given screenwriting contest. Because I know that those are hard to get into. They have a lot of story analysts reading the material. Vetting it. So if I get two unsolicited submissions from writers who email me and ask me to read their script and one doesn't have any story to tell me and the other says that they got their script into the Sundance Lab, and was also in this other program, and a semi-finalist in the Nicholl,

time being limited and scarce, I'm gonna start with the one that has been vetted a little bit.

Positioning Yourself for a Feature Writing Fellowship or Lab

By all accounts, screenwriting fellowships are seeking out serious, talented screenwriters with a unique voice and honed craft who are in it for the long haul. As part of their business model, these organizations seek to establish and reinforce their place on the forefront of talent discovery, sustain their reputation for taste and instinct, and are therefore looking to identify and accept screenwriters who are not only determined, but also capable of translating their fellowship or lab placement into a tangible step forward on their screenwriting journey, heading towards a genuine, long lasting and prolific career.

While there are no requirements as to how many completed screenplays a writer should have under their belt when they apply to any one of these programs, the underlying message for most of these fellowships and labs seems to be: novices, writers just toying with the idea of picking up Final Draft (or any other screenwriting software) for the very first time, need not apply. What is required as part of most submission materials is a completed screenplay, one on which the screenwriter could work during their residency, fellowship or lab placement, a screenplay that is far enough along in its writing process to show real promise and potential, yet offers opportunity for development with the guiding insights of program mentors.

As stated earlier, the mission of many of these programs is to support emerging writers in need of guidance as they reach the next step of their professional development. Therefore, and in order to show that you are indeed such a writer who is on the verge of making a splash in the space, establish indicators that would help you make a case for yourself: whether it's a high-profile contest win or even final-round placement, a well-regarded piece of produced content or an industry recommendation, your job is to be able to substantially and substantively indicate to these programs that while you may not yet be represented or have produced materials to your name, you are someone who is, for lack of better words, *right* there. You are a talented, respected screenwriter with some modicum of success, recognition or, in the very least, budding industry relationships to his name, to which the industry should be paying attention. You are someone who, with a little boost, the right support and quality guidance, could certainly reach that illusive next stage in your screenwriting career, and become the sort of alum that the program would be proud to have.

Upon acceptance into any one of these programs, little will be as important as your craft, and your ability to take, process and execute notes without being precious about your work. With programs that can last up to a full calendar year and intensives that run as long as a few weeks or as little as a few days, you need to be able to generate ideas, digest notes and identify potential fixes, and fast. In this sort of hyper-focused environment, you simply haven't the luxury of getting flustered or defensive about the criticism you receive about your work. If you do, it will irreversibly taint the impressions you make on the mentors, professionals and experts who may choose to champion you moving forward, or else let you figure it out all alone on your path. Therefore, once granted entry into one such program, it is your job to come in ready to think on your feet, and embrace the collaborative spirit of the fellowship or lab. It's in your best interest to study how to take notes, good or bad, to learn how to identify the note behind the note, to learn how to deliver on a schedule and to digest criticism that you may feel is unwarranted with a solution-driven mindset.

Perhaps most important for these programs is your ability to put your unique voice, point of view and distinctive storytelling skills on display. In these creative, supportive, incubator-like environments, where make-ability and sell-ability are not the most important boxes that have to be checked when considering the applicants at hand, a honed screenwriting skillset and powerful voice can go a long way for setting a lab, fellowship or residency aspirant for entry and success.

SCREENWRITER SPOTLIGHT #8: Melissa London Hilfers

Melissa London Hilfers is a graduate of the University of Pennsylvania and the University of Chicago Law School. She worked as a litigator at Cravath, Swaine and Moore LLP and began her recovery from law by developing an internet company, itsybits.com, from concept to sale. Melissa is now a writer who lives in New York City. Her projects for the screen include the thriller *Undone*, a feature film currently in development with Parkes/MacDonald and Black Bear Pictures; *Pop Culture*, a comedy in development at USA network as a movie for television, with UCP and Iron Ocean (Jessica Biel's production company) producing; and *The Recessionistas*, a book adaptation being developed as a limited series, also at USA. *Missing Piece*, a comedy-horror short film that she wrote and produced, premiered at the 2014 Phoenix Film Festival. She is represented by Paradigm and Alan Gasmer & Friends.

Melissa is a mother of three and has been active in various children's non-profits including Room to Grow, the Child Center of New York and is on the Board of the Speyer Legacy School.

Lee: When your feature spec *Undone* sold in a mid-six-figure-deal in March of 2015, there were comments online implying that you were a working NYC litigator who wrote a script on the side, and suddenly showed up and got rich. But that's not at all the reality, is it?

Melissa: Ha, no. I had been writing full time for about five years when I sold *Undone*. I had sold two other projects prior to that.

Lee: When you left litigation, did you do so with the intent of transitioning into screenwriting, or did that come later?

Melissa: I left the practice of law to be with my kids full-time. When my daughter was born, I had an idea for a movie, and I sat down and wrote it. I have no explanation other than it was in me and needed to get out, and it wasn't a novel, it was a movie. From there I knew this was something I wanted to pursue further. I have a close friend who used to be an assistant at one of the big agencies and I sent it to her. I knew she would be honest enough to tell me straight up whether this is something I should be doing as a hobby or something I should really go for as a career. She sent it to one of her former bosses, who eventually became my manager. But not before he read two more of my features.

Lee: Is there a connection between being a strong litigator and a successful screenwriter? Does one prepare you for the other?

Melissa: I actually think it does. Litigation is about telling a persuasive story and making people care, often within strict page limitations on crazy timelines. All of this stuck with me.

Lee: Once you set out to become a screenwriter, what steps did you take to develop your craft and inform yourself about the industry?

Melissa: I read a ton of scripts, took some classes at NYU and read several books, including Syd Field's. I also started reading whatever I could about the industry. Basically every minute my kids were in school I was either writing or trying to learn about the craft and business. That hasn't really changed.

Lee: From the time you decided to start working towards a screenwriting career and the time that you made your first sale . . . How long did it take, and what did you focus on during that time?

Melissa: I sold my first spec three to four years after I started. I wrote many scripts for both film and tv in that time.

Lee: While your first big splash was *Undone*, you in fact set up a TV show, *The Recessionistas* with USA Networks six months prior to your spec sale. You were primarily a feature writer up until that point. What inspired you to try your hand at television, and what was the learning curve like?

Melissa: I actually sold another feature spec, *Pop Culture*, prior to *The Recessionistas*. It sold as a movie for tv to USA Network, and that happened because I reached out to a dad from my kids' preschool who ran a show on USA. He mentioned they were looking for a romantic comedy feature, I sent it to him and they bought it. But I actually had been doing TV in addition to features for over a year at that point. My manager suggested it, since there's a lot of opportunity in TV compared to features.

Lee: What's the process of selling a TV show like?

Melissa: You have to create the world of the show, develop not just the pilot but a template for what the episodes will be, as well as the overarching themes, questions, etc. Arcs for future seasons. And then you go from network to network pitching, which is incredibly exhilarating and fun, but requires a lot of energy.

Lee: Can you walk me through the experience of having a spec go to market and quickly thereafter sell? It's every writer's dream!

Melissa: It was one of the most exciting weeks of my life. I believe it went out on a Tuesday. Wednesday I was at lunch with a friend (I am on the east coast, so it was morning in LA) and I got an email from my reps that the initial responses were extremely positive. I was like, "we like it, we'd like to meet with her sometime" positive? Or "we want to buy this" positive? By the afternoon I knew that a bunch of producers were taking it in to different studios. I was trying hard not to harass my reps, so I signed up for one of those Tracking Boards. The next night the Tracking Board called it a "blazing hot spec." But still, you never know until you get your first offer. That happened on Thursday night. By Friday we were doing a deal. It was absolutely surreal and crazy fun. A friend once told me of the business "it can be mind-numbingly slow or lightning fast." After five slow years, this was a fast week.

Lee: How does your life change after you sell a spec in Hollywood?

Melissa: Day to day, not that much. I got a lot of meetings with people who read the script, and have gotten opportunities for jobs as a result. But it's not like you sell a spec and the next day major studio jobs start falling at your feet. If I want a job, *Undone* may get me in the door, but I have to prove I'm the person for the job.

Lee: What have you been working on since you sold your spec script?

Melissa: I've been working on a book adaptation with a director, another spec, and I just pitched a new TV series. I also just went in to pitch on a book adaptation that I really love. Fingers crossed.

Lee: Now that you've sold a thriller, does your team want you to stay in the same space, or do you vacillate between genres?

Melissa: That's a tricky one. People definitely want to have a way of understanding what it is that you do and I do enjoy the thriller space. Folks also took note of the "complex women" in *Undone*, so I get calls about projects with damaged women. Yay! That said, *Undone* has a darkly playful side, and that sort of note tends to thread through all my projects whether comedy, drama or thriller, so hopefully that's the "brand" more than any particular genre.

Lee: You and your family live in New York. How often do you come to Los Angeles, and what is your time like when you are out here?

Melissa: It's been about once a month lately. It's not easy, but I try to make every moment count and pack in meetings the entire time I'm there. I've also found stores in LA that have good gifts for my kids (the boys love See's chocolates from the airport so that's great, the girl is tougher). Incentives. The time change thing is tricky too, but it is what it is. These are problems I am thrilled to have and remind myself of that often.

Lee: From one working mother to another . . . How do you juggle raising your children—all three of them—with your screenwriting career?

Melissa: My husband is incredibly supportive and helpful. I'm not sure I could do it, particularly the travel, without him. It's not as hard as it used to be because they're all in school now. But the bottom line is I am doing something that I love—something that brings me joy. I gotta hope showing them that you can create the life you want is good parenting. That and the See's chocolates.

Lee: Having known you for a while now, I know how hard you've worked at this. If there is one thing that you know now that you wish you knew then, what would it be?

Melissa: I would have liked to know how many things you need to be good at to succeed as a screenwriter. It isn't enough to sit in a Starbucks and bang out a great movie. You need to be able to sell yourself, negotiate, listen, play nicely in the sandbox, manage your time, make strategic decisions. I don't know that it would have changed anything, but it would have been good to know. Of course I might also have liked to have figured out sooner that I wanted to be a screenwriter. I would have avoided a lot of law school debt.

8

SELLING A SPEC SCREENPLAY

How Does Today's Spec Market Work?

Every aspiring feature scribe longs to see his screenplay graduate to a high-profile spec sale. But how does it happen? As the myth goes, a chosen script hits the market, creates a great deal of buzz, and before you know it . . . *Snatch*! The deal is done, the writer is made and the market moves onto the next. At least, that's how we'd like to think it happens. But the reality of today's industry is that it rarely works that way. Gone are the fat years of the 1990s when specs were moving in the market at a rapid, sometimes head-spinning pace.

For a dose of today's reality, I turned to subject matter expert Jason Scoggins:

> When I first started tracking the market there was this idea that representatives would take material into the marketplace without having any attachments. Basically, this is a great piece of material, buyers, you should buy it and package it yourselves and develop it—do your thing. What's happened since the writers strike is the shift of the burden on that, almost all the way down to the rep, where you almost don't want to even bother taking a piece of material out with the intention of selling it unless it has a significant producer attached, a director attached. Better yet if you have a lead actor attached (each of which is known as an ATTACHMENT or ELEMENT). Basically the package process sort of replaced the spec process. I don't want to overstate that—it's not like there's some new package market. But the activity really has focused around packaged material.

Jason went on to tell me:

> The studios are looking for very specific product, their strategy is really bigger and bigger projects and fewer and fewer releases. The smaller movies

the studios release, either directly or through their labels, tend to be acquisitions (*completed movies made independently*). So that's all happening in this independent space. On the studio side, they're looking for projects that are completely packaged up, by which I mean, they know the budget, they know the director, they know when it's going to go, they know the producers, they've worked with them all before, the material is strong. And on and on, even to the point where they have a lead actor, where all the studio has to do is decide whether to make it or not—not how to assemble it. I'm overstating that slightly, there's definitely projects that get set up with only a couple of elements attached, but by and large what the studios would love is if someone would just walk in with a ready-to-go package that they could just write a check for. Disney's brand strategy is a really good example of sort of the platonic ideal of most studios where, if they could get half a dozen franchises that they're just feeding every year and then augmenting with two or three or four non-franchise pictures, they would all do that. Not all of them have Star Wars and Marvel and the Disney brand, et cetera, obviously, but Paramount is doing that with Transformers. Everybody would love to be in that business.

But just because the studios have shifted their purchasing strategies, doesn't mean that the spec market is dead. I turned to Jason to discuss the avenues available for a spec script to stimulate interest.

The independent space has become very much sort of a free-for-all. There's definitely not a complete overlap between what used to be the spec market and this independent film space, but there's a growing one, I would say. The independent film space is sort of taking up that slot and, the premiere projects that would have sold to studios when the studios were making those movies, are being identified still and often will get set up and made, but, that number of spec sales every year has continued to diminish. I don't see that changing in the near future.

Like Jason Scoggins—and the industry at large—Paradigm's David Boxerbaum has been observing the current changes in the spec market:

It seemingly gets tougher every year based on what's happening right now with the movie going audience and what they're reacting to in the marketplace, meaning that most stuff getting done seems to have a brand appeal behind it. So, the Transformers of the world, the Marvels, DCs, it's all this kind of movies getting made, which takes more and more away from the original idea—the original spec—being something that piques your interest or you gravitating towards. So breaking in these days is not only about writing something that's high concept—that speaks to the mass audience—but also about something that cannot lack great characters, has to have great dialogue, it has to be something that's on the page. It used to be before that you could break in with a good piece of material that maybe lacked certain character work or certain dialogue work or certain structural work, but the conflict was so great that you could sell that for X amount of dollars, 6 figures, and boom, your client has broken into the business. These days it feels like breaking in involves having this really powerful piece of material that speaks to both of those things—being high concept and has great dialogue, great characters, great through-line, three act structure, everything is there to perfection.

While agents and managers are observing the challenge of getting "naked" specs—specs without attachments that have not been previously set up—to stimulate interest, industry executives are often lamenting the absence of great specs in the space. EuropaCorp's Chris Coggins elaborated:

> A good spec is so few and far between. Seven to ten years ago, the spec market was really big. Every once in a while, there's still a big spec that comes out and sells for a lot of money. More often than not, now there's usually an element attached—a producer attached, a director attached, an actor attached—which is still technically a spec, but they're fewer and farther between, they're hard to get your hands on, they usually go to the big studios . . . Where I work is a bit of a smaller studio, so I pay attention to the spec market—what's out there, did something sell, is it a big sale . . . I don't really go after them as much just because if it's a good spec that's going to sell, it's going to go for a lot of money, that's Warner Brothers, Sony money. Specs are always good to have. They're just not as big as they used to be, unfortunately.

Chris went on to say:

> It's not the goes-out-on-Tuesday spec day and everybody's clamoring to get their territory—it's just not that world anymore. I mean there's what, seven big buyers? A lot of financiers, but it's not the same spec market anymore, unfortunately.

Indeed, today's spec market rarely resembles that of the booming 1990s. Epicenter's Jarrod Murray echoed that sentiment:

> The era of going out with a spec on a Tuesday and you assign territories the next day and you hopefully have a sale by end of the week—that's just not the world in which we live anymore. That was kind of dying when I was starting. With something like Nick Yarborough's *A Letter from Rosemary Kennedy* (which you can read more about in Chapter 12) we're not going

to take this out wide. We'll show it to some people and see what happens. Going the packaging route is always preferable if you can get meaningful attachments. The goal is to get movies made so hopefully you find those producing partners who want to shepherd this project with the writer. With another project, we signed this writer from TrackingB (competition)—he won the feature contest with a sci-fi *Source Code* concept. We went out with the script and got the writer a lot of meetings—got him signed with UTA—but it wasn't the automatic sale. I thought it would be a little bit easier than *Rosemary* (which is a based-on-real-life tragic period piece). With *Rosemary*, we're partnering with Weed Road, which is Akiva Goldsman's company and are gonna try to package it. Our philosophy usually is to find the right partners who can help us shepherd the project along. We don't have the luxury of hanging back and saying, "lets send it to two people and see what happens" and wait a long time for these two people to respond.

Of course, there are exceptions. While—much like the market itself—the price tags for spec scripts has diminished in recent years, in 2016 the spec market was shaken up when Netflix purchased Max Landis's *Bright* for upwards of three million dollars. The project came complete with the high value attachments of Will Smith and Joel Edgerton. Netflix, still making the sort of bets that would help it establish itself in the feature space to the same effect it has in episodic content, has committed more than 90 million dollars for the production of the project. But that sort of price tag—upwards of 3 million for the spec—is very much the exception rather than the rule and arguably would not have put on the table if it wasn't for the elements already attached.

Bright is emblematic of the current buying conditions in the market, especially when studios are concerned. Bellevue's Jeff Portnoy spoke to that:

> It's very rare for a feature spec screenplay to sell to a major studio without any elements attached to it. It still happens. It's just few and far between and the reason for that is when the bubble was at its high, when spec sales were at their apex, studios were spending tens of millions of dollars a year on spec screenplays and very few of them actually got produced. So in hindsight they looked back and said, wait, we spent all that money on these specs but none of them are getting produced and the reason none of them are getting produced is that the studios will only greenlight a film if it has a director and an actor that they are happy with, otherwise it doesn't get a greenlight. So a lot of these movies never got made and all that money was wasted. So they started saying, let's let the producers package them and bring them to us so they are ready to go and then we can greenlight them. Why should we keep buying specs that never get made? Instead we'll let producers go out there and if they can get a director or an actor attached, great, we'll buy and immediately fast track it for production.

In the spec world there never was and never will be a sure thing. Of course, there are certain advantages a spec can have with the right attachments, or when packaged by the right agency. But for all the planning and strategizing that managers, agents and writers engage in, the reality is that there are no guarantees. APA's Ryan Saul told me:

> I've gone out with specs that I thought were home runs and didn't sell. And I've gone out with specs that I thought weren't that good and have sold. I think every time you hear that the spec market is dead there are specs selling. It's just that they're selling to different places now. It's always good to have an attachment. That's the advantage that WME and CAA and UTA have, they have more producers and directors who have deals. So packaging is a big part of it. I have a smaller movie in the $10–15 million dollar range, which I'm not really going to sell as a spec. There are a couple of places I could go to but I need to find a director. I need to find an actress. Before, it was like "it's the idea. It's the spec." I once sold a project when I first became an agent—I don't even know what the writer sold because it was four sentences and we sold this pitch for a couple hundred thousand dollars. That's not happening anymore. Agents are going out with less and less specs. I just sat down with an exec the other day who's like "there's no material out there. We need material." So there will be a new resurgence in the spec market.

Since everyone talks about the importance of attachments, I asked Ryan Saul to talk me through what happens once the spec is no longer a naked spec, but instead the anchor of a powerful package. He said:

> Once the package is there, I find financing. Or depending on the talent, I know where to bring it. For this one movie, we already had the financing in place so it's as simple as "hey we can make you an offer, at least a holding offer," which is generally 10–15 percent of what the actors' fee would be to hold them and give them a shoot date. And hopefully we hit that mark. So let's say we get this actress. Now I need to find a director. But if we have this actress than finding that director is that much easier. I have another project I've been packaging with a producer who has a deal at Warner Bros and we've been trying to put that movie together for 2.5 years. Jennifer Aniston read it, Cameron Diaz read it. We don't rep Cameron Diaz. We don't rep Jennifer Aniston. But the script is good enough that it's still about the material. So if I get one of them, well then I don't need anything else. That's a studio movie. That's Jennifer Aniston calling up Tom Rothman at Sony and saying, "hey I wanna do this movie." But with the smaller projects I have to find financing. I have to figure: what does this actress mean in the foreign market. Because it's all about foreign numbers now.

Where it used to be about how's it gonna do in the US. That's the big thing that's changed. And Cameron Diaz means a lot foreign. So if you get her, I know I can get financing for it. If I get Actress B who has some really great movies under her belt, you know, she may mean more in Japan or China or wherever but not mean as much in Latin America. So all of those things come into play. It's a jigsaw puzzle that you're constantly trying to put together.

It's important to remember that while it is possible for a writer's first script to be THAT good, to gather steam right out of the gate, to stimulate a package or get financed, the reality is that selling a first script is not something that any writer should expect. Ryan Saul's APA counterpart Adam Perry spoke to that:

It's very unlikely to sell your first script these days. You have to just think about percentages, how many people are writing scripts all over the world, then how many people are able to get representation, which are very few, and then of those the small percentage who sell the first thing they go out with. I know one guy for example, who's become very successful, and he said: "I locked myself in my room for basically a year in my apartment. I would drink Scotch and write scripts." And it was the 3rd or 4th script he wrote that year that got him signed on with a manager. Ultimately it attracted a big piece of cast. And then it sold for close to seven figures. But that is definitely the exception, not the rule. I mean it happens. And that is why everyone will continue to chase it.

While managers and agents work hard to introduce their feature writers to the market and gain traction for their specs, the truth of the matter is that not every single one of those writers will ultimately be able to break. But, hard as it is, the important thing to remember is that for many, it does happen. They do break in the feature space, and go on to build the sort of careers that last. Such was the case with Isaac Adamson, who wrote *Bubbles*, the script that topped The Black List in 2015. For further insight about what it took to break him, I turned to his hard-working manager, Lee Stobby.

Isaac wrote an R rated comedy that I read and really what I responded to most was that his writing was impeccable. The idea was commercial and I sent it around but I didn't get any points on the board for that. It was too commercial, it was trying to fit some slot, he wasn't being truthful to the kind of things that he wants to do. He wants to do something that is dark. That's provocative and interesting. So I've been working with him for two and a half years, we developed a few scripts and with every single one of the scripts that we were developing we were pushing the boundaries more and more. Then through a series of events and ideas he had, he pitched me: "What if I wrote a biopic of Michael Jackson but told from the point of view of his chimpanzee, Bubbles?" I was sitting in my apartment when he pitched me this idea and I thought: that's totally genius. It's so unique. I know that people will get a kick out of it. That's really where it started. So he goes away and writes it, literally in a month and a half I have a 1st draft. I read the script and I'm crying because of how good it is. I'm like, "Oh my God! People are going to freak out when they read this." I wasn't thinking about whether I was going to sell this script. I was just thinking: This is so good. I'm going to get it to every single person I have ever spoken to. And that's pretty much what I did. I made an obscene amount of submissions over a couple of days, and then it started this series of events and now he's got big fancy agents and he's been getting studio jobs. Screenwriting is magic.

Note that at the time we conducted this interview, *Bubbles* had yet to sell. Since then, the project was snatched up by End Cue and Dan Harmon's indie stop-motion studio Starburns Industry, which previously made *Anomalisa*.

But Lee is not a fan of writing scripts in order to sell them:

The worst note someone can give you is: "Oh, you should do this because it will make your script more commercial." Because the note is, "this note will help you sell your script." But it's not going to sell. Don't worry about it selling. Also, people are really bad at predicting what is going to sell. I'm bad at it. No one knows. It's not an exact science. And so the only thing you should be thinking about when you write a script is: "Why will someone love this? Not, well I should put a robot in it because people love stuff with robots in it. That's not going to work. Because we bought too many robot script and now we don't want any more robot scripts but then you're not going to know that. And it's like winning the lottery at that point.

Getting a Spec Out to Market

Every feature spec is expected to travel its own unique road; some are sent to the masses—others are distributed to a small group via 'exclusives.' But every time, when a feature spec is guided into the professional industry space, you are expected to find an agent or manager behind it, strategizing and informing its moves.

If a writer only has a manager on his team, the first step may be getting the feature spec to an agent, who has a wider reach and great caché in the space. Manager Scott Carr told me:

The first step (*to getting a script out to market*) would be getting the writer an agent because agents are essential in exposing material, and the credibility an agent or agency brings to the process is helpful in differentiating material going to the market. And just legally it's essential that you have someone who's qualified and licensed to procure and sell the material involved. So I try to align the material, the writer and the sensibility of the agent so that we have what feels like is going to sustain a career and not just the script itself. I could do an exclusive submission to an agent that I think would be perfect for the writer and try to make it feel like a real special connection or I might just play the field with several agents at several agencies and see what interest I get. And then once the writer decides on who they want to work with, as a team we would strategize on the best way to expose the material.

Ultimately, when being sent out to market, every spec requires its own unique strategy. Much like the writers who created them, no two specs are the same. Some are sent wide to every studio, every financier and every shingle, while others are sent to a small group of producers, with the hope that one of them will become its champion. Paradigm's David Boxerbaum explained:

> Every spec is treated differently. And it comes down to how it's going to speak to the marketplace. Whether it be something that should be shown to 50 or 60 executives—which is quite a lot, obviously, and kind of a throwback to the old days of exposing a spec—or something that should be handled differently and much more with kid gloves and given to 5, 10 people. I've gone every kind of way of either big, little or in the middle when it comes to how to get a spec out. I purely judge on the material. The writer may already have relationships or fan bases built in his career, so we go to those same people. Or the writer may be brand new so we have to build the fan base and the foundation of fans for him and introduce him to the marketplace. That entails going to 20, 30, 40 people. It really is a case-by-case situation based on the script itself and the writers and where they are in their career. If a writer is extremely established and writes a spec, you're probably not going to go to 50 people. There's already a fan base of executives and producers who you're going to go to with the script, before you have to go to a mass majority of people.

In today's market, a spec script is sent out for one of two reasons: the first and most obvious is to generate a sale, but in a retracting market a spec sale does not often turn out to be the case. Spec sales in today's market are possible, but not probable. The more popular reason is to introduce the writer—via an outstanding story told with a strong voice and in an original, unique way—to the marketplace. Ultimately it's those scripts—the ones that are sent to market and then start to move from executive to executive independently of the agent behind them—that are able to make the strongest impact in the long term. Adam Perry of APA shared:

I like the kind of script that if I pass it to my friend that's an executive, even if I don't think they are going to buy it, I think they are really going to love it and pass it to their friends. 'Cause it's one thing when an agent sends something to an executive because that's our job, to sell and to push, but if executives are sending it to each other that wall immediately begins to crumble. And they're just much, much happier and willing to read.

When Adam and I met, he was getting ready to take the script *The Builder* by Tom Cartier—described as a Donald Trump origin story, tracking some of the tycoon's early ventures and challenges that created the Trump of today—out to market along with Tom's manager, John Zaozirny. We discussed the team's approach:

I want to get this script as wide as humanly possible because I do think it's the kind of script that could be on the The Black List. I feel like a lot of people are going to want to read it just out of curiosity. So I think it's an easy one for me because Donald Trump is such a lightening rod of a character right now. And this is the calling card for the writer. So we've already outlined 70 producers we're going to send it to. Seventy is considered very wide. That's one day, 70 people over a day and a half getting the script. And that's only the ones we're sending it to, we're get another 20 phone calls once it hits Tracking Boards and people start passing it around. But this one is the writer's signature piece.

Tracking Boards have been around for some time. I asked Adam to explain how The Tracking Boards work:

The Tracking Boards are basically these websites that track the scripts that go out in town. And a lot of executives and managers and creatives log onto these websites just to see what's out there. So if something gets leaked onto a Tracking Board — sometimes it comes from execs, writers, etc, but agents and managers do it as well — it creates more incoming calls. Which is a good thing.

Just as each spec has a different strategy powering its approach to market, there can also be a different strategy behind WHY an agent or manager is sending the spec out to the executives working in the space. Gersh's Sean Barclay explained:

The new multi purpose spec submissions, it's all tied to whether you are launching a new voice, or giving someone a make over, or giving the market a fast ball that it expects from a writer, you are absolutely using that to jump start conversations and get writers in rooms for general meetings.

Lee Stobby talked about his approach when getting *Bubbles*, the unique script about Michael Jackson's chimp, out into the marketplace:

> I'm working out of my apartment so all I have is a phone and a computer. So I gotta start calling people. And if I don't try to drop a nuclear bomb, I don't know how else I'm going to do this, so I need to drop a nuclear bomb, and then through the rubble maybe we can work this out. Luckily it worked out but it was a very thought out process. Every single person wanted to meet with Isaac, it was a whole bake off with agencies, like something out of *Entourage*. But I could only do that because I knew how good the script was and I was totally backing it up. People are always terrified of sending something to someone because you get judged. Everyone gets judged. So you have to feel like I am going to put my head on the chopping block for this thing. You have to inspire someone to feel comfortable doing that. And that doesn't happen very often. It happens with several dozen scripts every single year. Right? And those scripts always end up on The Black List.

Manager Scott Carr, too, shared insights from specific cases taking specs to market:

> I took out a naked spec (a spec without attachments) that was on The Black List last year that was called *The Civilian* written by Rachael Long and Brian Pittman, which is a high concept spy thriller kind of in the vein of *The Fugitive* meets *Enemy of the State* in the *Bourne* space. The writers hadn't been exposed yet so we went to the usual suspect producers across town, Chernin and Stuber and Mary Parent, giving it to two or three producers per territory. And then each territory had a major producer interested, we got several offers on the script and then eventually sold the material to Millennium because they came in with the most aggressive offer. As a result the script got on The Black List. And then Brian and Rachael got to do all of their meetings at those studios that read and liked the script. Another example is a project called *Miss Sloane*, which is currently in production in Toronto. A first time writer wrote it, and once the script was ready, it was about getting him an agent. He was represented by UTA and I had shared the script with CAA as well because they have a lot of actors and directors that could make sense. And so, through the agencies themselves the material started to circulate to various clients, actresses, directors and then we facilitated an option of the material with Film Nation, again just trying to bring in producers and financiers that would help legitimize these 120 pages. And then CAA brought in John Madden (*Shakespeare in Love*, *Proof*) who ultimately became the director and he brought Jessica Chastain with him because they had worked together previously. So we had a package

before anyone in town had even heard of the script in a major way. The first announcement of the script was the package and then everyone clamors to read the material because they want to know who wrote this script that attracted all these elements. So from exposure of the script to the first person who read it to the cameras rolling was about one year—which is ridiculously fast. And I think that was a result of the material being of such a high caliber and put together in a way that preserved how special it was, it just really helped the writer get the most attention from it.

Manager Kailey Marsh added her experience:

I have a new script that could be sent to everyone because it is a great script and it is a thriller and pretty much anyone will make a thriller but I'm probably going to send it to ten producers, fifteen maybe, and that's kind of a lot. I'm going to send it to places and someone's going to want to do it. I just know it. And if that's not the case then I'll go out wider. I have my top tier and then my second tier producers. And that always just depends on you and what the competing projects are, who has which deals where, time commitment, there's just so many different factors that go into it.

And considering what it takes for the market to respond to material—and what sort of response you're looking for—manager Lee Stobby concluded:

The difference between a movie getting made and not getting made is like a handful of people really when it comes down to it. So it's about finding that handful of people who will really champion your thing.

The Anatomy of a Spec Sale

To help illuminate the various steps of taking a spec script out to market, I once again turned to my industry colleagues to identify the specific steps involved. Whether talking about approaching the different territories (i.e. companies with studio deals that can bring the project to the studio, or the studios themselves) or putting together a buyer's lists, I looked to them to break down their specific process. Here is what they told me:

Infinity's Jon Karas said:

On a typical spec script sales process, we work with the other teammates; primarily the agents and sometimes we intersect with a client's attorney if they have one as well. And we put together what I call a buyer's chart. A road map of who we are going to present the material to. Starting at the highest level of studios, then moving to mini-majors, then moving to independent production companies, then moving to foreign and foreign sales and other financiers and super independent people. At the end of the day, it ends up being somewhere between 75 and 100 people on one piece of material. The mission is always to create new fans and create engagement beyond just selling something. The mission is to have multiple producers competing to bring that script into each of the studios and then being wise about all the reasons why you would pick your partners, which one gets to go where. Who's hot at that studio? Who's got the movie that's about to come out or did just come out and was the big hit? If there's a bunch of people fighting, the ones that win are going to be really excited and tell the studio execs, and hopefully as high up as can be, that they had to fight to get that script and that it's in everywhere—and they wouldn't be lying.

John Zaozirny of Bellevue Productions shared his approach:

We put together what is called a territory list, which is essentially the major studios in town and you look at who has first look deals with them because those are the people that the studio wants to be in business with. So you'll go through the producers at that studio who are best suited to the project. There are people who are best for comedy. There are people who are better at action-adventure and so on and so forth. So it's, who's the producer that I think would be best for this? Do they have a relationship with me? Do they have a relationship with the writer? Who's the right executive to go to at a particular company? Who does the agent have a relationship with? And then you split up all those territories and you take it out to those producers in the first round. And then you might also go to the financiers, places like that. And then cross your fingers that people like it. Now, more often than not, the deal doesn't actually come on until months later. So when you're reading in the trades that something just sold, more often than not it actually sold months or weeks earlier. By the way, if you sell a screenplay you're not getting rich tomorrow. It's going to take 6 months for all the deals to get done because they're not going to pay the writer until they've made the producer's deal, there's underlying rights, they want to do due diligence that you actually control those underlying rights. There's a chain of title that's clear. So it can be very complicated.

Chris Coggins of EuropaCorp's shared spec sale stories from the Executive perspective from her days as VP at Escape Artists:

I was at a production company that had a first look deal with Sony. And usually Tuesdays is spec day and all the execs at the production companies are sent this script to see if they want to get a territory or not. Usually their home territory, for me it was Sony. So you would read the script, if you liked it you called the agent and said I would like it for Sony. But there's like ten production companies that have their deal at Sony so you're competing with the other production companies there. So the agent tries to fit that movie with the production company they think could be the best fit. If it's an action movie, it goes to Jerry's (Bruckheimer) company to take to Disney or what have you. So I would call the agent and say, "I really like this, I want it for Sony." If I get Sony, then I would call up the exec at the studio that I liked, that I thought would get this project. "Hey Warren Abrahams, I think this would be a great comedy because A, B, and C." She takes it, she reads it. Say she reads it, she hands it up to her boss hopefully by Friday. Best case scenario, which hardly ever happens: Amy Pascal would read it by the end of the day and put in a bid.

So I asked Chris: Once an offer is made, what happens next?

So then celebration. Not too much, though, because you're not closed. Then the writer has to wait for the deal to close, for the writer's agent and the business affairs exec at the studio or whichever company to close the deal. In the meantime, hopefully because it's gonna close, the production company, the execs there get their notes together: This is what we like, this is what we think works, this is what we think we need to work on. Get all those notes in a document, send those notes to the studio, make sure the studio signs off, get any notes from the studio that they need to send in, and then the writer can come in, have a meeting, talk about all those notes, and then the game plan is made. When the writer gets commenced they get their first payment—that's when they do their first rewrite. Say that's your first round of notes. Say best-case scenario you execute your notes, the new draft is great, you just need to do a little polish. You get commenced on your polish, you get paid on your polish, and then you get greenlit and start shooting. In between you probably get your director attached or your star attached. Get their notes. I worked on *Knowing. Knowing* was probably eight or nine years to get from beginning to end. But then I worked on *The Pursuit of Happyness* that was three years from beginning to end because we had Will Smith and he wanted to play it, so he was able to push it through. If you have that huge piece of talent or your studio that definitely wants to make it, that is pushing everything through, then you can get it done much faster. It can definitely take years. You might get rewritten. You might be off the project and somebody else comes on to write it. You might stay on the whole time and do production rewrites.

As Chris Coggins said, this is a best-case scenario. The alternative I often hear from my friends in representation these days is that they rarely bother to go out with a script that doesn't already have attachments in place. In other words: no attachment, no sale.

When A Spec Doesn't Sell—Measuring Success

In a market where as few as ninety scripts or as many as a 135 scripts sell every year, one might conclude that thousands of scripts, and by extension writers, fail to realize their screenwriting aspirations. On closer examination, however, you will quickly discover that this is not at all the case. And while every feature spec writer would love to find himself with a spec sale on his hands, it turns out that in the screenwriting space there is more than one way to measure success.

Take, for example, the case of the script *Bubbles* by screenwriter Isaac Adamson. The script is a biopic about Bubbles, the chimpanzee that was adopted by Michael Jackson in 1983. In it, we find Bubbles the chimp narrating his own story and detailing his life within The King of Pop's inner circle through the scandals that later rocked Jackson's life and eventually led to Bubbles' release. While manager Lee Stobby, whose invaluable insights you've read in these pages, had papered the town with it, sending it far and wide to studio and production executives, it took time for it to get set up. In fact, when I sat down with Lee in February of 2016, a deal for making the script was not yet in place. But just because the script did not sell immediately, it did not mean that the script was not a smashing success right out of the gate. Not only did the script make it to the very top of the very prestigious The Black List in 2015, it had also opened countless doors for its scribe, who has—since its release to the town—entertained endless meetings. In early 2016, the scribe was hired by Alcon Entertainment, the company behind such hits as *Prisoners* and *The Blind Side*, to adapt the psychological thriller *The Ice Twins* from the original novel.

While every screenwriter longs to write a script worthy of a sale, in an environment where very few works garner a lofty upfront payment (especially for specs that don't come complete with attachments) many screenplays become—rather than sale worthy—a valuable writing sample, one that can effectively introduce the writer to the town, and lay the foundation for a long and prosperous screenwriting career ahead. If screenwriting careers are built on the shoulders of relationships, then a strong writing sample becomes the conversation starter that launches many industry relationships. Therefore, you know that a particular script is working for its writer when it begins to "move on its own," i.e. get sent around, from executive to executive and from assistant to assistant, without an agent or manager behind every exposure. The script then becomes something that people within the industry are talking about and sharing with one another, instantly garnering the writer much needed interest. While in the long run this interest may eventually lead to writing assignments and interest in future spec work, its most immediate result is the writer being invited to a slew of general meetings, also known as generals.

For further insights on how one measures success in today's challenging industry environment, I turned to Paradigm's David Boxerbaum:

Success should never be calculated on the opinions of the marketplace. Success should be calculated on how you feel—if you're confident in your abilities, if you're confident in your script. So if I go out with a script and it's not received as well as it should have been, I deem success based on what my reaction to the script is. Because it's about my tastes and my judgment as well as the writer's work ethic and talent and what they do when they sit down and write the script. So I believe success is, you've written a script, it's gotten into my hands in a situation like this, and we've taken it out there and whether it sells, it gets well-received or not, success has been achieved because you've accomplished something that 99 percent of people cannot do. Which is write a screenplay. And a successful one, in that sense of getting to a place where we feel we should take it to the marketplace. To me, that's success. And everything else is kind of the cherry on top. Now, granted, if we're trying to make a career of it and we're trying to have financial gain, that's obviously important, right? And you want that next stage of success, which is the success of selling a script, the success of having a career, of getting opportunities in the marketplace, screenwriting and rewriting and all of that. But that first step to success comes with actually sitting down and accomplishing the writing of a screenplay, which I always commend any writer—any size, any shape, any age, any color, any gender who can accomplish that, to me, that is a success in itself.

EuropaCorp's Chris Coggins had this to add:

The worst-case scenario is the agents sends it out, nobody likes it, nobody wants to meet with the writer, nobody wants to take the project into a studio, and nothing ever happens with it. But that hardly ever happens. Just because writing is so subjective. Somebody's gonna like it. Somebody's gonna want to meet with you. Somebody's gonna want to take it in. Somebody's gonna want to take a chance on something. If you have a reputable agent who is going to send it out to production companies—to real production companies or real studios, you're going to get some meetings out of it.

Jeff Portnoy of Bellevue Productions shared his insight:

Right now, the best we can hope for when we take out a spec—of course we aspire to sell it to a studio but—we know that the odds are very low. We're happy if we get it on The Black List, we're happy if we get the writer an agent, or we're happy if we get them lots of general meetings, get them put up for assignments. If the script doesn't sell then it doesn't sell but if those other things happen then we're happy. If the studios are turning down packages with A-list directors and actors attached, why would they buy a spec screenplay?

The Prestige Lists

In order to make sure that the best unproduced screenplays are surfaced in town to studios, producers and executives every year, the industry has come to rely on its annual prestige "best-of" lists. These are:

- The Black List
  - The list, rather than the listing service
  - The list highlights the most liked material written on spec and on assignment in a given year
  - The list is aggregated by Franklin Leonard, and is considered the most prestigious of these lists

- The Blood List
  - The list is aggregated by manager Kailey Marsh
  - The Blood List highlights the most liked unproduced spec scripts in the horror, thriller, sci-fi and dark drama space in a given year

- The Hit List
  - The list is aggregated by The Tracking Board
  - The list highlights the most liked unproduced spec scripts in a given year

- The Young and Hungry List
  - The list is aggregated by The Tracking Board
  - The list highlights both up-and-coming and established writers making a name for themselves or hitting their stride in the industry in a given year

The above lists have all carved a name for themselves for identifying—via votes from industry executives including agents, managers, producers, development executives, studio executives and others—the best unproduced scripts and talent worth watching on any given year. While a spec script may indeed fail to sell, its appearance on any one of these esteemed lists garners the writer immediate caché.

I asked Jason Scoggins of Slated about the importance of these lists.

> In a word: Discovery. It's basically the consensus of the industry to a certain degree of what's good. As a writer or as a rep of a writer who has a script on those lists, you know it can be really helpful for their careers from a discovery standpoint. Every year there is a number of writers who

previously hadn't really been well known throughout the industry who, by dint of being on those lists, get a lot of traction and their careers get a boost. I don't know if I would go so far as to say that those lists can be gamed, but there's definitely an element where you know people make an effort to get on those lists, and there are definitely scripts every year where those efforts are helpful. I think at the top of all of these lists, the ones with the most votes, those are fairly bulletproof. It would be relatively easy to get five or six people to vote on a script, just because you asked them to. But to get 20 or 30 or 40 votes, that's a whole different thing. So certainly the top of those lists are bulletproof. And even the bottom of those lists is worth paying attention to. They tend to be up-and-coming writers, they tend to be scripts that haven't been well-circulated previously.

Manager Kailey Marsh started The Blood List, the prestigious annual list dedicated to highlighting the scripts written in the horror, thriller, sci-fi and dark drama space. Kailey told me:

I started The Blood List at the end of 2009 when I was an assistant. I was also hosting horror screenings. I've always been a genre fan. People seemed to like it and like most things that gain popularity in it so I just kept doing it. But I'm no longer just a genre person. I do tons of comedy. But I love doing The Blood List. I'm in the process of expanding right now—I'd love for it to become a production company where I have financing to make really cool left of center genre movies.

Madhouse Entertainment's Ryan Cunningham added:

There's a lot of validity to getting onto one of those lists. It certainly is a great feather in your cap, and it gives your script—and you as a writer—more exposure. And as a rep, it's a really great thing to say, Oh yeah, the client's script was on The Black List. It creates a shorthand for people to say it's legitimate. But I don't think it's the be-all-end-all. I don't think any of the end-of-year lists are. But I look forward to them every year. I like seeing what's on there. I like that I have clients on there. It makes them look good, and it makes me look good. But I see more and more from young writers that there is an undue amount of pressure they put on themselves to get on there. Look, the reality, too, if you look at the list of writers on The Black List every year, frequently it's younger writers who are breaking in. It's younger reps who are blasting material all over town. It's not the more experienced agents or more senior managers a lot of times. Because their clients are all working in the system anyway, selling stuff preemptively to one studio for a lot of money or they're doing assignments all the time. So I think the lists are great, you just have to be aware of what the context of them is. There are a lot of other aspects to a career, not just getting your name on the list.

I spoke to manager Lee Stobby, who got Isaac Adamson's *Bubbles* to the very top of 2015's The Black List, about the process of getting a script onto The Black List:

> It started nine months earlier with me calling every person I ever knew. If you want to get a script super high on The Black List, you have to have your managers and your agents truly behind the script in a very powerful way. I had never represented a script that had been read by more people. The awareness of the script was complete and utter. But as a manager I can only call so many people, so it was still only a small sub-set of the total that we're dealing with here because no one has a complete reach. The Black List was insanely helpful but at that point he'd already reached that point of total saturation. It wasn't that The Black List happened and then total saturation happened, it was the other way around. You don't get a script on The Black List without it being at complete saturation. It's a byproduct of all the work the writer and I, and the agents, had done to make sure as many people as possible were aware of that awesome script. You're not gonna know where the next job's gonna come from, so you have to be as open to as many different things as you possibly can. Having something that has that level of saturation should be your goal as a writer.

Positioning Yourself for the Spec Market

The one way to position yourself for the spec market, whether your script actually sells or goes on to become a strong and exciting writing sample, is to write a great, ORIGINAL, exciting screenplay.

When he sat down with me for this book, manager Jewerl Ross said:

> I was once at a restaurant and some producer told me: "You know, if there was a great script and you threw it into the middle of Sunset Boulevard, that script would find its way to someone who mattered, because finding a great script is so rare."

So what should you keep in mind when aiming to write a great, stand-out screenplay?

- **Create an original story.**
  Don't write the next *Die Hard*, *Titanic*, *Spotlight* or any other movie repeating what's been done well in the past. Those screenplays have already been written, those movies already been made. A strong original screenplay that is positioned to be sent far and wide and therefore have the desired effect

on the marketplace is just that: original. Something that is entirely new, that we have not seen before—be it the world, a particular key character or a conflict newly explored.

- **Don't anticipate the market.**

On occasion, you may see some blatant trends: multiple spec sales or placements on The Black List of scripts taking place in a particular time period, or set against the backdrop of a specific world event. That does not mean that your next script should unfold in that very same time or place. On the contrary, by the time you've completed the screenplay, written and rewritten it and gotten your feedback, the industry will have fatigued of that particular time period or subject matter, and those screenplays would have been produced or, worse, unable to stimulate the elements required to become a feature film, thereby invalidating any additional interest in scripts in that particular space.

- **Put your passion on the page.**

A few years ago, one of my long-standing clients started developing a new screenplay. We discussed a number of concepts, but she kept going back to one that she just couldn't seem to shake: a period piece. Set in Victorian England. Exploring the origin story of a beloved character in literature, who, only a short time before, was brought to the big screen by a major MAJOR director and his frequent A-list acting collaborator. While I knew the screenplay could easily be handicapped for a number of factors (period piece, straight drama, origin story of a character recently brought to screen) and questioned whether it would ultimately be able to find a home once completed, at the end of the day the writer just had to get it out of her system. Knowing all that she knew, she sat down to write. And what she generated is one of the very best feature specs I have read in recent years. The screenplay, a whimsical, tragic drama period piece set in Victorian England went on to win over the enthusiasm and dedication of a prominent management/production company, and gain the writer high profile representation. At the time this book is written a major international entity has stepped up to partially finance and produce, and the writer is now also slated to direct. Which just goes to show you that writing from passion, rather than from an anticipation of what the market may or may not respond to, is more often than not in the writer's best interest.

Paradigm agent David Boxerbaum concluded:

> Write from a place of passion, write something that is at least relatable in some way to the reader. So writing something that's a historic western set in the rural outback of New Mexico is tough. You know? You need to write something that has a relatable factor to it. But at the same time, you have to write from a place that you're passionate about, as well. So don't

chase genres, don't chase the box office—what's working at the box office, don't chase that—write from a place that you love.

SCREENWRITER SPOTLIGHT #9: Moises Zamora

Moises Zamora was born in Guadalajara, Mexico, and grew up in a town older than America, El Limón, Jalisco. When he was eleven years old, Moises's family immigrated to California. Moises graduated from Brown University with a B.A. in International Relations. A week after getting his degree, he moved to Paris to write a coming-of-age novel in Spanish. Moises's first literary achievement was the 2005 publication of the novel *Susurros bajo el agua*, complete with a national book tour and the Binational Literary Prize for Young Novel Border of Words. In 2008 he made a documentary film that followed the lives of young men and women from his childhood home. *Young + Mexican* premiered at the 2011 Oaxaca FilmFest and received the award for Best Documentary by a Mexican Director.

After having produced and directed various film projects, Moises enrolled in TV writing classes at UCLA Extension and Script Anatomy. In 2015 he earned second place in the UCLA Extension Screenplay Competition for his TV pilot, *Second Coming*. Moises is currently managed by Silent R Management and CAA, and staffed on the critically acclaimed anthology series *American Crime*.

Lee: When did you start writing? Did you always know that TV was where you wanted to be?

Moises: I wrote my first play when I was a sophomore in high school for English class. I had always been drawn to the stage and performance. What I didn't know at that time is that I would continue taking playwriting courses in college and then would pivot to prose. I wrote my first novel when I was a junior at Brown University. It was a time when I was figuring out my identity. I'm Mexican born and an immigrant. I came to the U.S. when I was 11 years old. For some reason, perhaps I was out of my mind or maybe it was a manifestation of my insecurity about writing in English, I decided to write in Spanish. I remember I was jotting down some emotional stuff in my journal and the language would change from English to Spanish. I felt that my writing in Spanish was raw and more poetic. My first novel was in Spanish and it was terrible. I had to teach myself how to write at a literary level in my first language, which had been neglected since sixth grade. After graduating from Brown, I moved to Paris to write the great Mexican novel . . . in Spanish. That was my second attempt. I won a literary award in Mexico and the book got a limited-edition publication. I moved to Mexico City for a modest book tour, organized by the Ministry of Culture. It was a magical time, but it was also heartbreaking. I was 27 and I couldn't survive as an author, despite being lauded. I returned to Los Angeles and I got an advertising job. I realized that

I had made a commitment to writing and storytelling. I couldn't go back to writing novels, so I decided to get involved in filmmaking; eventually, I ended up taking courses at UCLA Extension for feature and television writing. In my mind, breaking into television seemed more daunting than writing a feature. What I learned, however, is that I'm a good producer and I love working with people, or collaborating towards a specific creative goal. I think having always loved the classroom environment and excelling in advertising led me to truly embrace television. Once I did, my drive was focused and relentless.

Lee: Gotta ask . . . Why television?

Moises: I think that writing novels and loving long form narrative naturally pushed me to television. Seeing how a series develops over a season and its entirety is exciting to me. I want to be part of creating the bigger picture. When I was growing up in Mexico in the 1980s, we only had three channels. There was a Japanese animated series, which truly inspired me to start coming up with my own stories. It was a historical drama, too dark for children. It never made it to America, but after seeing heartbreak, death and harrowing scenes lived through the POV of an orphan girl, I couldn't really get into the Care Bears or the Teenage Mutant Ninja Turtles. I got obsessed with the series to the point I started drawing up my own "graphic novel." Now that I'm writing for television, I get this really warm feeling of familiarity, as if my inner child is finally where he needs to be.

Lee: Once you decided you wanted to write professionally, what steps did you take to become the best writer you could be?

Moises: I love learning. After having survived the tumultuous twenties, a time of fearlessness, invincibility, irrationality and egocentric harmful behavior, I knew it was time to take a different approach. I identified my insecurities and fears and I worked on them. I didn't know to write a script, so I took many courses at UCLA and made time at night and during weekends to get my assignments done. I was open to feedback. I suppressed my ego as much as I could. I knew that if I wanted to learn and improve at a moderate pace I had to get rid of my tendencies for self-aggrandizement. My first novel was earnest and terrible, so was my first TV pilot. I got torn apart by my fellow classmates, but I already knew it was going to be bad, so I was excited to write the second, third, fourth, and so on. My mantra is "Nothing is wasted." In other words, all writing adds up, it's cumulative. Of course, it's difficult to let your babies die, but the positive spin is that if they don't die, my writing doesn't thrive.

   I took classes at UCLA Extension, I joined an alumni writer's group from Brown, I attended WGAw panels and I've been going to the NALIP Media Summit, where I've connected with many Latino talented individuals. After a year of that, when I thought I was ready to take up a notch, I hired you, Lee Jessup, and started taking courses at Script Anatomy.

Lee: Your first introduction to the industry was through your pilot, *Second Coming*, which went out pretty wide. What was it like suddenly getting thrust into all of these meetings with production companies, studios and networks?

Moises: It happened pretty fast. The first and only manager who read my pilot signed me immediately and, a month after I made a few changes to the script, I got many meetings. The first thing that came to my mind was how grateful I felt to be able to express myself and have people interested in what I have to say. It's an incredible feeling; it wasn't about validation anymore, it inspired me to be better, work harder and prove to all those kind individuals I met that they didn't waste their time with me. Additionally, it was an opportunity to establish relationships with decision makers, which is truly a blessing—when driven, passionate people come together because of what I wrote on the page.

Lee: What did you learn from the generals you went on?

Moises: The generals taught me several things. It's a great starting point to begin speaking about yourself as a brand. Everyone asked me how I started writing and what kind of shows I like or variations of those questions. They want to know your story so they know where to place you or what project to give you or how they can work with you in the future. The same goes for your taste in shows. If you like dark dramas like I do, they're not going to give you a romantic comedy. In my case, they had read my pilot *Second Coming*; so they already had an idea about me. It was my opportunity to expand on that. I think the work comes after the generals. Keeping up with them, sending postcards, checking in on their projects. I don't pester, but I've also realized that I made a stronger connection with some. That's important to identify. They'll keep you in mind when staffing season comes around, or they'll be open to giving you a project. I had three projects to develop. One of them went as far as the financier, but he was looking for a different tone, a more comedic approach, to the project. In that case, there's nothing I could've done; however, the relationship with that executive solidified.

Lee: How do you work with your manager?

Moises: My manager is very hands-off. He doesn't note me to death. In fact, he prefers for me to run a few ideas through him and he then responds to what he likes the most. In a way, I like that I don't have to be 'manufactured' into a specific writer and he allows me to develop stories I love. However, now that I'm a staff writer and I'm about to hire an agent, the process will change. I'm expecting there will be a combination of passion projects and scripts developed with the reps from logline to draft.

Lee: In April 2016, without a writing gig in place, you decided to quit your full-time advertising gig. Why?

Moises: I held on to my advertising job as long as I could. I had negotiated a flexible schedule with the agency and I was permitted to work from home many days of the week. I wanted to take writing classes, have the ability to take meetings and spend my time more effectively instead of commuting. After getting signed with Silent R Management and having gone to many general meetings, I knew I couldn't squander the opportunity to get to the next level. I needed to spend more time writing. It was a difficult decision to make. I was leaving a stable six-figure job and I had nothing in place. I was making plans to work freelance. It was a scary time, but what pushed me into the unknown was my determination and the encouragement of people who know about my work ethic. I'm a hustler and I was confident I'd find one, two or three ways to make a living. What really scared me was the possibility of being too afraid and comfortable to pass on my dream. I couldn't let that happen, so I quit. Exactly a month later, I joined the writers' room for American Crime.

Lee: Your big break came through effective, targeted networking. Do you network a lot? And if so, what works for you when you network?

Moises: I don't network aggressively. I do put myself out there, writers' groups, conferences, panels and classes. Many working writers give back by teaching classes or a side gig, I look for those opportunities to learn from someone in the industry, improve my craft and build a relationship with that working professional. I think the hardest thing to do is to force a connection. It really is like dating in a way, if you're not a match, don't push it and figure out a way to come around. I think the quality of the connection is important but realize that not everyone you meet will work out. Acknowledging when there's an authentic spark and fostering that friendship is essential to your growth. I actually don't like the word 'networking' because it has a corporate ring to it. In this industry, you're building relationships, not just business or entertainment related, but friendships. People want good people around them. We're in the business of telling stories and there's nothing better than to tell a story to a friend and your friend loving it! That's how I see it. I'm the guy who wants everyone to circle around me and be enthralled by the crazy anecdote I'm about to share, but at the same time, I'm also the guy that listens. Being a good listener is key; everyone is giving you cues and insights to what's important to them. Paying attention is not a cold-blooded strategy, it's the foundation of an authentic relationship. When people see that about you, they'll want to work with you. Perhaps that's the biggest lesson for me: being a genuinely good person goes a long way.

Lee: Davy Perez was instrumental to your break. How did you two meet?

Moises: I met Davy at NALIP (National Association of Latino Independent Producers), a three-day conference for Latino Independent Producers. He was part of a panel of TV writers. I spoke to everyone at the panel, but Davy seemed to be more down to Earth and less standoffish. The other writers were great, but with Davy, I felt immediately that I could be my silly self. My conversation was brief and I said that I would love to ask him about his experience in getting into the ABC/Disney Writers Program. He told me to add him on Facebook. To me that was a clue as how to approach him, through social media. Some people give you emails, some take your card, etc., some don't give you any way of following up. I never actually asked him to coffee or tried to take his time to ask him questions I probably already had answers to. I personally don't like asking a busy professional for coffee; I think they know that you're asking them to like you and, if you're more naïve, you're asking them for a job. I prefer to develop relationships in a more organic way. I followed Davy on Facebook and Twitter, so I liked his posts. Normal stuff, no stalking behavior. When Davy posted a tweet about teaching a class on writing fellowships, I immediately signed up! I had gone through the process the year before, but frankly, it was about learning from someone and getting to know each other in a non-networky way. Besides, like I mentioned before, I love classroom environments. We were working on our bios and he immediately got to know my life story, my accomplishments and struggles. Additionally, he got to read my work. I was working on a spec for Black Mirror. That's all it took for him to ask me to put all that together along with my pilot *Second Coming* in an email he was going to forward to some ABC evaluator for a show that's looking for someone who has an immigrant story. I sent all the materials he asked for: bio-essay; letter of interest; resume; pilot and a PDF with press clippings of my successes. Three days later I got a call from the creative executive of the show to schedule an interview with the showrunner.

Lee: How did staffing for *American Crime* come about? What made you a specifically attractive candidate for that show?

Moises: When the creative executive called me to come in and meet one of the executive producers, I found out it was for the third season of *American Crime*, which had not been officially picked up. The theme included storylines about migrant workers and exploitation. My background and life experiences checked many boxes for them. They had read my writing sample and they liked the mechanics, but my ability to discuss personal, painful and harrowing experiences openly made me an attractive candidate. It is the nature of the show, thriving on raw human content and they thought I was able to provide that in a professional manner.

Lee: What did you do to prepare for your *American Crime* interviews, and how did that preparation pay off?

Moises: I prepared several personal anecdotes and experiences that I thought would be relevant to the theme. I also called my father and other family members to get more stories. My father works for a clinic as a Physician Assistant and he has treated many migrant workers who have shared horrifying stories about exploitation and abuse. I used real examples and I pitched them to Michael McDonald during my interview. I also spoke about intimate family issues and my personal journey and struggle with my sexual identity. In many ways, I shared the kind of stuff I'd share with a therapist; however, the difference is that I spoke about it as if it had happened to a third party and with a writer's point of view, almost as if I were pitching a scene. I watched both seasons of *American Crime* and I took notes, and wrote down dialogue lines that resonated with me so I could talk about them or allude to them casually. During the interview with Michael McDonald, he mentioned two books John Ridley was using as source material. I ordered the two books on Amazon and I read them carefully regardless of whether I was moving forward or not. I did get an email to set up a call with John Ridley and when I spoke to him I was able to pull a few examples from the books. I probably mentioned three sentences related to the book in total, but I do believe it made an impression on him. I was interviewing for a staff writer position, so in my mind, being resourceful and researching were going to be my contributions and I needed to make sure everyone knew that.

Lee: Once you started in the room . . . what was it like?

Moises: The *American Crime* room is a dream. We were assigned many articles to read and films to watch as part of the research. The days were short, five hours at most. We were all able to contribute and pitch, whether it was an article we found or something from personal experience. Everyone was respectful and wonderful. John created a very safe environment and even though he has a very specific vision and he's incredibly focused, he absolutely took in ideas and pitches that resonated with him and the storylines. We also worked very efficiently and ferociously. We broke eight episodes in less than four weeks. I was assigned to co-write episode three with the other staff writer and we were scheduled first in turning our outline in. The process was efficient and inspiring.

Lee: What have been your biggest lessons as you went from emerging to professional?

Moises: It's so important to be ready before you make the big push. There's no point of going around town networking with people if you don't have a stellar script to show for yourself, some sort of validation from the entertainment community (like winning a contest) or actual professional experience. In retrospect, I had many opportunities to break in, which I squandered because I was not ready and equipped with the knowledge and the script to take me through. I didn't worry so much about meeting the right person, instead I worked on my craft and kept myself ready. When Davy Perez asked me to send my writing sample and all the information he needed for him to recommend me to his bosses, I was ready: I had a killer script, I had some traction in my writing career after having signed with a manager and getting a production company attached to produce the pilot, I had won a writing contest and I was ready to talk about myself and who I am as a writer—I was ready. The interview process to get the job at *American Crime* was not daunting, because I was confident about my work and who I am as a person. That takes time and much self-reflection and awareness.

9

TELEVISION

Getting Staffed

Today's Television Landscape

There is no doubt about it: We are currently experiencing the golden age of television. With 409 original scripted programs airing in 2015, and as many as 450 original programs expected to hit the air in 2016, that simple fact can't be argued. We went from 29 scripted shows in 1999 to 409 less than 20 years later. Netflix—one of our outstanding growth examples—went from a big fat donut of hours of original scripted content to 450 hours in just over 2 years. There are more outlets for original episodic content than ever before, with more (Apple and Crackle, just to name a few) coming on board.

While we are in the thick of what FX Network president John Landgraf famously termed PEAK TV, there is also a growing sense that we are in a bubble, and that in the tradition of the tech and real-estate bubbles that came before it, this bubble, too, will burst. The *when* and *how* of it remain somewhat ambiguous, and although the high number of scripted TV shows is expected to—at some point, roughly around 2019—retract, there is anticipation that the number of original scripted shows on the air will remain significant. We will not be dipping below the 400 original scripted programs per year any time soon.

One of the complications born of this explosion in the television sector is that the industry has not been able to keep up with this intensive growth as far as generating competent and experienced showrunners to helm this growing number of shows. While in previous years showrunners traditionally worked their way up the television ladder for years prior to taking charge, today, the number of shows airing or getting ready to air via broadcast networks, cable outlets and digital streamers often outweighs the number of available, seasoned showrunners. Therefore, we are now finding ourselves in a situation in which mid-level producers and show creators are being promoted to showrunners potentially before their time. There have been occasions where the results have been successful; not every first-time showrunner who has not spent years upon years in the room as an upper-level writer is doomed to fail when given the reigns. But, on many occasions, because of the absence of a seasoned showrunner at the helm, some shows don't reach their full potential fast enough, and accordingly get cancelled or lose their viewership's interest before they hit their stride.

It is estimated that in 2015 more than 4,000 television writers were employed, in either writer or producer capacity, in a writers' room. But writers' rooms are also retracting. As Blondie Girl Productions' Ally Latman put it:

> I feel like maybe ten years ago there was a misconception that it was easier to break into TV, and I think now that staffs are smaller and smaller and smaller and there's a lot more shows like *Game Of Thrones* where there are like two people writing all the episodes . . . people realize that it's getting harder and harder as the staffs get smaller and smaller and more auteur driven.

Staffing new writers on television shows has changed and evolved as well. As the number of original scripted programs grew, so did the competition to get staffed on them. More and more writers have come to seek out the consistent and (relatively) stable employment that television has to offer, making getting that very first staff writing gig a challenging proposition.

Jarrod Murray of Epicenter told me:

> As a white male it's very hard to break in right now—unless you're a writer's assistant for a showrunner and getting promoted and getting bumped up to staff writer or you're coming out of the Warner's program. If we're reading something, unless it's the best thing ever, we have to kind of weigh whether we can we sell this person who's never staffed or has no experience other than having a good sample. Is it worth the trouble? You need to know the odds of it going in. You're probably not going to get staffed. It's probably easier for you to sell something as a TV writer having a good original pilot spec, although the need for original pilot specs has kind of died down a bit. We're at the point now where we (at Epicenter) take on people who have some TV experience or who've sold things, who have staffed before or are minorities or who qualify as diverse because that's the only way they're getting hired.

But the growth experienced in this sector over the past decade also brought with it opportunity. Echo Lake's Zadoc Angell brighter outlook on television staffing certainly reflects that:

> I think it's an especially wonderful time for writers who are minorities. There's such a demand at all levels, actually, not just the entry level finally,

for diverse talent. And because we've only cultivated it in limited ways over the last generation of writers, there's still a fairly shallow talent pool of available talent that are diverse and that have great writing and have built up a resume in television. There's just not enough people to sustain the demand right now, so that's a big area to win, and if you are a racial minority of any stripe, there's going to be opportunities. You know I find that there's especially a need for Latino writer talent, and I think as programming becomes more global and diverse, and niche audiences and whatnot, we're just going to have more and more programming aimed at Latinos and Mexican Americans and that kind of thing. So it's a really good time that way.

Staffing new writers has also been complicated by the industry's long-overdue push to diversify its writers' rooms and include writers with varying backgrounds, experiences and points of view. While white males originally dominated the profession (and effectively still do), today, as programing seeks to reach a wider audience, networks and studios are consciously making the push to include unique and varied voices in their writers' room. This is something that manager Mike Woodlief spoke to:

> From FOX, NBC, ABC, 33 percent of new writers have to be diversity or minority or however they phrase it . . . And it's fantastic—it's a wonderful thing. But it's the knee-jerk reaction of: it has to happen right now. You know you can't crack fifty years of bad behavior overnight.

Madhouse Entertainment's Ryan Cunningham talked to me about the demands of staffing a new writer.

> There are a lot of people who want to staff and they don't necessarily have any of those boxes (writing programs, working as writer's assistant, pre-existing relationships with showrunners) checked. They just have a script that they wrote that's good, but it hasn't sold and maybe it's not truly amazing—it isn't lighting the town on fire. Well, then, you've got to go back and write more and more stuff that eventually does make an impact. Otherwise, there are just too many people out there that want to be staffed. Big feature writers crossing over. People who have already been staffed on TV shows. Showrunners that are getting their shows picked up. And if I'm a showrunner that got my show picked up, who am I going to hire on staff? I'm going to hire people who are experienced, my friends that I really trust, or I'm going to hire basically those people or someone who is free, because they come out of a program of some sort. I'm not going to hire a writer who's never sold anything, who hasn't been in a room before—that's a huge risk. For me and for everybody else on the show.

One of the major barriers that new writers encounter when going after their first staffing job is this: they have never been in the room before. They are not familiar with how the room functions. They have likely never boarded an episode, pitched ideas in the room, or broke an episode with a group. They are probably not familiar with story areas, perhaps not as skilled at generating outlines, and potentially unfamiliar with episode one-pagers.

John Zaozirny of Bellevue Productions broke down the differences between working in film and working in television, which easily illustrate the challenge of getting a new writer staffed on their very first show:

> Being a writer in TV is like being a mechanic on a train that is currently in motion whereas being a writer in features is like being a mechanic on a car that's in the shop. You go in, you do the work. If you screwed up your work (on the car in the shop) someone else will go in there and fix your work. But if you screw up your work on the moving train that's going down the tracks, the train might derail, and so they can't take any chances. And so it's much harder to break people in there. But the good news is once you've broken in in television, the momentum tends to keep you going. If you're able to get a second job then you're 'in' essentially at that point.

The Hierarchy of The Room

Although there are exceptions—specifically when talking about shows for which one or two writers do all the writing on every single episode—most television shows are created in a writer's office, otherwise known as The Writers' Room or, quite simply, The Room. The room is where episode and season arcs are mapped out, where storylines are brainstormed, where episodes are broken, where writers go up to "board" their episodes, i.e. put storylines, acts and act breaks up in order to receive feedback from other writers in the room as they go from network story area to outline, from outline to rewrites, from re-written outline to episode.

Every room works differently, each adhering to the unique process that has proven productive over weeks, months and often seasons for the showrunner at the helm. While some shows focus on working—for the better part—in a collaborative environment where writers inhabit a large communal writing space, others situate their writers in individual writer's offices. Whether breaking story on their own at their desks, on beanbags and couches or surrounding a conference table, like any other office environment, The Writers' Room comes complete with its very own organizational chart.

Writers being staffed on a television show for the very first time traditionally come in as Staff Writer, the entry level writing position in the room, unless a previous high-profile pedigree, such as a much-talked-about spec sale on the feature side or a successfully produced project—or projects—are involved, and positioned the writer for a higher level entry point. Additionally, if the writer is also the original creator of the content, he may come into the room at a significantly higher level. A staff writer is not guaranteed their own episode during their employment at this level, and instead is often seen as more of a utility player, helping out higher-level writers with general story breaking, development of specific script acts, outlines, research, etc. on an as-needed basis. In cases where a staff writer receives a co-write (an episode co-written with another writer) or their very own episode (a sole written-by), the writer will not collect episodic writing fees based on contract terms and WGA guidelines. The writer will, however, receive a Written By credit for the episode on the screen, as well as re-run fees should the show have a long life that includes not only in-season repeats, but also licensing and syndication. An entry-level writer is not expected to take on producorial responsibilities such as sitting in on casting sessions or traveling to set to produce their own episode or anyone else's. However, even though WGA rules discourage it, I've seen it happen that a staff writer is ordered to pack their bags and head to set on many occasions.

With each year spent on a particular show, a writer hopes—and aims—to get single level bumps from show season to show season, each year escalating upward through positions, climbing the television writing ladder rung by rung. Many writers cite this as the reason they respond to working in television, besides, of course, the allowance for character development and world exploration facilitated by the format: it has a clear ladder for advancement. You succeed on one level, your show gets renewed, and with any luck you are promoted to the next rung. And while shows can be cancelled, executive producers and showrunners replaced and detours abound, there is indeed a clear path for growth and promotion in writing for television.

For a staff writer, the Story Editor position signifies one level up. While Story Editor is still a lower-level writing position that does include a pay bump and bears much of the same responsibilities as Staff Writer, a Story Editor is eligible for script fees for each produced episode that bears his or her name, either as a sole or co-written credit. The next level up from Story Editor is Executive Story Editor, the last stop on the lower-level writer train.

Mid-level writer positions begin with Co-Producer. As Co-Producer, the writer will not only be expected to participate in the room and deliver his own episodes (with some supervision from upper-level writers, of course), but he is also likely to contribute to casting choices, participate in editing sessions, and go to set for his episode's shoot. From Co-Producer, writers move up to Producer, a shift signified by the permanent appearance of the writer's name in the opening title sequence. Next up in the mid-level range: The position of Supervising Producer. Because supervising producers often supervise lower-level writers, some argue that they are still in the mid-level, while others contend that this position moves them to upper-level writer. Another upper-mid-level position that you may see—usually on procedurals—is Consulting Producer. The Consulting Producer may not be a writing producer, but rather a producer who oversees the technical accuracy of all episodes. Conversely, a Consulting Producer may have a deal with the studio or network behind the show, and therefore installed by them in the room.

And then there's the solid upper level. The higher echelon of television writing, where the responsibilities are plenty, as are the financial rewards. The first rung of the upper level is the Co-Executive Producer, also known as the Co-EP. While there may be more than one Co-EP staffed in a particular room, this is usually the showrunner's second-in-command, taking on some of the day-to-day responsibilities of keeping the show on track, communicating with the network and running the room. The Executive Producer is most often the big kahuna of the show, and on many occasions its creator: the showrunner. The captain of the ship. The person who oversees every aspect and element of the show. Of course, there are exceptions. There have been situations where the creator of the show was too green, and therefore given a Co-EP title while being paired up with a competent, experienced Executive Producer/showrunner in the best interests of the show.

In all of this, it's important to remember that there are also non-writing producers and EPs. These can be producers who are tasked with a lot of directing responsibilities, or producers who are overseeing the show on behalf of the network, and/or from a production perspective.

Getting Into The Room

With the golden age of television upon us, one could imagine that staff writing positions have suddenly become widely available, just waiting for talented new scribes to snatch them up. For good or bad, the reality of television shows, even brand new ones that have only just been announced, is that there is no "Apply Here" button, and most positions—specifically mid-level and upper level ones—are filled long before the show is officially announced. Whether new or returning, as a show gears up to make its pick-up official, showrunners and EPs are busy lining up television talent with whom they've had successful working relationships in the past, with whom they've taken meetings, whose personal story and experiences apply to a character, the world or a storyline and of whom they've become fans. In lieu of those, they are turning to their agents, managers and friends, seeking valuable recommendations for those to include in their writing staff.

In today's television market the competition for writing staff positions is not limited to scribes with previous experience or current aspirations in the television space. Many previously successful feature writers are migrating to this more secure format in light of the retraction being experienced on the spec market front and with writing assignments. These writers may garner almost immediate attention in the television space should they have notable success in the feature writing space already under their belt. As manager John Zaozirny once told me: Features are easier to break into, but harder to sustain a career in, while television is harder to break into, but easier to sustain a career in once you're in.

So how does it happen? How do unknown screenwriters break into television writing? There are those scenarios in which a writing sample or a personal story makes a staffing candidate such a perfect fit for a particular show, that the showrunner will take a chance on a previously unstaffed and untested writer. Such is the case with Screenwriter Spotlight #3 subject Marissa Jo Cerar, who was heavily promoted to the folks staffing up *The Fosters* due to a personal connection she had to the subject matter at hand, and also with Moises Zamora, subject of Screenwriter Spotlight #9, whose personal story and strong writing sample got him staffed on *American Crime*.

In most cases, getting into the room is an achievement pursued by prospective writers for years before they are named to a television writing staff. As Joe Webb, staff writer on *Sleepy Hollow* and the subject of Screenwriter Spotlight #10 said:

> In April 2010, I went on my first date with my wife, and I told her with all confidence that I'd be on a writing staff within the next year. Now, here we are, and by all accounts, my career progress to date has been remarkably steady, and I didn't land my first staff job until April 2015

. . . Five years later. It took THAT long. And this is coming from a writer who had pilots picked up by a major studio for development.

Unless coming in through the television writing programs, which have positioned themselves at the forefront of talent discovery, many aspiring television writers find themselves getting into the room via writer's assistant, showrunner's assistant, room PA and script coordinator positions. While those are not writing positions per se, they are support positions, which often allow the writer to forge meaningful relationships, learn the room's hierarchy and mechanics, and engage in the room's writing process (it is not unheard of to discover a smart PA contributing to a brainstorm, or an assistant doing research for the room), which could in time turn into meaningful opportunities. It's important, however, to remember that those opportunities for promotion do not come quickly; they often take seasons and years to come through. And rarely are individuals promoted directly from a PA, Assistant or Coordinator position to a staff writer opportunity. More often, you will see a PA, Assistant or Script Coordinator who had been able to impress the Co-EP or EP by not only finding ways to contribute but also by going above and beyond at their own job, get offered to write a freelance episode. Shows on broadcast networks require that a number of pre-designated episodes (usually just one or two) are written by a freelance writer every season, depending on the total episodes within the season order. Often, that freelance episode is given to a friend of the EP's or a writer who has left the room, but on occasion a freelance episode may be assigned to a room assistant or coordinator, and viewed as an opportunity to test the waters with in-the-room support staff. By most accounts, the freelance is given to the most tenured individual within the support staff. Think of it as a first-come sort of situation. If the freelance episode turns out to be successful, and the show is not cancelled from one season to the next, and the showrunner who assigned the freelance to the writer on the support staff is friendly to promoting from within, and there is no one else in line for a promotion . . . then the writer granted the freelance may be offered a staff writer position when plans are made for their return in the following television season.

Perhaps Circle of Confusion's Josh Adler explained it best:

> It is absolutely harder to break into television, especially if you're not here. Television is entirely a relationship business. At the very, very base level, if a show is looking for that staff writer level most of the baby writer spots go to either diversity hire for the room or if it's a show that's coming back from a previous season so the writer's assistant on the show gets promoted to that slot. So being an outsider with a script just trying to get a job on one of those shows is very difficult. Most of my clients that work in television started out as writer's assistants or PAs on shows. Again, it's the hard work adage. It takes a long time. Even these young kids who are staff writers that are 28, 29, whatever, they usually spend 7 or 8 years working as an assistant to this guy, an assistant to that guy, room PA, writer's assistant, and then one year they got a freelance episode and then their boss promised them that next season they would get the staff writer slot, and then the show got cancelled. And then they have to start all over again somewhere else, and they spend 6, 7, 8 years doing that before finally they are at the right place at the right time on the right show with the right relationship and get the promotion to staff writer. That's not to downplay what reps do, but in the world of television staffing, that first staffing job usually has more to do with the clients' relationships than the reps' relationships. Because the showrunner on whatever show, he's got his own baby people that he's been grooming as writers assistants and PAs—people that he feels loyal to. What you want to be is one of those guys. One of the guys that the showrunner feels some sense of loyalty to because you were there until 4 am everyday last year on the show, and he feels like he owes you one and he's willing to give you your break. Now, after that, once you've been in a room, you have a job on a show, then it's the reps finding different shows and different opportunities and making phone calls and making introductions to the networks and the studio execs, but that first job is typically the showrunner's choice, and you want to be in a position where that showrunner knows you and wants to choose you.

The bottom line is that once you get into the room, you better know what you are doing. That means having your writing chops down, and understanding how the system works. To this, manager Mike Woodlief said:

> A writer might have pecked out a script all by themselves in the solace of their room. Now you're going into a room with people who do it for a living. They're not going to suffer fools. So you have to have the same level of dedication. And it's a job. It's a twelve-hour-a-day soul-sucking job. And it's a grind. I don't think that's necessarily what everybody realizes.

The Cartel's Evan Corday told me:

> Maybe 12, 15 years ago there was this huge writer's assistant wave—that didn't really happen, when I was a kid. The assistants, or the PAs and script coordinators on shows, that was what you were, nobody looked at you as anything else necessarily. And part of that was because there were 3 networks and 21 hours or primetime and that was it. Now obviously the canvas has changed so dramatically that I think there's certainly more opportunity for more people to break in every year and to come from different areas. So there are script coordinators, there are PAs, there are writers' assistants that are getting bumped every year and sometimes showrunners will give them a script as a trial and then promise them a staff job on the next season, or something like that.

Manager Chris Cook added:

> It's that catch-22 of you can't have a job until you have a job, you know? You can work as an assistant to a producer, an assistant to the showrunner, or a writers' assistant, or a script coordinator, and then before you know it, maybe you can get a freelance. And if that goes well, then next year— if the show is on the air—you can get on staff. TV is more about working with others, working in a room, and because there's less specs, there's more of that groundwork. Now granted, there are people who have written a spec TV pilot and have had the right meeting and gotten in and never knew anybody and got staffed. But that doesn't happen as often.

Once a writer gets into the room—even at the staff writer level—he is expected to hit the ground running. That means that even on the very first day, he should be ready and willing to step up and contribute, pitch ideas and story arcs, and provide research and information that can be mined. But that doesn't mean that a staff writer should take over the show. While arriving ready to go, the staff writer is, for lack of a better term, the lowest on the totem poll. If not asked directly to pitch ideas right out of the gate, it is likely in the writer's best interest to learn the dynamics of the room first, then figure out how to tow the fine line of contributing just enough without taking up too much space in the room. If more senior level writers take the lead, the writer should focus his energy on forging friendships and relationships that will come in handy down the line.

A few things to avoid as a new writer in the room:

- Pitching problems without pitching solutions
- Hijacking pitches
- Interrupting others while they are pitching
- Riding dead pitches
- Providing notes to superiors without a direct request for them
- "Grading" or commenting on the overall quality of others' work
- Boasting about extracurricular activities outside the room
- Complaining when things don't go your way, or when you don't receive the assignments you think you deserve
- Getting involved with the rumor mill
- Tweeting or Facebooking commentary about the room, or anything that could be construed as questionable

Before getting into the room, a writer—new to TV writing as a whole or new to a particular show—should do all the research they can about their EPs and showrunner, learn what they can about their past shows, and—just as importantly—management style. If a writer is joining a show on a 2nd, 3rd, 4th or even 5th season, he should make every effort to study all available episodes of seasons past, and familiarize himself with previous story lines and character arcs, in order to avoid the embarrassing situation in which he steps up and pitches a story that has already been done. If the writer is staffed on a brand new show, he should seek out any source material that served as inspiration, and break down the pilot script every which way.

A new staff writer can be viewed as a utility player, or as a valued story contributor. It really depends on the room. But for the writer to succeed, and specifically if the writer is a diversity hire hoping to have their contract renewed and paid for by the show when his network-subsidized term is up, it is important that he is perceived as the hardest working writer on staff. That means being the first one in, the last one out, always willing to help and contribute, and sometimes—despite himself or what is wrong or right—setting his ego (and sanity) aside in service of his show, showrunner and even fellow writers.

Working Your Way Up: The Benefits

Many writers respond to the idea of working their way up in television. Not only does consistent work allow you to develop your chops, remain employed for at least part of the year depending on your show's episode pick-up and the consequent length of your contract and hopefully graduate from level to level, but it also provides you the opportunity to learn how a show is constructed and what makes it successful from the bottom up. In addition to being paid to write, you are also being compensated to learn on the job how to effectively build and sustain an efficient and professional multi-million dollar endeavor, which ultimately prepares you to one day run your own show.

While some television writers are content writing on shows created by others for life, most would love the opportunity to run their own show down the line. Though there have been cases in which content creators were able to sell their original pilot without working a day in the room and therefore bypass working their way up altogether and go straight to Co-EP or supervising producer level (though usually only with the guidance of a capable, seasoned showrunner at their side) as was the case with Mickey Fisher, creator of *Extant*, many prefer to work their way up and earn their stripes so that they are prepared to run the ship and are trusted by the network, cable outlet or digital streamer when their time comes.

In addition to learning the ins and outs of the job on the job, there are other, more nuanced added benefits to working your way up, rather than getting in at the top. I asked The Cartel's TV Lit Manager Evan Corday to elaborate:

> I think if you want to be a really successful, sought-after, adored showrunner, there are lots of things to learn along the way. How to treat your staff, how to talk to your staff, what the point of no return is. You know, several half-hour executives still want to run their rooms until one o'clock in the morning. And there just never is a healthy return on that. Something that is funny at 2 am, when you're kind of punch drunk, is never gonna be funny at 2 pm the next day, you know? You want to work for somebody who manages to make a 10–6 room completely work, get all the work done, board out this season, send people off to script. And then you have other showrunners who like to 'gangbang scripts' (a term referring to what is usually a late evening call in which the whole writing staff is summoned to bust out a script) and really keep everybody involved.

Evan went on to share with me some of the things you learn working your way up in the room:

> You have to find the style that works for you and you have to find the cadence that works for you in order to deliver your message to other writers. Nothing is more annoying to a writer than getting that vague note of "Act 2 just isn't working", right? Well why isn't Act 2 working? And if it isn't working, is there maybe a suggestion for a fix even if it's not 'the' fix? Really being able to dive into a script and help that writer elevate the material instead of just taking it and rewriting it yourself.

For a little dose of showrunner reality, Evan told me a couple of insightful anecdotes:

> I had a client on one of the most critically acclaimed shows on TV for the run of the show, she's an adult and perfectly capable of taking care of herself, but it astounded a lot of people that the showrunner would take credit on every script. Literally every single script. Over 6 years. You know, he was great in the room and obviously had an amazing show inside of him but there are ways to treat your staff and there are ways not to treat your staff. I was in a situation recently with a client who was the butt of many jokes in a half-hour room and it was a really unpleasant situation and it was a little bit of a mass exodus of the staff and so the showrunner went to one of the senior people and was like, "Why doesn't anybody want to come back?" and the senior person was like, "A, B, C, D, E, F . . . Like, these are things you actually said, in a room full of people." And to his credit the showrunner actually called everybody on the staff and apologized and became a human. I think some showrunners just get lost in the job and don't realize they are treating people in a certain way. And some showrunners don't have the balls to tell their writers that they're not doing a good job. You know, it's the reverse too. Where instead of giving negative notes they'll just take a script and rewrite it instead of being able to, again, articulate to that writer where we need more, where we need less, where the nuance is in this piece. There are some people that can't delegate at all, that need to do everything and they are incapable of running more than one show at a time because everything is important, they need to be in every score, they need to be in every post. And then your writers' room stalls because there are writers sitting waiting for you to approve stories and you're off listening to a song for episode 10 while they need to be writing episode 15 but the story hasn't been approved yet, so then your director comes in and there's no script. So showrunners have many, many ways of doing things—as we all do—and I think part of the beauty, just to bring it all back around, part of the beauty of getting that experience in the room is learning how you want to do it when it's your turn.

The Room: Compensation

Unlike the feature world, where a writer can receive script fees that may range anywhere from a few thousand dollars for a low budget feature—specifically if the writer is non-WGA and a first time writer—all the way up to the hundreds of thousands of dollars or even more if the writer is a WGA member and well-established, in TV, the numbers—at least in the early stages—are a lot more cut and dry. Writers in the room are compensated in two ways: weekly writer's fee, with a minimum set of weeks guaranteed per the contract as well as an option to extend, and script fees, available for Story Editor-level writers and up.

For a thorough compensation breakdown of the various levels of staffed television writers, I turned to Echo Lake's Zadoc Angell:

> Television is where a writer makes a lot of money. So I highly encourage everyone to do it. For a writer, you work your way up the ladder of television. You start out as a staff writer. The Writers Guild minimums for staff writer and story editor increase a little bit every year, but I think right now, the staff writer minimum is around $3,600 per week, usually for a guarantee of 20 weeks. And then once you graduate to story editor in the following season, it's somewhere above $8,000 a week for usually a guarantee of 20 weeks. And then as you move up the ladder and become a producer level person—co-producer, producer, supervising producer, co-executive producer—the rates become negotiable, but can never go below what you were making as a story editor. And so oftentimes, as a co-producer, you might make $14,000 to $16,000 an episode, and then as you move up the ladder, there's executive producers who are making $40–60,000 an episode. So you can make a lot of money, and that's not even counting the scripts that you write when your name is on that script, for which you get anywhere from $20–35,000 depending on whether it's broadcast or basic cable, whether it's half-hour or one hour. But you get paid for that script on top. And then there are residuals when that episode that you wrote repeats on traditional television and on cable television; you'll get residuals and checks that come in the mail for the life of that episode. Which is why if you write like a *Law & Order: SVU* or a show that repeats very well, it makes a lot of money, and it does well overseas. So an episode of a show like that is actually worth quite a lot in the long term.

According to WGA stipulations, a writer's weekly salary, specifically in the Staff Writer, Story Editor or Executive Story Editor categories, which are non-negotiable, varies slightly based on the length of the writer's contract. The longer the contract, the lower the weekly compensation. As network shows can span 24 episodes in a single season, those tend to be longest, ranging 40 weeks and upwards. However, some staff writers are initially contracted only for twenty weeks, with an option for the show to renew the writers' contract for an additional 20 weeks (or "back 20"). While some network shows do have a limited episode order (eight, ten or twelve episodes), the majority of short season orders (ranging from six to twelve episodes per season) can be found on cable and with digital streamers. Therefore, on shows with a smaller episode order, writers are likely to be hired for anything from a 7-week to a 15-week contract, with an option to extend.

However, before getting excited about the handsome weekly pay rate, writers are to remember three things:

1. Agent and manager fees, traditionally 10 percent each, are collected off the top, i.e. before taxes. That means that before the money reaches the writer, taxes and commission fees will be deducted off the top of the weekly sum.
2. In addition to paying taxes as well as agent and manager fees, writers on shows with contracts long enough to grant them entry into the WGA will be expected to pay their hefty WGA initiation fees, as well as their significant quarterly dues.
3. Writing fees are paid for the duration of the contract. Should the writer's contract expire after twenty weeks, there is limited likelihood that the writer will receive another staffing assignment until the following staffing season, if at all. Therefore, while the weekly pay may appear generous, it is made so in order to allow for significant stretches of unemployment, as they are likely to occur.

Positioning Yourself for Television Staffing

If television staffing is where it's at as far as you are concerned, and you don't live in Southern California, the first thing you can do to position yourself for television employment is get thee to Los Angeles. Television is a boots-on-the-ground, all-hands-on-deck sort of deal. You have to be here to build the relationships and make the connections that will one day get you to the promised land. Of course, if you're just at the outset of your writing journey, there is no need to pick up and move before you have a couple of strong writing samples on your hands, the sort of conversation starters that would make all the difference for your television writing career. Instead, stay put on your home turf, write like crazy without having to worry about acclimating and building a new life in a new location, then make your way to Los Angeles once you've got some work you're proud to show.

If comedy television writing is your desired space, supplement your writing with a variety of comedy classes including improv, stand-up and sketch. For comedy writers, training and pedigree are important, and when all things are equal it's often the writer who brings not only the funny pages but also the comedy chops who gets that coveted staff writer position.

Whether aiming to be staffed on a comedy or drama show, consider whether your writing is best suited for network or cable. While you won't necessarily have your pick of what show to get an assistant job or even interview to staff on, you do want to have a firm grip on what's the best fit for your voice. Are you network or cable by nature? Dark or feel-good? Fast paced usually implies network while series with darker, slow-burning, character-driven storytelling usually makes cable and digital outlets the writer's natural home. Once you have an understanding of the writer that you are, be sure to watch everything in the space that you would potentially like to write for. And don't only watch. Read. Get your hands on as many pilot scripts as possible, and get well versed in what is moving in today's market. If you are LA based, be sure to make regular trips to the WGA library to read episodes and catch up on writing styles, pacing and tone sown into the scripts of your favorite shows.

The Cartel's Evan Corday told me:

> In my personal opinion, the basis of all of it is your voice and your uniqueness and what you bring to a script. Because as we all know there have been a freaking hundred medical shows, but when Shonda created 'Shonda-speak', *Grey's Anatomy* took off. When ER created that camera style, ER took off. So what is it that you are bringing to the medical franchise that is unique and different and comes only from you? That's something that you can't learn or trade or buy, ultimately. Your voice is yours. And I always go to the writing first. And then there are plenty of talented writers, so the next thing for me personally, is that personality. Is this somebody that I really want to hang out with and spend time with? And when you're signing a writer you really have to think of all those things because you are going to go pitch them to sit for 14 hours a day in a room with a bunch of other people. So if they're not smart and they're not quick on their feet and they're not sociable and they're not able to handle themselves in that situation then they are not going to get a job. And if they do, they are going to get fired. It's that simple.

Once you are in Los Angeles, start making those all-important connections. You never know where your break or way in will come from, so get friendly with other writers, assistants, anyone and everyone you can find on your path to breaking into the television microcosm. As those job openings are rarely publicized and often go to referrals or recommendations—even at the lowest level of room assistant or room PA—you have to pursue all the relationships available to you and invest genuine time and energy in order to cultivate them. Recently, an emerging TV writer I've been working with was invited to apply for a room assistant job. The invitation came from a UCLA Extension Program classmate, who was an assistant in the room previously. When the assistant was promoted, she was tasked with finding her replacement, and naturally turned to her circle of classmates and valued writing friends. In television more so than any other sector of this industry, this is a relationship based business, so make sure to invest consistent effort into growing your television writing community. The writers in your writing class today (and by class I mean level, whether you meet them in a physical class or networking event) may be working writers in 5 years, and writers in hiring positions in 10. In time, they may become EPs and showrunners, responsible for hiring the writers in the room.

Echo Lake's Zadoc Angell shared:

> The personal is huge. It almost can't be underestimated. We work in a
> people business and because it's television, it's an ongoing longterm
> relationship, not just between agents and managers and our clients, but
> between our writer clients and their fellow TV writers, because TV writers
> hire other TV writers, and between networks and studios, who end up
> working with the same writers year in, year out, from show to show. So
> it's very much a small town kind of community, where you kind of rise
> up with your generation and your class, and then pretty soon you're all
> making television together. So the personal is very important. People have
> to want to invest in you. Other people have to be passionate about you.
> Showrunners have to want to work with you and hang out all day long if
> they have to get that script right. It's a very social business, so the personal
> is really, really important. And a big part of that, that I don't think writers
> always understand, is that you constantly need other people to advocate
> for you. You need your agent, your manager, your lawyer, writers you've
> worked with in the past, showrunners, executives that you meet on general
> meetings—everyone has to advocate for you so that you continue to work
> and continue to get jobs.

But building your community is not enough. You will also have to work on
your television writing, and specifically outlining, chops. Because of the
collaborative nature of television writing as well as its very fast pace, much of
the heavy lifting (writing-wise) happens in the story area, beats and outlining
stage, for which every writer eager to get into the room has to be prepared. So
take classes, read books and explore materials that breakdown television structure
in detail, and begin practicing this on your own work. Weaving in A-, B-, C-
and D-story, creating impactful escalations and satisfying resolutions all while
ingesting powerful act-outs are skills that you have to have down pat.

Perhaps the most important initiative you can take on if staffing on a television
show is your goal is the pursuit of the annual TV writing and mentoring programs. As most writers do not get anywhere close to getting in on their first try,
consider this a multi-year endeavor, and ingest the development of a stand-out
spec for a current show in the current season, one that can easily relate to your
brand, along with a fresh, great pilot and program materials such as personal
statements and essays into your annual writing schedule. While it is true that there
are only a few spots available year over year and that the odds are not great, it
is also true that those who do get in find themselves on something of a staffing
fast track. Although not everyone will get staffed right out of the gate, acceptance
into these programs will instantly increase your viability and desirability factor.

Remember this: landing a television staff writing position is not something
that can or will happen overnight. Therefore, in order to position yourself properly

for staffing on a television show, prepare for the long road ahead, and make ambitious plans to play and thrive in this long but potentially rewarding game.

SCREENWRITER SPOTLIGHT #10: Joe Webb

Joe Webb lives and writes in West Hollywood, CA. He has developed television pilots for Fox, Sony and Fremantle Media, and currently works on the staff of Fox's *Sleepy Hollow*. He is represented by WME and Primary Wave Entertainment.

Lee: Tell me your origin story—who were you before you became a screenwriter?

Joe: In the fall of 2008, I was a third-year doctoral student, and I was about to spend two years of my life writing a 400-page dissertation on American Literature that like twelve people in the world were going to eventually read. And there's nobility in doing that kind of work—but at the same time, I was also writing a pop-culture college advice blog that was getting a couple thousand hits a day, and I really liked having the bigger audience. So I decided to try my hand at a TV pilot—and it was . . . garbage. Like 100 autobiographical pages in Microsoft Word and, literally, there was zero plot—but it gave me the bug. And so I bought a copy of Final Draft, and I read every script I could get my hands on, and I wrote a string of bad pilots (that got progressively better with each try). And then in March of 2009, I was asked to be a contestant on *Jeopardy*, and I won enough money that moving to LA started to seem possible. So that summer, I packed two suitcases and my dog into my shitty Ford Focus, and I drove west to take my shot.

Lee: What brought you out here? And—adding onto that—do you think it's important for television writers to be in Los Angeles?

Joe: I'm from a small town in Illinois—you can actually see cornfields from my childhood bedroom. And then I went to school in Missouri. Needless to say, neither of these places is the ideal location from which to launch an entertainment career. So I moved to LA, which anyone who is serious about writing television ultimately has to do. You don't necessarily need to be in LA while you're learning your craft (there are certainly cheaper places to live), but when it's time to break in, you need a combination of good scripts *and* good connections—and the latter only come from living out here. One caveat though—before you move, have as much money saved as possible and a realistic idea about how you're going to support yourself. You need a day job. Because getting to the point where you can sustain yourself with writing income is going to take a lot longer than you probably think it should. It took me four years in LA before writing became my primary source of income, and I'd say that time frame is probably average (if not a little expedited) among my friendship group.

Lee: Gotta ask . . . Why television?

Joe: Just in terms of having a career and raising a family, there are structural advantages to getting a weekly paycheck. And there are currently way more jobs in TV than in features. According to a study I recently read by FX, there were 409 scripted shows on the air in 2015, which means 409 writing staffs, and in the feature world, there was a grand total of 330 films eligible for this year's Oscars. So TV makes a lot of practical sense as the bedrock of a career. That being said, TV also has an emotional appeal. I mean, you can tell stories on TV that stretch for hours and hours in a way that you can't when you're limited to 110 pages. For instance, there was something deeply magical about watching Jim and Pam fall in love across two full seasons of *The Office* that can't really be replicated in a ninety-minute rom-com.

Lee: Once you decided you wanted to write professionally, what steps did you take to become the best writer you could be?

Joe: Once I decided to go for it, I started treating screenwriting like a job. Grad school had been great for sharpening my writing skills and purging my procrastination habits (academia is too competitive for lazy people to thrive), but the teleplay is its own genre with its own rhythm and rules. So I spent my last six months in St. Louis reading every script I could get my hands on, completing a series of not-great pilot scripts, and trying to reverse engineer episodes of TV by transcribing them into Final Draft and then comparing my draft to the actual script (this was a great, if slightly insane, way to learn efficient action slugs). Once I got to Los Angeles, I made friends with a handful of writers who were better than me (*real* friendships; not "let me ask you for notes ten seconds after meeting you at a cocktail party" friendships), and when they gave me notes, I did my best to listen and learn.

Lee: Tell me about *Books*. How did that web series come to be?

Joe: Six months after moving to LA, one of my friends set me up for coffee with his manager, Brett Etre (who's still my manager today), and Brett got me started on a first round of generals in March 2010. My third meeting was with the fledgling digital division at a giant company called Fremantle Media, and I soft-pitched them an idea about two brothers who inherit their dead Dad's debt to the mob. Fremantle wanted to see a couple pages, so I dashed off a ten-page series bible, which they sent to Tyler Gillett, who signed on to direct the project—and all of the sudden, it was like, "Can you make this thing for 10 grand?" And we said YES. For me, the next year was film school. I wrote a thirty-page script, and with the help of our good friend Kate VanDevender, Tyler and I learned how to produce it on the fly. We ended up shooting for nine days in February 2011—including four days in Bakersfield —with a speaking cast of eighteen and a crew of another dozen, and when the thing was cut together, we had *Books*.

Lee: What inspired you to make a web series?

Joe: Honestly, our goal from the beginning was to make a polished, cable-ready thirty-minute pilot, even if it meant Tyler and I would end up supplementing the production with our own cash (which we did). The web series was a Trojan horse, which is why, if you watch it, the "act breaks" are artificial. Ultimately, I'm not certain how well *Books* works in five-minute chunks—the pacing never feels quite right when I watch the web version. But we've got a twenty-nine-minute cut of the whole pilot that won the Top Drama prize at the 2012 New York Television Festival, and the A.V. Club review said it was "as good as any new pilot on network TV this year"—which is definitely printed out and taped in my scrapbook.

Lee: What sort of doors did *Books* open for you?

Joe: So here's the depressing ending to the *Books* story. Tyler and I spent a year of our lives and thousands of dollars making it, we won three of the four fests we entered, and a national publication praised it effusively, and . . . we never got a single meeting. And in retrospect this was totally my fault. Fremantle's digital division was equipped to sell to networks based on the model of "check out this cool two-minute viral video; wouldn't it make a funny series?" And we gave them a thirty-minute dramedy with Thorstein Veblen jokes. It was a good first lesson in understanding the marketplace. That being said, I'd do it again in a heartbeat—because making *Books* at that larger scale of production was great prep for being on the set of *Sleepy Hollow*. Plus, during post-production, I wrote *Icon*—which was the script that really launched my career.

Lee: What was *Icon* about, and what do you think made it stand out?

Joe: *Icon* was a conspiracy thriller where this dying billionaire orchestrates a series of "miracles" to thrust a reclusive genius into the public spotlight. And on top of being a fast/fun read, it has a lot of twists and interlocking plot gears, which I think is why it jumps from the pile.

Lee: You have been lucky enough to set up a number of shows with FOX. Did those materialize through *Books*, or did it come about completely separately?

Joe: No, in 2011, Brett started sending out *Icon*—and it was clear right away that it was going to open some cool doors for me. During the next year, that script won Silver in the Page Contest, attracted my first agent, attached Jon Amiel as director, got optioned by Sony, and introduced me to Deb Spera and Maria Grasso, who gave really smart notes on the project and got me a ton of network reads. Ultimately, *Icon* didn't sell—(weird note: once you have enough access to pitch a show to networks, it's actually *way* easier to sell them a pitch than a spec)—but when it came time to develop in 2013, I knew I wanted to work with Deb and Maria again. So we took out a con-man project called *Takedown* that sold through 20th to FOX that summer, and I did a good enough job on *Takedown* in 2013 that FOX bought *Chicago* in 2014.

Lee: Could you walk me through the process of pitching a show at the network level? What are the general steps to that journey?

Joe: For most writers, the traditional model starts with a production company. You've probably had a great general there, you've hit it off with the exec, and either they've got a piece of IP that you spark to, or you've gotten them interested in an idea. Next, working with the producer, you take a month or two to flesh out the pitch. Every writer pitches differently—I memorize a twenty-minute story and then perform it like I'm doing the Moth Radio Hour— but once you're ready, you pitch the studio with whom the production company has their deal. If the studio jumps on board, there are more notes, and more rounds of polishing, and then the studio schedules the network pitch meetings. Usually, network pitches start with five minutes of small talk, which is them kindly allowing you to relax a little, but the chit-chat doesn't last long (because they hear a thousand of these things every cycle; and they also have to cover the stuff they've already ordered). Then you get thirty minutes to pitch your heart out and earn your annual paycheck.

Lee: You are represented by WME—how did that relationship come to be?

Joe: So, full disclosure, WME is my second agency—and getting a second agent is a little different than getting a first. But in both cases, my manager Brett was in charge of the early legwork. Basically, once my career was in a place where agents would be interested in signing me, he put out feelers to places that seemed like they might be a good fit, and sent them a script. In both cases, once agencies expressed interest, I sat down for a round of coffee/drinks. And this time around, WME was the obvious fit. Not only did my (soon-to-be) agent Blake already represent Deb and Maria, he was also really good friends with one of my best friends in LA—the same guy who had steered me towards Brett as a manager in the first place. If this all sounds a little familial, that's kind of the point. Careers are built by surrounding yourself with a network of people you trust, and it's not like you have to have those connections in advance. Six years ago, I moved to LA and didn't know a single person; now I have a full life here.

Lee: Could you tell me a bit about how you work with your representation? What do you expect from them, and what do they expect from you?

Joe: I think everyone handles these relationships a little differently; but what I need from my agents and manager is meetings—because meetings represent opportunity. And since quotes in this town are precedential, what I need from my lawyer is for him to fight for every possible cent every time I make a sale. What do they expect from me? I mean, I think they expect me to sell stuff and book gigs. Every time they send me out for something, in the back of my head I know they could have sent another client, so that's pressure. Your representatives need their writers to make money so they can make money. We're friendly, but we're also in business.

Lee: A lot of emerging writers think that everything becomes significantly easier once you have representation—did you find that to be the case?

Joe: Yes, definitely. And it would be disingenuous to claim otherwise. But, at least with agents, the relationship is probably more correlative than causal—they don't have the time or bandwidth to jump on board until you're market-ready. Managers, on the other hand, often get involved sooner and are more willing to spend a few years orchestrating your first round of generals. I think I paid Brett a grand total of 700 dollars in commission during our first three years together. But he was playing the long game, and step-by-step, we were making progress. Without him, I'm not getting the meetings that lead from *Books* to *Icon* to *Takedown*. So to answer the question one more time: *yes*, passionate representation absolutely makes everything easier.

Lee: You are now staffed on *Sleepy Hollow*. How did your staffing opportunity come about?

Joe: Coming off *Chicago*, which was my second script for FOX in two years, I had built a really good relationship with both the studio and network, and everyone wanted to stay in business—but the idea of writing a third straight "close but no cigar" pilot was potentially devastating. So finding a place for me on staff seemed like an obvious solution—provided the showrunner was interested in having me. Looking at the landscape of new and returning shows, *Sleepy Hollow* just made the most sense. I was already a fan of the show, American History is my academic jam, and a lot of the old staff was in the process of rolling onto new projects. So I sat down with (showrunner) Clifton Campbell, we hit it off, and two days later I was in the room.

Lee: What's it like, being staffed on your first show?

Joe: It's awesome. Before *Sleepy Hollow*, I spent six years writing a whole season's worth of Episode Ones. So it's pretty damn exciting thinking about Episodes 32 through 49, which is what we're writing this season. And I'm learning to flex new mental muscles. When I roll into the parking garage at 9, I know I'm going to help shape arcs for a show that millions of people watch all over the world. And then, every so often, I get to write forty-eight pages of that continuing story. Plus, writing pilots can be a lonely process. I really like having awesome co-workers.

Lee: When not in the room, do you find yourself going on a lot of generals? And if so, what are those like?

Joe: Right now, not so much. Other than a few scattered breakfast meetings, this season has been focused on the task at hand. But we're only a month from wrapping the *Sleepy* room, so come February, my calendar is going to get a lot busier. As for the structure, most generals stick to the script of: 1) introductory chit-chat; 2) the writer delivers a quick bio; 3) the writer soft-pitches projects they're working on; 4) the exec tells you about the company and 5) the exec soft-pitches the writer open assignments. That's the template. Every time. And this might sound formulaic, but it only feels that way when the meeting isn't going well. In fact, knowing the pattern in advance actually allows both the writer and exec to have a good time. You're less nervous, and you can have more fun with the interstitial beats, which is where you both get a read on whether or not this could someday turn into a productive working relationship.

Lee: If there was one thing you wish you knew when you got started that you know now, what would it be?

Joe: So I'm going to cheat and give you two. First, I wish I would have better understood how long of a haul it is to break into the business. In April 2010, I went on my first date with my wife, and I told her with all confidence that I'd be on a writing staff within the next year. Now, here we are, and by all accounts, my career progress to date has been remarkably steady, and I didn't land my first staff job until April 2015—five years after that bold declaration. Things just take time in Hollywood to develop, and you've got to be prepared to dig in and keep driving. Second, and this one is more tangible, I wish I had discovered sooner the podcast Stephen J. Cannell recorded with the USC School of Cinematic Arts. Seriously, his message is so damn inspirational— every aspiring TV writer should download it immediately, and then put it on once a week rotation as they commute to and from their day job.

10

SELLING YOUR TELEVISION PILOT

Bypassing The Room: Becoming a Television Content Creator

In today's booming television market, many writers have set their sights on bypassing traditional career-building routes of staffing on television and then working their way up, and instead seek to break in by selling pilots, much as the subject of Screenwriter Spotlight #10 Joe Webb was able to do. But is it really the open and highly accessible playing field everyone is hoping to find? For insights, I turned to my industry colleagues.

The Cartel's Evan Corday shared her insights about the evolution of the space with me:

> I think broadcast is a very different business these days. It's really about the package. I mean you will see people partnering that you can't imagine, you know, John Wells has to go out and get some feature director to get something on the air these days. It's just astounding, when he used to be able to just walk in and sell you a short and that became a show. I think the basic broadcast business is still very driven by the procedural, the soap. And now the package. You've got to have your John Wells, your J.J., some partner that can walk in those doors and say this is the one, this is the special writer, this is the person you have to get to know. Otherwise, you have to come up through the ranks and know all the executives and be able to pitch to a room full of people who are comfortable with you, that trust you, because they're handing you an enormous budget. These days those shows are so expensive. And they're really not for experimentation. CUT TO: The other side, which is cable and digital. Totally the opposite. We've had more people sell pilots that are supervising producer and under than

ever before, and that's really fun and exciting. That is a world where the idea is king. And that used to be on the broadcast side and now it's not. And so I think people are looking to the other side where, again, you can actually go shoot something. Put together a group of friends and shoot a sizzle to go with something. The dearth of anti-hero shows that we've got now never would have happened without your *Breaking Bad*s and your *Dexter*s and stuff like that, that came from cable and now run through digital. Some places are an anomaly. Netflix is not like that at all. They're just not. They want really fancy packages. They want underlying material. Leonardo DiCaprio just sold a kids' book series over there for a children's show because his President of Production has two little kids. That's how that happens. So writer/idea not really. Beau (Willimon) as talented as he is, never gets *House Of Cards* without Kevin Spacey. It just doesn't happen. So Kevin Spacey walks in the door and calls the head of Netflix and there you have it. They're very much the HBO model. Amazon is a little bit in between. Amazon, HULU. Obviously they would love the big package but they also have the other side of the coin, which is that they'll take risks and they'll take chances and they'll buy *Transparent* on a spec and put that together. Jill (Soloway) is a well-known writer but she's not a 6 time Oscar winner or anything. That wasn't a given at all. That's an amazing story. You know, even something like *Orange Is the New Black*, it took Jenji (Kohan) having hits already to be able to do that for them. So Netflix and HBO still are a little bit of their own universe and then there's everybody else. So now, HULU and Crackle and all of those places are spending some real money. AOL is planning to come in. Apple's coming in. So we're going to have a lot of places to sell. What that means in terms of the landscape and how many survive is a whole other story. You know, Amazon and Netflix had success built in already. So we'll see. But there are ways to get original programming on today that certainly didn't exist 10 years ago, even 5 years ago. So for the creator there are plenty of worlds now to just be able to create, you don't have to come up through a staff. But as somebody who manages clients, I personally would still like them to get that experience at some point.

Blondie Girls Productions' Ally Latman had this to say about writers breaking in by selling pilots when I visited her in her office on the Warner Brothers lot:

There's definitely a better market for people who are trying to break in who have a great spec pilot. But I also know that every time I've read a great spec pilot by someone who has no credits or is just really green or brand new or maybe came from features, the first thing is: okay, this is great, but we have to pair them with a showrunner. We have to pair them with someone. You know a baby writer, a brand new writer, a green writer, is not going to sell a show. Every network wants the bells and whistles to come with it. So you have to find a cool, great director or a great showrunner or somebody who's gonna get the project in the door.

While many writers hope to be at the helm of their very first pilot as it is picked up to go to series, this is an unrealistic expectation. To put it simply, the bigger the show, the more significant the network investment. Though writers cite Nic Pizzolatto as an example of one who was able to achieve this, they forget that Nic was staffed on AMC's *The Killing* before he got a greenlight from HBO on *True Detective*.

A more realistic example (though clearly best-case-scenario) is Mickey Fisher, who was plucked from obscurity when his pilot *Extant* won the TrackingB contest and quickly became a hot property. With such heavy hitters as Amblin Entertainment and WME involved in the project, Fisher was paired with Greg Walker, whose previous credits included *Without A Trace*, *X-Files* and *Smallville*, and who was now tasked with running the show, from pitching to networks all the way through to daily operations. In his widely-shared document 'Answers To Questions I've Been Asked,' Mickey Fisher shared that the knowledge that was imparted to him was that the first sold show for a writer is one on which they will learn the job, not one which will be truly theirs. As Fisher shared in this document, that same information was imparted in a WGA workshop for new TV content creators. Fisher said: "Basically they tell you (I've heard) that this first show isn't really your show. Your show is the next one. For this first one, your job is to help the Showrunner keep his/her job and be as helpful as possible in general."

But despite the boon of earlier years, where—for a minute—it seemed like anyone could sell a pilot, Echo Lake's Zadoc Angell is not a fan of new writers setting their sights on selling a pilot:

> It kills me when writers are just so focused on: how can I write a pilot that can sell? The likelihood of that happening is so low. And here's why it's low: in the feature world, the writer is not king. If it's a beautiful screenplay, that's all a studio really needs to acquire. They can buy it out from you. They don't care if you live in LA or Montana if the script is amazing so they acquire it, then they can have traditional Hollywood screenwriters do the rewrites for them, throw on a big director who's going to make it his vision, go cast it, shoot it, and the writer is totally out of the process. In TV, if you buy a pilot from a writer, you're buying that writer's vision, not just for one episode, but hopefully for 100 episodes. So you're investing in that writer in a much bigger way, and it's a long-term ongoing relationship. So that's why just writing a great pilot and hoping it will sell is sort of limited in its thinking, because they're not just looking to throw a bunch of great pilot scripts into development and see what happens, they're

looking to invest in writers that they believe in and who they think have a vision for the long term and that they can see executing that vision week to week. So I actually think a lot of wonderful spec pilot scripts don't sell not because they're not great, but because the writer is too junior and the networks are just risk-averse. They just don't have the confidence that that person can execute it over and over again because they haven't staffed, they don't have credibility, they're not a showrunner—because it's a multi-million dollar investment in one person's vision.

Zadoc went on to tell me:

If you're a totally green writer without any credits, selling a pilot script is very unrealistic. It's best if you don't think that way. Because if you worry about writing something that you think for sure will sell—something super commercial—you're probably not going to write something special and distinctive and that is uniquely you. And you also have to think, in a business where we live on ideas, the most commercial ideas they're hearing all the time are from big writers, writers that are already in the system. And they're going to buy from those writers because they're proven or they're already paying them under an overall deal or they've already had them write a movie for them in the past. They're going to go with known goods. So if they're going to buy a spec pilot from a complete unknown, it has to be something that's so special, that's so unique, that a regular writer working within the system wouldn't have come up with it. So that's actually empowering, I think, to new writers coming up through the system. Write something special! Write that script you're afraid of. Write from your personal life story. Tell the story that no one else can. You don't have to reinvent the wheel, you just have to tell it in your way and execute it in a way that only you can do. And that's—that should be empowering. And the beauty of writing for television, especially in the beginning is that you're also using it as a writing sample to staff on a new series or an existing series. Showrunners rarely hire people who write the exact same thing that they wrote. They usually want to hire writers who maybe have a darker voice than their pilot does or bring an edgier element to it than they have, or they just want to hire writers who have great, unique voices for their writing staff. It's not necessarily an apples to apples equation when you're hiring writers for a staff, and that should be freeing.

Manager Mike Woodlief agrees that for an unknown writer, selling a pilot is not going to be easy.

Frankly, it's nearly impossible. I mean, sure there's a 1 percent chance but the boom into TV has just meant that it's the rich getting richer. So you're taking all of the writers that used to be on the HBO list, who are now developing for Crackle. And so you have a glut of material and you have everybody writing pilots on spec. Brian Fuller wrote his first three projects on spec. You have to have a niche if you're getting started. Everyone is consolidating right now into the TV world. There is so much material in there, from people that are going to blow you away. And WME is in that business and CAA and UTA and ICM are there in that business because they package. There is no more development. WME comes in and goes "here, it might be a junior writer, but we packaged him with the showrunner, in this pod that we represent with this director we've already got this talent attached." Green light. Then you see a notice on it like "we developed this material for years." No. That's where the agencies are earning their packaging fee and quite frankly with all those elements they're probably losing money in commissions. Because the packaging fees have been capped at 3 percent.

Jennifer Au of Untitled Entertainment had this advice for writers eager to become television content creators some day:

> For any writer who wants to become a showrunner, it's important that they are aware and thinking about how to become producorial because that's not a skill that everyone possesses. But what you need more on the television side than the feature side is ultimately to be able to run that room, to deal with the politics. That is something that people aren't necessarily prepared for. There are skills that people innately have—it's being left- and right-brained. But also it's about taking a step back from (if you want to say) the microscope. If you're looking at the page—at your own work—you know, that is one thing. But if you're a showrunner, you take a step back, and you look at the room. You step back, you look at the studio, the network, all of the connections, and you are the epicenter. So I think the first thing that you can do is start educating yourself about the web surrounding you, so to speak. You want to be looking at the players—who's involved, the power dynamics, where you are, and that's different for everything. But it's really about honing those skills in yourself.

Jennifer also had this to add:

> A new writer selling a pilot is tricky. And you'll always be partnered with someone who is more senior to you—and that attachment process is similar to the attachment process in features—and that is a roll of the dice. Do you get the right person at the right time? Is there someone meaningful enough? The attachment game is tricky because there are levels, right? And I think that there are some people who matter to everywhere. It's going

to be, Wow! I will take something from this person in a heartbeat. And then the lower you get down on that list, some people have an in some places, others don't, maybe there's a tricky development thing over here and that place is untouchable now, and then you have someone attached to your show who doesn't matter. So sometimes you want to go into somewhere clean and have the buyers dictate that conversation of, "Okay great, we would buy this. Here's a list of ten people we want in it." But a lot of times, people just want the package. Then they'll tell you yay or nay, but you've already had to do the legwork. And, you know, we cut development in this town after the strike. And development, your R&D, is the backbone of any industry or business. And when you do that, it changes the infrastructure. So it's become trickier because you have to thread the needle so much on your own.

Ryan Saul of APA felt strongly that it's not out of the question for a new writer to sell a pilot in today's industry climate.

If it's on the page you can sell it, as long as it's not an idea that's already been done. I'm running into that with a script right now that's kind of in the tone of *Dexter*. Great script but *Dexter* is still in the zeitgeist. That's kind of the problem with the way we watch shows now. If I want *Dexter* I'll go watch *Dexter*. I don't have to go buy the DVD set. I'm just gonna go to Netflix and find season 4 and binge watch. So it's always there. If you want *Dexter*, you've got *Dexter*. I have a playwright and he created this series—he created this project called *Sold* and it took place in the high-end auction world and it became *The Art of More* on Crackle where he's the executive producer. Now off of that he just set up another project at NBC. He's a little older and he has more of a reputation being a playwright but that came out of a great script. It took us a year, year and a half to really put that one together but once the actors started coming in then we got the project going.

Jeff Portnoy of Bellevue Productions contributed:

If you have no staffing credits and no TV credits and you get representation and you write a great pilot, then your manager and/or agent, it's their responsibility to go out there and try to find a producer for that piece of material. And hopefully the producer will bring it into a studio, get it set up at a studio, and together with the studio find a showrunner and then bring the whole package into the network and sell it as a show. In which case the writer would get a 'created by' credit, they'd be a creator of the show and they would be staffing on their own show and working hand-in-hand as a protégé to the showrunner and getting a great amount of experience. Those are few and far between but it does happen from time to time.

Jeff also added:

> The networks typically won't buy a series unless a showrunner is attached because, with feature films, in the screenplay essentially all the work is done, if they like the screenplay, the whole project is right there. But with a TV series the pilot's just the first of many episodes. It's just the beginning of the creative process. So they don't typically buy them and order them to series without the showrunner who's got years of experience running a show and hiring writer's rooms and producing.

Jarrod Murray of Epicenter once again emphasized attachments, attachments, attachments:

> I find it's all about attaching that element that studios and networks want to be in business with who are buying shows. Look at all the shows that are on right now. Shonda Rhimes can sell this cup of coffee, you know? And it's already five seasons in. So it's trying to find those partners that are going to help us sell it because we've learned early on that no matter how good an idea is, no matter how good your writer is, unless it's someone—and not just us—bringing the studio the content whom they trust and who they've worked with in the past—that's important to them. Whether it's Dan Jinx or Kurtzman Orci, you have to be strategic about who you partner up with. We learned that early on. Our first pilot was, we were one-for-one with Jon Turtletaub, and that was a spec pilot. We sold it to CBS and they subsequently rewrote it and turned it into something else entirely. It was a good experience for the writer but even then they paired him up with a showrunner type who co-wrote it with him. *Mr. Robot* was a feature. It started off as a feature and I think that's a good example of someone who doesn't have that experience working his way up on a show, but who's voice is reflected entirely in the show. Now he's directing every episode this season. But, it was Anonymous Content—they're the producers –who were championing him.

About the current climate for selling pilots, Jarrod said:

> In 2014–2015 it was the year of the spec pilot and people were more open. I don't know if it's a confluence of network having a lot of material and a few of these things not working or . . . True Detective was a big package and you see the proof in the script. Is this resistance to pilots a backlash because of *True Detective*? Nic Pizzollato was a relatively new TV writer

who got a lot of power very quickly. Are people resistant to that now? I don't know. Also, networks are anti-period right now. There's another project we have that we have a showrunner on that we can't sell that's period that's about the first integrated neighborhood in Birmingham pre-Selma. But the response is, we have our civil rights thing. Any reason that anyone can give you to not buy something, they'll give you. So the trick is to try to make it as undeniable as possible. The trick is being as prepared as possible and hopefully you're able to control who you're partnering with and finding out whether or not networks want to be in business with your partners and making your pitch as good as possible. Doing any research, knowing if there's anything like this out there.

Constructing Your Show

A pilot script is not just a pilot script. It is—just as importantly—the prototype for the show that you are proposing. As Blondie Girl Productions' Ally Latman put it:

> Before we go to studio or network, we want to make sure that the idea seems like it's going to be viable beyond the pilot. And you can tell a lot from a spec script. If one of my biggest questions when I finish reading a pilot is, "What is the series?" then it's not a successful spec pilot.

Indeed, one of the comments I hear most often from consultants, reps and executives is that although they may like the pilot, they just don't see the show or how it will sustain over multiple seasons of programming.

Your pilot is not a stand-alone project. If done well, it will not only sow the seeds for the series to come, but also display the storytelling mechanisms you seek to deploy week to week on your show. Therefore, whether a premise pilot or a non-premise pilot, the show's launching episode has a lot to accomplish: it has to tell comprehensive A-, B-, C- (and often D- and E-) stories contained within the episode, complete with set up of goals, escalations, low points and resolutions, and also sow the seeds for the series to come, as well as set up our world, our main characters and their unique struggles or wounds, the show's engine and the core conflicts that we expect to explore episode after episode and even season over season. While your pilot has to be focused, it also has to provide a gateway into a world and characters that can grow and evolve into many television seasons. Not a short order!

I will not waste your time here preaching how exactly to execute the perfect pilot. Frankly, a single chapter in any book just won't do—this is something that serious writers learn and perfect over years of engagement in the craft. If you check out your nearest bookstore or your online book sellers, you will quickly realize that many books have already been written on this very subject, and more are being published every year as the television landscape, and the way in which we tell stories episodically, continues to shift and evolve.

To be perfectly honest, to me pilot writing is the most demanding and rigorous writing format there is out there. While fifteen years ago it was nearly unheard of for a writer not already established in the television space to write an original pilot, today, more and more writers are coming into the episodic space. The search for great content is intensifying as agents, managers, executives and producers seek out the sort of stellar, promising work that will stand head and shoulders above the rest. Therefore, pilot writing—because of all of its expectations and demands—is something that should be carefully studied. While previously television was produced by a select few, today the industry at large has grown wise, and learned to understand what to expect from a television pilot, much as it knew how to identify a good feature spec in the 1990s. So be sure to read books by Jen Grisanti, William Rabkin, Pam Douglas, Ellen Sandler, Kam Miller and the like, read other pilot scripts regularly, and take classes whenever and wherever those are available in order to begin to learn everything you need to know in order to generate an exciting, structurally-sound pilot. For the record: I am a firm believer that your television writing craft is something that should contentiously be developed over time. In fact, during hiatus, many of my working television writers tend to take television writing classes, in order to keep their craft evolving and their skills sharp. Additionally, many writers find that analyzing pilots and even speccing the occasional episode of an existing show is a good way to get a grasp on pilot writing—although, due to the limited audience for spec scripts, this should be done on a schedule and never ad nauseam.

Your pilot should set up the show, and clearly outline what it offers moving forward: a case-of-the-week procedural (such as *Blindspot* or *CSI)* a case-of-the-season (such as *The Killing* or *Damages*), or a serialized drama (such as *Breaking Bad*, *Orange Is The New Black*, *Bates Motel*, *Mr. Robot*, *The Path* and *Bloodline*). While many procedurals will have over-arching seasonal storylines (most recently seen in shows such as *The Good Wife*, *The Black List* and *House*), pilots for such shows are often tasked with setting up the world as well as delivering a "mini-case" emblematic of episodes to come. But make no mistake about it: Whatever you sow into your pilot is going to set the format for the show to come.

If you use specific mechanisms within your pilot, such as flashbacks or flash forwards, sectioned character-driven storylines, voice overs, or even teasers or tags adhering to a specific structure, expect to make a case for how those will be utilized, and remain fresh, in future episodes. Therefore: If you use flashbacks in your pilot, get ready to speak to how you will use flashbacks throughout the season. If you use voice over in your pilot, get ready to explain how it will not get annoying when viewers binge twelve episodes back-to-back. Of course, some such mechanisms can change over time: In its first season, *Sex and the City* included straight-to-camera, man-on-the-street commentary about that week's episode subject, but by Season 2, that device had been eradicated. To put it simply, every device you choose to utilize in your pilot should have clear and long-lasting purpose. It shouldn't be a stylistic choice, it should be a long-term storytelling choice. After all, your pilot is a starting point for what will hopefully become a long and prolific show.

In addition to delivering a strong pilot, many writers are asked by their reps—or later by the studio or network—to deliver a series doc (which may also be called a series deck) or else a more traditional bible before the pilot goes out to the marketplace. This document outlines where this series is going, not only over a few episodes but over multiple seasons in order to provide the executive reading the material with a more complete breakdown of the writer's vision for what the show is about, from its unique world to its layered and dimensional cast of characters, to what are its driving thematic principles, and how one should expect it to progress not only from episode to episode but also from season to season. If you have done your job right, in most cases this will have been figured out long before you sat down to write your pilot. While seasonal storylines may evolve and change over the course of time, the crux of the show and what is driving it should have been established in brainstorming and outlines.

Most importantly, remember that although you are presenting—and potentially pitching—an original pilot, what you really are selling is a show, and your vision for how to keep it fresh, interesting and exciting over multiple seasons. Television is a rigid format—every character, every storyline, every bit of your world must serve a greater purpose, feeding into the whole of the show. Pilots that have done this successfully have included such masterpieces as the *Breaking Bad* pilot, which sets up a show about a man who gets in over his head and yet gets away with it time and again because he is constantly underestimated, as well as more recent staples such as *The Night Manager*, *Mr. Robot* and *Unreal*.

Should you be so lucky to find yourself on the verge of a sale, keep in mind that the network is not only buying the document at hand, they are buying you: your vision, your ideas, your clarity and creativity for the project, even if those are then entrusted to a more experienced showrunner. Therefore, the material you present has to be original and carefully thought out in order to give it a real shot at going from script to a pilot, or even a series.

Pilot Pitch Meetings

Writers already established in the television space may be able to bypass having to write out the entire pilot, and instead go directly to pitch meetings. During such meetings, writers are expected to pitch the beat-by-beat of the pilot itself if not every moment and nuance (a pitch usually lasts anywhere from twenty to thirty minutes), while also delivering a comprehensive overview of the show starting with the world and characters at play, as well as the overall vision detailing the material's narrative progression over seasons. The rule is that the more known the entity pitching, the more loose the pitch itself can be. In general, these pitches are carefully mapped out and rehearsed, putting all of the writers' storytelling skills on display. Some writers go in with a vision board or a pitch deck in hand; others prefer to go in "bare," with nothing but a powerful story to make their case. Oftentimes, a writer will be invited in to pitch more than once; while the first pitch may be to a VP or development executive, a second pitch may be presented to company heads for final signs offs.

For new writers who have written the pilot before the concept is introduced to the space, the situation may be a bit different: while the executive with whom they are meeting had likely already read the pilot script itself, they are now invited to pitch the show, and speak about their long-term vision for the material at hand. At the end of the day, television shows are all about characters and world. Therefore, the writer may opt to speak to a specific character's evolution over multiple seasons, or the growth and development of the unique world in which a show will take place. But through and through this is where the writer will put his vision, and his strong feel for the work at hand, on parade.

Blondie Girl Productions' Ally Latman cautioned:

> Pitches are no longer enough, because you hear "pitch" and you want to know, well, okay, it's a great pitch, but I want to know that this can be executed well. So people are just executing it from the start (i.e. writing the pilot) instead of pitching it.

Echo Lake's Zadoc Angell shared his perspective about what goes down with a pilot pitch scenario, from pitch to pick up:

> You take the pitch, you work out the idea, and then you try to marry that to auspices that could help build the so-called package around it. So if the pitch is ready I would have the writer usually meet with a bunch of producers that are meaningful in television, maybe a director, maybe an actor that we think is perfect for the role. But you try to find other elements you can bring onto the idea so that when you take it out to buyers, it's not just one writer in a room—although I have sold those, too. But it helps if there's more layers on it. It's just more people believing in the idea and saying, when they walk into a network, "We believe in this, we all think it's great, you should, too." So then once you get the producer on board, or your director or some attachment, traditionally you go to a studio and try to make a deal.

Which, if you ask me, sounds a lot like the packaging that's happening on the feature side of things.

The Cartel's Evan Corday had this advice:

> I have actually had clients in the past take an acting class. I think that if you don't believe it, why is the buyer going to believe it? If you're not

passionate about it, why are they going to be passionate about it? You have to be able to say, this is why I have to get on the air, this voice has to be heard, this point of view has to come across. Half hours are a little bit different. But in the hour side, either you've found a new way to combat something, again that cop show that falls from space, or you know, the legal show that has a spin. And I think that as the writer in a room, you've got to be able to get all that across. You have to be able to sell the person sitting across from you not only on you but also on the actual idea. And most of the time you have to be a little bit flexible. It's very tough to get 100 percent of what you want to get across, across. And there, again, cable/digital are places where you can go the indie route and do it exactly how you want to do it and if people see it, great. Broadcast: it's not gonna work that way. But my actors are the best pitchers. Not even a question.

Jarrod Murray of Epicenter also shared insights from his client's experience in the pitching realm:

> I have a client who sold two pilots the year before—one to CBS, one to CW and neither one got picked up but he went out with another one this year that we thought was a great idea. It's kind of like Party of Five meets Bloodline. We partnered with Amblin but we took a bunch of meetings at various production companies trying to figure out who is the best fit for him. This guy is like, ace pitcher in a pitch scenario. He's a beast. He's so good and he treats it like a performance. He rehearses it like a performance 2, 3 times a day until it's second nature. It's not enough that you're coming in with this good idea, you have to really sell it. He does this whole board that he spends his own money on and as he introduced his characters he'll Velcro them up to the board. I think probably the biggest thing that trips execs up in a pitch is keeping track of all the characters, and this alleviates some of that.

Any pitch scenario, whether pitching the series or the show itself, is the writer's opportunity to excite and inspire others to get on board with him. The key to success is not only knowing the work and feeling passionate about it, but also being able to communicate that passion to others in a clear, focused fashion that—hopefully—provokes them into action. Incidentally, many of these skills will come into play both in the room and in a general meeting scenario.

The Anatomy of Setting Up a Pilot

Once there is "buy-in" for your show . . . What happens next? How does it go from being just a script, or an elaborate pitch tied to a great deal of hope, to getting picked up?

First, it's important to understand the various roles that the entities involved—production companies, studios and networks—play. Blondie Girl Productions' Ally Latman explained:

> If you're at a studio, let's say you're at Warner Brothers, they will work with the writer, get the pilot into really good shape. Sometimes there's no studio. Sometimes it's just a production company. But let's say there's a studio. The studio is the one that makes all the calls to the networks to get your project heard. They form relationships so they can call and be seen and be like, I have a show about this, and NBC says: "Great, bring it in." The studio is critical in that part—in heading off any possible things that will turn off a network. They're really there to be the cheerleaders and to mold the pilot into the perfect show before it ever gets into a network room to be pitched. And then going forward in the series, it's sort of the same thing. The studio is the first stop before it goes to network. Networks are the buyers, studios and production companies are the sellers.

Madhouse Entertainment's Ryan Cunningham also broke it down:

> In television, you're selling your project to a studio who then shops it to multiple distributors (that are called networks, of course). So you have more layers you're going through. And separate from that, it's a little bit riskier buying a TV show from an unknown, because if the show gets picked up and goes, they're not buying a one-off project, they're buying essentially a business they want to open for five or six years. And you've got to have the right people to know how to run that business, which is the TV show, to make it sustain.

The writer's agent and/or manager will likely determine where to take the material to first. If there are pre-existing relationships at studios, that will likely be the material's first destination. Or, if a high value attachment such as a showrunner or producer who has a deal at a studio or network has come on board at the outset of the project's lifecycle that again will likely be where the material is taken first. In lieu of those, the reps will likely take the writer's new pilot out to the existing fan base, or else use the material to forge new relationships on the writer's behalf in the material's corresponding space. After a round of reads, the writer takes meetings with companies and executives who have expressed interest in the work. During those meetings, the writer may elaborate in more detail about his grander vision for the work, while executives may share any notes or suggestions they might have, which could entail minor fixes or major re-direction. With any luck, more than one producing entity becomes interested, allowing the writer and his team a choice in partner that would best support their vision for the work. During this time, the writer will be in close communication with the rep, and any decision should be made in harmony. Then, a strategy is set, identifying whether to go straight to a studio or network, or vie for meaningful attachments first. In all likelihood companies with studio deals will be approached first. After all, these are the companies that the studio already wants to be in business with. From there, the writer can hope that the studio will bring his project into development.

Echo Lake's Zadoc Angell shared his insights about what happens when a studio comes aboard the pilot:

> It's a lot of hoops from there. The script goes into development, often competing against a bunch of other scripts that the same studio has in development, so you are in competition the whole time. And then the networks will develop a batch of scripts, and then they'll decide which of those they want to shoot and actually produce as pilots. Sometimes they pick things up straight to series, but still more often, they shoot a pilot. And then you get a pilot pickup—hooray, hooray, hooray, you're going into production! At that point, as a writer, you still might be doing some small rewrites on the pilot script, but you really shift from being just a TV writer to becoming a TV producer. And at that point, you're going into casting sessions and you're hiring a director and you're going location scouting and you're meeting with line producers, and your show is going into production and you have to wear different hats. And then your pilot shoots, you're on set, you're doing rewrites, you're working with actors, you're working with the director to create the best creative product possible. Once the shoot is done, you go into post, and then you have to deliver a cut to the studio and then a cut to the network, and then the network will test their pilots that are in contention and decide which of those pilots they want to pick up to series.

Zadoc went on to tell me:

> Oftentimes, there is a sort of step before they pick up their pilots to series where the ones that they're seriously considering, they will go to the writer/creators and ask them to tell them where the show is going—give us your episode ideas for season one. Tell us how the season ends. Sometimes the writer has done that work a lot earlier in the process, but it can be a bit of a curveball at the tail end of the process, and you have to have that vision and have those ideas about where the show is going beforehand so that you're not blindsided by that. It only makes sense that they want to make sure there's a plan of where the show is going because they and the audience have been burned in the past. So they try to head that off at the pass.

It's important to remember that what Zadoc speaks to above is very much a blue sky scenario, in which your show is one of the lucky few to not only get picked up to pilot, but also go all the way to series. But at every stage of the game, things might not go as planned: You may get a studio on board, but then not get any bites from network. You may get bites from network to go into development, but never end up shooting the pilot. You may even shoot the pilot but then not get picked up for the season. In short, nothing is guaranteed. It's been said that 5,000 pitches produce 500 viable scripts; 500 viable scripts produce 20 viable pilots; 50 viable pilots produce 25 new shows, and of those 25 shows, 2 go on to a successful run.

What is important to note is that television is a microcosm in which you fail up. Even if you had a show in development at the studio level that never got any bites from network, with your next outstanding pilot you are likely to get that much more interest as you've already established your capacity in the past.

Selling a Pilot: Financial Expectations

While every emerging TV writer with a great new pilot on his hands hopes to get a sale, not every writer has a clear understanding of what that sale would mean in financial terms. Like everything else in television, making big money on your pilot is very much a long game. You may end up doing work for free up front if a standard If/Come deal is in place, only to reap the rewards later in the process. But what sort of money are we talking about?

Here's what Zadoc Angell of Echo Lake had to say:

> In pilot writing, if you sell a pilot in development, you're usually paid somewhere between, on the lowest end, like $25,000, or on the higher end, I would say $150,000 for that pilot script. I mean, there are some writers who are premium writers that are getting paid $300,000 or $400,000 to write a pilot script, depending on their cache in the business. So you're paid to write the pilot script and then if that goes into production, pilot production, you're paid a pilot producing fee for your producing services on that, which might be, I'd say $20–50,000. And then when it goes to series, you're paid per episode as a producer on the series. At the lowest I've ever seen, if you create a show but you really have no credits, you're probably going to be a supervising producer on your own show that you created. Normally even green, young writers get co-executive producer, but getting that executive producer credit title on a series that you created is hard to do unless you've already achieved like a supervising producer or co-ep level through traditional staffing.

However, selling a pilot is not the writer's only path to TV compensation outside of staffing on a show. Another path to financial reward is cutting a studio or network deal for the development of a new agreed-upon pilot. I asked The Cartel's Evan Corday about the "Blinds" or "Blind Deals" we often hear about:

> There's two meanings now. It used to be a pretty cut and dry situation where a studio wanted to be in business with a writer, they didn't have a

show to put them on and so they would negotiate this blind deal. The writer would get paid to write something that both parties agreed on. So typically the studio pitches you 3 ideas, you pitch them 3 ideas, out of those 6 everybody likes something enough that that becomes the thing and they basically pay you to write an original spec pilot of. And then they own it, to be able to take it out or to be able to put it together as a television show. That still happens. The bad news is, let's say 8 times out of 10 these days they are going to be an If/Come deal. That means that you go through the whole negotiation just the same but the money isn't guaranteed. That means that you have to go set the pilot up at a third party, at the network, or at the digital or cable company, or whatever it is, to be able to get paid. So you'll still have to do all the work to come up with the pitch and all that kind of stuff and make your lawyer or your agent or whatever go through all the steps of making the deal but the money's not guaranteed.

To break it down further: unlike a Blind Deal, with an If/Come deal the project usually originates with the writer, and the studio comes on board to provide support as the material is developed and prepared to take out to buyers. Additionally, in an If/Come deal, no money changes hands unless and until a buyer comes to the table. As long as the material originates with the writer, the rights to the material will likely remain with him should the studio decide to pull its support or cease the selling effort, unless otherwise negotiated. However, if the concept originates with the studio or production company, then the rights to the material remain with the originating entity even after all buyer options have been exhausted. This is similar to a speculative writing assignment, or a situation in which a writer develops an original screenplay or pilot from an idea given to him by representation, a producer, or a production entity. Even if the writer and the producing entity part ways, the producing entity will likely remain attached to the material as producer, if not retain the rights to the material altogether.

At a higher level, television deals for writers include:

• OVERALL DEALS—these deals are usually forged between the studio or network and a showrunner or EP, where the content creator (in the caliber of a Vince Gilligan, Kurt Sutter, Matt Weiner) signs a deal under which he is obligated to bring anything and everything he is developing to their studio, and work on it under the studio umbrella. Overall Deals are also known as PODS (Production Overall Deals). These deals are lucrative for the content creators, who often collect an upfront fee, an annual fee and additional writing and production fees for anything the studio picks up during the term of the deal. Additionally, the content creator is likely to receive funds for overhead costs, and potentially on-the-lot office space. As the studio is eager to foster and cement its relationship with the sought-after content creator, it is incentivized to help the deal holder develop, package and sell his shows. If the studio rejects every single show the showrunner presents, then the showrunner is likely to pack his bags once the deal has lapsed, and go make a home at a studio friendlier to his storytelling sensibilities and overall brand.

- FIRST LOOK DEALS—Ordinarily, a content creator or production company can have a single deal with a major entity, or multiple deals for work done in different spaces. For example, Bad Robot has its feature deal with Paramount, and a TV deal with Warner Bros. In such a deal, the production entity receives annual funds to cover all or some of its overhead costs, may receive on-the-lot privileges and offices, and in return make the studio with which they made their deal the first destination for any new project it is looking to develop. Unlike Overall Deals, content creators and production companies holding a First Look Deal are allowed to shop their projects elsewhere should their home studio or network reject it. However, many holders of a First Look Deal tend to develop material with their specific deal partner in mind as their home studio is incentivized to give priority to any of their projects in order to justify the significant cost of the deal and preserve a prestigious relationship.

SCREENWRITER SPOTLIGHT #11: Barbara Curry

Barbara Curry holds an MFA in Screenwriting from UCLA and a JD from Northwestern University School of Law. Her produced writing credits include the feature film *The Boy Next Door*, starring Jennifer Lopez, and the television movie *Anything But Love*, starring Erika Christensen. She was hired by Fox 2000 to write the feature film *The Jury*, yet to be released, and by Screen Gems to rewrite the feature film *The Perfect Guy*, starring Michael Ealy. Most recently, Barbara sold her legal drama *Reversible Error* to NBC with Chri Morgan attached to produce. Barbara is represented by APA and Heroes & Villains.

Prior to becoming a screenwriter, Curry spent nearly ten years at the United States Attorney's Office in Los Angeles as an Assistant U.S. Attorney in the Major Violent Crimes Unit where she prosecuted federal crimes such as murder-for-hire, prison murder, racketeering, arson, kidnapping, bank robbery, money laundering, conspiracy and fraud. She also taught Advance Trial Advocacy at the U.S. Department of Justice in Washington, D.C. and at the FBI Headquarters in Quantico, Virginia.

Lee: Before you became a screenwriter, you were a federal prosecutor. What inspired you to pivot into screenwriting?

Barbara: I didn't intend to quit law to become a writer. I had two children while I was at the U.S. Attorney's Office and as they got older, I felt they needed me more and more at home. But the law is a jealous mistress, as they say, and working twelve hours or more a day left me little time for family. I decided to take a break from practicing law to consider my options, fully intending to go back once the children became a little more independent. But while I was at home, a funny thing happened: I realized I loved being with them and that practicing law would never be a career that would allow me the freedom and time to be the kind of mother I wanted to be. I knew there had to be something else I could do. And that's when I discovered writing.

Lee: Interestingly, you are not the only writer profiled in this book who was a lawyer before she was a successful screenwriter. Is there a connection between being a good litigator and being a good screenwriter?

Barbara: It's funny you ask that because I recently sat on a panel for the American Bar Association where the topic of discussion was entitled "Using the Art of Storytelling to Frame Your Case." I think litigators, especially trial lawyers, recognize that it's their job to fit the evidence into a believable plot and then to shape the plot and its outcome by choosing which facts to emphasize, how much weight those facts should be given, and the meaning that should be derived from them. If you read the closing arguments of famous, well-regarded trial lawyers like Clarence Darrow or Gerry Spence, you will quickly see they are master storytellers.

Lee: When you decided to pursue screenwriting, what steps did you take to learn your craft?

Barbara: I started with a UCLA Extension course. At the time, UCLA Extension had a great contest called The Diane Thomas Screenwriting Awards. Extension students were able to submit a script they wrote in class, and a panel of judges would choose the top ten scripts. Mine was one of the ten. Each of us finalists was assigned to one professional screenwriter who worked in the genre of the script we wrote. The professional writers gave notes and we were given one shot to rewrite the script and submit it again. The writer I was assigned to was Ehren Kruger, who wrote *Arlington Road* and *The Ring*, among other great movies. He was very supportive, and he told me that I had the talent to pursue screenwriting, which was monumental to a newbie like me at the time. That experience really motivated me to become serious about my writing. After that, I went through UCLA's Professional Program and then UCLA's MFA Program in Screenwriting.

Lee: Your time at UCLA was beneficial—not only were you able to hone your craft, you also won its highly regarded contests. Did that open many industry doors for you right out of school?

Barbara: I got a manager as a result of winning a contest at UCLA with a romantic comedy I'd written. But the real benefit to attending UCLA for me was that I was able to really focus on writing. We had to write a new script every ten weeks. That taught me a lot about showing up and doing the work even when you don't feel inspired. I think it really put me in the mindset of being a professional writer.

Lee: How did the trajectory of your career change once you had an industry advocate on your side?

Barbara: It's great to have representation because they can get your material out there better than you can alone and because it gives you a sense of legitimacy. But the reality is, they can't get you work. You have to do that. You have to keep writing and pitching and jumping through hoops. It seems interminable, and you often think all this writing and meeting and driving around town isn't doing any good. But if you do it long enough, it will amount to something.

Lee: Shortly thereafter, APA came onto your representation team. How did that relationship come about?

Barbara: My manager introduced me to several agents. I chose APA because they were really excited about me. They had a whole team of people assembled and ready to work with me. They were all really nice, to boot.

Lee: Tell me about *The Boy Next Door*. What was the process of getting that script out into the industry? Did you get the impression that it was going to sell right away, or did that happen over time?

Barbara: *The Boy Next Door* was one of the first scripts I wrote (although that was not the original title). It got me a manager right away as well as a "hip-pocket" deal with an agent. They sent it out, and it was optioned almost immediately. I thought, "Well, that was easy." I really thought I had broken in, and that it would be smooth sailing from there on in. Boy, was I wrong. The movie was not made, but I got the script back when the option expired. I was very disappointed, but I didn't want to wallow in my pain, so I turned to other ideas I had and started writing other scripts. I put that script away for a while, and it was probably the best thing I could have done. After I got out of UCLA, I sat down and read it with fresh eyes. I decided there were a lot of things I wanted to do to it—character development, plot changes, etc. that would make it better. I ended up making major changes and doing pretty much a page-one rewrite. The two versions really share nothing but the premise. The one thing you come to understand when you start writing seriously is that no script is ever really finished. There is always something more you can do to it to make it better, and there are always new, exciting things you discover when rewriting, especially if you've let it sit for a while. After I completely rewrote it, I sent it to my new manager and he sent it around. At that point, I really thought that this script was going to be the one that would jumpstart my career. I thought it would sell right away. But the industry had changed a bit since that first manager and agent had taken the previous version out. At that time, there was a bigger, more active market for spec scripts. When the new script went out, the spec script market was no longer so vibrant. So it took another couple of years before it finally sold.

Lee: Can you give me the play-by-play of getting a spec screenplay sold? It's an experience that—these days—not every writer gets to have!

Barbara: I'm not certain about the specific steps my manager took to get that particular script sold. But every once in a while, I would get a call from a producer or someone at a studio who had read it and was interested in buying it. One time in particular, a producer from a mini-major called and said he wanted to purchase the script. He was very excited and assured me that he would send a purchase contract to my lawyer by the end of the day. Naturally, I was thrilled. But then something happened internally within the company, to which I was not privy, and instead of receiving a contract at the end of the day, I got an embarrassed and apologetic phone call from him telling me they weren't going to buy the script after all. It was really crazy. After a few of those kinds of experiences, when someone tells you they love your script and want to produce it, you say to yourself, "Yeah, right." You become a little cynical as a way of protecting yourself. Eventually, the script made its way to Blumhouse Productions. They have an interesting model they use to get movies made quickly and on a tight budget. At that point, there was a lot of momentum behind the project, and it went into production not too long after that.

Lee: The script ended up on the prestigious Blood List. Did that accelerate the screenplay's trajectory and give you more name recognition?

Barbara: I think it probably did give me some name recognition. As far as accelerating the process of selling the screenplay, it's hard to tell, but I think it might have, because it sold not long after it appeared on the Blood List. I really have a wonderful producer named John Graham to thank for nominating me for the list. He read it while at Screen Gems and became passionate about it. He is the one who got the ball rolling for me by recommending it to others in the industry.

Lee: *The Boy Next Door* went from a smaller, more nuanced movie to a bigger movie that went in a different direction from what you originally wrote. What was that journey like for you?

Barbara: It was difficult. I felt really fortunate initially because a director whom I admire greatly and who shared my vision of the movie as a nuanced thriller was attached. He made some suggestions for rewrites, and I happily executed them. We were really on the same page. But at that point we didn't have a star, and your movie isn't going to make money if there isn't a big-name actor who is passionate about the role involved. We finally got that actor, which I am very grateful for, but as a result the movie changed because she and her people had a different idea about what the movie should be and who should direct it. And, you know, I totally get that. Movies are big business. People invest a lot of money and time making your script into a movie, and it's a very risky investment. I was not happy with some of the changes made to my script, but in the end who am I to say that that wasn't the way to go with it? The movie went on to make a lot of money. I will never know if my less popcorn version would have done the same kind of business. Still, it was quite a shock to me as a first-time writer. I was not fully prepared for it, and it sunk me into a deep depression for a while. I think now I'm more prepared for the process because I realize that once you sell your script, it's not yours anymore. You have to let it go and move on to the next thing.

Lee: Since *The Boy Next Door*, you've been working consistently on writing
          assignments for studios, mini-majors and production companies. What sort
          of writing assignments do you seek out?

Barbara: I don't personally seek out assignments because I don't have any way
          of knowing what's out there. My manager and agents seek them out. They
          send a writing sample and pitch me as a suitable writer for the job based on
          my writing credits, my writing samples and, I assume, my background as a
          criminal prosecutor. I think generally, my representation seeks out thriller
          projects that involve a woman in peril and/or projects that have some legal
          aspect to them. But I recently sold a romantic comedy, so I have just now
          started getting offered more writing assignments in that genre.

Lee: As there is no place to go and apply for open writing assignments when they
          become available, how do you get those jobs? Do you have to do a lot of
          preparation and take a lot of meetings before you are given the assignment?

Barbara: This is one of the most time-consuming aspects of the business. Going
          after a writing assignment involves multiple meetings and a lot of preparation
          so that you can go in with a fully formed pitch that will lay out specifically
          the story you intend to write. You're basically breaking the story, which to
          me is the hardest part of writing a script. After pitching your take to lower
          level executives, you most likely will get their notes and suggestions, which
          will necessitate your revising the pitch so you can pitch it to someone else
          higher up in the chain of command. Sometimes this can go on for months
          with no guarantee that you will get the assignment. Because it can be such
          a huge time commitment, with no payoff in the end, I now only go after
          writing assignments I feel passionate about or ones that I feel I have a
          likelihood of getting because I have a unique take or a unique background
          that can add something another writer might not be able to.

Lee: Can you walk me through the experience of working the writing assignment
          itself? Obviously each one is different but . . . What are the usual steps and
          parameters?

Barbara: Yes, they are all different and depend on what has been negotiated
          beforehand. Generally though, there will be some sort of schedule including
          steps in the process and deadlines for accomplishing those specific steps. For
          instance, some contracts call for a written outline so that the producers can
          give you notes before you start writing. There will be another deadline for your
          first draft (which of course is not truly a first draft, but a quite polished second
          or third draft). After they read that first draft, and share it with other people
          in the office whom you've never met, you will most likely be called in for a
          meeting during which they will give you their notes. You will usually have a
          far shorter amount of time to do the rewrite than you had for the first draft.
          You will often be asked to do another set of rewrites, which might involve some
          new ideas someone has thought of, or it might turn out to be just a polish.

Lee: What can new writers expect of writing assignments that nobody tells them?

Barbara: One thing that you should anticipate from writing assignments is an expectation that you will not dilly-dally. This isn't a time for you to succumb to writer's block or a bout of procrastination. You are being paid to submit a quality piece of writing in a timely fashion, whether you have contractually imposed deadlines or not. That is not to say, there isn't some leeway involved. Most producers understand that life gets in the way and most don't hold you to rigid deadlines. They understand that writers need time and space to create and that every writer has his or her own process. It's important to think of the people who hire you as members of your team and not an antagonist. They want you to succeed and they will want to help you in whatever way they can to do that.

Lee: How do you juggle your writing assignments with your original work?

Barbara: To be honest, I haven't mastered that juggling act yet. I tend to get so wrapped up in getting that assignment done well and on time, that I end up spending most of my time on it. As a result, my own original projects fall by the wayside. Every time I get an assignment, I promise myself this won't happen, but it always seems to. I picture the executives sitting around, holding their breath waiting for me to hand in the assignment, which of course they are not. They have their own juggling acts to perform. Nevertheless, you want to do great work and submit it in a timely manner, so that puts a lot of pressure on a writer. I am to the point, though, (partly thanks to your advice, Lee) that I am really making an effort to push the ball forward on my own work even if it means just writing a few scenes a week. It's very important to be constantly generating new work of your own, even when you are doing an assignment. That's something I am trying to make a priority.

Lee: If there is one thing you know now about being a working screenwriter that you wish you knew then, what would it be?

Barbara: Not to sound negative, but getting there is hard. No matter how smart, talented or hardworking you are, you will face rejection and failure. Many of us are not prepared for this. Our system of schooling and our experience in most "normal" jobs and professions, sets us up to believe that if we are smart, if we do the work, if we get the grades, we will see a rather immediate reward. We will graduate, get a steady job, get the promotion, get the raise. It doesn't always work like that in this business. You can be talented and hardworking, and still toil in obscurity for years before getting your movie made or being able to make a living writing scripts. I think that before getting into this business, you have to ask yourself if you will be okay with that. There are exceptions to this, of course. But generally speaking you should prepare yourself for a long haul with many moments of despair and hopelessness. What separates those who make it from those who don't is their ability to overcome the despair, to reignite the hope, and to just keep going.

11

GENERAL MEETINGS AND WRITING ASSIGNMENTS

General Meetings

General Meetings—or "generals" as they are more widely known—are effectively meet-and-greets between a producer, development executive network or studio executive, and the writer whose work the individual behind the desk has taken to. The formula bringing a writer to these meetings is deceptively simple: a great spec—whether for a feature or television pilot—inspires a rep to take the script out to market, whether as a writing sample or for a potential sale. The market responds to the writing style, the voice, the concept, or all of the above. Even if the spec script fails to sell, with any luck a slew of generals are set, and the writer begins building and/or extending his fan base.

Manager Jewerl Ross told me:

> The building of careers is really about—it's a cliché, but it's true—the building of relationships. If I'm going to send a script out to everyone in the business, I want my client to take a lot of meetings. I send out a script to 80 people, 40 people are going to want to meet, so it's setting 40 meetings and getting the client into 40 rooms. The hard part comes with the client. How do you build relationships with someone you sat down with for 45 minutes? Why do you have reasons to keep in touch with them? How do you create creative common ground in that room, whereby they are inspired by your worldview or your thinking or your writing or your new ideas?

Jewerl went on to say:

> Meetings are all about the love affair. How do you get someone to fall in love with you in 45 minutes? For the client, that's where the magic is. If

the client doesn't have these skills or they're too young or too new, they don't know how to handle this room well, I can only teach them so much. If they've never done it before, they can only hear a portion of what I'm saying. So I don't necessarily have expectations that after 40 meetings this guy or girl is going to have a host of relationships that they can now use to build their career. That they're going to know how to maintain a relationship with seven of those executives—have creative common ground and then build a relationship worth something where that person is going to want to hire them on the next thing or that person is going to want to refer them to the other person or that person's gonna want to put them on a list for something or call them when they have an idea. When you are not that writer who has the ability to foster relationships, it's really about what is the next thing. And will that be worthy enough to send to 80 people? And will I have the ability to set 40 more meetings? Will the people who read you previously want to read you again? Will they want to sit down with you a second time? When I have situations where the client doesn't have that ability to build relationships and I send out the second sample and none of the people who read them previously want to meet them a second time, that's telling. If a lot of the people who met them want to see them again, that's telling. Best case scenario is someone like my client Sam, who I can set ten meetings for and 8 of those people are going to want to be his best friend because he's so dynamic and interesting. He has so much to say. He can take any idea and regurgitate it back to you in a way that is exciting. So yes, my job is about finding people who are going to write well on the page. But can you also be a personality? Do you have enough inter-personal skills to build a relationship with someone? Are you also sexy enough or interesting enough or smart enough to get people to fall in love with you? Can you take an inherently un-intimate thing and make it intimate? That's where magic happens.

Echo Lake's Zadoc Angell provided his unique perspective:

Selling yourself, I think for most people, seems so ick. Right? I mean, that's a total turnoff. That's why I hire agents and managers, right? They're doing the selling. And yes, we are. And that's a big part of what you have us for. But we can only open doors and put you in rooms, and you have to get it across the finish line. I advise clients to be interested in their own lives, be able to talk at a moment's notice about where you grew up, where you came from, what's your family like, what's your college like, what was your first job, what's the worst job you ever had, how did you break into the business, why did you want to become a writer, what are you passionate about . . . it's less about selling yourself than having something to talk about that interests you from your own life, that other people will find interesting, and then in talking about those things, you will connect. The people you're talking to, that you're trying to win over, that you're trying so hard to sell yourself to will, in all likelihood, open up and share their own stories and their own life experiences, and then you're bonding and you're talking, and you're becoming memorable to that person, and it doesn't feel like you're selling yourself. And the person who's on the receiving end doesn't feel like they're just being sold, too. That's the art form right there. Agents and managers do it in our jobs all the time, too. At all the business lunches with executives or producers, we'll spend the first hour just catching up on each other's personal lives, finding out what's going on with their families, what are they working on lately. And then oftentimes, the hard sell portion of the meal is the following half hour, where we know we gotta talk business, and I'll find out what they're looking for, and then I'll pitch my writers, and they know what the deal is, and we walk away satisfied. But so much of it is treating the other person like a person at the front of it so that you're vesting in each other beyond this particular sale.

In general, the executive on the other side of the desk will seek to answer one simple question: Is this a scribe that I am interested in working with? Is this someone I want to get into business with? The answer to this question is usually derived from a combination of elements, including personality, disposition, professionalism, pitching ability, talent and creativity.

Adam Perry of APA said:

> Being good in a room … I think it's personality, it's likeability, it's information in your mind, are you well read, have you done your research, it's charisma, it's communication, anything that would make the writer good in any room in life carries over to the writing.

General meetings have a loosely formed flow to them. After an initial introduction, the executive is likely to ask the writer to share some personal stories, wanting to get to know them. Any number of questions may be asked: Where are you from? Did you always want to write? It is the writer's job to put his interpersonal skills on display, talk about himself in a focused, specific, compelling fashion that makes him memorable and sets him apart from the rest.

Manager Lee Stobby weighed in about the importance of interpersonal skills:

> They're more important than they should be. That's what I'd say. You're a writer, sitting in your apartment all day, writing away, but then you're told you also have to be social. It is important. But the most important thing is if that's not your thing, you have to figure out what you're good at. Let's say you know you're really really not good at that, then you know what? You need to be a better spec-er, you need to be better on the page.

If you're better on the phone than you are in person, then you know what? You should make sure that you do more phone calls than in-person meetings. If you're better in person than you are on the phone, then vice versa. You have to be very self-scrutinizing. If you know that you're not gonna be prepared, you're gonna have to practice that many more times before you go in. It doesn't matter how old you are, you gotta figure it out. Some executives really want to feel like the writer is their new best friend and others don't care. Some executives want to get along with writer and some love the awkward nerd. The most important thing is that you have to know who you are and you have to be authentic to it. People don't respond to fakeness . . . If you are the nerdy quiet writer that's fine, you have to embrace that. Be that awkward weird writer and choose how you can make that fun when you are going and talking to people. Executives and producers just want to sit in the meeting and be in business with people that they like. You don't have to be, "I'm such a smooth talker and I'm so powerful and I convinced all these people of all this stuff." You can be heartfelt and quiet too and that can be just as effective.

Manager Scott Carr chimed in on the role that a writer's personality plays in these meetings:

I think it's over 50 percent nowadays. The days when you could just be an introverted writer and write a spec draft and sell it and then go and write another spec and sell it are gone. Now the personality of the writer has to be on a level that they can hold their own in a room with very outgoing and well-spoken people, be it representatives, directors, producers, talent. If a writer ideally wants to make the most money and have the longest career they have to be able to stay in the process as long as possible. Or be someone that is brought in in the late stages of the process, which are the highest paid people and usually are the ones who have the strongest personalities and work well with other personalities. Navigating the system—the business of Hollywood—is of the upmost importance these days and to me reading a great script is half the battle, the other half is meeting a great writer and assessing that they really have a good head on their shoulders and they're coachable and they look like they can handle the rigors of what the job entails outside and beyond the keyboard.

Manager Kailey Marsh added her perspective:

It's getting harder and harder to sell scripts—whether people believe that or not—there's just too much competition out there so if you're a weirdo, it makes me as the manager hesitant to put you in the room with other people because I don't want to get feedback that you were weird. Writing is collaborative, especially if you're working with other producers and having to get notes from potentially up to ten people at different levels. So you have to be able to interact with people of all ages, you have to be really comfortable, you don't have to be a showboat but . . . Don't be weird basically.

While I was lucky enough to be able to rally many of my industry colleagues in representation and development to participate in this book, I also went into offices I've never been to before, and spoke with agents and managers whom I've never previously met. And more often then not, the first request made of me on such occasions was: TELL ME ABOUT YOURSELF. Folks working in this industry understand that part of their job is connecting with the person sitting across from them, no matter who it is, and attempting to do so every which way.

Remember, executives often meet with dozens of scribes a week. Therefore, it is the writer's job to tell his personal story effectively. But personal exploration doesn't have to go one way; the writer is encouraged to ask the executive where he is from and what brought him to this line of work, in order to create a real dialogue and more opportunities to connect. After all, meetings in which the writer monologues and never asks any questions do tend to end fast. The last thing you want to be remembered as is the writer who couldn't stop talking about himself.

Evan Corday of The Cartel told me:

> When you're going into meetings with Executive A at Warner Brothers television I'm gonna call you beforehand, I'm going to tell you what they're covering, I'm going to tell you what you need to have seen so that you sound smart in the room and you know what that person is up to, but also, if they went to Syracuse and out of nowhere their team's in the final four which never should have happened and maybe you could mention something in the room how you're gonna watch the Syracuse game on TV tonight . . . Whatever the tie-in, that's already going to put you higher up than the person that came in before you, in the executive's eyes. Having confidence in the room is a huge thing, again that's where actors—they may not be confident but they can put on that face and they can pitch the crap out of something and make you sit up and be like, "oh, you know what, I'm so sorry this show is not for me but I want to be in business with you." Or they pitch you a book or something like that and a relationship starts and boom, you're off and running.

When it comes to prepping for these meetings, Twitter, Facebook, Instagram, podcasts, industry blogs, print interviews and any other information you can find are all game! The point is to find common ground on which you and the executive can connect.

Once the get-to-know-you-chit-chat is out of the way, the writer is likely to be asked about the piece that the executive already read—which could include questions about the show as a whole, or about what brought the writer to this particular piece of work—or else what he is working on next. Whether it's a script half way through the development process or an idea still in its infancy, executives are looking to hear if the writer is going to continue to generate work of interest, and explore whether there is a particular idea in the writer's arsenal they may respond to.

If a connection is made and the executive is eager to explore the relationship further, he may bring to the writer's attention particular ideas or materials that the company has been exploring internally. This may be a short story, a magazine article, a blog post or even a novel that the company is seeking to adapt. The executive may ask the writer to tailor a story around a core idea, or else develop their take on pre-existing work. While these opportunities may sometimes appear to be fool's errands, they can eventually lead its writers to bona fide industry work. Said Erin Cardillo, featured in Screenwriter Spotlight #1:

Take the smaller opportunity and turn it into the bigger opportunity in whatever way you can. And I don't mean aggressively. You don't want to be forceful in that way. But be strategic. Know who you're meeting with. Know what they're looking to do. Ask questions. Get excited about ideas that they have. And find your way into ideas that maybe they are already interested in.

EuropaCorp's Chris Coggins, who takes generals regularly, shared this with me:

When a writer comes in I definitely want to talk about work, talk about how they started writing, why they started writing, what they want to write in the future, what movies they like, what television shows they like, what they do in their spare time, family, school if they went to school. But really for me, I've already read your script, I already like your writing. I want to start a relationship with a writer so that I'm able to give notes that they're going to take and not take personally, and I want a writer who I can have a conversation with so they can tell me, "I'm really having problems with this. I really disagree with this thing," So we can talk about it and not feel like it's one versus the other, because it's a relationship. I hope. I just want a good conversation. We don't have to talk about work if you don't want to. We can talk about anything. We can talk about dogs. We can talk about movies. We can talk about space. We can talk about whatever it is, as long as it's a good rapport back and forth.

Madhouse Entertainment's Ryan Cunningham told me:

> Everyone I work with is always generating new material. You never want to go into a meeting holding your hand out. You want to go in there showing all this great stuff you're doing, and if they want to jump on board, great, and it not, you'll see them some other time down the road.

Epicenter's Jarrod Murray had this general-meeting advice:

> Don't be a cold fish in a room. It's knowing and preparing yourself for the fact that the executives are just people and they want to hear good things and meet interesting people. You get better at it as you go along. I didn't get good at meetings until I was a few years into this. You learn how to put people at ease and just not be a weirdo. Just look at it as a conversation and be yourself. We've read people we liked who haven't been great in rooms and that's a factor we've taken into consideration when we're signing them. It reflects badly on us if we're sending them into a room and they're embarrassing themselves. We try to prepare our writers as best we can but there's only so much we can do. Being good in a room is a combination of being relaxed and looking at it as a conversation between two people—one of whom can potentially pay you money. And knowing your material and being prepared for every question that you might get asked.

APA's Ryan Saul provided his insights for a successful general meeting:

> You have to give off an energy that is positive, confident, but not egotistical. Affable. If I'm an executive or a producer and I'm gonna be working with you for the better part of a year, I want to enjoy that experience. So if you're a young writer, you're selling yourself. You're selling your personality. It's not just about the writing. You'll have plenty of time to become an asshole and be a great writer. There's a handful of writers who are just curmudgeons and are like "hey just give me the project, I'll work on it, I'll deliver it, leave me the fuck alone." And they can do that because they have the street cred to do it. But when you're first starting out and you're not Aaron Sorkin or David Mamet or Zack Penn, you've gotta play to your personality.

Manager Jennifer Au of Untitled contributed:

> Just like in any other business, we are interactive. Our business is built on synergy. There are multiple hands in everything that we do, so that means you are a part of that. You're not just an island. So you need to go into

that system and work with it. People like to hire people they like, that they want to work with. If you make a great impression and you end up having a rapport with an executive, they're going to want to hire you down the line and remember you, and those things are important.

Whether emerging with actionable next steps or just creating a new fan, general meetings and the impression the writer is able to make in them are instrumental for the career to be built or built upon in the weeks, months and years ahead. Once again, if screenwriting careers are built on the shoulders of relationship, these generals are where those all-important relationships begin to take shape.

Finally, John Zaozirny of Bellevue Productions said:

> The reason you do a ton of generals connects back to this: they're not going to offer you an assignment if they haven't met you because if you're going to work with someone on assignment it's going to be 3-, 6-months, maybe even a longer process. They want to meet with you and see that this person seems reasonable, this person seems that they are open to collaboration, this person has an interesting point of view, this person and I, we connect, we vibe. Would you want to work with someone sight un-seen? No. You'd want to meet with them. Especially if you are going to have to work with them for a number of months and it was important for your job security. So the first thing they'll do is they'll meet you and be like, OK, do I like this person? Do I connect to this person? Do we like the same things? And then after that, once they've met you then they might in the room, or afterwards, be like, hey I really liked "Writer X", this book might be a great fit for them. We talked about it in the room. Or down the road, "Oh, you know, I really liked Writer X, here is a comic book we just found, see if this might be right for them" and so on and so forth. And then you're going back and you're pitching your take. So it's kind of a multistep process but certainly you're building your profile in town through generals first.

Which brings us to . . .

The Road to Writing Assignments

Every once in a while, a writer with a recent contest win or fresh interest from representation just under their belt will approach me and say: "I would like to get some writing assignments now. How do I go about that?" The answer, and the process, are much more complicated and trying than many think when they come into the space.

Perhaps manager Chris Cook put it best when speaking to today's industry climate and process:

If you have the material that people want, people will buy it, and then they will want to go to you to rewrite every other project under the sun. Now, how do you get to that point? It takes the time it takes to create the thing that's gonna knock everybody on their butts. Then you go in the room and be smart and listen to what else they're looking for. Or let them know what you're working on next. So it's not like an on/off switch. It's not necessarily like, Oh, you just sold something for a big amount of money, and now you've made it. There are variations in between. But I don't know of a way to break a writer without great material, let's put it that way.

Writing assignments, or OWAs (Open Writing Assignments) represent the brass ring for many a screenwriter. Sure, every feature writer would love to sell spec after spec, but in a retracting spec market that is not always a highly accessible or widely achievable reality. Similarly, in television, where getting staffed or selling an original pilot both seem like tall mountains to climb, writing assignments can be an entirely attractive proposition. Many TV writers partake in feature writing assignments in their off season. Television writing assignments are becoming more prevalent as well, specifically when a production entity seeks to develop new material based on a concept generated from within. Writers just emerging into the space may find that they are considering assignment work that comes without up-front pay in order to get in with a prominent production company, studio or mini-major. After all, if the material is well executed, the writer stands to end up with a powerful ally championing his work in the space.

Jason Scoggins of Slated, Spec Scout and The Scoggins Report told me:

> From talking to agents and managers over the last couple of years, there's this newish situation where the studios bring in lots of different writers to pitch their takes on projects, and it's almost like a bakeoff, where they're getting a lot of professional writers to spend time thinking about projects that a given studio is developing, come in and pitch their takes and then not get paid to do that work. Another thing that's happened before the strike, for writing assignment deals, it was customary to pay a given writer for multiple drafts of a script. So you might negotiate a several hundred thousand dollar fee that gets broken up into chunks, with the first draft, second draft and a polish, which gives the screenwriter a bunch of time to do good work, basically. I think everybody can relate to the idea that the first thing you write is not the best thing you write and that editing and the development process can really bring a fuzzy draft into complete focus. It's a much more successful thing for everybody involved. Well, after the strike, that shifted a lot, where those second and third drafts within a given deal are not guaranteed, so a writer might write a first draft, and then not be allowed to write a second draft, let alone the polish, and that's a

problem as well, not just from an income standpoint, but also from an industry perception standpoint, where a given writer might be perceived not to have gotten the job done on that first draft and that can be damaging to their careers.

If the formula is that a strong writing sample leads to general meetings and the construction of a fan base, then the next part of the formula is that the fan base then leads—hopefully and over time—to securing a writing assignment. But that's not always as easy an A-to-B-to-C-formula as it may seem. As Gersh's Sean Barclay explained:

> It's all about [insert sports metaphor here] know what I mean? It's about being aggressive and strategic. Getting a little bit of attention, that's easy. Again there's a formula. You make 50 calls, you make 35 submissions, that's 20 meetings, right? Your piece of material comes in. You will eventually build that fan base and be recognized for your talent. No doubt about that. Getting the job is more of a sniper's bullet than a shotgun blast.

Sean went on to elaborate:

> For 18 years I've only been hired by people I know, so the idea that there's a job out here and we're going to send this new person, new idea, new sample, you've never heard of them, let's send them in for this job . . . They're not getting that job. The fan base is built, the decision makers have lists of people that they've been tracking, writers they really love, with tons of notes on Excel spreadsheets about what these technicians did well.

Bellevue Productions' Jeff Portnoy added his insights regarding the way that the assignment world works.

> The realistic road to getting a writing assignment is getting your manager and/or agent to send your best writing sample to producers, to studios, to companies that have writing assignments. So usually it starts with a manager and/or agent sending a sample to a producer or studio executive. And the producer or studio executive then meets the writer for a general meeting. Then after the general, the producer following up would say, hey I think your writer would be great for this book that we have—I'll send you the book. The manager/agent sends the book to the writer. Writer reads it, and if it's something that they would like to do as an assignment, the writer then develops a pitch or "take", goes back into the studio or producer's office, gives the pitch to them and if they like the pitch then they take the next steps towards getting paid to write the assignment. It's very competitive

and for any given writing assignment usually there's multiple writers or writing teams going up for it. So it's just a matter of doing your best pitch and having a great sample. But it's hard. It's not necessarily hard to get invited to pitch on something, but getting the assignment is hard. You're always up against other people and you've just gotta do your best and hopefully if you're up for enough of them you'll eventually get one inevitably, and then off to the races.

Manager Scott Carr added:

Writers who write for hire, which means that they are spokes in a wheel, have to be very good at working within the construct of development. Which means they have to bring ideas to the table while also being open to other people's ideas, also being able to take notes and improve on those people's notes, because they usually come from people who don't consider themselves writers so they always want to be surprised by having a better result coming out of their notes. So it becomes not just about being a good writer, it becomes about being a good listener, a politician within the system and I find for writers, it's generally not as fun. Because you're not really just writing anymore, you're doing a job and you're being paid and thus you're an employee and so you have to take instructions. You have to be willing to compromise and be delicate and diplomatic and those skill sets are what writers who want to write on assignments need to embrace and have and develop further. Because it's not just sitting at your computer and trusting your instincts as a writer.

However, Scott went on to caution:

Personally, I think a writer should first adopt the desire and the muscles to be coming up with original ideas that they can at least pitch and get paid to write versus always waiting reactively for people to pitch them ideas, bring them books, bring them articles, I think that is a dangerous territory for a writer to have a sustainable career from the outset. People at the highest echelons, like the Aaron Sorkins of the world and the Billy Rays of the world, they can sit back because the food will always be there. Those guys will always be hired to adapt books, close on scripts and whatnot. When you are in your first few years, if you take on that mentality, it will be a very frustrating process because there won't be enough work to sustain writing and therefore those muscles of a writer will start to atrophy. Writers need to write always. Otherwise the muscles are just gonna shrink. And there won't be enough writing if you're just starting out and waiting for things to come to you.

APA's Ryan Saul provided his two cents:

> If the writer has a great spec that either sold or didn't, they're getting those meetings, and those assignments will come to them. My job is to find the assignments that aren't cattle calls. Where there isn't like "hey we're bringing in 20 writers for this." Now if you're a new writer, you're gonna do the work because you wanna get in the room. You wanna show that you're easy and great to work with. And being a screenwriter or television writer is unique in the writing world because it's also a social game that you're playing. If you deliver on an assignment, that writing work will keep coming. I have a couple of young writers who are television guys, I share them with people in the Television Department. They have a feature assignment at Fox Animation and initially it was just some punch up work, some joke polish, whatever. They did such a great job, a phone call came in saying "hey we have two more things we want them to take a look at that are going to be a more expanded assignment." I had this other writer who delivered two movies for a distributor and they keep coming back to him for assignments. If you deliver, the work just keeps coming in. But getting that first assignment is the toughest thing. And if you don't deliver, getting that second assignment is probably even tougher.

Of working the writing assignments themselves, Ryan went on to suggest:

> Executives want you to challenge them but not on everything. There's the note behind the note. They'll give you the note "this needs to be funnier" which is a shitty note. Or "on pg 35, this dialog is not really working." It's like therapy—they're not gonna give you the answers but they want you to figure out those answers yourself. That's why they're paying you. You're the writer. And there's a give and take too. It's like, I'm gonna get 10 notes. Of those 10 notes I'm gonna deliver on 7 or 8 or them. But there are 2 and if I don't agree with them I'm not gonna do them. And then they'll ask "why didn't you change this?" And then you have to give your explanations as to why. So it's being intelligent. Being smart. It's reading the room. And that's the big difference between screenwriting and television writing and writing a book or writing poetry or whatever. You are writing for an audience. You are writing a screenplay or a pilot because you want someone to not just give you money to write it, but it's gonna take millions of dollars to turn that script into a movie. And there's no other writing that's like that. You write a book and you have a publisher and you get paid but it doesn't cost 80 million dollars to distribute or make a book.

Initially, OWAs were made available on the studio level. A studio would invite a slew of approved writers, as well as the occasional hot new writer in the space, to come pitch their take. However, those studio-approved writers' lists are hard to crack. Manager Chris Cook explained:

> Across the board, studio assignments are just not available to somebody that's won a contest or hasn't been produced or doesn't have the script du jour that everyone is talking about. It's just always gonna go to people who have done a pretty good job fairly often. You're still an unknown quantity until you've done it a few times. The studios are making fewer movies, and the movies they're making are bigger. So the amount of jobs out there is lesser and lesser. And because you're talking about a $250 million proposition, the list of writers that you want to go to—that you (the studio or executive) would feel comfortable going to—gets whittled down from maybe 30 writers to 7 writers . . . There's a cover-your-ass mentality from a studio point of view in the sense that if I'm a development person at a studio and we need a rewrite as we're heading towards a greenlight, if I go to someone off the beaten path and it doesn't work out, I'm gonna look like an idiot and possibly lose my job. If I go to one of the "usual suspects"—the people who have come through in the past—if the draft doesn't come out, the stink won't come out on me because I can raise my hand and say, Well, what do you want? I hired so and so off the approved list, not the writer I had to convince you to hire.

But studios are not the only microcosm in which Open Writing Assignments are available. In today's market, and in lieu of waiting and hoping for a script that's a perfect fit for their company's unique brand and vision, many production companies have taken to developing their own unique materials from within. This is nothing new—movies such as *Wedding Crashers* came about in just this fashion. Such product development can come about—traditionally—in one of two ways:

The first one very much follows the studio Open Writing Assignment model, in which an executive sets out to develop a specific idea either as a pilot or a feature, and invites a slate of previously-identified writers to come in and pitch their take. To clarify, those lucky writers would have likely been flagged off of previous writing samples or high profile spec or pilot sale, followed by a general meeting in which writer and executive were able to meaningfully connect.

The second path through which OWAs often come about is a much more organic one: During a general, the executive may share with the scribe a few new concepts that his company is interested in exploring. If the writer sparks to one such idea, a conversation would develop around its development, and the executive would then invite the writer to draw up a treatment or outline detailing their specific take on and vision for the material at hand.

But open writing assignment opportunities are not exclusive to new material developed from inception. These prospects may also include rewrites, polishes, punch-ups, as well as the adaptation of books, newspaper articles, magazine articles, short stories or documentary material for the big or small screen. Without a doubt, the most popular of these opportunities is book adaptations, scenarios in which production companies, mini-majors or studios bring in a writer to adapt a book for screen, provide narrative focus and cinematize its vision. Such opportunities, which capitalize on that all-important pre-existing IP, usually come about when the producing entity approaches a rep in search of a writer suitable for the material, or else when a producer or executive makes the opportunity available to a scribe who has come in for a general and positioned himself as a good fit.

I asked Circle of Confusion's Josh Adler what writers can expect when going up for OWAs. He told me:

> They can expect to do a lot of work for free. It takes everybody going above and beyond to move a project forward, and that includes the writer. And especially if you're a young writer trying to get noticed, to break through the ten other writers that they're out to on a project, go above and beyond.

However, manager Chris Cook warned:

> If you realize the amount of people that are going up for writing assignments, whether they're official or less official, you would then look at writing a spec screenplay as a much more desirable thing. Because the amount of work you have to do in order to get one of these jobs is getting a little bit ridiculous.

Developing Your Take

A few months ago, one of my writers—just broken in off a hot TV pilot—set out for a general meeting with a studio executive. The writer, I knew, was eager to hear what the company was interested in developing, and asked for a coaching session that moment to help him prep. But as we talked, I quickly got the sense that perhaps the writer's expectations were not set properly. So I asked him: "What is the expected outcome here?" He thought for a moment, looked at me and said in complete earnest: "To walk out today with a writing assignment and a paycheck."

Going up for open writing assignments may sound simple: You are given a great idea, around which you develop your very own fully fleshed-out take, go into the room and dazzle the executives with your storytelling and pitching skills, and . . . you're in! Or else, you walk in with your very own set of perfectly developed, ideally suited ideas, deliver a stellar pitch, and before you know it . . . You're in business! Sounds great, doesn't it? But the reality of landing writing assignments is much more involved and often takes a lot more time to make happen.

Consider Screenwriter Spotlight #1 subject Erin Cardillo; while she originally arrived on the scene in 2009 with an attention-worthy feature spec and had been busy creating her own television show since, Erin did not land her first open writing assignment until 2015. "It's like the longest audition of your life," said Erin. "It's months of work to develop the pitch, and then you go in, and hope that you get picked out of however many writers they're seeing . . ."

If it's a brand new idea you're pitching on, you will be asked to develop your cinematic take on the material. If this is for a feature, the executives will expect to hear your three-act vision for the material, complete with twists and turns, characters and world descriptions. While you are not expected to develop a full outline, you should be able to speak competently about each and every significant story beat and general plot progression. If it's a television show that you are being considered for, your take will be needed not only for the pilot episode, but also for the show's overall long-term, multi-season vision. Additionally, you will be tasked with laying down the groundwork for characters and world building.

If you are developing a pitch from a short story, news article or blog post, you will likely be asked to produce a treatment that will outline how to develop the material from a straightforward, contained piece of limited material into a complete cinematic or television-oriented dramatic narrative. You will have to figure out how to take the core elements of the material that attracted the executive's attention, and transition them into a multi-dimensional feature script or television pilot that honors and highlights the core concept while supplementing it with enough story meat to make the story rich and viable.

When book adaptations are on the table, the writer's very first task is to read the book at hand. All 400 or 500 or 600 pages. Next, you will have to identify which elements of the book are important to incorporate in the screenplay or television show, and which threads can be left off. This stage is all about focusing your vision: You can't convert a 400-page book into a 120-page screenplay without making some tough but important choices. Additionally, most books are not positioned to seamlessly transition from book to screen. What may be viable story in a book complete with character insights, internal monologues and author commentary is likely not to easily transition to feature script or pilot form as is. Not only will you then have to figure out which threads or secondary storylines to keep, which to discard and how to contain your A-story for the screen; you will also have to offer up fixes for elements that may have worked in the book, but don't transition well—if at all—to a script.

When rewrites are on the table, the task at hand is all about offering up solutions. Your job is to take the elements that the executives love about the work, fix characters, story points and escalations that got in the project's way, and make all of it sing in harmony. Vying for the assignment, you will have to speak to the elements in the material that you connected to (i.e. why you're the perfect writer for this job) as well as the elements that require fixes and improvements, with real, thought-out suggestions for how to address those. While inspiration is important, this will be a practical exploration: you will be required to come up with fixes that not only dazzle in conversation, but can also be executed seamlessly on the page, preserving the material's original strengths and bolstering the project's overall cohesion.

Circle of Confusion's Josh Adler had this advice:

> Wow people. People want to be excited about what they're doing, and they want to be excited about who they're working with, and they want to be working with people who are excited as well. So if you're going in to pitch on a project and you go in and you sit down and you're like, "Yeah, these are my three ideas, and we could do this, or we could do this, or we could do that, what do you think?" It's not really all that exciting. Another guy who comes in and says, "Listen, I know you guys are thinking about this over here, but I had this crazy idea—let me tell you about it," and you spend 20 minutes talking through with examples and things really fleshed out, and there's passion behind it—and by the way, maybe that's not the direction they want to go—you'll get noticed, and you will separate yourself from the pack. Maybe not for this particular project, because that's not the direction they wanted to go in, but you always want to be separating yourself form the pack, whether that's in the idea or the direction you're taking something or the amount of work that you're doing and the amount of passion that you're putting into something. If there's an open writing assignment—it's a cattle call—and there's 50 people going in for a job, and I know everybody is going to be giving basically the same pitch on it, the same take because there's 2 or 3 ways you can go, I'll say to a client, "Listen, go the exact opposite direction. Do something fucking crazy. Maybe you won't get the job because it's too crazy, but also at the same time, maybe you will because they'll just say, 'God, we heard the same thing over and over and over again, and then you walked in the room, and it flipped us on our head. We saw this in a whole new light." So I would rather a client have a 50 percent chance of getting something by going way off the reservation in some crazy take on something than just being one of 20 people pitching on something with a 5 percent chance of getting it.

Going up for and getting these jobs rarely—if ever—happens in a single shot. Multiple writers—from three or four all the way up to a dozen or more—are brought in to pitch their take, each one competing for the job just like you. Writers who successfully completed writing assignments before have an immediate advantage walking through the door. They are proven quantities, bringing with them a track record that includes successfully working with executives to deliver on such jobs. During or following your initial pitch, you are likely to be given executive notes, which you are then expected to incorporate into your materials. If you make it through the initial round—which means that the executives in the room responded to your take—you will likely be invited to come back and pitch again, potentially to the upper brass. There is no limit to how many times you may be called back in to pitch your take, tweak and pitch again. On some occasions, the writer may be asked to elaborate further on the work—provide more detail or expand on certain areas of story, before a final decision can be made.

The downside? All of this work is expected without pay. You may be engaged in reading books and developing your take for weeks and even months without any guarantee of payment in the end. And if the producers decide to go in a different direction? You have no right to the material at hand. So not only did you not get paid for all this time, effort and work, you also lost time that you could have used to work on your own original work, which is instrumental to staying relevant in a crowded marketplace.

Nevertheless, once attained, writing assignments represent a path to a sustainable, long lasting screenwriting career. In addition to—eventually—getting you paid, they also provide a fantastic opportunity to build and reinforce meaningful relationships with executives as well as the possibility for adapting IP that you love, while simultaneously bolstering your reputation and honing your skills.

SCREENWRITER SPOTLIGHT #12: Diarra Kilpatrick

Diarra Kilpatrick is a native Detroiter. She studied drama at NYU's Tisch School of the Arts. Diarra is the creator and star of the web series *American KoKo*, which received the Best Web Series Award at the American Black Film Festival and has been featured as a web series standout by Essence.com and others. She's also an award-winning actress, having garnered a host of theater awards and nominations including, LA Weekly, LA Drama Critics Circle, NAACP and LA Ovation. She also received an NAACP Theater Award nomination for Best Playwriting for her one woman show. Acting TV/Film work includes *Mike and Molly*, *Southland*, *Private Practice*, *Hart of Dixie* and *Lila and Eve* opposite Viola Davis and Jennifer Lopez. She worked as a staff writer for NBC's *Mysteries of Laura*, co-writing three episodes in season one. She is currently developing original scripts for F/X and Amazon streaming and is repped by CAA and The Gotham Group. She lives in LA with her husband writer/director Miles Feldsott.

Lee: You started by studying over at the Tisch School in New York. Were you studying acting or writing or both?

Diarra: The program that I was in was called Playwrights Horizons Theater School, and it was a full, comprehensive theatrical experience. So like 360 degrees of theater. We studied a conservatory program, acting, voice, speech, movement, but then also directing, stage management, not-for-profit theater (which I wish I hadn't studied, actually), design. And we did that for two years. And then there were some electives, and I did take a playwriting elective there, as well.

Lee: What brought you out to LA?

Diarra: I'm a theater person at heart, but there wasn't a ton of straight theater on Broadway. It was mostly musicals. One thing I will say about NYU is that it helped shape the artist that I am, but the business person that I am, it did very little for. And that is something that I'm just figuring out today. Ten years later. I didn't even know how to make a career of it there. I knew how to be very passionate and work very hard and dig into a role and all that kind of stuff, but I was like—How do you break into this business? And I did very foolish things when I first started out, like being super young and taking headshots with tons of makeup and hair and glamour. Why would you do that? You could actually play under 18 at this point! So I didn't see the opportunity on Broadway in straight theater, so I thought, I'll move West, there will be more opportunities, there will be more auditions. That was my initial thought.

Lee: And did that prove to be true?

Diarra: Yes. It did. I think it was true there, too, I just didn't know how to find it. New York to me represented so much fun and enthusiasm but it didn't represent nose to the grindstone. So coming to LA was a fresh start. It was a way to really focus on my career.

Lee: At that point you were just acting full-time.

Diarra: Yes, but I had written a one-person show. And I still didn't know what to do really. I had this one-person show that I did in New York, and I was like, Oh, I'll put that show up. So I put the show up, and that's where I found my first community out here, which was the theater community. We did the show, and people started coming. And I got an NAACP theater award nomination for best playwriting. That should have been the first sign to start writing more, but I didn't take it. I did the casting workshops and just scraped to get my first credits, did live theater, did some TV, some indie movies, until finally I was like, Okay, I'm going to really take some time to write a piece again.

Lee: What inspired you to take some time to write?

Diarra: It's interesting because Tonya Pinkins wrote this really inspiring article about being a black woman in the theater and being hired to play certain roles and not really having a voice in terms of how the character is being portrayed, really. And so I think I got angry about something that I couldn't help. I wasn't writing it, I wasn't directing it, and I felt like the character wasn't fully realized. And I was like, I'm going to write something! And I also felt like I wanted to make something. I wanted to offer something. I wanted to give something. And so I started thinking about the fact that I have a really unique point of view. I'm from Detroit, but I'm from so many different aspects of Detroit, that I felt like I had a really unique POV and I wanted to express it. And with theater, the beauty of it—and also the thing that kind of sucks about it sometimes—is that it's a moment in time and it's done. I wanted to make something that people could see over and over again, that I could send to my parents or that I could send to friends.

Lee: Was that first thing that you created *American Koko*?

Diarra: I had previously written something called *The Dirty Dozen*, which went on to be one of the WGA Writers Access Project Honoree Scripts, but it was just a webseries idea. I had started writing that first, and it was building to this big battle on a bridge, and I realized that if I was going to make something, I needed to write something that I could produce. That was my first cue to start thinking like a producer. So then I wrote *American Koko*, because I knew I could probably use this hallway and this school, I know I could use this office, I know I can use my own home. I didn't write anything that I didn't think I could produce.

Lee: Can you tell us a little what *American Koko* is about?

Diarra: It centers around the Everyone's A Little Racist Agency or the EAR Agency, and it's about a woman, Akosua Miller, who is a lead agent there, and they seek to solve sticky racial situations. And Akosua Miller is recently recovered from Angry Back Woman Syndrome, so I was really looking at things like *House* and *Scandal*, where the fixer or the healer is broken in some way. And I also love *Law & Order*. I could get lost in a *Law & Order* marathon any day of the week. And so I just took all those hours and hours of watching those procedurals and turned it into this fun, quirky satire about what happens if we seriously attacked these small micro-aggressions. The season ends on a heavier note, but it started in my mind as thinking about, how do we solve these really small issues? Good people, you know, there's no malice in anyone's heart, it's just sticky and messy sometimes when we are in a post-post-racial society. When Obama was elected, everyone said, it's a post-racial America, and then we realized very quickly that that wasn't true, and so I like to call it the post-post-racial America, which is—we want to do the right thing. For the most part—aside from the Trumps and the crazies—good people want to do the right thing. They don't want to offend anyone. But we've spent so long as a country denying that race was an issue, which is an act of aggression in its own right, so I thought it would be a fun way to talk about it. It's something that I always talk about with my friends and family. Black people talk about race more than white people do historically, because it comes up in every aspect of our day and in our interactions and the way we raise our kids. So I thought this would be a fun way to get into that.

Lee: How was the show received?

Diarra: The reception was great in terms of people recognized me as a voice and a talent and a hybrid. I think because I actualized that for myself, people were really able to get on board—and when I say people, I mean producers and agents and studios. And that was really cool. Right away, I was out on meetings and was repped and all that kind of stuff.

Lee: Did your talent agent become your lit agent or did you bring on a new lit rep to your team?

Diarra: I just moved across the board. I just had a theatrical rep before, and then I went to a place where I could do it all in one swoop.

Lee: How did *The Mysteries Of Laura* come about?

Diarra: I put *American Koko* out in April, and by May, I was on *Mysteries Of Laura*.

Lee: Wow, that is really fast!

Diarra: It was really fast. And completely unexpected. I was repped probably by the beginning of May, and I went on a couple of meetings, one with Michael Patrick King for *Two Broke Girls* and the other was for *Mysteries Of Laura*. And meeting Michael Patrick King was like a dream come true, but that show was very joke-joke-joke-joke-joke. And even though I think *Koko* is very funny, it's not necessarily joke-joke-joke. But Jeff Rake (Showrunner of *Mysteries Of Laura*) watched the webseries. And then he said, "Do you have anything that's written?" And I had that script that I had written before. It was perfect because I had this kind of quirky, what could have been a half hour (which was *American Koko*) and then this hour-long, gritty drama, and so he hired me.

Lee: And what was the experience like, being in the room the first time?

Diarra: In a word, it was great. Really empowering and interesting to see how a show gets made from the bottom up, from the very beginning. From the logline, from the sentence, to the paragraph that gets sent to the network, to the outline, to the script—that was very fascinating for me, and it really opened up my mind because as a writer, I think from small details that will inspire me, whether it's an outfit or one news article or the way a woman smiles at her husband or something. But for network, it seemed like you start with very big concepts and then those details get filled in later, and so that was really mind-expanding to work that way. Because I read Shonda Rhimes' book, and she was talking about being a pantry kid (being in the pantry and creating in the pantry), and it totally revitalized all these memories of me being in my bedroom and making up all these worlds and shows. What it really taught me was working with other people can be really amazing. It was a tremendous learning experience.

Lee: Did you get to produce any of your episodes?

Diarra: We had one producer that was always in New York—the writers' room was in LA, the show was in New York, and our showrunner flew back and forth, and there was one producer who was always there. So the network did not send writers to set like they normally would.

Lee: Do you now think of yourself as a writer first?

Diarra: I think of myself as a creator first, and sometimes that utilizes my skills as an actor, and sometimes it utilizes my skills as a writer. What really helped me was when I was thinking of everything that I'm doing now is an extension of that little kid in her bedroom, and so I don't really have to get bogged down with like, I'm this first and that second, and I'm this percent this, and

I'm half a singer and this a writer—I don't really think about that at all. If there were no society, if there were no money, if there were none of that, what would I be doing? I'd be creating. If I lived in a little, small village, I'd be the one gathering up the kids to write a song for them to celebrate the birthday of the old woman at the end of the block, or at the harvest, I'd be the one doing a little performance, or I'd be the one visiting a sick person and trying to make them laugh. That's who I am. And so that, to me, falls under creator. A friend of mine gave me creatrice, which is like the female version of that, and that's just how I'm rolling right now.

Lee: You talked earlier about coming out of NYU and feeling like you had a good creative experience, but not having gotten the business acumen. What are the business secrets or truths that you learned when you came out here that you wish you knew way back when?

Diarra: You have to be able to sell yourself, that's one thing. There's this notion—and it might come from being a woman, too, it might be a societal thing that somehow imprinted on me because I'm a woman—which is if I'm good, then I never have to say I'm good. I never have to take much stock in it or be real bold about it. I'm just gonna be good, and it will find me. You know? The cream will rise to the top, and I just have to smile and be lovely along the way. Because Beyonce does it, right? Beyonce is like this bold, badass, take-no-prisoners on the stage, and then she comes off, and she's smiles and she acts like, Oh little old me? But it doesn't really work that way. You have to toot your own horn a little bit. And that's something I'm just really learning to do. And then there's also—and I hate this word—but it's branding. I think even writers are branded, and I never thought about it that way. This is my story, this is who I am, this is who I am as an artist, you know, really having a clear-cut understanding of those things and then going after it. What I've discovered is you have to come in with some sort of product, some sort of idea—if you're waiting to be "discovered," that's not going to happen. I mean, it might—there's that lovely story of Charlize Theron in the bank, and she was cursing someone out in the bank, and the guy behind her happened to be a manager. I don't even know if that story is true, but I've heard it, and maybe that happened for her. But I probably would've just been the angry black woman yelling in the back. You know what I mean? I think you have to create. That is when I felt a huge shift. Everyone that I know who has brought something to the table—Hollywood has been like, Oh I get it! And they open the door. You have to create yourself and arrive. You know what I mean? Who are you? And what do you have to offer the business? You have to figure that out on your own, and you have to make it happen. It doesn't even have to be a linear outcome. I have a friend who made this trailer for a pilot—and it was like, this is who I am and this is my sense of humor. And next thing you know, she did get this dream role. She got cast as a series regular. And I think the business responds very, very strongly to that.

Lee: What's next for you?

Diarra: I'm developing a half-hour for FX, and we'll see how that goes. It's been really cool, I'm working with Color Force, they produced *The Hunger Games*, and they're producing *American Crime Story*.

Lee: How did that come to be? The FX deal?

Diarra: A lot of it comes back to *American Koko*. My agent at the time sent them *American Koko* and they said, we love this character, we love this point of view. Do you have something that's not so race specific? So I started thinking about these kinds of characters being young in LA and the kinds of issues they were having and just opening it up a little bit. I still like this idea of this person doing the fixing who has no idea how to fix, so I came up with this idea for a woman who works at a Buzzfeed-like website, and she is the sexpert. But like most online experts, there are really no qualifications whatsoever, it's just gospel after that, so she's this deeply unqualified sexpert. She knows just as much as you if you watched all the seasons of *Sex & The City*. But fun and brash, like if Larry David were a black woman, from that same sort of POV. We've also gotten some offers to continue on with *American Koko*, so we're trying to figure out if all the parties are going to congeal. And I'm also developing another half hour comedy for a streaming service.

12

ADDITIONAL PATHS TO BREAKING IN

Query Letters, The Black List, Live & Online Pitch Opportunities

When conducting interviews for this book, there is one thing that was communicated to me emphatically, again and again: the industry consensus is that there are more avenues for discovery available to screenwriters today than in previous decades. Conventional wisdom is that if you do the work, if you write that outstanding script, there are more avenues than ever before to ensure that you will be discovered as your work—of outstanding quality—will rise to the top. But what are those avenues for discovery, and what sort of stock does the industry put in them?

Manager Scott Carr told me:

> The unsolicited query route is a game changer in the world of the internet. Everyone's information is online. So all resourceful writers need to do is get an IMDB Pro account and then see which reps have emails and accept queries and send off well structured loglines. And then also there are screenwriting competitions or The Black List website. Access is no longer the problem. I don't think a writer out there can complain that they don't have access to Hollywood anymore, we are all one click away from seeing and hearing what they have to say.

Query Letters

The most traditional of discovery channels is the query letter—the tried and true, long-established written format for writers to reach out to potential producers or representation in hopes of piquing their interest. Query letters themselves peaked in the 1990s, when agents and managers in search of the next hot spec became overwhelmed by the sheer volume of queries landing on their desks on a regular basis. At that time, many QUERY DESKS started popping up—desks dedicated to sifting through query letters, requesting scripts, reading unsolicited screenplays as part of the ongoing search for a needle in the haystack. However, because those desks had no real direct Return On Investment (ROI), they were usually manned by interns and assistants, ones who either returned to school at the end of summer, or graduated to more important—and therefore time consuming—roles within the company, and accordingly were unable to stay on top of incoming scripts requested off of queries with any consistency. As the spec market waned, so did the dedicated query desks, though some agents, managers and producers have continued to read query letters nonetheless.

While query letters are still read in the industry today, they are now read by individuals with many other to-dos on their list, be they assistants, reps or executives. Following a series of intellectual property theft lawsuits in the 1990s and early 2000s, few producers and production companies read unsolicited material, depending instead on submissions made by those on the frontlines of talent and material discovery: agents and managers. While there are a number of query sending services still active in the space, the sort that blast a stock query letter to hundreds of recipients, what my clients found to be more effective in this day and age boils down to two things: targeting and specificity. Know who it is that you are querying, and be able to state eloquently why it is you are approaching them.

One service that has positioned itself above the rest is Virtual Pitch Fest, which allows its writers to query the agents, managers, executives and producers on its roster with targeted, tailored query letters. An element that makes me appreciate this service is that its recipients are paid to respond to the query rather than just read it, ensuring that every query submitted is given its due consideration.

I spoke with Jennifer Au of Untitled Entertainment about the art of querying. She told me:

> People forget when they write a query letter (or even when you're writing a note to someone) that writing is a reflection of your writing, too. So if you're a comedy writer, your query letter should be funny. Your query letter shouldn't be filled with typos. That is a reflection of your work and your work ethic. Don't send me a query letter addressed to someone else—that happens a lot. Take the time to put my name on it. It makes a difference. It's more rare for someone to infuse a type of writing like that with their voice. It's much harder. But it does stand out.

Jarrod Murray of Epicenter wholeheartedly agreed:

> If you're writing a query and you don't use my name or you spell my name wrong—if it's a to whom it may concern or you're spelling my name with an "e" instead of an "a"—there's less reason for me to respond. You're

sending it out to everyone—"dear sir." I've only signed on one person off a query letter who we don't actually represent anymore. So chances for me to respond to a query letter are pretty low. I don't want to dissuade people from doing it because it does work for some but during the day I'm dealing with these other 30+ people who need my attention. Chances are I'm probably not going to respond. Don't take it personally; I just have to prioritize the day as much as possible. And don't send query letters on weekends. That annoys me so much. Sometimes you'll get a bite but know that those are probably going to be few and far between. It's better to get a referral if possible. Queries are the lowest of the priorities on the reading.

Manager Kailey Marsh added her perspective:

For every ten queries I get I request maybe one, and I might read the script and I might not. And that's totally my prerogative. So the more I like you, the more guilty I feel about not reading your script. That's a fact.

Chris Coggins of EuropaCorp had a good experience that started with a query letter:

I found a spec script that I sold to Overture with my friend Lance, who was my colleague at Escape Artist, we sold this script to Overture that we got from a query letter, and it was the funniest query letter we've ever read. The writer's personality just popped off. We called her and were like, "We love your letter. We want to read your script." And we sold it. We actually had a couple of directors interested in it, and we had Brie Larsen interested to play the lead, when no one knew who she was. So it can happen. It's rare. But it can happen.

John Zaozirny of Bellevue Productions added his two cents:

I don't read the screenplay if it's sent to me without my asking. But I will read the query. If the logline doesn't excite me, or if I get confused after the second sentence, I'm out. The query letters I hate most are the ones that say, "Hi! Do you accept query letters, or do you accept screenplays?" I don't want to have to follow up and say yes and get into a whole conversation. Or when they write, "Hey, I'm a writer, would you like to read my script?" There shouldn't be any follow up work for me (other than requesting the script), because if there's any follow up work for me, I'm not going to do it. Sometimes, I actually prefer things when they're designed towards me. There's not just, "Dear Sir or Madam. I've written a screenplay". That is not a great thing. It doesn't mean that I won't ask for the screenplay but it doesn't set things off on a great foot. It's better if the query says: "Dear John, I think you're a great fit for this, here's why." But it's all about the logline. If the logline seems intriguing, then I'll ask for the script. And then people have to be able to sign a release form. If people don't want to sign a release form then I'm not going to read their screenplay, because I just have to protect myself.

I asked John to elaborate about why release forms are so important—and widely used—in the industry: If I do not like your screenplay and then later on I develop a screenplay that has any similarities, and lord knows there's only so many stories under then sun, then I've opened myself up to a scenario where you could sue me for stealing your idea.

> So if I want to develop a script about an Ambassador on the run for a crime he didn't commit and you sent me a screenplay years ago about an Ambassador who was investigating the murder of his wife, you could argue that the two things are the same. There's very little to gain on my end for reading some random screenplay unprotected, there's much more to gain for the writer. Because if you are querying me then I'm probably in a more established position than you are. It's all downside for me if I read the script without the release form. The second thing is that if you're worried about signing a release form then you're probably not somebody I want to work with because you're coming at it from a position of mistrust and I understand that "people have to protect themselves," but that's what copyrighting your screenplay is for. If I read a screenplay and I thought there was something good in it, why wouldn't I just develop it with you? Why would I go and try to back door something? What's the upside? No one's trying to mess you over, they have way too many things going on, and it's kind of arrogant for you to think otherwise. Too many amateur writers are concerned with trying to make money off their "genius" screenplay and not concerned about trying to make a career. They treat their screenplay like some lottery ticket when really the best thing it can do is get you in the door with a rep who cares about you. Odds are the screenplay you've written is not going to be the one that makes you rich. Not the one you're sending me at least.

The Black List Website

In October 2012, Franklin Leonard, founder of top prestige list The Black List—which, as noted in Chapter 8, lists the most highly regarded unproduced works of the year as voted on by industry professionals—launched The Black List website, which invited screenwriters to list their projects, have them evaluated and scored by readers from The Black List, and viewed by industry professionals on the hunt for strong new voices and material.

While listing services are nothing new in the space (for an example, look no further than industry veteran InkTip), The Black List quickly gained a strong reputation for surfacing quality work and discovery-worthy writers relevant to the marketplace. For a monthly fee, writers are invited to post a profile of their project, and upload their screenplay or pilot to the website. Evaluations generated by readers (for a fee, of course), provide the listing a score or score-average if multiples are paid for or inputted from industry professionals downloading the material, singling out material that garners high scores.

For industry professionals, The Black List offers regular featured scripts complete with a movie poster designed for a particularly high-scoring, high-performing script, as well as a newsletter featuring loglines for the most highly scored scripts available on the website. In addition, The Black List brings its writers a number of contests, fellowships, labs and other initiatives, as well as an active blog and live script readings. Manager Scott Carr told me:

> The brand of The Black List that Franklin created through the list itself definitely is something that the entire industry has come to revere. And leveraging that into a paid website was a really strong business model that has not lost any of its brand equity in terms of writers. I personally see it as a website that is now no different than any of the other websites that did that, be it InkTip or whatnot, largely because they accept all material and put it all on the website. Franklin and his team do a good job at having certain material stand out. They are making smart strides in differentiating the glut of material that is on there to find what is the stuff that can rise above the noise. And I think that's important because otherwise it's very difficult for anybody who has a business to spend much time on the website culling through 20–30,000 screenplays on there. Because of the steps The Black List is taking in differentiating the material, compounded by the value of the brand, it has become probably the strongest resource for writers who don't have access to the industry. They are trying to truly connect the writers with the town.

From early days, and with the help of a slew of high profile success stories, The Black List effectively made its case to the industry that, through rigorous evaluations and algorithms, it had developed the ability to vet, identify and surface superior writers and screenplays. And the industry wholeheartedly agrees:

Epicenter's Jarrod Murray recently signed Nick Yarborough, a writer whose screenplay *A Letter from Rosemary Kennedy* was discovered through The Black List website. When we sat down to talk, Jarrod told me how it all came about:

> *A Letter from Rosemary Kennedy* was a featured script on The Black List website. Consequently, the script was later named to 2016's The Black List, that is the prestige list, rather than the website. They feature one script per

month on their site and they do a poster and then everybody who is on the mailing list gets that email stating "this is the featured script for the month." *A Letter from Rosemary Kennedy* was a featured script in November 2015. I read the script on the plane ride back home for the holidays—and straight through which I never do with anything. My partner and I met with the writer as soon as we got back from the holiday and then there was about a month of us just sending the script around until all of a sudden it just kind of blew up when the writer signed with WME. People who had passed on the script said, "man I kinda missed the boat on this."

Jarrod went on to explain what made the script hit in such a big way:

It's a really emotional read. It's brutal. The story of Rosemary Kennedy is about her being lobotomized and it's an inherently sad story but it's beautifully written. You have agents calling to say "this script made me cry". It's a story about an underdog. It's a story about this woman who had ambitions but her dad does this barbaric procedure that was en vogue then. It's resonating with people on an emotional level—how could someone do this to their child? It's definitely not a feel-good script by any means but Nick was able to write that character in a way that made her so sympathetic and kind.

The story of the script, which effectively began on The Black List website, doesn't end there. Emma Stone became a high-profile attachment in March 2016, and the script was going out to directors. Jarrod went on to tell me:

It's on a fast moving train, hopefully, Nick has gotten a ton of fans and a lot of actresses want to work with him because he was able to write such a compelling character that happens to be female. He's meeting with Margot Robbie and Elizabeth Olsen and Elizabeth Moss. I read a lot of featured scripts on The Black List and I don't think any one of them has gotten quite this much attention off of that site. I was lucky to have found this one thing.

For manager Lee Stobby, The Black List website produced tangible results as well:

I signed Isaac (Adamson, writer of *Bubbles* which topped the list in 2015) off of The Black List.com. You pay to put your script on the site, they have some readers read the script, they give it an evaluation, and I get an email saying what are the top ten scripts of the week. And Isaac's previous script was one of those.

While the script that Lee signed Adamson off of was not the *Bubbles* script, the website was the avenue through which Adamson was discovered by his manager.

John Zaozirny of Bellevue Productions is a fan of the website and all it can do for emerging writers, as well:

> The best thing you can do is get your script on The Black List website. *Nightingale* (starring David Oyelowo and released on HBO in May 2015) was on The Black List.com, which got made and won awards. That was just right on there, you know? I think of it as a way to find writers who have talented voices, I don't think it's a way to find amazing concepts that sell for a million, zillion dollars to a studio. You get a weekly email from The Black List and I definitely read every single logline. I was just talking to a writer last week that I met off The Black List.com. So it's definitely a place where I look for talented writers. I don't necessarily go trawling through there, so it's a lot easier when you're getting a weekly email that tells you: here are the scripts that we're excited about that kind of match with your preferences.

While none have the shine of The Black List, other listing services remain active and productive for screenwriters as well, most notably Jason Scoggins's Spec Scout, which is a hybrid coverage, qualifying, listing and scouting service housed within an active marketplace website. The service offers high quality coverage provided by three vetted industry readers, who deliver ratings and in-depth analysis of eleven separate attributes of the script, which are then combined into an overall script score. A score of seventy-five or above allows the writer to have the logline for their qualifying screenplay on the spec-market-centric website, and the information is also marketed (or scouted) to SpecScout's industry audience.

Live and Online Pitch Opportunities

One-on-one pitch opportunities—usually offered as part of a larger screenwriting conference or convention—first became popular with Screenwriting Expo's Golden Pitch Festival, which has now been defunct for years. Since, many players have tried their hand at offering a pitch event dedicated to connecting emerging screenwriters with industry professionals. The ones that remain most consistent in the live pitching field today are Hollywood Pitch Fest and ScriptFest (formerly Great American Pitch Fest), which take place in Los Angeles in the summer months. While other events, such as Story Expo, have sprouted up—and gone away—HPF and SF have continued to offer writers the opportunity to pitch their wares and connect with industry professionals year over year.

Although there may be outliers, most such events take place over a single weekend, during which writers are invited to participate in short pitches (usually five to ten minutes) conducted in a variety of formats. Some events require that writers sign up for pitches in advance; others stipulate that the writers line up for the executives they are looking to meet with physically in the live event. Whereas some events offer an educational component as part of the weekend (usually classes and panels, or one day of classes and panels and one day of pitching), others are all-pitch-all-the-time, as is the case with The Hollywood Pitch Fest, which has made its reputation for bringing in a high caliber roster of executives into the pitch room.

Over the years certain events have touted success stories, prompting some of today's writers to attend them hoping to sell a script or gain representation in the room. The truth of the matter is that I rarely—if ever—find those sorts of aspirations to be realistic. Regardless, that does not mean that these events are without value; it may just not be the value advertised. In most scenarios, these are pay-to-play networking opportunities, which could one day lead the writer to meaningful relationships with industry executives, the sort of relationships on the shoulders of which careers then get built. These events also offer the writer a great opportunity to get comfortable speaking about his work, something that for most does not come easy. Simply by participating, these events force the writer out of his comfort zone and push him to find ease with talking to executives about himself and his work. Practice makes perfect, as they say.

Candidly, I will admit that for years I was not the biggest fan of these events, as I felt that they set the wrong expectation for the writer. But over time, I've come to recognize the valuable opportunity they do represent for a scribe who has little to no industry contacts. After all, where else can you find a room full of willing industry folks, ready to sit down and talk to you, even if just for a few moments?

And these events have produced results: some years ago, my client Scotty Mullen pitched to industry executives at Great American Pitch Fest. Scotty went on to forge a meaningful relationship with the executives from The Asylum (*Sharknedo*, anyone?) who were in the room that day. Within just a few months, Scotty landed a writing assignment with the company, and the feature he wrote for them was released the following year. Scotty's relationship with The Asylum now runs four movies deep, and he has also gotten involved with the company's casting department. However, such stories are not the rule; they are the exception.

Madhouse Entertainment's Ryan Cunningham had his own perspective, a mix of positive and skeptical:

> I think that pitch events are a really good way for interns and assistants to network with other interns and assistants. As for the writers, I'm sure there's some networking value for all of the different writers who go to those, but if you're going to go to any events, festivals usually have panels that are great, and you can network in the same way without paying money to pitch. Rarely are the decision makers actually hearing your pitch. The problem, too, is that the pitch fests tend to attract a lot of crazy people, so even if you're totally normal and great, you're going to be associated with the crazy people. If you're going into it and you just really enjoy the process, great,

but I do think they create unrealistic expectations of what's going to come out of it. Personally, I'd rather see those things turn into networking, relationship-building events that you pay for, because there is benefit to meeting the assistants or interns or occasionally the junior exec or manager that's there. I could hear the pitch in 30 seconds and tell you if it has merit. I'd much rather talk to somebody for five minutes and get to know them more as a human being and who they are and what their process is and what types of material they're into. And I'm going to be a lot more likely to say, "Great, well, send me some stuff to read." Because how many pitches—legit pitches—actually sell going into studios? Let alone a two-minute pitch you hear at some event. No. You're not going to sell your project. All you're going to do is maybe endear yourself to the person you're talking to.

At its peak of popularity, there were as many as five live pitch events in Los Angeles every year. Additional pitch events and pitch opportunities—such as those conducted in association with the Austin Film Festival and London Screenwriting Festival—continue to take place every year, and provide a great deal of value and insight for their attendees. However, that number—and specifically the number of Los-Angeles-based pitch events—has declined over time. The reason? Online pitch opportunities, which allow writers to connect with industry executives from the comfort of their own homes, year round and at a fraction of the cost.

While different services have popped up (and often folded) over time, offering writers the opportunity to submit pre-recorded pitches or participate in live online pitch sessions, Stage 32's Happy Writers, guided by the capable hands of S32's founder Richard Botto, has been on the forefront of revolutionizing the pitching space, making this avenue available to every writer, local or remote. Through Stage 32, writers are offered the opportunity to pitch (for a fee, of course) to a revolving door of reputable agents, managers, producers and executives via Skype or phone, or else submit written pitched for consideration. Each pitch receives an evaluation from the listener, allowing the writer rare insight into what worked—and what didn't work—for them in the pitch. Additional service providers, such as Roadmap Writers lead by Joey Tuccio who works tirelessly on behalf of his writers now offer online pitching to those seeking to connect with executives, aganets and managers.

Jeff Portnoy of Bellevue Productions is a fan of what Stage 32 has to offer.

Stage 32 is a good, unique resource, it's another one of these resources for people who don't live in Los Angeles. If you don't live in Los Angeles you're limited to The Black List website, InkTip, Stage 32, these are websites and organizations that get writer's material to people in the business, managers, agents, studio executives, producers. And also get the on the phone with the executive. And that's something Stage 32 does more than anyone else. Stage 32's specialty is the pitching. Stage 32 is "we're going to put you on the phone or put you on Skype with a manager or an agent, producer, executive etc., and you can pitch to them." I've listened to a lot of pitches on Skype or over the phone through Stage 32 and people are calling from Africa, Australia, China, Japan, and today, if you don't know anybody, there's no other way to get face-to-face, or phone-to-phone time with a manager or an agent other than through that.

Web Series and Short Films

In recent years, web content has become a new, exciting and valid path for writers to gain visibility, attention and traction through, as was the case with Erin Cardillo, subject of Screenwriter Spotlight #1, and Diarra Kilpatrick, subject of Screenwriter Spotlight #12. Certainly, they are not the only ones. Perhaps most notable of these stories is Issa Rae, creator of the standout web series *The Misdaventures Of Awkward Black Girl* who went on to sign a development deal with HBO for her new show, *Insecure*.

It is important to note that engaging in the creation of a web series has practical benefits, not just strategic ones: by working with a team on a web series, the writer can gain a significantly better understanding of what it takes to get material in the proverbial can, without too much financial downside, due to the affordability of digital equipment. Not only would the writer develop a better handle of the collaborative process, but he or she may also begin to build a creative community that may one day prove both informative and beneficial.

In addition to the web, many writers consider investing time, energy and sometimes resources in the creation of short films. However, in my experience (and strategically speaking), short film is very much perceived to be a director's or writer-director's vehicle, rather than an avenue through which a writer is likely to gain attention or be discovered. Unless the short film ends up on the Academy's short list of nominees for that year's Academy Awards or is able to win Sundance, it is significantly less likely that a writer would be able to gain the same sort of traction via a short film as they would through their contribution to a web series.

While the internet offers a valid avenue for exposure it is also, in many ways, highly saturated. There is so much content out there! Outside of word of mouth or viral videos, how do you make sure your content is found? Because of this, the challenge for many an online content creator is not the creation and production of the content itself, but rather the ability to surface it online, be it a single clip with the potential of going viral à la *Too Many Cooks* or a web series such as *Notary Publix*, *Carmilla*, *American Koko* or *Eastsiders*. The question ultimately becomes: In a space overwhelmed with content, how do you make your web series stand out?

For insights about the importance of creating web content, I once again turned to my industry counterparts.

Infinity's Jon Karas had this to say about creating web content:

> It depends on where you are in your career. If you're already successful it looks like you've failed. If you're on your way up, it's OK. If you want to do something in a different medium or something that is going to be radically creative—go for it. It's really a case-by-case analysis. Writers gotta write. Writers write. We read. I read really quickly. I still love it. I read 5–10 feature scripts a week. I have now for 30 plus years.

Manager Mike Woodlief added:

> There are avenues now as a writer/creator to go into—there's the social media platform, create your own channel, create skits, get your friends together, be an advocate for change instead of sit on your ass whining about how tough it is. Instead, go do something. Go film it. You can film it on your iPhone now. Holy shit! Take advantage of technology. Unfortunately the television world hasn't caught on yet. But Amazon doesn't want to do business with a young unknown writer. They want stuff that they can market and promote off of just like everybody else. So go use the YouTubes, go use Tumbler, go use these avenues that are there and available. Somebody's making money off of it.

Faced with the same question, manager Jennifer Au of Untitled Entertainment told me:

> If you are someone who wants to direct and you've never directed anything? You've got to direct something. Ideally, you've made your own feature. Can you make a web series? Sure, there are the web series that transition, like *High Maintenance* that HBO picked up. Again, those are the exceptions. I think it's still a bit of a wild west. There's incredible opportunity on the digital side, but it's about, does it make sense? If you're looking to be able to automatically pluck a series out of one format and throw it into another, you're still going to have to rework it. But I think success in any field, being able to point to something else that you're doing is helpful. Saying, "Hey, I did this over here" matters to all of us. You create something on YouTube that gets a million views, people are liking it—those are substantial numbers. But to create to create, that's not a business. And the thing is that when you're a writer in this town, you are a business. It's not a hobby. You have to look at what's going to be building that business.

Manager Jewerl Ross brought this perspective to the table:

> Have I ever seen a good web series? I haven't watched dozens and dozens of web series. But the few that I watched were terrible. And keep in mind

that I throw out the word terrible a lot. If it's not good enough, I think it's terrible. And so I've seen a lot of web series that aren't good enough. I personally think that the only work that should be produced is work that will blow someone's mind. So if you have the ability to produce a web series that's going to blow someone's mind, do it. But just because something is produced doesn't mean it should be seen. I often will be approached by someone who says, "Oh! Check out my web series! Check out this script! And check out this pilot! And check out this animated thing I did!" And let's say this person came from a referral that's respected. So I look at all this shit. And most of it is . . . not good enough. What's the point? I'd rather someone send me one thing that is extraordinary than ten things that are not good enough.

Evan Corday of The Cartel added:

Because of all the digital platforms and the FUNNY OR DIEs and the Crackles, there are so many places to create content that there is absolutely no reason that you couldn't take your iphone and go out and shoot a little something, that may or may not get some attention and that could launch something.

Evan went on to tell me,

The studio executives are coming up in a different world and so they're seeing these things that are happening in digital, where they want to have 'that guy', they want to work with 'that person' and even though it's digital, even if you made it independently, even if you shot it on your iphone, there's something there that somebody can see that gets you to the next level.

Added Jeff Portnoy of Bellevue Productions:

The digital space is blowing up right now. There are a lot of new companies that are offering these paid subscription services to go online and watch original content, and it's a good platform for writers to either get discovered, or to develop, to get your work sold. You've gotta think of a YouTube as a vetting source. Someone reached out to me and said "Hey I wrote this script that got produced as a digital series on YouTube and it's gotten 10 million hits"—I'm more likely to take them on. It's a good way to showcase your work and get attention. You need to be proactive and do it yourself until you get momentum. Don't wait for someone to come to you and say "Here's the money." Go out and do it yourself, do it through YouTube or Awesomeness TV, Makers Studios. That's a way to get people quickly to vote on it. And it could be really helpful.

But would managers and agents prefer to watch a web series or read your script? To that, Madhouse Entertainment's Ryan Cunningham said:

> It's usually much faster for me to read something, so if you're a great writer, I would just lean on the script. If you want to be a writer-director or a director, then I think shooting something is proactive and you're flexing your muscles that way and that's part of what somebody is going to judge you on. Even if I saw something great—let's say I saw a short or web series that I really liked, but I was looking at it for the writer, not the director, my first conversation with the writer would be, "Can I read some of your stuff?" Because I need to see the words on the page to know what it is. So much changes in the shooting process, I don't always know how much is the writer versus how much of it is the director or other aspects of it. Going back to voice, how somebody smiths words on the page is a huge part of if I want to sign them or work with them, because that's part of what makes reading scripts entertaining and that can be the difference between an idea selling or not selling.

Different web-driven companies seek out different project types in varying formats. For insight about how a digital show gets off the ground in a particular incubator, I turned to Jennifer Titus, Senior Vice President, On Air & Digital Programming at CW who also oversees CW Seed, the CW's digital arm. Sharing with me her individual experience and opinions—rather than those of CW Seed as an organization—Jennifer told me:

> CW Seed is the digital studio that's affiliated with the CW. It has a couple different initiatives, but it really is an incubator for three main areas. One is technology, one is content, and the other is kind of to supply comedy in a way that our broadcast can't. So it's the comedy answer to the prime time drama and genre brand that we have.

I asked Jennifer how they source their content and what it is—format wise—that CW Seed looks for:

> In general, the writers come to us through a traditional path, so we get pitches from a lot of the agencies, agents and managers, so a project comes to us already having begun the development process. So it's usually writers that are repped and projects that have already begun some ideation and maybe even done a one or two-minute sizzle or shoot—a proof of concept—or have a developed show bible or a pretty developed pitch. We don't have a format, and in fact on the site right now, we have a variety of mediums, formats, some that are serialized, some that are sketch comedy, some that are animated. So partially what we're looking for is someone

with a really singular point of view—a creator and a producing team that have a very, very specific and passionate idea about what they would like to do. We have some series that are 20-episodes, we have some series that are 6-episodes, and then range from 2-minutes to 14-minutes. The lucky thing is that we don't have to meet a format, unlike a scripted drama or comedy when you're trying to hit act breaks or have everything come in under a broadcast schedule hour. We can flex a lot more.

I wanted to know more. Specifically, I was eager to find out whether one listens and looks for the same things in a digital pitch as a pitch for a traditional format and platform. What gets the good people over at CW Seed excited? Jennifer told me:

Because comedy is our number one priority, we get excited when it's funny. When it's funny from a millennial perspective, so you want people who are consuming content with that psychographic of a millennial. Our age is quite young, much younger than broadcast. A lot of people are watching on their devices, right? So we want to make sure it translates well. And then, also, our unique take on it is that we are always looking for projects that, after they have a singular point of view, have a natural marrying or intersection point with something that we're doing really well in primetime. So that could be genre. It could be a piece of talent that has equity in our primetime. It could be tone, like we're working on some musicals for CW Seed, based on the success we've had with both *Jane The Virgin* and *Crazy Ex-Girlfriend*, which involve a lot of magical realism. So we're looking for the intersection point so that we can confidently say to our viewers, If you like something in our broadcast, we can recommend to you the funny or the light or the parody version of that on a digital channel.

Not all shows that start on CW Seed are destined to end up going to network. Jennifer explained:

I think it's very possible. We've had two series already that have gone from the digital realm to the broadcast realm in different formats. One was a series called *Backpackers*. Season one ran on the digital channel and then we ran season two in broadcast. Then we had a series called *Significant Mother* (formerly bearing the broadcast unfriendly title *Motherfucker*) that was developed for the digital channel and we re-developed it for broadcast. And we just did another, more of an experimental series that was an alternative series called *Mortal Combat*, so that was a reality series that had five digital episodes and then finished with a broadcast hour. While it isn't a requirement for us to pick up a series, we are always looking to see how we can migrate. It's all about what we're trying to do well. So it's not just necessarily, is your series gonna go to broadcast? But is the production company a great partner? And now is the door open to them to develop an hour-long? So it's kind of testing all the different levers for us. In fact, the pair that developed *Significant Mother* ended up with an hour-long script in development here this last spring.

My next question: What is the step-by-step process of getting a proposed digital show pitched and developed with CW Seed? Jennifer said:

A lot of time we'll start with an email pitch, and then the three of us (Jennifer and her counterparts) will discuss it, and then it goes to your standard in-the-room pitch which different people do different ways. We respond very well to visual aids even if it's a slide show or a tonal document. The more you can show us, the better. And then, generally, the three of us talk and say, you know, where does this fit into our slate? We don't have a season like network TV has, we are developing constantly for opportunities as they come up, so sometimes we're developing for when we don't think we'll have a lot of content. Sometimes we're developing because we think we have a great opportunity in primetime to draft off of, so the temperature does change a lot, and we're also getting to experiment a lot. Once we've had a pitch, then the three of us meet and then it's sent to business affairs. It can be a long process, but there's not many people involved in it.

CW Seed also works with digital partners.

Alloy was the studio for *Significant Mother*, and BlueRibbon is the digital studio in Warner Brothers that's one of our partners. And the *Mortal Combat* project, that's through Machinima, which is one of our corporate partners that Warner Brothers might have either a stake in or they have an arrangement with them (Warner Bros has invested in the company). *Vixen*, which is one of our biggest hits, that's through BlueRibbon, which is Warner Brothers. Everybody's overlapping.

I couldn't help but ask: What are digital outlets looking for?

Every streaming outlet is looking for something slightly different, and they have their different core competencies. What we would love is to have a whole slate of serialized comedies that match our drama slate. So I would encourage people to think of it the same way that they write for network television. It's smaller, but you still need to build those arcs in. There are going to be different outlets that need different things because those are going to be more stand alone, more sketch-based or more personality based, but for us in particular, we are more open to serialized storytelling than I think some of the other outlets are. We are the incubator for the mothership. So we're not going to be as different or as weird. We want unusual ideas but we want them produced in a really professional way and so with us the experimentation should take place before the stories are getting shaped, rather than with some of the other outlets that I think have more play because they're populating everyday with a lot of things. For us, because we are more selective in the way we roll out series, we usually have between 7 and 9 series a year. It does have to have some kind of coherent beginning, middle and end.

Finally, I inquired: What should content creators keep in mind when developing content for the web?

It's still the high-level storytelling. It's going to be your craft, your writing and your storytelling skills. If you're a visual storyteller, then work on that. And then, also, make sure that you understand the difference between whether you're a good storyteller or whether your story is interesting— because those are two separate things—and require two different skill sets. For a while, the web was really encouraging people who had interesting personal stories to tell. Now I think it's encouraging people who have interesting storytelling abilities, which is different. Also, you have to think about your audience. What are they doing? How are they even ingesting your story? Are they doing it on an iPad? Are they doing it on a plane? Are they doing it with headphones on? Are they doing it while exercising? You should be telling the story that you're passionate about, but you should really be thinking ahead of the curve on how quickly people's brains are adapting to absorb these stories like sponges. So, your story—does it need to be an hour? Should it be 9 minutes? Should it be a movie that lasts 100 minutes? Should it be a podcast? Should it be a visual podcast? There are so many ways you could break apart your particular imaginative story, and the more fluent you are in those different places, the more successful you'll be.

Other Avenues for Recognition: Novels, Plays and Other Supplemental Materials

In today's industry, the cream rises to the top not only by developing traditional materials—namely feature scripts and television pilots—but also by putting voice, vision and storytelling skills on display through a myriad of less screen-specific literary materials.

Novels and memoirs have become fertile ground for talented scribes seeking to gain industry attention through generated IP. During the time I've been working on this book, one of my comedy television writers, the very talented Ayser Salman, has been toiling over a comedic memoire, *The Wrong End of the Table*, about growing up Muslim in the United States of America, utilizing her unique voice and specific sense of humor, expanding on the personal stories that informed a hilarious pilot inspired by her life and family that she recently wrote. While the pilot itself has garnered great feedback, (it was a finalist in the highly regarded Austin Film Fest screenwriting competition) it could be argued that it is too niche to gain the wide audience and necessary traction to take it from paper to screen without a proven showrunner or content creator behind it. Building momentum for the writer's memoire and establishing her comedy brand in another medium will not only cement her following and grow her audience, but also increase her relevance in the television writing space with the help of additional IP. Ultimately, it was the advice of her manager and the guidance provided by an ABC executive that brought her to this unique prose-driven project, one that falls outside of her writing comfort zone but ultimately makes a solid case for her wit and unparalleled point of view.

Going novel-first or even novel-only is not new for writers eager to get crafty as they seek to create excitement for their work, their voice and their unique brand of storytelling in both traditional and unconventional avenues. Whether the material is easier to sell as a novel first, or simply creates a following and brand recognition for the writer at hand, real, tangible success in the long-form literary space (i.e. work published by a known press, or if self-published then selling tens of thousands of copies) can translate to screenwriting momentum in the traditional space, be it for the writer himself or for the material he created, which could be published and monetized on its own, or, upon success and adaption, parlayed back into the entertainment space.

However, it is not only publishable material that can be monetized that could help make a writer's case in the professional space. In today's industry marketplace, many agents and managers are recommending that their writers explore writing supplementary material to go along with their original screenplay or pilot to help make their screenwriting case. Such material may include short stories, essays, sketches, one act plays, graphic novels or even novellas, which may put the writer's voice and storytelling skills on display.

When it comes to supplementary materials, The Cartel's Evan Corday is a fan:

> I represent playwrights. I represent a couple of short story authors. And they've all transitioned based on their material into television. And so, I also feel that the writing doesn't always have to be a pilot. You know? Write that one act. Write that short story. Write the thing that is going to, in 5 pages, tell somebody who you are. Because frankly, most executives aren't reading 62, 63 pages. And that's the truth. The beauty of cable and digital changing the way that we see television and the landscape in general is you can do that in 10 pages, open on the big explosion and then cut back. Or open at the end of a story and then cut back. Whatever it is that grabs the reader and keeps them turning the pages is the most important thing, for us.

Manager Chris Cook shared his perspective:

> I look at things like web-series or one-act plays or short stories or essays,
> as a rep, that's something I love to read and I love to watch because it's
> different from slogging through another feature. Often it will show another
> side of the writer. I think, as a sample for your body of work, they can be
> a good thing. There's not much in the way of monetizing these things.
> I'm not gonna hire you to rewrite a feature because I like your web-series,
> without a feature sample. So I think it can be a good arrow to add to your
> quiver—but I don't think it's the be all end all.

And Madhouse Entertainment's Ryan Cunningham told me:

> Short stories can be a great supplementary piece of material for television
> staffing. So someone is reading something other than a pilot, but it's short.
> Short stories, if they're great, could be adapted into features or TV shows,
> as could web content or graphic novels. It really depends on what the piece
> of material is. It even more so depends on—what's the strategy? Where do
> you want to be in five or ten years? And if you say, I want to be a working
> studio feature writer that is doing a lot of assignments, that's different than,
> I just want to write specs. That's different than, I want to be a writer-director
> and I want to be directing material. That's different than, I want to be on
> a TV show. There's a version where, depending on what the idea is, creating
> the ancillary materials that aren't just TV shows and feature specs can be
> great and can be totally additive. And there are a lot of situations where it
> can just be a distraction from what you really want to be doing and how
> you're getting there. If those things fit into your overarching plan of what
> you want to do, then great. If they don't, then I think you should hold
> back and keep that creative juice for something else that is more appropriate.
> There's a lot of writers who I hear say, "I just gotta write, I just gotta write."
> Which is great and I totally get that, but if you start diving into those
> supplementary materials and you use up your energy on those, it can actually
> hurt you more than help in the long run, sometimes.

SCREENWRITER SPOTLIGHT #13: Tawnya Bhattacharya & Ali Laventhol

Tawnya Bhattacharya & Ali Laventhol are a writing team. They recently finished
a season as writer/co-producer on NBC's *The Night Shift*, and formerly wrote on
TNT's *Perception*, *The Client List* at Lifetime and on USA's *Fairly Legal*. Their most

recent credit is as writers/producers on Freeform's *Famous In Love*. The team is NBC Writers on the Verge Fellows. Before partnering up with Laventhol, Tawnya was a FOX Writers Intensive fellow. The duo is repped by ICM Partners.

Tawnya Bhattacharya (BAT-tuh-CHERRY-uh), of Native American, Mexican and Caucasian descent, hails from Washington State where she survived growing up in a reservation town near a nuclear power plant, the explosion of Mt. St. Helens and high school. Upon graduating from Cornish College of the Arts in the Acting and Original Works Program, Bhattacharya lived and worked abroad in Vienna, Prague and India, before landing in Los Angeles permanently. Tawnya has taught screenwriting for ten years and is the founder of the go-to TV writing school, Script Anatomy.

Ali Laventhol started in the industry as a flame artist, composting visual effects for countless commercials, music videos and feature films. After transitioning to her first love, writing, she and partner Tawnya were selected for a coveted spot in **NBC's Writers on the Verge** program.

Lee: Before you two became a writing team, you were writing individually. Could you tell me a bit about what each of you were doing before you decided to partner up?

Ali: Sure! I had gone through the two-year program at Writers Boot Camp in which I wrote three feature scripts. I got to know Tawnya during that time and had a lot of respect for her story skills, her humor and her work ethic. We had expressed interest in writing something together someday but were both busy with other things at the time. A year or so after finishing WBC, I realized I might have better luck breaking into TV than features, so I tried my hand at a few TV specs and a pilot after taking a TV writing class at UCLA. These samples led to a few network generals, which really taught me I had no idea how to take a meeting. And walking into those rooms alone was fairly terrifying. It was around then that Tawnya and I met for lunch during one of her trips to LA from India, where she had since moved. In the time she'd been gone I had co-written a comedy feature and had a second feature idea brewing with my co-writer and our producer. But the other writer decided he wasn't interested in the second idea, and I was debating tackling it on my own. It was when Tawnya and I were talking over lunch that it dawned on both of us at the same time . . . let's do it together. She also had a feature project optioned with the same producer, so it worked out beautifully. We wrote that script together and the rest is history.

Tawnya: I was teaching feature writing at Writers Boot Camp as well as writing features when my husband got a job in India and we moved to Mumbai and then Delhi where we lived for two years. I kept a guesthouse in LA and would fly back every three months to work on a couple of projects with producers and a feature assignment for a director. None of those projects got made. During that time I also wrote my first pilot that landed me a spot in the FOX

Writers Initiative—at the time it was called FOX Diversity. As Ali said, we met for lunch and decided to work on a feature together, which we did over Skype because after finishing the FOX program I was on the east coast for about nine months before convincing my husband to move back to LA. Because the feature went so well we decided to become a partnership and began with the Nurse Jackie Spec that got us into Writers on the Verge.

Lee: What motivated each of you to try writing with a writing partner?

Tawnya: I had worked with a partner early on when I was writing features and loved collaborating and being able to talk things out. I worked solo for a while, but for me going through the process with another person is more alive—it ignites ideas and creativity and is fun. You have to have the right combo in a partnership, though. You have to respect each other as writers and as people and for me, Ali is "the one."

Ali: I was motivated by the "two heads are better than one" theory, and to be honest I was motivated by Tawnya herself. I could tell in our creative conversations that collaboration between the two of us held an exciting world of possibilities, and I wanted to explore that world.

Lee: Initially, you collaborated on a feature film script—what made you pivot to television?

Ali: Even though both of us started out writing features, we understood there was increasingly sophisticated and inspiring work being done on television. And if we wanted to be working writers, which we did with every ounce of our being, we'd be foolish not to give TV a shot.

Tawnya: For me it was the FOX Initiative. I had been writing features and was frustrated by how long it took—not to write, but to take a project to the screen. Getting into FOX and the experience I had there made me think TV was a strong possibility.

Lee: Together, you got into NBC's Writers on the Verge Television Writing Program. What was that experience like for you?

Ali: It was fantastic. And challenging. Writers go from concept to completed script on a new spec and a new pilot within the twelve-week time frame. It's fast, the feedback is immediate and insightful. In addition, WOTV exposes you to executives and showrunners who help prepare you for meetings, staffing and pitching, all the while giving you a leg up on the networking aspect of the business.

Tawnya: What she said.

Lee: Tawnya, having previously gone through the FOX fellowship, is it different participating in a program with a partner? And, if so, how so?

Tawnya: Actually, I don't know. I had a partner in that fellowship, too, and unfortunately we weren't a good match. We wrote the one project, did FOX together and that was it. This person was not someone I could work with in the business long term. You have to be okay with the way someone else is going to conduct themselves, how they are going to get along with fellow writers, handle the pecking order . . . At times I spend more time with Ali than my husband. It's a marriage. If the marriage isn't working it'll end in divorce.

Lee: Does being part of a writing partnership give you an advantage when being considered for staffing?

Tawnya & Ali: It's hard to say. There are some instances where a showrunner might see two brains for the price of one as a good deal. Or they might imagine a team can turn an outline or a script around faster than a single writer, simply because of the sheer (wo)man-power. But it could work the other way, too. Staffing is so much about balancing the levels and genders in the room—so adding two female mid-level writers instead of one, let's say, may prevent us from being the ideal candidate in certain situations. You just never know because when you don't get the job, nobody tells you why.

Lee: Is staffing easier when doing it for the first time with a writing partner?

Tawnya & Ali: Any time you walk into a meeting with a writing partner, you know there is someone there who has your back. Obviously, that is comforting and immeasurably valuable. So, probably, yes. It's also wonderful to be able to discuss and vent and process and obsess (!) with a writing partner when you're going through such a stressful and unknown time.

Lee: Once you are in the room—do you always write together, i.e. on the same episode, or are you sometimes separated into different episodes?

Tawnya & Ali: When episodes are assigned, we have always been considered one writing entity. Therefore we've always written episodes together.

Lee: What is the division of labor between the two of you when you write?

Tawnya & Ali: It varies, depending on the project. Usually we brainstorm, develop and break story together, then split up the outline and draft. Or, outline together and split up the draft. We tend to come together along the way to put the pieces together, read out loud and rewrite together. However, there have been a few projects where it hasn't worked out that way simply due to schedules, or maybe one of us has more passion for a project than the other and in that case it's natural for the inspired member of the team to lead the charge. In the case of our first feature, we outlined and wrote the first draft completely together, scene by scene, line by line. Conversely, there have been times where we were on a show and one of us covered episode rewrites while the other finished a pilot draft because staffing season was approaching and we just had to get it all done. Now, six years into our partnership, we trust each other enough to split things up more often, knowing we'll talk it through if there are any questions or issues.

Lee: Does one of you take the lead when dealing with representation and other business contacts, or do you both participate equally?

Tawnya & Ali: We try to participate equally, though we're not militant about it. Whoever is the first available to handle something usually does. But being in constant communication means that we're always tossing around ideas and options when a situation comes up with our reps or other business contacts regarding how we should respond. It's like any good relationship—healthy communication is key.

Lee: How are pitch meetings different for a writing team vs. an individual writer?

Ali: I've never pitched on my own, so I can't say. But my guess is those meetings would be much scarier alone!

Tawnya: Memorizing 6 to 7 pages of a pitch is difficult enough—sometimes I don't know how a solo writer manages 12+. When executives ask questions after your pitch, it's nice to know there is someone else who can jump in.

Lee: Yours is a strong and stable writing partnership—you write most everything together. What do you think has made your writing partnership successful?

Tawnya & Ali: We started out with a similar drive and determination to really make this career materialize out of thin air. That, together with complementary creative preferences, has been a huge advantage. We also benefit from a mutual respect and a genuine friendship that has helped us work through any bumps if they come up . . . though we've been lucky, we don't have very many of those.

Lee: What are the challenges—and advantages—of writing in a team vs. writing individually?

Tawnya: Navigating a career or a script or a job or a scene or a meeting with your friend who wants a successful outcome as badly as you do, is enormously advantageous. And it makes the whole thing a lot more fun. We laugh a lot. We talk each other out of funks, we are each other's unofficial therapists, we bounce ideas off each other constantly, and we drink way too much coffee and wine together, too. We've been in the trenches side by side experiencing some very stressful and difficult moments together. This shared history has cemented our bond in ways that are hard to explain. Diving into any new career situation with the strength of that bond is a huge asset.

Ali: Tawnya never ceases to amaze me with her determination, talent, wealth of ideas and a million other positive qualities. It's a big advantage to be in a partnership with someone who impresses you on a daily basis because it pushes you to be better, which is something I constantly feel.

In terms of challenges, for me, I think there are very few. But if I had to come up with something I'd say: there are stories I would like to tell that I know are outside the area of overlap in terms of the creative preferences Tawnya and I share. Those stories will have to wait, and I'm absolutely fine with that since I know they are not career-building ideas anyway. They are softer concepts that wouldn't bring us attention as writers so it wouldn't make sense to work on them now anyway. And I guess it's not that much of a challenge since it leaves me something to do when I retire. Beats Bingo and shuffleboard!;)

Tawnya: I do feel badly about that—about some of the ideas Ali is interested in that are beautiful stories but maybe hard sells because of where we're at or because the appetite is smaller for those types of stories. But at this point in our career we are definitely going a certain route to shake things up, and it's probably one I'm more comfortable with, but Ali is an incredible writer, and she, though she doesn't always think this, can kick ass in any genre.

Lee: You've now staffed on a number of shows together, and rose through the ranks to mid-level producers. What advantage does being a part of a team give you in this journey?

Tawnya & Ali: Producing requires keeping track of lots of details and coordinating those details with the rest of the production team. It means covering meetings and being on set and in general, making sure the episode turns out as you, but more importantly your showrunner, wants it to. Having two of us instead of one has definitely been an advantage in this process because again—two heads are better than one! We each catch certain things and remember different bits of important information and put out fires, which makes us more effective. Additionally, Tawnya has an acting background while Ali used to work in vfx and post, so we bring a different but important skill set to the writing/producing process.

Lee: What challenges exist for being in a writing partnership, and how do you resolve yours?

Ali: The best way to resolve the very few challenges we've faced has been through healthy communication. Being willing to hear how the other partner feels, without judgment. Being willing to talk through possible solutions together. Recognizing that as the years pass, we're not always going to have the exact same wants and needs at the exact same time—and that's okay. I'm no expert on relationships but I think the same guidelines that apply to healthy friendships or romances also apply to writing partnerships.

Tawnya: It probably helps that we're yin and yang. Ali is so chill that her feathers don't get ruffled that much. I'm super vocal and say whatever is on my mind— I like to work things out and resolve them quickly. I don't like any weirdness or tension to linger. We were once described as: a wild river that's a fun and exciting and dangerous adventure (me), and a tranquil, peaceful pond that you could dive into to be cleansed and refreshed (Ali). We didn't disagree. And it's a nice balance.

Lee: Would you recommend to other writers that they become part of a partnership?

Tawnya & Ali: If they find the right person, yes we would recommend it wholeheartedly.

Lee: What should writers consider before becoming part of a writing partnership?

Tawnya & Ali: They should realize it's really about much more than just collaborating in a creative way. It's also about making every business decision with the other person in mind, if you plan to have a successful career together.

13

EVERYTHING YOU CAN DO FOR YOUR SCREENWRITING CAREER TODAY

Preparing Yourself for the Industry

As you consider your screenwriting career, remember this one simple fact about the entertainment industry, which has already been mentioned throughout this book: you can't cram for it. When Hollywood comes knocking, you better be ready to show up as a professional in the know. What is topical today will be gone tomorrow, and reading a backlog of *The Hollywood Reporter* magazine is not going to be efficient enough to get you immersed in the space and effectively caught up. Therefore, use the time during which you develop your craft, voice and skillset to also develop your knowledge of the space in which you are aiming to work.

Speaking of how writers should keep themselves busy in the years it takes for a screenwriting career to take off, Untitled Entertainment's Jennifer Au told me:

> I think it's a combination of writing for yourself—of figuring out your voice—and learning your craft, so reading as well. If you want to be the next Aaron Sorkin, read a lot of his work. It's almost like learning through osmosis. And know where the bar is at for your writing in general, but your particular world. Learn everything if you're a specific genre type of person. Learn what genre works best for you. And the thing is you can write everything—but you can't write everything well. Some people can truly go across the board, but you know, I can very much tell when I've known a writer in one space, and they try to write in another genre, so they went from dark drama to comedy, that they're stronger in one side than they are in another. Do they want to hone that? Maybe. But maybe just naturally they have an affinity for one style. I think that it's important to get to know yourself. It's trying to figure out the themes that really inspire you as a writer. I think that people do cross genres and I can see a throughline of their work,

whether it's, "I love working with really nuanced female characters," or "I like working with men with emotional handicaps," or whatever it is. There's going to be something where, if I looked at the breadth of someone's work, there's going to be connective tissue somewhere. It's learning what's going to make you stand out, because the business—it's always been difficult, but now I would say it's more difficult than ever, and good isn't good enough. You have to be great. So it's what is going to make you great. And that's tapping into what you're best at.

Ryan Cunningham of Madhouse Entertainment added:

Because we're looking for new writers all the time—I think putting in the work, honing your voice, making sure your stuff is actually excellent before you put it out there, that's the best first step. And I think as a means of doing that, it's prolifically writing tons of stuff. Don't assume your first or second thing is going to be the thing that takes off. It could be. It happens. But a lot of times it isn't. Join writers groups, whether you're in LA or you're in Iowa. It doesn't matter. Find the five people who are interested in screenwriting who will read your stuff and be honest with you and give you criticism to make you better. Read screenwriting books but don't take them as the word of God. Read books on writing in general, but don't take them as the word of God. Network, which doesn't mean you have to hit every party out there, but once your body of work is good—meaning your fellow screenwriters that you've shared stuff with in confidence or the Lee Jessups of the world have told you this is ready to go out there— then don't be afraid to send your stuff out. You're going to get more nos than yesses even if it's an excellent piece of material, and you just have to stick with it. And then when your stuff is out there, keep writing at the same time. Don't just wait for the responses. Put it out into the world, let it go, continue to send it out, but almost assume nobody is ever gonna respond to it and start working on the next thing. It's a good habit to be in for when you are a working writer. Even if the thing you put out there catches fire or does really well, you want what's next to be ready anyway. It hopefully keeps you distracted from waiting for responses, too.

It is imperative that you get to know the space in which you are writing. Screenwriting is a difficult and challenging craft, which means that you will constantly need to find new ways to access and get excited about the work again and again. Therefore, you can never consume enough books about screenwriting craft. Whether you read the masters (Robert McKee, Syd Field, Linda Seger, Michael Hauge, John Truby, Chris Vogler and the like), or newer staples such as Blake Snyder's *Save The Cat*, Pam Douglas's *Writing the TV Drama Series*, Pilar Alessandra's *Coffee Break Screenwriter* or Jen Grisanti's *Storyline*. As Ryan

Cunningham put it, don't take any of these as the word of God, just take what works for you from each, and move on.

Another one of your responsibilities as a screenwriter is to get familiar with other material in your particular space, be it in script form or book form. In the simplest terms (and as mentioned in Chapter 2), part of your job is to become an expert on the work in your genre, so that when the opportunity presents itself you can hold your own in a conversation with other industry folks. For example, if you were a thriller writer in 2014–2015, it would not have been enough to read recently sold scripts such as *Matriarch* by Eric Koenig, subject of Screenwriter Spotlight #5 and *Undone* by Melissa London Hilfers, subject of Screenwriter Spotlight #8. In addition, you would have had to read the ever-popular dark thriller novel *I Am Pilgrim*, watched *The Jinx* on HBO and listened to the first season of *Serial*, just to name a few.

Watching television shows and movies obsessively is just one of the perks of the job. You want to be ready to walk into any meeting and talk about the content out there with knowledge and authority. That only comes from knowing the material and the space inside and out. At the end of the day, you want to contribute to the conversation you are having with an agent, manager or executive, rather than just show up as a student, being told what to read and what to watch.

In addition to getting familiar with your space, become familiar with the marketplace. If you are a television writer, it is your job to become knowledgeable of pilots currently being shot, or in active, going-to-pilot sort of development. Thanks to endless Google Drive repositories, such pilot scripts can usually be uncovered. On the feature side, be sure to read the screenplays that are moving in the market not only for content but also for style. The easiest way to get your hands on such scripts is through The Black List, Hit List and Blood List scripts, which are usually made available through links plastered all over social media.

John Zaozirny of Bellevue Productions told me:

> It's important to be someone who reads screenplays a lot. Someone who's aware of the form. Who's aware of the other people before them, the incredibly talented writers, the William Goldmans, the Tony Gilroys. You become a better writer by becoming a great reader as well.

Build on your knowledge base by exploring the companies, large and small, that are developing the sort of material you write. If you are a thriller writer, ask yourself: Who are the production companies, studios or mini-majors that would be right for your work? And who would be the premiere producers in that space? Much like writers, most companies have their unique brand, and have made their names in a particular space.

Study other screenwriters and showrunners as well. For scribes writing for the big screen, prepare to speak about directors old and new that you would love to work with. Be able to answer questions such as: Who are some of the screenwriters working in the industry today that you admire? Or Who are the showrunners for whom you'd love to work? Professionals want to work with other professionals, and industry knowledge is one sure fire way to impress.

Manager Lee Stobby shared:

> The question you need to answer which always seems so stupid is: "What are some of your favorite movies?" It seems like a stupid question but you have to answer that. That's what these general meetings are. They're about talking about movies. And talk about the kind of movies you want to be making. And talk about how that script that you wrote represents the kind of movies you want to be making. And you like these books and you like these people and you like these historical figures. And you have to be able to know what that is, and have thought about it. That's a good giveaway to me of a casual writer, someone who is casual about this because they haven't ever thought about these things. They're not thinking all day long: I'd love to be in business with this director and this is why, I'd love to be in business with this actor and this is why, I'd love to be in business with this producer and this is why. You have to be aware of your surroundings. If you're an executive at a production company or studio, literally your job is to think about movies all day long. So, if you're a writer and only think about movies an hour a day, then you're not going to have a very interesting conversation with somebody who spends their entire day thinking about these things. You're going to run out of things to talk about really quick and they are going to have an infinite well of things to talk about. So be more knowledgeable.

Writing Partnerships

I started writing this section on a bad week for my writers engaged in writing partnership. One writer, breaking up with her writing partner at the conclusion of their fifth year of staffing together, had to create a whole new body of work—including supplemental materials—to convince her agent that she is just as desirable on her own and worthy of a full writer's salary (rather than splitting it with her writing partner) before she could be sent out for staffing for the following television season. Another, an emerging writer, finally had a screenplay place in a contest: Top 5 in Tracking Board's renowned Launch Pad screenwriting competition. The only problem? The script that placed was co-written with a writing partner. The writing partner was repped, and the writing partner's manager had no desire to take the script out. My client then was faced with a depressing proposition: the inability to do anything with the biggest success he's had in his screenwriting career so far. He couldn't send his contest winning script to managers or agents, as no one would sign him alone off a script co-written with a writing partner. The only option was to get a producer involved, a long shot, as the script was not highly makeable. In just a few days, I was reminded why writing partnerships should be entered into with great consideration and caution.

Don't get me wrong: I am not down on writing partnerships as a whole. Like the case with Bhattacharya & Laventhol featured in Screenwriter Spotlight #13, those partnerships can be incredibly productive and powerful. This industry has a slew of writing partnership success stories: Larry Karaszewski & Scott Alexander (*The People Vs. Larry Flynt, Big Eyes, Ed Wood, The People Vs. O.J. Simpson*), Terry Rossio & Ted Elliot (*The Lone Ranger, Pirates of the Caribbean, Shrek*) and Thomas Lennon & Robert Ben Garant (*Night at the Museum, Balls of Fury, The Pacifier*) to name just a few. And I too work with writing teams: one of my pairs went on to win one of the biggest competitions in the space and would never imagine writing separately, while another has been working together through marriage and divorce and writing for some of the biggest names in comedy. But despite these very successful duos, the reality is that most writing partnerships end in divorce.

If you do decide to enter into a writing partnership, it is important that you do so with your eyes wide open; aware not only of the immediate benefits, but also the challenges you may face down the road. Therefore, if you are considering a writing partnership, contemplate doing so for one, if not a combination of, the reasons below:

Complementary Skillsets

The other writer brings a skillset to the table, which complements your own. You're great with structure, and your writing partner is a rock star with dialogue. You shine with ideas and twists; your writing partner is a magician wordsmith. In time, you want to develop your own skillset so that you may not be perceived as an impediment. But from the partnership's inception, you want to complement rather than overlap.

Similar Long-Term Goals

It's critical that you and your writing partner share long-term professional goals. In order for the journey to be satisfactory and successful for you both, confirm that you are excited to head for the same destination. Do you want to write for features, or television? Staff and work your way up, or break on an original pilot? Generate spec after spec, or write on assignment all day? Of course, plans can change, but if you at least start with a common goal, it is that much more likely that the partnership will last for a substantial period.

You Are Better Together than on Your Own

If two brains are not better than one in the proposed partnership combination, don't do it. It's that simple. The partnership is supposed to bring added value into any writer's room or development scenario. If one writer is always doing the heavy lifting, and the other is only cheering him along, consider whether or not it's the best thing for you.

You Get Along

While your writing partner doesn't have to be your best friend, if the partnership is to last you are going to spend a significant amount of time together—potentially in very small rooms—for years to come. Therefore, it is critical that the relationship is built on a foundation of connection, trust and mutual respect. Otherwise, the partnership is likely as good as doomed.

The Challenge

The challenge of temporary or single-screenplay writing partnership is this: if the writing partnership breaks up, neither one of the writers involved is going to be able to continue to use any of the co-written material written within the partnership unless one of the writers agrees to remove his name from the title page, and relinquish any future rights to the material. In other words, any work done within the partnership is no longer available to you, even as a writing sample. As no one knows what makes the "secret sauce" of a particular partnership, agents, managers, executives and producers will be skeptical of whether an individual writer is going to be able to repeat on his own what he had previously done successfully as part of a writing partnership. Therefore, as the partnership comes to an end, you will have to re-establish your body of work and your brand, which for many may mean starting all over from scratch.

Additionally, writers trying a few different writing partnerships on for size (writing multiple scripts with multiple partners) convey that they have yet to settle on their winning career combination. Don't engage in writing partnerships because you hate asking for notes, because you need someone to hold you accountable or because you dread the thoughts of facing the industry alone. Instead, consider a partnership only when you meet a writer with whom you can go toe to toe, who complements your skillset and shares your sensibilities and with whom—because you make each other better writers—your screenwriting career is more likely to take off.

Every Screenplay is a Brick: The Three-Step Approach

As you develop your body of work, remember that each one of your completed screenplays is another brick to lay in the road to your screenwriting success. As such, each screenplay must be thoughtfully strengthened and reinforced in order to make sure that it does as much as possible for you.

Whether you are a professional or emerging writer, take deliberate, specific steps in order to make the most of each screenplay and utilize it to create opportunities. It's a wash-rinse-repeat method, one that every screenwriter seeking to move their screenwriting career forward should adopt and apply.

Vetting Your Screenplay

The first, and perhaps most critical step to making the most of every screenplay, is the vetting of the material: making sure that your feature script or original pilot is technically and logically sound, emotionally impactful and overall beyond reproach. Or as industry folks like to say: undeniable. While not everyone is going to agree about the "worthiness" of the material (this is a business of opinions, after all), there should be some level of consensus about the quality of the writing deployed. Beyond that, it's all about taste level, and whether your screenplay is able to hit the reader's sweet spot. So in order to ensure that you are giving your screenplay the very best chance in the market, before you get it out there, it's all about getting feedback from known sources.

As stated earlier in the book, I have always been a fan of exposing your work early and often. The sooner you start getting feedback, the more efficient your writing process. Whether you put your outline, beat sheet or early draft in front of critics in the know, the more you will be forced to step outside of your writing bubble, the more informed and thoughtful will be your writing process. Early-and-often exposure, if done right, is sure to help you effectively move your project along. Until, finally, you arrive at a draft that you suspect could be ready for wider market exposure.

Said manager Scott Carr:

> Based on a lot of the material I read, I assume that a fair number of writers are submitting material to representation without doing enough due diligence to make sure the scripts are ready to be represented. And going to a representative, be it a manager or an agent, it is an access point that will be a first bite at the apple. So the writer should either get thoroughly educated on the craft of screenwriting and whatever that looks like for them, they should be writing screenplays, getting feedback on screenplays from people that understand the craft and they should be taking that useable feedback and either reapplying it to that script or to new scripts, until they really feel not just intuitively based on their own instincts that they have something special and something great. And that their intuition is actually confirmed by a volume of people that they trust. Then they'll come forth with an even stronger confidence in making those submissions.

If you are a writer just starting out, it is likely that you don't have many industry insiders ready to read your work. If such is indeed the case, secure the services of experienced, well regarded industry readers who actively read in the professional space, or else work with a consultant who has a number of success stories to their name. While opinions of friends not in the business could provide insight and support, it's the discernment of professionals who read scripts day in and day out that is going to make all the difference when it comes to elevating your work.

Equally, if are a part of a writer's group that includes writers whose skillset and taste level you respect or even a member or two who are just a couple of steps ahead of you in their screenwriting trajectory, their ongoing insights and feedback could become invaluable.

For writers working in the industry or possessing pre-existing industry relationships, turn to your trusted circle of industry friends, be they members of your writer's group or other working writers, for insights and feedback.

Whether you are professional or just emerging, vetting your script is often a process that needs to happen over and over again. Get a set of notes, rewrite, get feedback again, until the comments you get back become less critical, and there is general consensus—for the most part—on the quality of the work. While screenplays and original pilots can be written and rewritten every which way, you want to continue to seek out feedback and notes until you arrive at the point of diminishing returns, where the notes are not about sweeping changes or character correction, but rather about adjusting that line or tweaking that character.

Remember: for the most part, vetting your work is NOT about getting a confirmation that the work is great. Instead, getting feedback is all about identifying the flaws and ironing out the kinks. Of course, it's wonderful to hear that people love your work, but that ultimately doesn't help you become a better writer. Instead, it's constructive criticism and being challenged to make the work better that is going to push you to the next level.

Creating Pedigree for Your Work

Pedigree comes to answer the ever-present question asked by agents, managers and executives facing an ever growing pile of scripts in their inbox, on their desks or on their iPads: "Why should I prioritize this script over others in my pile?" This is when those extra incentives to read—a valuable referral, a high score from a listing service or placement in a high profile contest—could push the executive to read your script ahead of many others.

For writers just starting out, pedigree is built through more traditional channels, namely high-profile screenwriting competitions and listing services such as The Black List and Spec Scout. As you've read in these pages, the industry regards these providers as filtering services, destinations that are able to pluck the best scripts out of thousands. Success in these avenues provides a screenplay or original pilot a seal or approval, while offering the writer something of a short cut to the top—or at least the middle—of the pile. Rather than convincing and explaining why the script is worthy of a read, now the writer can effectively say: "See? A service or competition that you trust already likes it."

For writers on the way to being established in the professional space, that pedigree is likely to come in the form of a referral, although those high scores from The Black List website or placement in competitions such as The Nicholl Fellowship never fail to provide a useful boost of confidence. Writers who have representation will send that new script to their agent or manager, receive additional notes and prepare the material for their reps to take into the marketplace.

Remember, the industry is a bit like the mafia in that we need someone else to vouch for you.

Exposing Your Work

Once your screenplay is vetted and potentially possessing a little bit of pedigree, it's time to get it out to the industry.

Repped writers will likely lean on their agent and/or manager for exposure strategies, while cherry-picking industry contacts with which they previously had productive generals to whom the script should be sent. Writers who are without representation but connected in the industry space will likely reach out to pre-existing industry contacts with news of the newly completed work and any pedigree that comes along with it, in the hopes of stimulating interest. A new script is not only a path to reconnecting with old contacts; it's also an opportunity to reinvent yourself in the space.

Writers who don't have contacts in the professional space will likely rely on some of the avenues suggested in Chapters 6, 7 and 12: targeted query letters, The Black List, Spec Scout, live and online pitching opportunities as well as television writing programs and feature labs and fellowships to help put their work in front of a professional audience. After all, once your script has been completed and vetted, your job becomes getting the material read.

Networking and Your Screenwriting Community

The word NETWORKING has such an awful sound to it. Everything associated with it feels . . . entirely unappealing. However, in the entertainment industry, networking is synonymous with relationship building, and as you've read in this book many times before, screenwriting success is all about relationships. It has been said that the very best networking is done in the spirit of generosity, and when networking is done effectively, favors will be offered, rather than asked for. Consider that to be the standard towards which you should be striving.

It is integral for writers, whether in Los Angeles or remote, to interact with other individuals, professionals or emerging, in the space. In Los Angeles, there are more opportunities then ever: mixers, conferences, meet-ups and panels connect emerging writers with those who are steps ahead of them, be they working writers, showrunners or producers. Los Angeles-based opportunities to network can be found through such organizations as:

- WGA Foundation
- ScriptWriters Network
- ISA (International Screenwriting Association)

- Final Draft
- Stage 32/Happy Writers
- The Black List
- Chicks with Scripts
- Writing Pad
- Script Anatomy

Many articles, books and blog posts have been written about effective networking. I won't bore you with those same guidelines and instructions. Instead, I would like to once again turn to my industry colleagues, who provided their valuable insights:

Circle of Confusion's Josh Adler told me:

> This entire business—and I know everybody says it—but this entire business is relationships. So if you're trying to start your way into this business, be here. And start networking. Start going to things. Start playing in the kickball leagues and going out to the parties and the get-togethers and whatever and start mingling and being in the business. When I started out many years ago I was in the entertainment bowling league with a bunch of assistants and there were 144 people in the league, and it was all Hollywood assistants. We all started out together and everybody was at the end of a long day, and the league didn't even start until like 9 or 9:30 pm on Wednesdays because that was the only time we could start when everybody could make it from their jobs once their bosses left and they got everything finished up. It was the greatest networking thing ever. And a good number of those people still work in the business now, and they're studio execs and they're managers and agents and producers, and a lot of the people that I do business with, that I developed a relationship with.

Josh continued:

> To young people who want to get in the business, move out and start networking and start working. If you can get a job as an assistant at an agency or a management company, a studio, get your foot in the door, even if it means sidelining the writing to early morning, late night, weekends. Spend a year or two meeting people and working in the business and getting an understanding of how the business side of this works, because at the end of the day, this—while writing is an art form—is a business. Somebody that just knows about the art but has no idea how the business works will probably have a harder time. And then after a year or two, then you've socked away a couple bucks, go off, get a clerical job doing data entry and then the rest of the time write. And then when you have something that's ready, you'll know people, you'll know the people who

you need to get it to. They may not be the decision makers, but you'll at least know the guardians at the gate to at least get it in somewhere.

Epicenter's Jarrod Murray agrees:

If you can, get an internship or get an industry job that will help you. It's not just enough to be a writer, you need to be networking and those people that you meet are going to be very helpful to you at some point along the way. You need to be meeting people in the industry so try to network with as many people as possible. It's not enough that you're focusing so much on just what's on the page—which is most important—but you have to be getting out there and meeting people. If you have the means to take an internship or work at an agency and it's still something that offers you the ability to write while you do that and you're able to meet a million people who are going to become your base then do that. Obviously if you don't live here you can't do that.

Blondie Girl Productions' Ally Latman shared:

Work as hard as you can to meet as many people as you can. Because you never know who you're going to meet who's going to help you get a manager, get an agent. There's a writer that we both know who needed new management, and because he was a known quantity to me, I sent his material around to try and get him new representation. If you're trying to break into the business, just be the squeaky wheel. Just meet people. Ask somebody to just have coffee. Or offer to go to their office and just talk to them for twenty minutes. Because the more people you meet, the better the chance that one of those people is going to help you out at some point.

And Echo Lake's Zadoc Angell told me:

If you're a prospective writer reading this, and you're in another career, but you really want to be in this career, don't wait too long. Because what happens is people wait too long, and then they move out here, you know, not when they're 22, but when they're 30 or 40, and they haven't done the years of being an assistant making no money in Los Angeles and going out to drinks every night with the other assistants in town, and getting to know kind of their generation of people who are coming up the ranks in Hollywood at the same time they are. And that generation is essential to long-term success, because those are the people that you became friends with. You knew each other and cared about each other when you were nobodies, and then years later, when you are in positions of power, you can call on each other, help each other, work with each other, sell TV shows together. It's one of, I think, the most wonderful pleasures of our business that that happens—that you rise up with your class. But if you wait too late and you do it when you're much older, than your class, it doesn't gel as well, because you're 35 and married with a kid, and you're trying to hang out with some 22 year old who just graduated college and is at a totally different stage of life. It's just harder to cultivate that foundation of relationships. And you probably have less tolerance for working a job that has you working at all hours for no money, when you're starting at the entry level. So it's something to consider. It's really helpful to have life experience and to have other things to write about. But you also can't escape those really important early years of networking.

For those not in Los Angeles, look to film festivals, local screenwriting guilds and online opportunities to network with industry professionals or consider traveling for concentrated events such as the Austin Film Festival or the annual Produced By event in which you can make a number of meaningful contacts over a short period of time. Explore how to utilize Twitter and Facebook with consistency and purpose to reach industry professionals and contribute to meaningful exchanges, building your network over time with thoughtful engagement. There is no question that being in Los Angeles gives you a relationship-building advantage, but there is networking that can be done otherwise, as long as you are willing to stomach the finances involved or make a regular investment of time.

In addition to networking with industry professionals, it is critical for writers to establish a solid and dependable screenwriting community for themselves. A writers' group that will grow with them, understand their struggles and help them prepare for the industry and constantly evolve and improve their craft. A writers' group that will be able to not only help celebrate the small wins, but when the time comes, (and it will), commiserate. For good or bad, this is an industry like no other, one that is often hard to understand for those looking at it from the outside in. Therefore it is integral for writers to create a space for themselves where they are understood, supported and—in the best ways—challenged to write on and keep going.

Said Europa Corp's Chris Coggins:

> I know so many writer groups—like big name writers—who still send their projects to each other and still help each other and give each other congratulations and accolades. There's a really great sense of community here, I know with writers and some executives and some producers, so it's not as scary as Hollywood sometimes can feel. It is still a very small town and it feels like it's getting smaller every day.

Writers' groups, made of like-minded individuals at a similar stage of writing development, can become instrumental for the screenwriter's success. Not only will these groups—if made of equally dedicated, focused members—hold their members accountable to deadlines, they will also support their writers through the trials and tribulations of navigating the entertainment industry. Many writers have come to build bonds with their writers' group members; when one gets ahead, hopefully he is able to help respected members of his group along. It is not out of the ordinary for me to hear that any one of my writers has gotten their script in the hands of a network executive looking for new fresh voices, landed a writing assignment or went up for a staff writing job because of a recommendation made by a member of their old or existing writers' group.

In their best iterations, writers' groups are there to challenge your craft via early-and-often exposure, inspire you to write your best, help you decipher the industry space and become an expert presenter of your work. With any luck, your group will become instrumental for the development of your craft and your network's growth. For a group to succeed, specific parameters have to be installed: once identifying group members, determine how many times you want to meet per month, and how often one may submit pages. Is it a set number of pages, or a full script? And what sort of notes—written, verbal or otherwise—does one expect? For a writers' group to work, it's important that each one of its members continues to both get and give with generosity and consistency.

Today, screenwriters are everywhere. Whether through your local screenwriters meet-up, an online community or a local screenwriting guild, there is no reason why every writer should not be able to find or create such a community to participate in.

Your Industry Education

As mentioned at the beginning of this chapter, this industry is not one you can cram for. Therefore you need to study it, consistently and methodically, until you are able to speak to what's happening in it on command, be it in a general meeting or a casual networking scenario.

Said Gersh's Sean Barclay:

> You want to move towards the core of the business. And I do think that by understanding more of the mechanism of the business you will be able to breathe into your work a little bit more, maybe shift genres, maybe throw out that idea that doesn't feel like it's connected to the Zeitgeist. You know, all that good stuff. So absolutely, writers should absolutely be studying the business.

So how does one study the business? In earlier sections of this chapter, I spoke of the importance of reading unproduced industry scripts, of knowing the material in your space, of networking and participating actively in a writer's community. But there is more. There is industry commentary, insights and news—and you don't have to look too far to find them!

The industry's go-to news sources are: Deadline.com, the longstanding industry blog that changed the way Hollywood gets its news; staple publications *Variety* and *The Hollywood Reporter* (I am a sucker for THR's weekly glossy and the think pieces that it offers) as well as outlets such as *The Wrap* and SSNinsider, a useful news aggregate that delivers a twice-daily news rollup to your inbox.

For those with less time on their hands to sift through news online and more time commuting, podcasts are a great way to catch up on what's happening in the industry space. KCRW's *The Business* and *The Spinoff* provide an overview of what's happening in their unique business sectors, while podcasts such as *Children of Tendu*, *Scriptnotes* and *Nerdist Writers Panel* provide the listener with insights from the front lines, as experienced by working writers themselves. If you're looking for a rep, or more industry interviews, listen to podcasts on such outlets as *Scripts & Scribes*, *On The Page* and *Selling Your Screenplay*, all of which provide extensive interviews with industry professionals, the sort that can become invaluable when targeted query letters are concerned.

Josh Adler of Circle of Confusion told me:

> I always say to everybody: Learn the business! Read The Black List. Read the books. Go to seminars. Get a job in the business. Get a job at an agency or management company—the information hubs of the business—and learn how it works. That will at least inform somewhat your writing, and you'll know the steps, and you'll know the people, and you'll develop the relationships.

And manager Scott Carr added:

> This is a business. I think it's important to understand and appreciate that it is a business and it is ultimately about commerce and that writers are liabilities until movies get made and that's when they become assets because they are now making other people money and not just taking money. Their goal should be to write a movie not a screenplay. So really studying film and reading scripts and watching the films thereafter and trying to get a real strong sense of what films look like on the page and look like on the screen goes a long way. And just doing all of their due diligence to better educate themselves on how the business of Hollywood works. Don't just read books on screenwriting, or the craft of screenwriting, read books on production, read biographies on people who have made it through the process, that can share with the writer their experiences, because the screenplay is just the tip of the iceberg. To get to the movie screen you have to go all the way down to the depths of the ocean, but I think if

you've got the time while you're writing, and you want to learn about the industry, study it. Really come in like someone who has done their due diligence because that work ethic and that grit will go a long way and impress people. It just shows that a writer is more dedicated to being a screenwriter versus just writing scripts.

SCREENWRITER SPOTLIGHT #14: Isaac Gonzalez

Isaac Gonzalez is a Mexican-American comedy writer who was born and raised in Oceanside, California. The son of Mexican immigrants, he received his B.A. degree in Communications from UCLA in 2008. Isaac is a proud alumnus of NBC's prestigious Writers on the Verge Program. He is currently a Story Editor on *Legends of Chamberlain Heights*, an animated sitcom on Comedy Central. Past credits include *Community*, *Welcome to the Family* and Seth MacFarlane's *Bordertown*. Most recently, he sold a pilot to NBC about a dysfunctional Mexican family called *The Great Brown Hope*. Isaac is repped by CAA. When not writing, you can find him in Echo Park watching sports, gambling and eating burritos.

Lee: When did you start writing?

Isaac: English was always my best subject growing up, but I didn't start screen-writing until college. I was a lost junior at UCLA with two boring majors and in need of some direction, so I took a shot in the dark and enrolled in an introductory screenwriting class (130A with Richard Walter, still remember the class). I was hooked right away; it was the only class that I was taking that felt fulfilling and "cool."

Lee: Did you always know that TV was where you wanted to be, or did that reveal itself later? And if so, how?

Isaac: At UCLA (and most colleges I assume) the focus is always movies, not really TV, so I started writing screenplays. The first screenplay I wrote fresh out of college was a horror movie and it was absolutely terrible—a complete dumpster fire. But instead of quitting, I decided to take a shot at writing a comedy. That screenplay turned out a lot better and gave me the confidence to keep going. Turns out I was writing in the wrong genre and that comedy was more my bag. As for the switch to TV, that came about when I learned there were more opportunities for comedy writers in TV than movies. Once I figured out I was a comedy guy, pursuing TV and sitcoms just felt natural.

Lee: Gotta ask . . . Why television?

Isaac: For comedy writers it's a no brainer. Getting into the film world is tough—studios don't make that many comedies, they are riskier and don't sell abroad (and the ones they do make usually come from veteran comedy writers—it's a club). So basically, if I wanted to make a living, TV was my only route. I learned that every year there was a TV "staffing season" where comedy writers could get jobs—that was very appealing to me. I just had to figure out how to get in the door.

Lee: Once you've decided you wanted to write professionally, what steps did you take to become the best writer you could be?

Isaac: I read everything. I made friends with some Hollywood assistants who would send me comedy scripts (both existing shows and pilots) and I just studied them. I learned different joke structures, how to create funny characters and funny stories, basically how TV comedy functions. And obviously I wrote a lot—I started writing pilots and specs of my favorite comedies. The first spec that I wrote was for *South Park* and I got great feedback on it. After that, I decided to do one for *It's Always Sunny in Philadelphia*. That was the spec that got me into NBC's Writers on the Verge Program. It's cliché, but I think it's the Malcolm Gladwell thing, you put in the 10,000 hours and you will get better. You have to write a lot and read enough scripts so you are comfortable with the language and conventions of TV comedy.

Lee: If you could retrace your steps . . . what did you do to prepare yourself for a career in the industry?

Isaac: As a comedy guy, I think it was all about getting my comedic education. I supplemented my writing by doing other stuff—I took improv and sketch classes at the Groundlings and UCB, I did stand up for about a year all over LA, basically I became a student of the craft of comedy in all forms. I think it is very important for comedy writers to also do these other things—they will only help you become better and funnier on the page. Comedy writing is its own animal, you can't just be a good writer—you also have to be funny and understand what makes people laugh and how to do it in a way that is unique to you and your sense of humor.

Lee: You first surfaced through Writers on the Verge; what was that experience like for you, and how important do you think the television writing programs are for breaking into television?

Isaac: I got into Writers on the Verge when I was 25 and the program launched my career. It was pretty much like grad school for TV writing. I got coached through a couple of scripts and the pilot that I ended up writing in the program changed my life. The script got me an agent and my first job; in fact I still use it as a sample today three years later. Landing a fellowship is like cutting the line and getting a VIP entrance into the TV biz—obviously writers should shoot for them. However, there are different pathways in. The assistant route is another one, and I have many writer friends who took that path, however that comes with its own set of politics and challenges.

Lee: Did you go directly from WOTV to staffing? And if so, what was that experience like?

Isaac: I did. I ended the Writers on the Verge program in February and went straight to staffing season and was lucky enough to get hired on the fourth season of *Community*. It was a crazy transition. I went from working in a film storage warehouse in Hollywood with fat guys named Bubba to driving through the Paramount gates every morning and writing on a sitcom. It was a difficult transition because I was so green, but I am still working today so I guess I didn't screw it up that bad. The downside of going the fellowship route (if there was one) was that I didn't have room experience as a writer's assistant, so it was a lot of on-the-job training.

Lee: When and how did representation come into your journey and how did you decide to go with your rep?

Isaac: I got repped right after the fellowship. The pilot that I wrote in the WOTV program was submitted to all the agencies around town and the first one to contact me was CAA (it's crazy how thirty-five sheets of paper with jokes on them can really change your life). I didn't meet with any other agencies because I really liked the guys at CAA—they still rep me today. Also, when you are 25 and a huge agency comes knocking, you don't really say no.

Lee: How do you work with your reps—what do you expect from them, and what do they expect from you?

Isaac: I expect them to keep me employed. Every staffing season they submit my samples to all the TV shows that are hiring and get me what are called "showrunner meetings"—basically interviews for writing jobs. Their job is to keep their ear to the ground and find projects that are right for me. They are connectors and I use their Rolodex so I don't have to go out there and schmooze on my own. Recently, I've been developing (creating my own pilots), so they are responsible for getting me pitch meetings and brokering the deals if I sell to a network. Some people have more of a creative relationship with their reps and like to get script notes and bounce ideas off them, but I find that my writer friends are better for that purpose, so I use my agents strictly for business and career advancement. What do they expect from me? I don't know, not to suck haha. Just to keep doing good work I guess so it makes it easier for them to pitch me to the town.

Lee: Tell me a bit about the experience as a first-time TV-staff writer. How was it for you?

Isaac: It was daunting but very rewarding. I was on a show that already had a fan base so that made it extra difficult, the added pressure and standard to live up to. But the main challenge was just learning the dos and donts of a writers' room (when to speak, when not to speak, how to pitch jokes in a room, how to provide solutions to story problems and not just throw wrenches, etc.). There were definitely moments when I thought I was in over my head and that "this wasn't for me" but you just work through them and keep pushing. That first job put hair on my chest and I was much more prepared when I landed my second staffing gig the following season.

Lee: How does your life change after your first staff writing position—are jobs just
        handed to you, or do you have to work for them? And—assuming you do
        have to work for them—what does "working for them" look like?

Isaac: It depends on many factors, mainly your performance on that show and your
        agents. I have great agents so I went out the following season and got staffed
        on another NBC sitcom. Jobs are definitely not "handed" to you. It's about
        making relationships on shows you've worked on and finding jobs that you
        are right for. For example, being Mexican-American, I have a unique back-
        ground for a TV writer, so when a Latino-themed comedy comes knocking,
        my reps are usually all over it. It's my agent's job to find me work, but during
        the "offseason" (whenever I am not on a show) I keep writing so I have newer
        and better samples to send. I also develop and try to raise my clout in the
        business that way—by selling pitches and getting paid to write pilots.

Lee: In addition to your Story Editor credit, you now also have a show in
        development with the network. Could you walk me through the process of
        setting up your own show?

Isaac: I had a meeting with a production company called 3Pas, run by Mexican
        actor Eugenio Derbez. This is what's known in Hollywood as a "pod,"
        basically a studio signs a deal with a big name actor to help them develop
        projects for that studio. I pitched 3Pas some ideas and they liked one of them.
        From there, we started working on the idea and crafting a pitch. Once we
        got it tight, I pitched it to Universal TV (the studio that had the agreement
        with the pod) and they loved it. Universal gave me notes on the pitch and
        then we shopped it to all the networks. I sold it in the room to both Fox and
        NBC and we ended up doing it at NBC because Universal had a relationship
        with them. If you are a young writer, a pod is the way to go. It doesn't matter
        how great or funny your pitch is, if you don't have the clout nobody is going
        to buy it. Veteran comedy writers with tons of credits can go in and sell
        pitches, but if you're young like me, you need to piggyback off people who
        are more successful, be it a huge actor or a producer. That's just the nature
        of the beast.

Lee: Is it important for TV writers to live in Los Angeles? And if so, why?

Isaac: Yes. All the jobs are here. There are shows that shoot in New York but they
        are few and far between. I know a guy who lives in Minneapolis and goes
        back and forth to work in TV. That man is crazy.

Lee: In your estimation, how long did it take you to break into the industry from
        the time you set your sights on a career writing for television, and what did
        you do during that time?

Isaac: I decided officially that I wanted to be a TV comedy writer after college when
        I was 23. I was 25 when I got my first writing job (please don't hate me
        haha). My path was not the norm, in fact there is no norm, it is unique for
        every individual. I will say though that I worked extremely hard during these
        two years. This was the time when I dove head first into the comedy world.

I was doing stand up and improv, in addition to reading and writing comedy scripts on my own, all while working a soul-sucking day job.

Lee: If there was one thing you wish you knew when you got started that you know now, what would it be?

Isaac: This one is hard. I will say there are some things I wish I did better back then. I could've been better at removing my ego from things. TV writing is a collaborative medium, so people will reject your ideas and your jokes; it's just the game. You have to learn not to internalize these criticisms. I wasn't very good at that in the beginning. I wrote mainly by myself and it took time to adjust to the rejection that comes with being a writer in a group setting. Now I am not precious with jokes or ideas at all. I almost have a business-like approach to comedy.

14

THE KITCHEN SINK

Insights, Guidance and Advice

Over the course of the many interviews conducted for this book, a great deal of wisdom and knowledge had been generously imparted to me by the agents, managers and executives who agreed to share their experiences with me, as well as the writers who so generously stepped into my Screenwriter Spotlights. While not all of it fits neatly into a particular chapter, a lot of it seemed all too valuable to leave out. With that in mind, I'm sharing it, organized by topic, with you here.

General Advice from Industry Professionals

Manager Chris Cook told me:

> I've seen so many people who have struggled for so long who then made it. And then I've also seen people who have struggled so long and then didn't make it. And I see the difference—it's the work you put into it. You know what I mean? Most of the people that have made it in this thing aren't the overnight successes.
>
> Every screenplay that you embark on has to be an infuriating puzzle that you can't wait to solve. Maybe you don't like banging your head against the keyboard, but you like the victory you get that came out of banging it. If you ever stop loving it, you shouldn't do it.
>
> If you love it, 99 percent of making it is hard work. And by the way, there's a lot of other things in this industry that aren't just hard work. And that's one of the things that I love about screenwriting. I can be an incredible actor, but if I look a little too much like George Clooney, good luck to me. We have a George Clooney. I can be an incredible director,

but if I can't go out and actually make films to prove it . . . Writing is something that, with $300 for the screenwriting program and 10,000 hours—whatever the Malcolm Gladwell thing is—of hard work, it can be done. So it's all about hard work.

David Boxerbaum of APA shared:

My advice to screenwriters is so simple. It's just not to give up. Too many writers who are too talented and have a career they don't even see in front of them yet, who are going to be very successful, give up too early. And I think the key is to be creative and express yourself through the vision of storytelling, and there are too many writers just giving up too soon and taking no and taking that and running with that. And running away from the business. I think people should run towards it, and more writers should stick in there and continue to work on their craft and try to chase that dream if they truly believe in it. I know it's a train that's hard to grasp sometimes, but I think if you really do want to be a writer and really want to be successful in this business, the only way to achieve it is to continue to work on it and believe in yourself and be passionate and don't let NO stop you. You know? Knock down every wall possible. And I think if you look at most of the success stories in our business, it's writers who have achieved that from never taking no and never stopping and never saying "This is not for me." They believe this is what they should be doing in life, and they've chased it. I think that's the most important thing you can do in our business.

Infinity's Jon Karas mused:

You can't control how much talent you have, but you can control how much originality you have. If what you are doing resembles anything that anybody is doing, stop. Think it through again. Come up with a way to be fresh, unique, original. Look at things like Zombieland for example. There's a reason why that movie was so successful. It was cool. It was fun. It was unique. Think about things that are different, things that are special in some way. Don't say, "Oh these Young Adult movies work really well, why don't I just write one of those?" Well, if it wasn't some hit book, nobody is going to care about your script. Think about whatever you're doing, make it special, make it fresh, make it your own voice. So if you can do that it will establish your entire career. Recently people are doing it with shorts. There's a short that every one of the readers of this book should take a look at, you can find it on the internet super easily, it's a CGI short called THE RUIN. Really stylish, really cool, kind of post-apocalyptic little chase kind of thing. Really well done. That short led to its writer-director Wes Ball first getting this movie called *Maze Runner*. He's directed all 3 of those. And now he has a deal at 20th Century Fox. So doing something that is cool, special, unique, original, is the essential catalyst to breaking in. It may not be the first thing you do but it will be the thing that makes the difference for you. So be fresh, be unique, be original.

Josh Adler of Circle of Confusion added:

The first thing I always say is, if you have a backup—if there's anything else that you could see yourself doing and being happy doing, save yourself the time, energy, effort, and go do that thing now. It will save you a few years of difficulty, heartache, blood, sweat, tears. If you can't, if there's nothing else you can see yourself doing and being happy, then this business is for you, because there are many times during when I was coming up in this business, where I was beaten down, it was a horrible day, whatever it was, and if I had something else where I could have said, "Fuck it! I'll just go do that," I would have gone. But I always got to that moment and was like, "Fuck it! What else am I going to do? This is what I want to do." And so I stuck with it. So yes, it's a very hard business to break into. My piece of advice is if you have anything else that you would want to do, go do that. If you don't, go for this full bore and don't stop until you make it.

Chris Coggins of EuropaCorp had her own unique advice for screenwriters:

Write every day. Keep writing. Write a bunch of different things. Try to find your voice. Don't be afraid to try anything. And it's nice to write something that sells. For sure. But really write something that shows your voice and shows what you can do. That's what gets you on The Black List.

Definitely pay attention to what's going on in the world. It might not seem like it's important to the movie business, but it is. What's going on in China economically is important for Hollywood, especially right now. What's going on in Europe economically and socially is very important to what's going on right now. Because movies aren't just in a domestic space anymore. They're definitely international, and oftentimes more important internationally than here. So, you know, studios don't make something about ISIS because it's controversial. They don't make political stuff because it's controversial. You don't want to make anything that alienates part of your audience. Which can be unfortunate, because different strokes for different folks. But always pay attention to what's going on in the world. And try to notice trends, to see if you can project a few years in the future to see what's there, just to be aware of it.

I think the most important thing is to stay optimistic. Stay productive. Have a full life. Don't be writing all the time. Maybe write five to six days a week. Because it's your job—creating is a job. But you have to have fun with it, too. You have to get out. And always make your own stuff. You have an iPhone or an Android. You could make a movie on that. So write it and make it. Write something small and make it. The important thing is to just to keep going. There are people out there who want you to succeed. And try to find your community, because it makes it so much easier and plus, you can commiserate.

Jennifer Au of Untitled Entertainment provided her unique advice:

Your work is a reflection of you. Yes, being personable is important, but before you get that chance, someone's probably reading you, so make sure that it's stellar. Take the time to put in the work. Be students of the game. Be really thoughtful about reading and don't be lazy about your own careers. It's finding your voice, it's knowing yourself, it's having passion for what you do. And that is reflective. And guess what? A lot of us have worked in the business for years. We've read a lot. I think passion is contagious. If you can captivate us and bring us into your world, and make us fall in love with that, that means everything. So love what you do, and have that come across, and through that love, take the pride in your work and your career. And then hopefully it will come.

Evan Corday of The Cartel provided this insight:

Figure out a way to come out of your shell. A lot of writers write and are not comfortable talking, and in any room you've got to be ready to jump in or your voice is never going to heard and you're not going to get the episodes that you want to advance your career. Or you are never going to be able to sell that original the same way that somebody who can even fake it for half an hour is going to be able to do. You know those opportunities are few and far between and you really want to take advantage of them.

Manager Kailey Marsh told me:

The biggest thing with writers these days is they're always stressing out over what to write. If you want to break into the industry you should just write something that you really, really need to write. The longer I've been doing this the more I realize who the true writers are, and who are the people who just want to be a screenwriter, it's not a fine line at all. I have friends who have been writing a screenplay for two years and have never let me read it. So I just feel like if you really are a writer then you need to have something to show for it. If you're telling me you're a screenwriter and I'm like "Cool, send me your script!" And you tell me it's not done yet, then you're not a writer. I don't start talking to people about scripts, most of the time, unless it's so close to being done or it's ready. When I call an exec I'm like "Hey I have something I want to send you" not "Hey I'm going to send you something in a week and a half" because why wouldn't I just call him in a week and a half when it's done? Once you start to tell people you're a writer you need to be 100 percent ready. Or at least as close to 100 percent as possible. So have that piece of material that's really strong, and really work on your pitching skills. Know your pitch for your project because if you can't pitch your own project you're done. And also just be polite. And be cool.

APA's Ryan Saul instructed:

Don't worry about being typecast or put into a box like, "Oh I'm a thriller writer or a romantic comedy writer." You'll eventually find your voice. And if you're a great character writer, you can write anything. To me, when I read a script, story's great and I want to find something unique, but if you can show me a voice either in dialog or with characters that are three-dimensional and rich and every character makes a difference, every scene leads into the next scene . . . I'm looking for writers who understand what it means to have a well-structured screenplay with really rich characters.

Manager Jewerl Ross had this to say:

I think that people who are talented, who are meant to be successful, are going to be. I just think it's a matter of time. Time plus talent equals success. The only variable—if you have the talent, so the talent is invariable—the only thing that's variable is time. Is the time going to be a month? Or a year? Or ten years? Or twenty years? But I think with the appropriate amount of time, plus the talent that you have, it's impossible not to be successful. That's just my view of the world. So if you're one of these people with talent, you just need to be in the circumstance where you can grow your talent. Where you have a job that allows you to write—instead of working 40 hours, you can write 40 hours a week. So you're growing your talent. If you are talented and you go to one of these schools—USC, UCLA, Chapman or something—and you're sitting in a room, a seminar, where a professor has 15 students and he's reading your writing, if you are talented, that professor is going to fall in love with you and help you and connect you to someone like me. Because for people who are that incredibly talented, someone is going to help them and invest in them along the way.

Manager Lee Stobby provided these insights:

> I can't do anything with a B+ script. I can't do anything with an 8 out of
> 10. I don't think anyone in Hollywood can. There's no marketplace in
> Hollywood for scripts that just exist. Or are 'fine'. There's no room for
> that anymore. If you want to break into Hollywood, you have to be writing
> the best script that an executive read, not just that day but that month.
> That's what you have to be striving for. If you want to break into
> Hollywood that's the deal. If you are a more established writer this doesn't
> necessarily apply but if you want to break in you have to establish this base
> of "no, this is the best thing in my abilities, I can't make this any better
> than it is, this is as good as I possibly can make it." You have to constantly
> be pushing it to the next level.

Mistakes Writers Should Avoid

Throughout this book, we heard a lot from agents, managers and executives
musing about what you should do, what you should write. But what are some
of the mistakes that a writer should avoid, or the things that can turn an agent,
manager or executive off?

EuropaCorp's Chris Coggins shed some light:

> Writers need to work on their female characters. They really do. And I'm
> sure it's a hot topic right now and the strong female character is definitely
> a cliché, but there's a reason why. So often they give a masculine name to
> a female character because apparently that means they're cool or whatever.
> That really bugs me, when it's Alex but it's really Alexandria or Alexandra.
> Or Billie. Think of Lucy. Lucy is such a nice, friendly, female, very feminine
> name. And she's this badass who kicks ass and takes names. And don't ever
> describe a female character as beautiful without makeup, beautiful but doesn't
> know it, gorgeous and she's the only one who can't see it. Beautiful but
> broken. Clumsy but adorable. No. As an executive who's reading script
> after script after script and reading the same thing after the same thing, it's
> a cliché and it just automatically turns my brain to be like, "Well, if you're
> going to write this cliché, then your script will be full of other clichés, so
> why waste my time?"
>
> What's the other thing I hate? Oh. I really hate when writers put in
> scene numbers. Your script is not a shooting script. You do not have your
> greenlight. This is not scene 23, this is page 12. Unless this is your shooting
> draft—your white draft—leave out scene numbers. Also you don't need
> to use CUT TO: very much.
>
> Another mistake to avoid . . . Not speaking up when something doesn't
> feel right. Always tell me if you don't get something, if something isn't

reading, if you don't want to do it, if it doesn't make sense . . . Always speak up. Always over-explain instead of under-explain. Don't necessarily write something that you think is going to sell. If you're just starting out, you're not going to sell your first script most of the time. You're just not. Writers often try to write for the current marketplace. They try to write something that sells. I don't think that's the best use of their time. I think it's much better to write a sample, to write something that shows your voice, and to remember that whatever it is that's popular now in three years, when (best-case scenario) your movie gets made, same thing isn't going to be as popular.

Adam Perry of APA cautioned:

I think a lot of people will come right out of film school, get one good script and get an agent, get a manager, get an entertainment lawyer and sell it and then they ease up a little. They say: "I've got a manager, I've got an agent, they're going to do everything for me." Without material we can't do anything. We can put you in a ton of rooms. And the other thing is ideas. People who don't have a lot of original ideas. And they're just kind of asleep at the wheel. And say, "Oh, people are just going to bring me stuff." No. You have to generate. So, I would say, self-generating is the thing that lots of new writers lack. And the mistake is having one good sale and then resting on it.

Jennifer Au of Untitled Entertainment told me:

I don't want someone who's one and done, you know? I want to read other work. But don't give me something that you don't stand behind. Don't give me something that you haven't polished for ten years, because I'm going to look at that as a reflection of your current skill. Part of my job as a rep is to educate. But I want my clients to be students of the game and reading and networking and all that. But make sure that you stand behind the work that you're sending out. Constantly be thinking about ideas. Generate for yourself. It's a mistake if you don't. This is a proactive business at its best. If you sit back and are purely reactionary about your own career, no one is going to do it for you.

Madhouse Entertainment's Ryan Cunningham warned:

A lot of people end up reading way too many articles on Deadline and other websites. They get a lot of misconceptions looking at people around them and assuming what their path was and then feeling bad about themselves because of it, and usually it's not at all what you think it is.

Some people do it for the money, thinking, "Oh I could write a script. It's only 100 pages. It's a lot of white space." Like it's a lottery ticket, and that's not what it is either. A lot of people do it thinking that they're going to have more control over the finished product than they do, and it drives them nuts because of it. There are a lot of misconceptions about the way reps sign people or the way business fucks over writers. Writers sometimes think that it's some kind of a conspiracy, like it's an old boys club that you can't break into, and honestly, everybody out there, they just want to find great stuff. You know, the mechanics of it and how the stuff comes to the surface can seem kind of weird, but at the end of the day, everybody wants unique stuff. Look, it's a business. Everybody has to make money and everybody has to sell the product to somebody else, all the way from the top, which is the studio selling it to the American public or to the world to make money. You know, backtracking through the executives that have to sell to the studio head, the agents and managers that have to sell it to the studio, the writers that essentially have to sell the idea to their reps to get it out there, and I think a lot of people look at that and they say, "Oh, well, the system is only built to do one thing, and it's not what I want to do." But it could be, if you're smart and you look at different avenues of how to get your stuff made, it's not a conspiracy against the writers. And that's where I go back to: have a passion for it. Write great material. Continue to churn it out. Show it to people when it's ready. Almost do away with what your expectations are, but put the work in. And if you're really doing great work you're going to find success eventually.

Ryan Saul of APA suggested:

Don't send the first thing that you write out . . . that's the biggest mistake you can make because you get one crack really. That first screenplay that you write, burn it. It's not ready. The first one you write, that's for yourself. Put it aside. Write the second one. Maybe then you kind of find the voice a little bit. Put that one aside. The third one you write, you're gonna learn a lot from the first two you've written. The great thing about being a screenwriter is it's a fluid document that you're writing. If you put that first screenplay aside and you realize something that you're writing in the third screenplay would work in the first, steal from yourself. Go back to that first screenplay and then hone that one. Re-write it. And maybe that screenplay that you wrote—maybe burning it is an overreaction—that first screenplay that you wrote becomes your first spec. But only after you've gotten to understand your craft.

Bellevue Productions' John Zaozirny advised:

If I am suggesting something and at the other end you are like, "no, I'm not going to do that," I'm not excited about working with you because you don't seem really open to collaboration. Also, I don't want to put you in a room with my friends who are executives, my friends who are agents, because you're probably going to tell them the same thing that you are telling me. Nobody wants to be in the scenario where they're working with someone who's not collaborative. Not open to making something better. Who's closed off. Generally, the more experienced a writer is, the more open they are to collaboration, to ideas coming from anywhere. Let me put it this way: not all amateur writers are closed off to other people's ideas but most writers who are closed off to people's ideas are amateurs.

Manager Lee Stobby reiterated the importance of learning how to take notes, and further told me:

Not being open to notes is a problem. From my perspective, my clients have an audience of one person—Lee Stobby. And I'm their biggest fan. I'm the most helpful, I'm the most invested of anybody, but if you can't do my notes and be open to them, how am I going to feel comfortable going and putting you in a room? 'Cause, honestly, my notes are gonna be the best you're ever going to get, because I understand you. You have to be respectful of notes. And we can talk them through and we can break them down and we can argue about why we should or shouldn't do those but you have to be very open to that kind of thing. And writers who think that their scripts are perfect documents that don't need to be changed— unless they are actually perfect documents that don't need to be changed, which is very rare—need to be very open. It's very collaborative and you need to be very collaborative in that process. It's really hard if I'm going to read 17 drafts of a script, I'm not going to read 17 drafts of a script for an asshole, I'm just not. You have to be very pleasant. You have to understand that this is a very hard business and you have to be very easy and understand that it's going to take forever and be collaborative and fun to hang out with.

The number one mistake that anyone makes is that they haven't actually studied writing, at all. The number one traits of all of my writers is that they've been writers for a while, in various capacities. None of them are people who said, "Oh yeah, sure, I have no experience writing anything, why don't I write a script?" That doesn't work. You have to understand prose. You have to be able to tell a story. You have to be able to put words down on a piece of paper. You have to have written enough that you know what you are good and bad at. Just because someone has a good idea doesn't mean that you can write it well.

Living in Los Angeles

Over the years, whether or not a writer has to reside in Los Angeles in order to gain traction and get his screenwriting career off the ground has been a hot and often contentious topic. I myself got called out more than once for saying that living outside of Los Angeles is a handicap for writers who are eager to make it. Is it possible? I believe so. But is it preferable to live in Los Angeles? Here is what my industry friends said:

Manager Jewerl Ross provided his perspective:

> It's hard to build relationships living somewhere else. Skype and phone aren't as good as meeting in person. Skype and phone are poor tools in comparison. And yes, someone can fly here four times a year and meet people and whatever, but it's just not as good. Now I've signed and worked with writers from all over the world but if you are in your 20s and 30s and childless, you should be moving to LA if you really want to have a career here. I understand if you have two kids and a dying grandmother and you live in Ohio and you don't want to uproot your life. But I think one of the components of having and getting a successful career in Hollywood is ambition and putting yourself first and people in their 20s and 30s have the ability to put themselves first, get on a plane, and move to fucking LA. Some people who don't have the life circumstances to do that or the ambition to do that or the will to do that won't make it. It's not just a function of being in LA, it's a function of: do you have the will? And not everyone does. People can talk a lot about it—and I know this from my own experience in my own life growing up poor in Inglewood and creating this business for myself and going to Yale and all this shit—I know what kind of ambition that took. So I know it takes similar amounts of ambition to have success in this town. And everyone can TALK about having ambition and passion, but where the rubber meets the road is about DOING it. Can you forsake all that you know and move to a town where you don't know anyone and make it happen? Not everyone has the will.

Blondie Girl Productions' Ally Latman told me:

> If you're a TV writer who is only interested in developing and you're willing to come out here whenever you're needed—I don't think it's a must. But if you're a TV writer who is interested in staffing? Yes. You have to live out here.

David Boxerbaum of Paradigm said:

> I think writing can be done anywhere in the country. It's helpful for sure to live here—for on the spot meetings, opportunities to brand yourself and

meet people here in Los Angeles, submerge yourself with people who are doing the same thing you're doing—I think that's helpful. But it's not a necessity and I would never tell anybody to pick up—especially with a family, when they're trying to make a living as well as writing—until they can get to that point where they're making a living writing. I'd never tell them to pick up and move here without knowing that they have that backing already in place. That financial backing. Being here is helpful, but it's not necessary. I have writers who are all over the country—and the world.

Manager Lee Stobby felt strongly about it:

Living in LA is really important. It's super important. It's not an absolute. I do represent people who don't live here. Isaac Adamson doesn't live here. But at the same time, if you wrote something like *Bubbles* then you can live wherever you want. Right? You have to show Hollywood—"I'm serious about this." I don't represent people who are casual writers. It's not a hobby for me. It's all consuming. I spend every moment of my life thinking about it. If you want to be a writer in Hollywood and you don't spend every moment of your life thinking about it, you probably should try to do something else. It has to be the thing that you want to do all the time. You have to love writing. So if you don't live here, it just sends a signal of—to me—how serious are you about this? Three days after graduating, I drove my car to LA because I am super serious about it. So, if there's some reason that's preventing you from being here then you have to over-compensate, you have to be that much better of a writer, you have to be that much more on social media, you have to be that much more aggressive in your query letters. And so you are going to be that much more limited and therefore at a disadvantage compared to the competition of the writers who do live here. And again, that feeds into my ability to help you.

Infinity's Jon Karas provided his take:

It's really important to be around to network, to take a meeting at a moment's notice, to hang out with your peer group—peer group meaning more executives from the studios, your team, etc—you can't do that if you live some place else, you won't succeed. Or let's put it this way, you will have the odds go way against you. Is it because LA has nice weather? No, it's because the industry is here.

Circle of Confusion's Josh Adler provided his two cents:

My advice would be to get here. I know it's not feasible for everybody, it's not an option for everybody, people have families, people have jobs, whatever—but, and it may not be fair to say, but for the most part, if you're trying to break a new writer into the business, they need to be here. It makes it easier, and it shows that this isn't a hobby to you. That you're passionate about this, and this is your goal, and you're sacrificing and risking everything to try and make it, and you're not just a weekend warrior writer. It's not playing second fiddle to some other passion that you have. So most of the time, I would say, if you can, be here. It's the easiest way to start.

Ryan Cunningham of Madhouse Entertainment shared his thoughts on the location question:

It's not essential, but it certainly helps speed up the process because you're in a place where everybody's at least aware of the industry and has those connections and a lot of times, it is those weird connections that lead to finding a rep or finding a producer that likes your stuff. And if you're not there, it's gonna be harder to make those connections. And yeah, you can reach out over email to people and try your best to wave your hands and get their attention, but still a word of mouth referral from somebody you trust, whether that's an industry colleague or a family member you just want to shut up and not have to answer their phone calls about their cousin's friend's brother's script anymore, that's a lot better than an unsolicited email or a phone call from somebody I've never met before when I'm extremely busy all day to begin with.

Finally, manager Kailey Marsh told me:

I don't think it's a hundred percent necessary to live in LA. But the face time value is invaluable. Really. You know I developed a book with one of my clients over the past year and we're editing it right now and it's beautiful and I can't wait for people to read it but she lives in Florida and it's been difficult because I know she's a gorgeous girl and has a great personality and is so sweet, and I just know if I were able to put her in rooms with people, people would respond to how great she is. I feel like you don't really get that over a Skype session. I can't imagine not living in LA working in this industry and I feel like the same should go for writers.

Overnight Successes and How Long Building a Screenwriting Career REALLY Takes

Every once in a while, I meet a writer who just finished their first script, who neither worked in the industry before, nor knows anyone in the space, but expects for the script to sell and for him to become an overnight success nonetheless. But does that really happen?

Untitled Entertainment's Jennifer Au told me:

> That's . . . One in a million? I don't know what the odds are. This is the thing: It's rare. It is rare. But I'll also say this: you don't necessarily want to be that person. It's not about having the sale, it's about having the career, and it is about creating the infrastructure to have that career, and your body of work, and your skillset to match that. So, yes, I would love for people to sell overnight and for all of that to happen. But it is rare. And that is because of the nature of the business now.

Delving further into the sought-after concept of becoming an overnight success, I turned to my longtime friend, manager Chris Cook: "You hear about all of these overnight successes. Nine times out of ten, it's not true. I've worked with people for years and they were then dubbed an overnight success just because nobody heard of them."

Circle of Confusion's Josh Adler told me:

> Does it happen? Sure. I'm sure that you could walk out and you can go around town and you can find stories of people that signed at an agency or management company, got a rep, and 3 weeks later, their spec sold or they got staffed on this show based on their sample or whatever that might be. But for every one of those, there's others that it took five or ten years, you know, to really find that piece of material that broke them through or whatever. So, with this as well, there's no tried and true way.
>
> It's so funny to me, the overnight successes that everybody talks about. It's almost like everybody knows the term ten-years-in-the-making overnight success, but every time it happens, everybody just assumes, "Oh, this is the one that was an overnight one." Every client that I have, they're not 22-year old kids straight out of college with their first script that sells and becomes some huge thing. Most of them worked at it for a long time and they had a bunch of misses, close calls, their scripts got past the gatekeepers and went all the way up, and right at the last minute—right when they were going to get that yes—they got a no or a whatever, and they've had a lot of heartache and disappointment and a lot of nos. And then they get the yes. Very rarely is it that 22-year old kid off of their first script that gets a yes. It may seem that way. You may see some 28-year old that sells a script for a million dollars and say, "That's an overnight success," but chances are that that 28-year old has been here for 6 or 7 years, writing nonstop and that was not their first script. They've probably had two or three different reps and been dropped by one or things didn't work out or they were so close on this one thing but didn't get it and lost out to someone else or whatever. And then finally they get one through, they get a yes, and it appears like an overnight success, but it was 6 or 7 years in the making.

So how long does it really take to build a screenwriting career, to go from emerging writer to working professional? I usually say three to ten years but . . . what do my friends in the industry think?

Gersh's Sean Barclay said:

> It's very unpredictable. I think we throw out the extreme as a little bit of a gut check to people. Hey—Are you in this for ten years? Is this a business trip or is this your business? And I think the answer is it takes different people different amounts of time but be prepared for a fucking journey. There's a reason why people get compensated so well when they make it at the highest level because it's a process, it is a multi-year journey, just to get in the conversation. So, you are right.

APA's Adam Perry shared:

> I say 3 to 5 years. You should have another way to supplement your income. If you sell a script early, it's still a battle. Very few people just launch in a huge, huge way. Even when you sell your first one, maybe you make 50 grand that first year and then maybe the next year you make 75 and then the next you make a 100. You're still fighting. Until you get to a point when you are one of the few writers in town that's 4 or 5 films deep, 4 or 5 TV projects deep, and that's when you've truly hit as a writer. And then it's a battle to sustain. But you have to weather the storm in those first few years, or otherwise you're in trouble.

Manager Jewerl Ross added:

> When someone has failed to produce great work over the course of four or five years, maybe this isn't for them. They usually will recognize it before I have to tell them anything. And maybe after four years of not being able to produce something as stellar as that thing they produced four years ago, maybe they need to go write prose or a book or short stories or poetry. Though it is my goal to make all of my clients famous writers and directors, that's not going to be everyone's path. And I accept the fact that most will fail. And some of the ones who make it may surprise me, and that's okay. I don't need to know everything.

Manager Chris Cook imparted his knowledge and experience:

> Some of the biggest writers I know didn't get a paying gig until four or five years into working their butts off . . . You also have to give yourself the time. To say, giving yourself a year or two seems just kind of foolish. I'm not going to tell you to forgo a job that is going to put food in your

kids' mouth because you want to be this screenwriter. You have to have a comfortable day job. But you have to sacrifice your free time and put in the hard work to write. And writing when you don't want to write. Writing even when you're stuck and figuring out what else you can do to move the ball forward.

Madhouse Entertainment's Ryan Cunningham told me:

It can take a long time for some, it can take a short time for others. I don't think anybody should put an artificial clock on what that is. I think you have to use your own barometer of, do you love what you're doing? Are you seeing a continual evolution of your craft? Are you getting better as you're doing it? There are a lot of barometers you can use for that, both personally and externally. Are you enjoying what you're doing? And does your lifestyle and what you want outside of your career accommodate that still? It's no fun to be writing if your husband is bugging you that you have to get a real job, and God, we've gotta have kids now or you don't spend enough time with your kids because you're always doing this. That's not going to be fun, and whether you're getting paid or not, that's not a good career, probably. So I think you have to be very cognizant of how it works in your own life. Some people could take a year, some people could take ten years. It's unique to everybody's situation.

Bellevue Productions' John Zaozirny cautioned:

Scripts are not a lottery ticket, it's going to take you years and years and years to make any money from screenwriting. There are exceptions but those are just what I said, those are exceptions. The general rule is it will take you years to make money, let alone a living as a screenwriter.

And Untitled Entertainment's Jennifer Au told me this about how long you should keep trying:

The idealistic answer is you do it as long as you can't imagine doing anything else. And I say idealistic because I'm not looking at somebody's mortgage or they just had kids—I can't speak to that for everyone. But it takes a hunger. Every one of my clients' first films, their first sale, hit at a different point. Because it's about their personal development and their relationships and the tone of the town. And sometimes there's no rhyme or reason why it's not working. For the amount of time it takes to build in this town, it is harder to walk away and come back. It does happen. But I will say that that's a very personal discussion about looking yourself in the mirror and saying, "Is there anything else that would truly make me happy?" And also, what would it take to get there? Am I willing to do that? Or am I willing to see what I'm doing here through? I once sat down with someone, a potential client meeting, and I said, "Are you in it for the long haul?" And they said something like, "I'm giving it two years, and then I'm out," and my response was, "Great, well, I'm out right now." That's as long as it takes to get me a draft and for me to get it out there and for me to get you some fans, and maybe you haven't even written the second piece by then.

Jeff Portnoy's Five Things that Every Writer Should Know

When I sat down with Jeff Portnoy of Bellevue Productions, who started out at CAA, went on to now-defunct Resolution, and from there graduated to literary manager, he shared with me his best comprehensive advice for screenwriters:

- **Number One:** You have to love the process of writing. Whether it's TV or features or fiction, short story, novel, memoir, non-fiction, whatever the genre may be, you have to just love it so that you're excited to get to the computer or the typewriter. You can't wait to get up and do it. If you don't have that passion, that natural love for it, then writing is probably not for you. And that's why I'm managing and developing and not writing myself, because I just didn't have that compulsion to wake up and run to the computer. And then, of course, you have to rewrite, which is very tedious. You've already lived the story once and now you have to go back and rewrite it and rewrite it and then that's very fatiguing and so in order to endure that tedium you have to have that natural passion that really burns bright.
- **Number Two**: If you have the passion and love for the game and you're able to move to Los Angeles, you should do that. It's not easy for people of other nationalities to get here and do that. If you live in the States though, and you really love it, you should be here, that's it. You have to get here.
- **Number Three:** Until you find a representative you have to be your own rep. So you have to be proactive. If you love writing, you love it enough that you move to Los Angeles, you can't just sit in a room and write. You have to try and get in the game. Get into the festivals. Get into the fellowships. Get into the competitions. Reach out to people. Network. Work in the business. It's gonna help you. Once you have your representation you can go back to writing and just focusing on writing and not have to work on all the politics and all the other crap that no-one really likes to do.
- **Number Four:** If you do all these steps and you eventually find yourself in a room for a general meeting, you've got to project that you're an easy person to work with, you're a fun person to work with, you have to project charisma, smile! No-one wants to work with someone who's not going to listen to notes, not going to accept notes, that's going to be hard-headed,

that's cynical or pessimistic. When you finally get in the room with someone and they have a book they need adapted or a show they need a staff writer on or an article or it's a rewrite on something, you want to go in there and make them like you. That's all you have to do. You have to make them like you. Personality is everything. So it's being charismatic, it's being funny. Be open to anything. That doesn't necessarily mean you have to roll over to every note that they have but you have to consider it and if you don't think it's going to improve the script then you have to state your case.

- **Number Five:** Read as much as you can, watch as much as you can, stay in touch with what's happening in the business, if you write for TV you should be watching as much TV as you can, if you write features, read as many scripts and watch as many movies as you can. And just stay in tune with what's going on in the business and what people are looking for.

Advice from Working Writers

As this book draws to a close, I wanted to share with you final bits of advice provided by the talented and generous writers featured in these pages. These writers went from emerging to professional not by some indefinable, smoke-and-mirrors magic act, but by perseverance, focus and hard work. Here is the advice they had to share:

Erin Cardillo, creator and EP of the CW's *Significant Mother* said:

> Don't be too precious about anything. Writing is way more collaborative than a lot of writers think it is. When you start out, you're like, It's me and my vision and this is what I want! I've found that all of the collaborations I've had have actually elevated the material, not taken anything away from me. So if you can come from a collaborative mindset and have the mindset that that's going to help you and not take from you, then I think it's a good perspective to go into everything with. Even notes— I used to get really frustrated with notes, and now I get excited about notes, because I'm like—whether we like the suggestion or the fix, they're going to point out what isn't working and what isn't coming across. So it's interesting to get to a point in the process where you're not dreading somebody weighing in on your material, but you're excited for the collaboration. So distill that to get excited to collaborate and don't be too precious about your brilliance.

Kirk Moore, a NBC Writers on the Verge alumnus and working TV writers with credits including *American Crime* and *13 Reasons Why*, advised: "Never stop writing. If you believe you're supposed to be working in television, then you have to keep writing specs, pilots, short stories, etc. And, I would have to say, get comfortable with being vulnerable."

Marissa Jo Cerar, who made The Black List, The Hit List and the Young and Hungry List, sold a feature spec and spent three years on Freeform's *The Fosters*, told me:

> You need people who will inspire you to keep writing. My writers group offers unconditional support, and we've seen amazing successes in the years since we've formed. We help each other break stories, craft stronger characters, and when we have a crappy day we know there are six other writers we can call who will get it.

Terrell Lawrence, who wrote on *Your Family and Mind* and *Undatable*, shared:

> One of the things that helped me with networking was, when I would go to networking events, instead of bumping from one person to the next, I would find one person and talk to that person for almost the entire night. Sometimes that person would know somebody and then they'd introduce you to other people, and it gets a little bit easier.

Greta Heinemann, a Story Editor on NCIS New Orleans and a past participant in CBS's Writers Mentoring Program as well as the Humanitas New Voices program, contributed:

> If you don't write, it doesn't matter how many people are pulling for you. Nobody can get you a job. So my big advice would be to write your ass off. And be tough on your writing, but don't be tough on yourself. At the end of the day, what matters is what you write. But then you also need to be aware that there's a big business part to it, too, so strike that balance between writing your ass off and realizing that you're still a business person. And treat it like a job if you want this to be your job.

Chandus Jackson, a Universal Picture's Emerging Writers Fellowship alum, whose script *The Muti Killing* appeared on The Hit List, suggested:

> One of the things that's been consistent in this journey is that you're going to have those moments that are very rewarding and you're going to have those moments that are very disappointing. Don't get caught up on that. Just focus on what you're here to do, which is write—to be a storyteller. And know that you can have those days when you're up, those days when you're down, and you just have to find a way to stay steady with it. Because none of that makes you a writer. Getting back to sitting in a chair and sitting in front of a typewriter or a computer, doing it day in and day out, that makes you a writer. Don't get caught up in the ups and downs of it. Just focus on that process and enjoy where you're at and getting it out there.

Melissa London Hilfers, whose spec script *Undone* sold to Parks/McDonald, and who is also developing a pilot for USA, contributed:

> The best advice I can give is to meet anyone you can in the business and know, when you meet them, that you have something valuable to offer. I used to avoid reaching out to people because I felt like they were just doing me a favor by meeting me or reading my work. Now I know that every meeting is an opportunity for us to help each other and it shifts the whole dynamic.

Moises Zamora, who broke in on the merit of his pilot *Second Coming* and is a staff writer on *American Crime*, shared:

> My advice is to be patient and believe in the process. To do it for the writing, it is a life commitment. My journey began exactly twenty years ago and I hope it goes on for another twenty and more. I don't see myself doing anything else that gives me as much meaning. I'm not in it for the fame or the money. I'm in it because I don't see myself being happy doing anything else. I'm aware I may evolve as a writer and may end up writing poetry in thirty years. I think that's something no one can take away from you, your true passion for storytelling, and, frankly, it's the first thing people notice about me—my face lights up and my heart beats faster. It's the best feeling in the world.

Joe Webb, who developed pilots for Fox, Sony and Fremantle media, and whose credits include *Sleepy Hollow*, offered:

> At the end of the day, it all comes down to structure—because there are very few geniuses working in this industry; and almost all the successful writers I know are grinders. They write every day, and they just keep producing pages. And they know the second draft will be better than the first, and the third will be better than the second. And they know creating a good script, and a great career, is about water bashing away at stone slowly over time. So you've got to learn to structure your day to accommodate your writing. And then you also have to learn to structure your scripts. Because people who don't outline are either lazy or insane.

Barbara Curry, whose spec script *The Boy Next Door* appeared on The Blood List and was released by Universal Pictures, recommended:

> Assuming you are doing the hard work of writing, I would say it's important to meet other writers who are trying to do what you're trying to do. Take classes and go to conferences, not just because you might actually learn

something, but in order to meet other writers. Start or join a writers' group with people you genuinely like and trust because these are the people you will need to give you feedback on your work and to support you emotionally through the tough times. Personally, I think having a core group of fellow writers whom I trust to read my work and with whom I feel safe in sharing my successes and failures is the main thing that has sustained me throughout the years.

Diarra Kilpatrick, who created the web series *American Koko* and wrote on *The Mysteries of Laura*, advised:

> Make something. The ADD of our culture is pervasive. It's not just singular to kids or people who play video games. That extends to studio execs, to everyone. So if there's something they can click on their computer and get your voice in five or ten or fifteen minutes, I think that's much easier than getting someone to read 120 pages. So that's the first thing—make something. And then, more specifically, I would say make something that is so specific to you—make something that no one else could ever write. I think sometimes we fall in love with these things that are in the canon that we grew up watching and we're like, I want to write the next *Citizen Kane*. I want to write the next *Godfather*. But that's not your experience. And I think the thing they can't take away from you is your voice, your experience, your point of view. And so define yourself in three words. Write your biggest secrets down. Your opinions that you say at a party and everyone laughs. Or your opinions that you say at a party and everyone goes, I have never heard anyone say that before! Zero in on those things that are you, you, you and write from that place, and make it. Whether it's three minutes, whether it's shot on an iPhone, put your work out there, and it will work more for you than you ever could trying to beat on a bunch of doors with a 120 pages.

Writing team Tawnya Bhattacharya & Ali Laventhol, who have written on such shows as *Perception*, *The Client List*, *The Night Shift* and *Famous in Love* after coming out of NBC's Writers on the Verge, advocated:

> There are so many ways to break in, so don't give up if the traditional methods aren't working. In fact, that is our best advice: if you really want this, don't ever give up. Continue to read scripts, write scripts, get feedback, watch TV and movies, meet people in the business, write and produce a short or a web series . . . and live life. Life experience is as important as the rest of it because it will enrich your writing and make your storytelling more authentic.

Isaac Gonzalez, an alumnus of NBC's Writers on the Verge whose credits include *Community*, *Bordertown* and *Welcome to the Family*, recommended:

Be honest with your work and don't be precious. You won't get good until you allow people to tear your writing down and until you learn to take notes and constructive criticism. Don't get mad when people don't like your stuff, try and look at your work objectively, and figure out ways to get better. If you are doing comedy, study it and try to understand your own sense of humor. Do some comedic soul searching (What shows make you laugh? What are your influences and inspirations? Are you into more subtle comedy or are you broad?). Try to blend these influences together with your own experiences to form your own comedic voice. Growing up, I was heavily influenced by *South Park*, which was my absolute favorite show. It is no coincidence that my writing is very dark and irreverent—because that's what I think is funny. Don't worry about what others think is funny, you have to be honest with what makes you laugh. At the end of the day, you are selling YOUR sense of humor. When you pitch a sitcom, they are not buying your brilliant idea (let's face it all comedy premises are pretty mundane) they are buying YOU and the way you tell jokes and the way you see the world.

Danny Tolli, an alumnus of the NHMC program and a writer on *The Catch*, advised:

> Never give up writing. Always be thinking of new ideas and putting words down on the page and finishing projects—and finishing projects that you're really proud of and coming up with stories that you want to tell and that you feel really passionate about. Characters that you love and that you feel have something really important to say because they're an extension of you. And you have something really important to say. The obvious advice is, "Move out to LA and be a PA in a writer's room!" But I'm not going to pretend that so many people can easily do that and upend their life and move out here. So if you're in Michigan and you've just graduated from college and it doesn't make sense for you at the time to move out here, don't just give up. Keep writing. Find a way to put yourself out there. With social media now, with new media, with Crackle and Hulu and YouTube and even Netflix and Amazon to an extent, there are so many channels for your voice to be heard. But you've gotta write. And you've gotta write from the heart. Otherwise those stories aren't going to get told.

Michael Perri, who has written on *State of Affairs* and *Blindspot* and is an NHMC and Writers on the Verge alumnus, told me:

> Your first drafts are always crap. In fact, everyone's first drafts are complete crap . . . from the most experienced writer to the first time writer. It doesn't matter, you just have to get something on the page . . . JUST WRITE! Then and only then, you can mold and shape your story so it can become even better than the last iteration.

SCREENWRITER SPOTLIGHT #15: Danny Tolli

Born in Queens, New York, to Argentine immigrants, **Danny Tolli** had a passion for storytelling at an early age. Following his graduation from NYU's Tisch School of the Arts, he moved to Los Angeles to participate in the National Hispanic Media Coalition's TV writing fellowship. Danny's big break came at Vin Diesel's production company One Race Films, where he wrote an episode for the company's first foray into episodic series, Crackle's *The Ropes*. Shortly thereafter, Danny worked for Kevin Williamson as his assistant on the hit shows *The Vampire Diaries* and *The Following.* He was promoted to writer's assistant on Williamson's CBS procedural *Stalker*, where he wrote and produced a freelance episode. Danny is currently a Story Editor on Shondaland's *The Catch* for ABC and is repped by Verve.

Lee: Hi Danny! Let's start from the beginning. Are you an LA native?

Danny: I am not. I was born and raised in Queens, New York, in a neighborhood called Elmhurst, which is one of the most diverse neighborhoods in the country. My parents are Argentinian and moved here in the 1980s, and I am first generation.

Lee: And you went to NYU, right?

Danny: I did. Yes, I studied film and television, and the first couple of years there I really struggled with what I wanted to do. I started off thinking, "Well, I'm a director!" And then I was really into cinematography and thought I was going to be a DP, and I realized I didn't want to do that. I did the same thing with editing. But the whole time I was writing and taking screenwriting classes and taking TV colloquiums and liberal studies regarding TV. In my senior year I realized, "Oh! I am a TV writer, and that's what I want to do."

I graduated in 2008, and a good friend of mine who moved out to Los Angeles was applying to a program called the National Hispanic Media Coalition—a TV writing fellowship—and he said, "Hey Danny, I know you're in New York, but check this fellowship out. It's just a couple weeks here in LA, it might be fun." I applied to it, and was accepted into their program. They flew me out that November of 2008, and I lived out here in Los Angeles for six weeks, and got to meet all of the executives who run the ABC Diversity Programs and the person who ran the NBC Diversity Program at the time. So it was sort of like a meet-and-greet, but we also developed specs so that we could then submit them to the ABC Fellowship and to NBC Writers on the Verge the following year. That was my first taste of the business and working here in LA.

Lee: Once the fellowship concluded, you went back to New York. What ultimately brought you back to Los Angeles?

Danny: At the time I thought I was a comedy writer—and *30 Rock* was still on the air, and I said, "You know, I'm a native New Yorker, I'm never going to move to LA, LA is stupid and everyone is so sunny and cheery. I'm going to be a dark and twisted comedy writer who's living in New York and I'm going to work on *30 Rock* and blah blah blah." The people who ran the NHMC program said, "That's cute, it's not going to happen that way. You really need to move to LA. You need to be a PA. You need to work from the ground level up. That's the only way to break into the business." I wasn't working at the time in New York, and I never lived so far away from home. Even when I was at NYU, I was only fifteen minutes away from home. So I thought it would be a fun journey. I moved out to LA in 2009, and I started interning at Vin Diesel's production company. I met Vin through his father who was one of my NYU professors who I worked with for years, and when I moved out here, Vin's producing partner Samantha Vincent hired me as an intern. That turned into an assistantship there and a mentorship for a couple years before I actually broke into TV.

Lee: During that time, what did you do beyond your assistant job in order to keep developing your craft and develop your industry relationships?

Danny: In my free time when I wasn't working, in the evenings, on the weekends, I was just writing—perfecting scripts, coming up with new ideas, and actually completing them, which was the most difficult thing to do after working a thirteen-hour shift everyday. There was a lot of me working on my craft but then also seeing how the entertainment business works. What sells, what is a good story, what isn't a good story, how to tell stories that people will be engaged in, that will want to bring you in for a meeting. I was learning that through work, and I was applying that to my own personal writing, and it only helped my craft grow.

Lee: When did your agency Verve come into the picture for you? And how?

Danny: Verve came into the picture just last year. My agent, Melissa Darman I have known for years. About two years ago, she and I were having coffee. I sent her this script that she was obsessed with and she loved. And at the time, she was an executive at Lionsgate TV on the comedy side, and she took me out for breakfast one morning and we talked for an hour just about our lives, and then we started talking about my script, which she really loved, and she informed me that she was ready to make a career move and that she was actually thinking of going into representation. And she said that, wherever she landed, I would be one of her first calls. And I was like, "Great! That sounds nice—we'll see if that really happens . . ." And then it did—she landed at Verve. And a couple months into her working there, she let me know that she shared my material with the people who would be my team— Bill Weinstein and Felicia Prince—and they loved it. They brought me in for a meeting, and it just clicked. I was actually taking other meetings around that time. I met with Paradigm and with WME and ICM, and everyone was saying great things, but I felt that Verve were the ones who really wanted to hear what I wanted to do with my career and wanted to know where I wanted to staff and wanted to know what shows I was watching and what material I was interested in writing. At the time, I was Kevin Williamson's assistant—

and so many places wanted to just capitalize on that and say, "You're Kevin Williamson's protégé, let's put you on a horror show!" And I love horror, but that's not really my sensibility. And so I thought that, with Verve, I could say, "This is the type of writer I am," and they were like, "Yes! We love that, and we're going to help you become that kind of writer."

Lee: What was it like being Kevin Williamson's assistant? How did you come into that job?

Danny: It's funny—the same friend who told me about the NHMC program is the friend who hooked me up with the Kevin Williamson job. He was working as one of Kevin's assistants at the time, and he knew that Kevin's Executive Assistant—the one that is the day-to-day on all of Kevin's showrunning duties—was getting promoted. I was desperate to work in TV after working at Vin's company. I had been such a huge fan of Kevin from the beginning of my childhood—I love everything that he's done, so it was a total, *This is never going to happen. This is a pipe dream!* And then I got the interview, and I was so giddy and such a fanboy, and we sat down and had a really long interview. I loved that he was open to mentoring his assistants and really letting them be a part of the process and see how you produce a show and deal with writers and behave in a room and how you get to pitch story. I worked with Kevin for almost three years as his assistant, and that was on *The Secret Circle* and *The Following* and his latest show *Stalker*, which I was involved with on the pilot. And then he and I sat down and had a serious conversation where he said, "You have been such a fabulous assistant, and you've learned so much from me, it's time that you get room experience." As a showrunner's assistant, you don't really get a chance to sit in the room and be a part of the storytelling process. He really wanted me to learn that component, and he brought me in as his writer's assistant on *Stalker* and awarded me a freelance episode, and it was just life-changing. Because I already felt like I went through one school with him. And then writer's assistant was a completely different, other beast. Just getting the chance to see him do his thing in the room with other writers, watch him break story live in person, was phenomenal.

Lee: Tell me how you went from *Stalker* to *The Catch*.

Danny: *Stalker* only lasted for a season. In February (of that year) I was done with writing my episode, and we were hearing rumblings that *Stalker* might not come back. And my agents were like, "We're gonna get you out. We're gonna introduce you to the executives at the networks and the studios, and push you really hard for staffing because you're in such a great position—you just came off an episode, you just produced an episode, which is so rare for a writer's assistant to do by themselves, so we've gotta build on this momentum." One of the things they asked in my first meeting with them was, "If you could work anywhere, where would you work?" And I said, "I would work on a Shonda Rhimes show. I eat, breathe, sleep her, I worship her at the altar. I would just love the opportunity." And then, sure enough, this show called *The Catch* got picked up in May, and I got a call saying, "Do you want to meet there?" And I was like, "Yes! Of course I want to meet there!" I met with the showrunner at the time and got hired like three weeks later.

Lee: What is it like, being a first time staff writer in the room?

Danny: It's very exciting, but daunting. It's so amazing to have a job where you sit in a room with super talented people and just bounce ideas back and forth all day. It's also incredibly exhausting because I don't feel like I have ever really worked as hard a job than I have as a staff writer, because your brain is always on and you're always observing and absorbing everything. You're thinking about other writers' ideas, and you're thinking about your own, and you're finding ways to fix a problem and solve puzzles and come up with cool stories that have not been seen before and find times that are appropriate to pitch them and then make sure that you pitch them in a way that is confident and that you feel proud of your idea so that it comes across as a good idea. It's a strange dance, where you've got so many things you're trying to juggle and then six o'clock rolls around and you're like, "Wait! What did I do all day?" But the great thing about our show that I don't think lots of shows do is that all of the writers are hands-on on every single episode. We break our outlines together in the room. We do a lot of group writing for specific episodes. Everyone is allowed to pitch. There's never a sense of— you're a staff writer, don't speak. Everyone is welcome and all of the ideas are put into this big melting pot.

Lee: You fell in love with TV early and figured that was your avenue. What was it about TV that causes you to speak about it with so much passion?

Danny: On the creative side, I've always loved how collaborative it is, how it's not just you in a room typing away behind a blue screen. It's bouncing ideas off of each other. A good TV writer isn't an egomaniac. It's someone who can pitch an idea and respond well to the fact that someone else might re-pitch that idea with a better twist or have a fix for what you just pitched. I love the whole passing the ball back and forth that happens in TV.

I grew up watching TV shows. My parents didn't hire babysitters. They just said, "Okay, you get home from school at 4 pm. We'll be home at 7. Entertain yourself in front of the TV and don't burn the house down." So I grew up watching soaps that I probably shouldn't be watching—*Melrose Place, Beverly Hills 90210*. My favorite show of all time that solidified the kind of writer that I wanted to be was *Buffy the Vampire Slayer*. And I was also a WB kid, so I was watching *Dawson's Creek* and *Felicity* and *Charmed*. As early as I can recall, TV was always on in the background. I've just always loved that you can live with a character for so long and take them on a journey for years.

Lee: Do you have a manager or are you agent only?

Danny: I do. I'm with Rain Management Group. And actually—my husband is my manager. [*Laughs*] He started getting hands on in my development process and I really respect his opinion, not just because he's my husband but professionally he's one of the smartest people in the business. He watches everything, reads everything. He can look at a character and really understand what works and what doesn't work in a script and where they're at emotionally. He knows me so well, knows the type of writer that I want to be, so he is the best choice to help me build my career. And that's honestly the most important part of picking the right representation. Not just that Verve said all those nice, great things—but the fact that they understand the type of writer I want to be, and aren't forcing me to do something just because we're going to make money out of it. I think that, when you're a young writer, you really have to look out for who is going to have your best interests and who is going to treat you like a person and not just like a moneymaker.

Lee: Do you think being in Los Angeles is imperative for anybody who wants to break into TV?

Danny: Oh yeah. I really do. Studios and the networks are here, the big heavy-hitters are working out here—and those are the people who you want to meet in some capacity, who you want to work for as an assistant so that they can help mentor you and introduce you to other people . . . You're only going to get those relationships living out here in LA.

Lee: If there was one thing that you wish you knew then—when you first moved from NYU—that you know now, what would it be?

Danny: I wish that I realized that first year how much of a social industry this is. I spent the majority of my first year here really having a hard time adjusting to LA life and feeling like, "Oh, this is just temporary. Oh, I'm looking to get a job and hopefully spend a couple years here and then move back." It really hindered me from making friendships and relationships with people and it really put me in a bad place. And at the end of the day, this business is about who you know and working with your friends and being a good person and having a good reputation. An executive is going to get you in front of a showrunner because they remember how great you were in the room and how nice you were and how you know so-and-so. For me personally, a lot of the executives who I met this first go-round—we grew up as assistants together. And that first year, I wasn't realizing that like go out to drinks. Do dinners. Hang out with people on the weekends. Don't just use people for whatever personal gain you may see. Really build good relationships because those people are going to want to go up to bat for you at the end of the day. They're the ones who are going to get you jobs. You can be the world's most prolific, talented writer, but if you don't have someone who's going to want to take a chance on you because they know you personally, it's going to be a very hard path for you to succeed.

15
FINAL THOUGHTS

Even though my instinct is always to leave the last words to those wiser than me, because, frankly, I already know what I have to say so I would rather listen to others, it's a three-layer cake I promised, and so a three-layer cake you shall receive.

Which in other words means . . . one more time . . . drumroll please . . . Little ol' me.

As mentioned in the very beginning of this work, this book has been—by far—the most comprehensive, ambitious and thereby gratifying project I have ever taken on. But as I come to its final pages, and my final hours with it before I send it out into the world, I can't help but recall a moment from the very earliest of moments in this book's lifecycle: in the fall of 2015, before I even put together a book proposal, I floated the idea to my friend Jason Scoggins for a temperature gauge. Maybe the three-layer cake metaphor had not been introduced as of yet, but the overall concept was very much what you have in your hands—or on your iPad or Kindle—today. Jason, supportive and enthusiastic as ever, asked me why this complicated approach, which involved coordinating and conducting countless interviews, not to mention sifting through, editing and organizing significant amounts of information. Why not just write it on my own, from everything I already know?

I didn't tell him my secret: that at heart I am an information hoarder. That— put quite simply—I just love this stuff. But what I did say was equally true: that I wanted to write this book in a fashion that would not only allow me to share my own knowledge, but would also permit me to take other opinions and points of view into account. In other words, I wanted to write this book in a manner that would allow me not only to share what I already know, but also to learn, and continue my quest to information gather. And now that it is—in industry speak— in the can, I am happy to confirm that it has absolutely allowed me to do as much.

Indeed, this book has extended me a great deal of opportunity to ask a great many questions of my generous, knowledgeable and remarkably candid industry colleagues and friends, old and new. I crammed as much as I could of what I gathered into this book, while inevitably having to leave some precious nuggets, anecdotes and quotes on the cutting room floor. And yes, some statements did get taken out in order to protect the innocent. After all, if I shared those with you, I would have to kill you. (Note: I am writing this at 2:49 in the morning. Is this what Evan Corday was talking about, the diminishing returns you get as you write deep into the night, which don't always quite hold up in daylight? Time—and the readers of this book—will have to be the judge).

However, before it's all said and done, before the file is locked and sent to my publisher, I wanted to lean into the inspiration given me by the writers I spoke with, by the agents, managers and execs whose stories and insights have been deposited into the micro-recorder that for six months became my steady companion, and share with you a few final thoughts, my last bits of guidance and advice:

- **If you want to be a writer, write.**
  I believe that it was manager Lee Stobby who said—and I am paraphrasing—that unless you are actively in pursuit of a thing, which in this case is writing, you can't claim the thing as your own, i.e. call yourself a writer. So if you are a writer, it is critical that you are indeed actively and consistently writing. Take classes. Take many of them. Don't assume that just because you can shell out $200 for Final Draft your scripts are going to be great right off the bat. Therefore, study the craft. Participate in writers' groups. Develop new material. Hone your skills and develop your style. Bottom line is: screenwriting is serious stuff. Real writers write. It is not something they just talk about; it's something that they do. Actively, determinedly, with focus and purpose.
- **Be unrelenting about WHAT you write**.
  In today's competitive, ever-changing industry reality, mediocre, half-baked or even just "good enough" simply won't do. It all starts with an idea that is fresh, unique and original, a story only you can tell, unlike anything else out there. So if you want to make a screenwriting career your new reality or push a stalled career back into motion, challenge yourself to greatness by putting in those 10,000 hours, by exposing work early and often, by getting up early or going to sleep late, by skipping out on random drinking nights with your friends and buckling down to write instead, by being unyielding and unwavering as you challenge yourself to your most unique, most interesting ideas and to the most seamless, stellar execution, as you write script after script, identify, define and develop your voice, and seek out constructive criticism ensuring that when the cream rises to the top, eventually that cream may indeed be you.

- **Think like a writer.**

  Don't write to trends. Don't attempt to anticipate the market, to write whatever you think the industry is looking for that day. Even if you are right, whatever the industry is looking for will change ten times over by the time you finish new work. Therefore, write the stories you have to write, the themes you are driven to explore, the characters and worlds that you can't seem to shake. Write material that is deeply meaningful for you, material that excites you, that is original and unlike anything else out there, to which you are able to connect. Write it because you have to write it, not because you think it will pave your path to a career or even a sale. Passion inspires. Careers are built when a writer is able to put passion on the page, marry it with craft and tell a powerful story that will set you apart from the rest.

- **Screenwriting is not a lottery ticket.**

  Screenwriting is a job. And as with any job, you're going to have to prepare yourself for it. You're going to have to work for it if you stand a real shot of making a go of it. It's going to take time. Even if and when you do get interest in your work, you will likely not get any sort of significant money up front, so get clear on that ahead of time. It will take time to build up. You are going to have to prepare for what one of the writers interviewed in this book called *the longest job interview EVER*. So study the business, and your particular business sector. Develop and bolster your body of work and thereby your craft and skillset. Learn everything you can about the players—production companies, producers, showrunners, directors—in the space. Watch movies. TV shows. Read books. Listen to podcasts. Become a student of the game. And always continue challenging and working on your craft. That's the only way to ensure that when your opportunity knocks, you stand a chance of showing up prepared.

- **Personality matters.**

  Sure, the work you produce has to be superior. Inspiring. Undeniable. But even if you're shy, reserved or potentially socially awkward, love it or hate it, you're going to have to figure out how to show up in a powerful way for generals and pitch meetings or even face time with agents and managers. Reps have no desire to work with writers who lack business savvy, who will not represent them well, or are just straight out "weird"; showrunners, producers and executives are looking to hire and be inspired by writers who are composed, informed, knowledgeable and passionate. Writers with whom they want to spend time and work with. So do what you have to do in order to present well when the opportunity comes: practice your pitches, work on your personal narrative, or take an acting class. You don't have to be everyone's best friend, but you do have to show up and make the most of every opportunity, every potential relationship when the time comes. After all, opportunity rarely knocks twice.

- **Treat your writing like your job.**
  Until your writing becomes your "job" job, the one that earns you regular income, you have to treat it as a bona fide second job, one that you will be paid for—and eventually handsomely—later on. That means that writing once in a while, when time permits, when the muse strikes or when the stars align is not going to be enough if an actual long lasting screenwriting career is what you have in mind. That means hard work, less sleep and some semblance of sacrifice in order to balance paying your rent or providing for your family while consistently developing and working on your craft. And once your writing becomes your job . . . You have to be writing all the time. Create structure. Commit to discipline. Don't wait for the writing to come to you. Writers in this business are most successful when they are proactive. Like every other job, there will be days you love it, and there will be days you love it less. But if you want to keep it, like every other job, you're going to have to make sure that day after day you're getting things done on both the creative and strategic fronts. If you don't want to do it, there will be plenty of other writers who would happily step in for you.
- **Go big or go home.**
  Seriously. Don't go for middle-of-the-road. Challenge yourself to aim as high as possible, and then go even higher. If you've learned nothing else from these pages, I hope that you learned that building a screenwriting career— while difficult, challenging and long-gestating—is also very much possible. Writers are doing it all the time, inventing their unique paths to screenwriting success with hard work, determination, talent, courage and focus. If you rise to the challenge, if you inform your own choices and business decisions using what you've learned from those who came before you and those who work on the forefront of discovering new writers, then the next writer to break in could very well be you. But it's going to require that you challenge yourself, that you don't try for short cuts, that you put in the work, that you don't spend time devising your next Hail Mary while doing little else and that you step outside of your comfort zone when networking, exposure and rejections are involved. A career in screenwriting comes with high competition, but also serious rewards: if you staff on television and make it to the second season or your next show, if you sell a spec screenplay or make it onto The Black List and land writing assignments from there on, if you sell a pilot and go on to become a Supervision Producer on your own show, you will be well compensated to do what you love down the road. So if that is what you want, give it the sort of fight that—win or lose—you will be proud of.

As said and demonstrated in this book, the industry might have shifted and changed, but writers are still breaking in, going from emerging to professional, on a regular basis. In fact, in the thick of PEAK TV, the explosion of web content, and some hope for features in the independent space, screenwriting, at the moment, is a growth sector. Writers out there are working hard, developing their craft, reaching for those original ideas, trying to set themselves apart. They are networking. They are shooting web series. They are applying to television writing programs, feature writing fellowships and labs and submitting their completed materials to screenwriting competitions as well as listing it on The Black List website. They are finding ways to attract representation, and showing up prepared for generals, whichever way they come. And if they're not in Los Angeles, they might even be making the cross-country move. So embrace the fact that if this were easy, everyone would do it. If not for the realities—good and bad—of screenwriting, then for the fantasy of what it means to be a screenwriter in Hollywood. But if you really want to break in, to become a working screenwriter, to dig out your place in the trenches and for a living get to do what you love, the one thing that you have to ensure is that, no matter where you are in your screenwriting journey or where you are in the world, every day, bit by bit, both strategically and creatively, you are finding smart new ways to move your screenwriting career forward.

SCREENWRITER SPOTLIGHT #16: Michael Perri

Michael Perri is a dramatic writer who was born Emmanuel Pedro, until his adoptive parents changed his name when he was ten. Growing up in Chicago's foster care system, he wrote plays and asked (okay forced) the other kids to act them out. Before moving to LA to write full time, he traveled the world as a technology and cyber-security consultant. In 2013 through 2014, Perri was awarded a coveted spot in the NBC Writers on the Verge Program and was also a finalist in the Disney ABC Writing Program. Prior to that, Perri was also a part of the National Hispanic Media Coalition's Television Writers Fellowship sponsored by ABC Creative Development and NBC's Talent Inclusion Programs. He attributes his success to the same resolve and optimistic attitude he displayed as a child in foster care. Perri's characters often reflect his own upbeat and positive attitude, persevering to overcome their obstacles no matter the odds. As a nice Catholic boy, his dream was always to marry a sweet Jewish girl, join the enormous family she puts up with and have a family. Recently, Mike's dream came true and he looks forward to raising his children to be guilt-free "Cashews" one day. Perri was a writer on the NBC CIA Conspiracy Series, *State Of Affairs* starring Katherine Heigl and Alfre Woodard, and most recently staffed on the NBC hit *Blindspot*. He is represented by Kaplan Stahler Agency and Echo Lake Management.

Lee: When did you start writing? Did you always know that TV was where you wanted to be, or did that reveal itself later? And if so, how?

Mike: Ever since I could talk, I've always been coming up with "make-em-ups." Growing up in the foster care system outside of Chicago, I used my humor, wits and mouth to help keep the bullies at bay . . . and also as a protective layer against the jumbled and volatile emotions that consumed me when I was a child. And, because of the constant bouncing around between my biological mother and adoptive parents, I often wrote about escaping to far-far-away worlds in other galaxies or would put on plays with the other kids and act them out. Maybe, the escape would prove to be a stable endeavor, or not. These dreams, skits, story ideas I would create all helped me come to terms, much later in life, with the identity and abandonment issues as a result of foster care. So, storytelling was my refuge and my savior. It kept me sane.

Television writing revealed itself much later, after trying to do improv comedy and acting in Chicago. Eventually, I found that, although I had something to say on stage and was funny in person, on the page it didn't translate so well. It actually was drama writing where I had really had something to say and, I guess, that all stood out.

Lee: Gotta ask . . . Why television?

Mike: The TV was another parent to me growing up. I can't tell you how many life lessons I learned from Kevin Arnold on "The Wonder Years" or even Sam from "Quantum Leap." Although, later, this career made perfect sense, I really had to tap into my voice and listen to my gut, because I didn't know what kind of writing I wanted to do. Honing on my voice and working my TV writing muscles over time was a long process, because, at first, I really thought I wanted to be a performer/writer on SNL. SNL was also another parent, a baby sitter and even my best friend all rolled up into one while I was growing up. More importantly, after my adoptive parents passed away around the age of 30, I was working in this really crazy job in technology and I just didn't know what to do with myself anymore. I was lost, so I went back to what made me feel like "me" again . . . writing.

Lee: Once you've decided you wanted to write professionally, what steps did you take to become the best writer you could be?

Mike: At first, I did what every writer does in Hollywood: I faked it, till I could make it and then I took a zillion classes and workshops, but that was a huge mistake. I basically fooled myself into thinking I would, by osmosis, absorb the knowledge I needed to become successful. The truth was, writing means you have to write . . . a lot. So, I had to pen a metric-shit-ton of samples before I finally "got it." Practice made perfect. It took YEARS to find my voice and to create great samples that would be worthy of either representation or being something I was really proud to have in my arsenal of scripts. Soon, friends, with connections, started to help and my work got noticed. Plus, my then girlfriend (now wife) asked me what my "brand" was . . . It threw me for a loop, but I decided I needed to specialize in something and that brought my "voice" into my writing even more. Since I had a twisted family upbringing and love technology, I found myself writing about twisted families or twisted technology . . . and then, things really started clicking.

After gaining more confidence and honing my brand, I started applying to fellowships with my sample specs and original work (The NHMC Program, Writers on the Verge, CBS, WB, ABC | Disney, etc.) And, in 2012 (after writing at least ten samples in the past four years) I was accepted into the NHMC Program where ABC and NBC (sponsors) took note of my writing. I kept plugging away, which meant more writing, and in 2013, I was accepted into the NBC Writers on the Verge (WOTV) program along with being a finalist in the CBS and ABC | Disney Program. That entire journey took about seven to eight years. From 2005 when I moved to LA and then in 2012, when my writing took off . . .

Lee: If you could retrace your steps . . . what did you do to prepare yourself for a career in the industry?

Mike: It really was persistence. I had to find time to write, work and be a husband . . . and eventually, also a father . . . all while constantly trying to write something better than the last. Surrounding myself with too many critics with lofty opinions was also something I had to wean myself from as I was moved up the food chain. I decided to find working TV writers (like Tawnya Bhattacharya & Ali Laventhol) who could critique my work and help me become better. I felt like I had to listen and apply everyone's notes in my large circle of friends. Ultimately, I had to find a trusted group of people who got my writing and me. Also, I read a TON of PILOTS and specs so that I can learn how the masters of television do their job. I'm still learning. That's what I love about writing . . . there's always a new story to craft as well as compelling ways, on the page, to tell it . . .

Lee: You first surfaced through the TV writing and mentoring programs; what was the experience like for you, and how important do you think these programs are for breaking into television?

Mike: Fellowships were CRUCIAL for my success. I recently read an article where someone said that getting into Writers on the Verge is harder than getting into Harvard. I am very proud and humbled by achieving such a tough feat. As far as importance goes . . . Look, it's a crapshoot. I was extremely lucky. It did help, there's no doubt. Eight out of 2,000 who applied made it the year I was accepted. The application numbers are through the roof now and keep rising. I feel that great writing will surface no matter if you're in a fellowship or not. Connecting with people in the industry, working your way up on a show from PA to Staff Writer are also other ways I've seen people make it. It just takes time, tenacity and talent. A great sample that makes people jump out of their seat . . . that's what I would first focus on, then I would focus on replicating your writing process in a way that can help you write even faster, better and with even more to say.

Lee: Did you go directly from Writers on the Verge to staffing? And if so, what was that experience like?

Mike: In my fellowship class, only three writers were staffed. One was actually staffed during the program itself. That year, it was a bloodbath for new writers and shows that didn't get renewed or picked up. The pressure was on. So, I thought I wouldn't get staffed no matter what, but I was very fortunate. It takes a village . . . okay . . . it takes an intergalactic federation to get staffed on a TV show these days. It was NBC, my reps and various connections to showrunners that helped get me meetings for available staff writer or diversity spots. I was up for two shows, *American Odyssey* and *State of Affairs*. *American Odyssey*, who looked like a shoe in, changed their game plan. So, I was out. At the last minute though, I got a meeting with the first showrunner of *State of Affairs* (Ed Bernero). Ed and I clicked and I was offered a spot in the room . . . so, I was on cloud nine. I got to quit a temp tech gig and I became a staff writer . . . full time. I've dreamt, ever since I was a child, that I would write something that would air on TV and now, I was getting my shot. I jumped up and down in the elevator after the meeting and called my wife, crying. Next to seeing my son be born and marrying my wife, that's my top three moments in Mike Perri history that I will always cherish and remember.

Lee: When and how did representation come into your journey and how did you decide to go with your rep?

Mike: Thanks to the NHMC and ABC, I found my managers at Echo Lake . . . that is after I left another manager who literally went MIA. I still don't know where he is . . . JK, if you are out there, please call. I'm worried about you. Anyway, while doing WOTV, my manager introduced me to Shan Ray at Kaplan Stahler and we began a great "bro-mance." I love them all. I wanted lovable "pit-bulls." People who would be tough as well as go the distance, helping me stay relevant, grounded and excited to be a writer.

Lee: Now that you've been represented for some time—How do you work with your reps—what do you expect from them, and what do they expect from you?

Mike: My managers are my creative partners. They work with me from concept to final draft. My agent is the final link, he reads the later drafts of my work and together "Team Perri" puts a game plan in motion for staffing or pitching opportunities.

Lee: Tell me a bit about the experience as a first-time TV-staff writer. How was it for you?

Mike: I have to say that it was both AMAZING and TOUGH. *Amazing*, because I was getting paid to learn how to produce television, write professional drafts, generate story and season arc ideas, all while watching and collaborating on how a very expensive TV show gets put together from the ground up. There's an art to everything . . . everything! From pitching ideas, to breaking story to even tech scouting locations, it's the best time ever. It was also *tough*, because politics came into play a lot, and it clouded some of my experiences. Of course, I wanted everything to be puppies and unicorns all the time, but the reality of the situation is that people are people . . . even if you have the best job in the world, you're still going to face obstacles that you need to overcome in order to thrive and get ahead in this business no matter what.

Lee: How does your life change after your first staff writing position—are jobs just handed to you, or do you have to work for them? And—assuming you do have to work for them—what does "working for them" look like?

Mike: The first thing to note is that you're still considered a "Baby Writer." Even if you were staffed, you have to work even harder to prove you still belong in the next room should you get staffed again. Jobs are definitely not handed to you. Writers are only as relevant as their last show or latest writing sample. You have to constantly generate new material . . . always. Working is writing. A LOT. This year though, due to life (child and other stuff I won't go into) I had to really refocus. Especially after not getting staffed this past year again, it bruised my ego. After I licked my wounds, I promised my wife and my reps that I would complete at least two new pilots in the coming months to make up for everything. So, that's what I am doing now. Writing new pilots, meeting new creative execs and coming up with pitches so that I stay relevant . . .

UPDATE: Shortly after this interview, Mike got staffed on NBC's *Blindspot* so the new pilots must have done their job!

Lee: How do you keep yourself busy (creatively and professionally speaking) between TV seasons and staffing gigs?

Mike: My personal life comes first . . . I get so much of my inspiration from my son and wife. That fulfils me and then pushes me to do the three most important things as a TV writer. 1) Write. 2) Write. 3) Write. In between those three things, my reps set me up with meetings that could lead to landing a pitch or a future staff spot down the road. So, I always have to stay on top of the latest shows, scripts or production deals. Plus, Deadline.com is my start page. Every morning, I look at what has sold or what's going on in the industry.

Lee: Is it important for TV writers to live in Los Angeles? And if so, why?

Mike: I think LA is the hub. You have to come here to excel. New York has many rooms as well, but LA is where the majority of the work resides. Therefore, I think, if you're truly serious, you need to be here, to meet the decision makers, movers, shakers, established and aspiring storytellers who can help show you the way.

Lee: In your estimation, how long did it take you to break into the industry from the time you set your sights on a career writing for television, and what did you do during that time?

Mike: Eight years. In that time, I studied with every teacher or consultant in town, wrote about twenty scripts (TV, film) and "lunched" with way too many people. Honestly, what helped me the most was finding trusted sources who would give me brutally honest feedback. I also tried creating and filming my own pilots or web-series and that was eye-opening and terrifying, but I learned valuable lessons that require way too many beers to get into it all . . . :)

Looking back on it, I felt like I did the shotgun approach, writing both comedy and drama. I didn't tap into what I had to say as a writer. Once I focused on drama and cut back on the money I spent going to "experts" (and therapy), I started to see results. Writing is re-writing. You need to always generate new material, and I believe by doing so, you'll tap into your voice. Your POV starts to really come out. It took a very long time, but I am very lucky that I now have showrunners, established TV writers and even a novelist who help me when I need it.

ABOUT THE AUTHOR

Lee Jessup is a career coach for professional and emerging screenwriters, with an exclusive focus on the screenwriter's ongoing professional development. Her clients include working screenwriters who have sold screenplays and pilots to major studios and booked writing assignments, staffed television writers, best-selling authors, television writing programs and feature fellowships participants, contest winners, as well as emerging screenwriters just starting on their screenwriting journey. In her role as career coach, Lee serves as a sort of industry guidance counselor, adviser, drill Sergeant, cheerleader, confidant and strategic partner.

Born to a film producer father, Lee grew up on film sets and became a production gypsy right out of high school, working on a series of low-budget films back-to-back into her early 20s. Eager to find her niche, Lee then tried her hand at screenwriting, and was fortunate enough to have her feature screenplay picked up by Tapestry Films (*Wedding Crashers*, *Wedding Planner*) when she was just 23. Through the development process that involved the William Morris Agency packaging the project, Lee quickly realized that she had no desire to build her own screenwriting career, and instead turned to working with writers herself, first as a development executive, and then as the director of leading coverage service ScriptShark.com. While at ScriptShark, and troubled by the missteps that she saw writers make again and again, Lee launched a national business-of-screenwriting seminar series sponsored by *The New York Times* and in partnership with Final Draft. Through the seminar series, screenwriters both local to Los Angeles and all around the country started seeking Lee out for industry advice, inadvertently launching her coaching practice. Lee began coaching screenwriters privately in 2008, and in 2012 opened her coaching practice to the screenwriting public as she took on coaching full time.

Lee's knowledge and expertise in the space have been utilized by such entities as the WGA, NBC International, UCLA, ISA, NYFA, Story Expo, The Great

American Pitch Fest, London Screenwriting Festival as well as film festivals across the United States and around the world. Her previous book, *Getting It Write: An Insider's Guide to a Screenwriting Career* is a bestseller, and she has been the interview subject of countless podcasts and screenwriting-centric websites. With her husband, two children, a dog, two cats and hippie parents living upstairs, Lee currently resides in Los Angeles, where she continues to shepherd, champion and challenge her stable of talented, ambitious and dedicated writers.

APPENDIX

While there are endless resources for professional and emerging screenwriters out there and an entire book could be written on those alone, included in this appendix are those proven, vetted, valuable resources that I regularly turn to and recommend to my coaching clients.

Screenwriting Classes

- Pilar Alessandra's OnThePage Studio (features & TV)
- Script Anatomy (TV only)
- Jen Grisanti's Annual Storywise Teleseminar (TV only)
- Corey Mandell Professional Screenwriting Workshops (features & TV)
- UCLA Professional Program

Screenwriting Consultants

- **Pilar Alessandra**/OnThePage
- **Jen Grisanti**/Jen Grisanti Consultancy
- **Tawnya Bhattacharya**/Script Anatomy
- **Michael Hauge/**Story Mastery
- **Ruth Atkinson**
- **Hayley McKenzie**/Script Angel
- **Ellen Sandler/**Sandler Ink
- **Danny Manus/**No BullScript Consulting
- **Erik Bork**/Flying Wrestler

Script Readers

- **Andrew Hilton**/Screenplay Mechanic
- **Rob Ripley**/The Third Act

Screenwriting Competitions

- Final Draft's Big Break Competition
- Tracking B's TV Script Contest
- Tracking B's Feature Script Contest
- Script Pipeline's Feature Competition
- Tracking Board's Launch Pad Feature Competition
- Tracking Board's Launch Pad Pilot Competition
- Austin Film Festival Screenwriting Competition
- PAGE International Screenwriting Awards
- The Nicholl Fellowship
- ISA Fast Track Fellowship

Television Writing Programs

- Sundance Episodic Lab
- The Humanitas Prize—New Voices
- Nickelodeon Writing Program
- CBS Writer's Mentoring Program
- Disney ABC Writing Program
- NBC's Writers on the Verge
- WB's Television Writers Workshop
- FOX Writers Intensive
- NHMC (National Hispanic Medial Coalition) Writing Program
- Cape (Coalition of Asian Pacifics in Entertainment) New Writers Fellowship

Feature Film Labs and Fellowships

- Sundance Institute Screenwriting Lab
- Film Independent Screenwriting Lab
- Project Involve
- Universal Pictures' Emerging Writers Fellowship
- Hamptons International Film Festival Screenwriting Lab
- Outfest Screenwriting Lab
- Hedgebrook Screenwriting Lab
- New York Women in Film & Television Writers Lab

Screenplay Listing Services

- The Black List
- Ink Tip

Additional Discovery Services

- Spec Scout

Podcasts

- KCRW's The Business
- KCRW's The Spin Off
- Nerdists Writers Panel
- ScriptNotes
- Children of Tendu
- OnThePage with Pilar Alessandra
- Curious About Screenwriting ISA Podcast
- Selling Your Screenplay
- The Q & A with Jeff Goldsmith
- Scripts & Scribes
- Screenwriter's Rant Room

Industry News

- The Hollywood Reporter
- Variety
- Deadline
- The Wrap

Screenwriting Websites & Blogs

- ScriptMag.com
- Go Into the Story
- Done Deal Pro
- LA Screenwriter
- Stage 32
- The Black Board
- ScriptChat
- Wordplayer.com
- Roadmap Writers

Screenwriting Books

- **Story** by Robert McKee
- **Screenplay** by Syd Field
- **Writing Screenplays that Sell** by Michael Hauge
- **Story Line: Finding Gold in Your Life Story** by Jen Grisanti
- **The Hero Succeeds** by Kam Miller
- **The Coffee Break Screenwriter** by Pilar Alessandra
- **Rewrite** by Paul Chitlik
- **Save the Cat** by Blake Snyder
- **Writing the TV Pilot** by William Rabkin
- **Writing Movies for Fun & Profit** by Garant & Lennon
- **The Hidden Tools of Comedy** by Steven Kaplan
- **Writing the TV Drama Series** by Pam Douglas
- **The TV Writer's Workbook** by Ellen Sandler
- **Good in a Room** by Stephanie Palmer
- **The Script Selling Game** by Kathie Fong Yoneda
- **Hollywood Game Plan** by Carole Kirschner
- **How to Manage Your Agent** by Chad Gervich

INDEX